BRIGADIER GENERAL ADAM R. JOHNSON,
1863.

THE PARTISAN RANGERS

OF THE

CONFEDERATE STATES ARMY

MEMOIRS OF
GENERAL ADAM R. JOHNSON

edited by William J. Davis

STATE HOUSE PRESS
AUSTIN, TEXAS
1995

Library of Congress Cataloging-in-Publication Data

Johnson, Adam Rankin, 1834-
The Partisan Rangers of the Confederate States Army : memoirs
of Adam R. Johnson / edited by William J. Davis.
p.   cm.
Originally published: Louisville, Ky. : G.G. Fetter, 1904. With
new preface.
Includes index.
ISBN 1-880510-29-4 (alk. paper)
1. Johnson, Adam Rankin, 1834- . 2. United
States—History—Civil War, 1861-1865—Personal narratives,
Confederate. 3. Confederate States of America. Army.
Kentucky Cavalry Regiment, 10th. 4. United
States—History—Civil War, 1861-1865—Regimental histories.
5. Morgan's Ohio Raid, 1863. I. Davis, William J., b. 1839.
II. Title.

E564.6 10th.J64 1995
973.7'82—dc20   95-16738

Printed in the United States of America

dustjacket design by David Timmons

STATE HOUSE PRESS
P.O. Box 15247
Austin, Texas 78761

Publisher's Preface

The Partisan Rangers of the Confederate States Army chronicles the exploits of a most remarkable regiment, the Tenth Kentucky Cavalry, and their brilliant commander Adam Rankin Johnson. The breadth of Johnson's character and the esteem in which he was held by his men were evident throughout the war, but they are exemplified most dramatically by his actions near the end of the war.

Captured by the Federal Army in August 1864, General Johnson was exchanged as a prisoner in early 1865 and returned to Virginia for orders to rejoin his brigade. In his Richmond hotel room he was visited by Governor Lubbock of Texas, General Breckinridge and President Davis, who all believed him too disabled to return to duty and encouraged him to retire and return home. He told them he was less maimed than many and that, if given his orders, he would find his men; if *they* believed him too disabled and would not follow him, then he would resign.

Reluctantly they gave him his orders, and in Mississipp he located 150 men of his old unit who received him with enthusiasm. They were preparing to leave for Kentucky when the news came of Lee's surrender at Appomattox. Had the war lasted a bit longer, Johnson might have given us one of the most spectacular examples of military leadership to come out of the war, because he was preparing to lead his men even though he was *totally blind*. We will never know if he would have been successful as a blind leader, but his successes during the remainder of his long life indicate he would have done well even without sight.

Adam Johnson was born in Henderson County, Kentucky, on February 8, 1834, the son of a medical doctor who had married a doctor's daughter. Johnson later said he spent a third of his youth in the outdoors but learned much from the books he read at night. At the age of twelve he began to work in a drug store owned by a friend of his father and soon was managing the business on his own. By age sixteen he was a factory foreman with eighty people working for him.

In 1854, at the age of twenty, he went to Texas and settled in the Burnet area on the Indian frontier. There he worked as an Indian fighter, stage driver and as a surveyor.

With the outbreak of the Civil War, Johnson hastily married his sixteen year old sweetheart, Josephine Eastland, before leaving for Kentucky to join Nathan Bedford Forrest as a scout. He eventually became commander of the Tenth Kentucky Cavalry Regiment, and in June 1864 he became a brigade commander with the rank of Brigadier General. Among the exploits detailed in *The Partisan Rangers* is the capture by Johnson and twelve of his men of a large garrison of Federal troops at Newburg, Indiana. Their ruse of mounting two joints of stovepipe on the running gear of an abandoned wagon, that from afar appeared to be a large cannon, won Johnson the nickname "Stovepipe." He was with General Morgan on his famous raid but escaped capture by swimming the Ohio River.

On August 21, 1864, Johnson attacked a Federal encampment at Grubbs Crossroads in Kentucky but was rendered totally blind from an accidental shot by one of his own men. For the next several months he was a prisoner of the Federals until his exchange shortly before the end of the war.

After his return to Texas, Johnson settled first in Llano County and then in Burnet County where he remained in the livestock and land business for the remainder of his life. His young son Robert served as aide and eyes in his travels around the area. Back in the 1850s while surveying the Colorado River, Johnson had identified a site where he believed a dam should be built; the place he located became the dam at Lake Buchanan and the entrance to the locale is designated by a marble slab dedicating the Adam R. Johnson Parkway.

Johnson founded the town of Marble Falls, which became known as the "Blind-Man's Town." Near Marble Falls is Granite Mountain, the quarry for the red granite used to build the Texas State Capitol; Johnson donated some of the railroad right-of-way for hauling the stone to Austin.

General Johnson and his wife Josephine had nine children, three of whom died in early life. Their son Robert served as mayor of Marble Falls for several terms, and Adam Junior was Austin's city manager for seven years. Johnson spent his last years at "Airy Mount," a two-story stone house built in 1884 just east of Burnet. Pictured at page 204, his home has been recently restored as a Texas Historic Landmark and has become the Airy Mount Inn, a bed-and-breakfast owned and operated by Rosanne and Charles Hayman.

Adam Johnson died in 1922 at the age of eighty-nine. His body lay in state in the Senate chamber of the State Capitol, and Governor Pat Neff read the burial service. Both Johnson and his wife are buried in the state cemetery in Austin.In 1963, on the grounds of the Burnet County courthouse, the state of Texas erected a granite marker dedicated to General Adam Rankin Johnson. One of Johnson's men, Colonel Thomas S. Miller of Austin provided a fitting epitaph for the life of Adam Johnson:

> No man in the Southern Army, no matter how high his rank, displayed more military skill or intrepidity than General Adam R. Johnson. . . . He was literally the "Swamp Fox" of Kentucky.

PREFACE.

✿ ✿ ✿

My motive in publishing this work has been two-fold:

First, to pay merited tribute to the Kentucky boys, who, most of them gently born and nurtured, left home, family, friends, fortune behind them, and, enlisting in my command, fought for the Cause of the South. I do not dwell on these sacrifices; it is enough to say that the young Kentuckians cheerfully bore every privation and freely offered their lives in defense of principles they held to be right and for the sake of the cause they loved. This story of their services is my tribute to their memories. May it not also be regarded as a minor contribution to the history of the war between the States?

Secondly, to aid the women of the South, who, under the name of United Daughters of the Confederacy, have organized local societies, or Chapters, in the several States, to care for the poor, to nurse the sick, to relieve the distressed, to help the aged and infirm among the survivors of the Lost Cause, to bury them when they die, and to mark their graves. Another purpose of these noble women is to place in the hands of their children and their children's children truthful histories, so that the memory of the Confederate soldier shall not perish, but be rightfully held in honor.

I have long wanted to help this work. I therefore propose to donate to each chapter one-third of the proceeds of the sales of this book made by it, and to the National Association "U. D. C." one-third of the proceeds of all other sales. I wish I could give more.

I feel that I should not close this prefatory note without rendering thanks to the friends who have encouraged me and who have assisted me in the preparation of this book, especially to Colonel James W. Bowles and Major Frank Amplias Owen, whose kindness and courtesy have been great.

CONTENTS.

PART I.

Capture of Colonel Jim Jackson's cavalry horses—the McFarland girls—two "nice young men"—the requisition—the joke on Field— General Crittenden's good humor—Mrs. McFarland has her inning.

At Henderson—military headquarters—brothers in the Federal army—Colonel Holloway—suspicion—pursuit—combat—en route to church—"You must leave this town to-night"—the sergeant's horse— return to Forrest.

A fortunate horse-trade—within the enemy's lines—information leads to enemy's repulse—behind the Federal general's tent again— the three scouts—fight with the gunboats—a successful ruse—third scout into the Federal camp—preparing for battle.

The battle of Fort Donelson—Forrest's part—Hanson's brigade— Generals Buckner, Pillow and Floyd—encounter with a Federal lieu- tenant—Martin asleep—talk of surrender—Forrest determines to escape—his scouts find the way—discussion at headquarters—justice to Buckner—Floyd's guide—panic at Nashville—Forrest restores order.

With dispatches to Texas—at the Burnet home—return to active service—Bob Martin's prisoners—a renegade Southerner—an "Indian thicket"—"too shrewd" to be entrapped—on Van Dorn's staff—fight at Farmington—Bob Martin's feat.

General Breckinridge sends for "the two young scouts"—a lesson in "cipher"—scouting for Breckinridge—the railroad cut—the mission— John C. Breckinridge—the sick Confederate—a smallpox stampede— Federal pickets—David R. Burbank—the message delivered—"too young for a leader"—stay-at-home Confederates—an army of three— the Federal major and the Kentucky girl.

"Three hundred guerillas" attack Henderson—"Bloody war on the Border"—resolutions—a mild communication—Bob Martin as envoy— Jimmie Quinn on duty—the amende honorable—recruits—the black- list—an army of seven attack Madisonville—occupation of Henderson— flying the Confederate flag.

An army of twenty-seven—the stovepipe battery—surrender and capture—a colonel of home-guards—gunboats pursue—home-guards as avengers—repulse of gunboats—"Stovepipe Johnson"—effect of the expedition.

The army of three becomes a battalion—Indiana home-guards invade Kentucky—are happy to get back safe—proclamation to Kentuckians.

Capture of Hopkinsville—capture of Clarksville—citizens rejoice— Miss Tennie Moore—presentation of the flag—the old black mammy— results of expeditions—Federal forces kept from the front.

Capture of Madisonville—an unprincipled Union officer—battle of Geiger's Lake—one of Martin's feats—Federal discomfiture—artillery mules in action—improved prospects—the "River Robber"—the band of three becomes a regiment—"The Partisan Rangers of the Confederate Army."

En route to Richmond—a Tennessee host—"Stovepipe Johnson"— too many counsellors—a Federal passport—in Buell's camp—meeting with Forrest—a change of plan—Kentucky ablaze—the turning point of the war in the West—evacuation of Kentucky.

In Richmond—synopsis of first report—the Tenth Kentucky Cavalry—promotions, appointments and commissions—Jefferson Davis— a thorn in the side—Bragg sets a trap.

Morgan's Christmas raid—feint against Lebanon—mission to Texas —capture of wagons—another of Martin's feats—crossing the Mississippi—General Albert Sidney Johnston's wound—reorganization of the Tenth Kentucky Cavalry—mutual compliments—St. Leger Grenfell— Morgan's division of cavalry—Basil W. Duke: his ability and reputation; unanimous desire that he command first brigade; second in rank to Morgan; "the ablest officer of his age"—command of the second brigade—skirmishes—another of Martin's feats; his wound— Major G. Wash Owen.

Across the Cumberland—skirmishes—defeat at Green river bridge —capture of Lebanon——demonstration by Major Davis—across the Ohio—agreement broken—encounters with home-guards—Cincinnati flanked—General Zachary Taylor's nephews—"the danger line passed;"—"troubles are over"—disastrous mistake—ammunition exhausted and men worn out—struggle in the Ohio—rescue of Neil Helm —Federal soldiers forbear—three hundred escape.

In Richmond—Kentucky representatives—Shall Morgan's men be dismounted?—E. M. Bruce and Adjutant-General Cooper—Colonel William Preston Johnston befriends the command—President Davis—the camp at Morristown—bushwhackers—Morgan's men at Chickamauga— Bragg's enmity and Forrest's friendship—Bragg's failure after victory —Forrest makes a speech—renewed efforts to dismount Morgan's cavalry—"the old man" again checkmated—in camp at Decatur—Morgan escapes from prison and resumes command—ordered to Richmond—an important work.

The "thin gray line"—Kentuckians in council—secrets of State— en route to Kentucky—department of western Kentucky—Burbridge routed by Breckinridge—proclamation to Kentuckians—a Federal officer's review of Confederate movements in Kentucky—promotions and commissions—rapid recruiting—the Sons of Liberty—plans frustrated—battle of Grubbs Crossroads—wounded and put hors du combat—daring feats—Colonel Chenoweth takes command.

Narrative of Colonel Chenoweth: recapitulation—grief over the body of his wounded commander—General Johnson's loss of sight and imprisonment—an incident at Grubbs Crossroads—Waller O. Bullock— atrocities of the Federal General Payne; his "foul memory;" Federal General Meredith's opinion—after the battle of Grubbs Crossroads— personal adventures—Dr. Mathewson and his family—General H. B. Lyon commands the department—fight with a negro regiment—a guerilla band—Adam Johnson's brigade as reorganized—guerillas outlawed; Bob Gillaspie—a grand ball at Hopkinsville—encounter with Federal troops—Lyon and McCook—a winter raid—cut off by a gunboat—a Confederate colonel mixes with Federal cavalry in pursuit of his own men—General Lyon's daring escape—news of Lee's surrender —surrender to General Meredith; his courtesy and kindness—enemies become friends.

Personal narrative resumed: hospitable amenities; kindness of friends and relatives during convalescence—imprisonment—exchange—application for re-assignment to duty; interviews with the President and the Secretary of War; their remonstrances; orders issued—rejoin wife and old friends—death of Neil Helm—journey to Mississippi—welcomed by remnant of old command; preparations for return to Kentucky; news of Lee's surrender; "all is over"—journey to New Orleans—sudden trip to Kentucky—kind offers—return to Texas—the greatest and best man of the Confederacy—Davis and Lincoln.

Bad conditions—"reconstruction" and confusion—Honey Creek Cove—the old Dancer home—the poisoned arrows of the Comanches—murder of Dancer—an oath of vengeance—the Brazeal boys—the new home.

Adventures of Miller and Morrow—raid on Honey Creek Cove—Pickett's adventure—struggle for existence—courage and endurance of Mrs. Friend—Indian captives—misplaced sympathy; "philanthropists" encourage crime—the Shegogs and the Menascos—Indian thieves and white marauders—minute men—story of the Dillard brothers.

On the ridge of Burnet county—escape of Mrs. Johnson and friends —the Whitlocks—story of Brit, the famous negro—the frontier in arms; no aid from the government; misrepresentations of sutlers and Indian agents; correspondence with officials—the Kiowa chiefs, Sattanta, Big Tree and Satank—trial of Indians by a civil court; the only instance—the Reconstruction Administration; its failure and overthrow—Indians beaten; troubles ended.

Return to Burnet—a land office and a "country store"—build a school-house—establish a newspaper—physical resources of Burnet county; granite and marble quarries opened—Marble Falls; its growth and development—public spirit of its citizens—rich and well-watered valleys; water-power; building-stones; factories—"The Little Gem City"—happiness and peace.

PART II

ILLUSTRATIONS,

PART I.

Memoirs of General Adam R. Johnson:

AN AUTOBIOGRAPHICAL NARRATIVE.

CHAPTER I.

Adam Rankin Johnson was born in the town of Henderson, Kentucky, on February 8, 1834. He is the son of Thomas Jefferson Johnson, M. D., and Juliet Spencer Rankin, daughter of Dr. Adam Rankin, who settled in Henderson county during the early part of the year 1800. Dr. Johnson removed from Frankfort to Henderson in 1823, and, four years thereafter, on the fifteenth day of February, 1827, married Miss Rankin. Dr. Johnson was a man of strong mind and positive character, and during his early life enjoyed a prominence few young physicians of his day attained. Mrs. Johnson was one of the noblest of women, and was beloved by every one who knew her. Dr. and Mrs. Johnson lived to a ripe old age and reared a large family, all of whom succeeded in life and became prosperous.

At the age of eight years, I was allowed the use of a gun and spent many happy hours roaming the forests and fields of Henderson county, where game was still plentiful. In course of time, I became an expert shot and was considered one of the best hunters in that country. I also learned to swim well.

In this outdoor life I acquired health, strength and activity and the habits of close observation and prompt action. Probably more than a third of my days up to the age of twenty had been spent in the open country, while evening hours were devoted to reading history, biography and tales of romance and adventure.

At the age of twelve years I went into the drug store of Ira Delano. He was fond of society and soon left the business to my care. The responsibility thus thrown on me was thought to

1

be a misfortune at the time, but I have since learned to regard it as a blessing, for I had to make extraordinary exertion to learn the business. Having become familiar with it in all its details, I virtually controlled it for three years.

At sixteen, I accepted a position in Burbank's factory and was put in charge of about eighty hands. Here, too, the responsibilities were serious, but, by close application, I succeeded in accomplishing the best results that had ever been attained, making the best "average," as it was called. To properly handle the men under my charge, I had to study human nature, and in this school I learned to control men, which experience, in after years, served me in many a desperate strait, and, indeed, on many occasions thereafter, acting on intuitive perceptions, I trusted my life to total strangers; nor was I ever deceived. In this association with Mr. Burbank, I derived another advantage, though unforeseen. This gentleman was a warm personal and political friend of John C. Breckinridge; they visited and entertained each other at their respective homes and were congenial spirits. As will be seen in the course of this narrative, my association with Mr. Burbank strengthened the opinion of General Breckinridge that I was the right man to convey an important secret message to Mr. Burbank and his friends during the Civil War. Thus do single threads unite to form the woof of our lives.

When twenty years old, I went to Texas and settled in Burnet county, then called Hamilton Valley, in the western part of the State. Texas at that time had a population of only a few hundred thousand people; now there are three million and three hundred thousand.

The Indians had not yet been driven from this part of the State and were still resisting the advance of the white man, but with little success.

Soon after my arrival, I became acquainted with a party of surveyors and attached myself to them, thinking it the best opportunity I would find in a new, sparsely-settled country to make a living, and reflecting that increasing immigration would bring many men into the community, and that perhaps the majority of these would acquire ownership of land which a surveyor would have to lay off.

I found the red men roaming over the plains in large numbers, industriously endeavoring to live without manual labor, for they rode hundreds of miles to steal a few head of stock, when, with millions of acres free to them, northward or westward, they could with more ease and no danger raise all the cattle they needed.

I devoted myself chiefly to the business of surveying lands for the ensuing five years, and enjoyed the friendship and had the hearty co-operation of neighboring settlers. Among these neighbors and friends were three old soldiers who had fought with General Sam Houston at the battle of San Jacinto—Captain W. H. Magill, Logan Van Deveer and Noah Smithwick. The first two were from Kentucky and were very kind to me. These old soldiers were typical frontiersmen and great bear hunters. Their stories of war and hunting profoundly impressed me.

Once while hunting a bear they had wounded, they followed him until, coming upon him suddenly in the bush, where they had heard the almost human scream of agony from one of their dogs, the intrepid Van Deveer, impelled by the desire to rescue his dog as well as to kill the bear, impetuously rushed in, brandishing a long, keen knife which he drove into the heart of the bear just in time to save his faithful dog, which was almost crushed between the powerful arms of his enraged and relentless adversary.

At another time, these men had a contract with the Government to feed a large body of Comanche Indians, whose hunger must be appeased to prevent them from attacking the settlement. The Indians, nevertheless, became dissatisfied and, led by a fierce and truculent chief, had plotted to murder the white men in charge of the cattle. At daybreak they surrounded the camp and were in the very act of attacking the herd when Van Deveer, who was coming from the fort, dashed on horseback up through the crowd of savages to the spot where Yellow Wolf, their chief, was standing, alone. Dismounting hastily, Van Deveer seized him by the throat and, flashing his big knife before the startled Indian's eyes, exclaimed fiercely: "You old yellow scoundrel, I'll cut your throat, if you don't make your Indians put up their bows and arrows."

The Indian chief, astounded and overawed by the boldness and impetuosity of a single white man in the face of his band of braves, surrendered at discretion and quickly obeyed his command, and thus the guards and cattle were saved. Indians admire bravery in a foe as well as in a friend, and despise cowardice, and as long as any of these redskins lived, when they chanced to meet a citizen of Burnet county, they were sure to ask: "You know him, Logan Van Deveer? Him heap, big brave—skeer Yellow Wolf!"

It was not long before I found it necessary to protect myself against an attack of these treacherous marauders. Once, while surveying along a creek that I had named "Yellow Wolf," after the old chief, and near Fort Chadbourne, with four companions, I was nearly surrounded in the night and attacked by a band of Indians. Drawing the horses into the thicket where we had been camping, and instructing the little force to keep up a continual firing, I crept through the tall grass, and, winding my way to the rear of what seemed a large body of men, opened fire upon them, at which they were so surprised and disconcerted that they made off hurriedly, fearing that they in their turn were about to be surrounded.

Soon after the occurrence of this incident, camping at Kickapoo creek with four men, we heard a large flock of wild turkeys flying past. Here was a great temptation for men whose meat was salt pork, and Neil Helm and I together followed them up the bottom for some distance, but then separated for the better search. Ere long, I saw a fine, large gobbler and brought him down at the first shot, and then ran forward and placed my foot on the neck of the fluttering bird; but, having learned to be ever on guard, took the precaution to reload my gun before dispatching the game. Just as I had finished renewing my charge, I saw dimly in the dark some one approaching. I slipped behind a tree, "Indian fashion," and called out for Helm, who answered on the outer edge of the creek bottom. Fearing that the Indians were gathering around my friend, I seized the turkey and, slipping into a ravine, made my way to the outskirts of the timber and gave a signal for Helm, who, recognizing the call, soon came rushing up, exclaiming that he had just caught a glimpse of the biggest Indian he had ever seen. Right in front of our camp was a low island, covered with high grass and cat's tail flag. One of the men who was on guard opposite the lower end of this island saw an Indian and promptly fired at him. Another was seen at the upper end, and, apprehensive that the savages were trying to surround our little party, I set fire to the heavy dry grass and reeds, whereupon they vamosed and troubled us no more.

Having a wagon heavily loaded with provisions for some of our men on the plains, we pushed forward and late the next evening encamped on Antelope creek. Selecting a small but dense thicket, we drew the wagon in so that we could tie the horses to the wheels farthest from the road, and all, being greatly fatigued, soon fell asleep. I was accustomed to sleep in my clothes, revolver buckled around my waist and gun by my side, so as to be prepared for any sudden emergency. About four o'clock next morning, I was awakened by a fierce but low growl of my little dog, as if it were meant for a signal of danger. This little dog was my constant companion, following me everywhere, and always sleeping at my feet; he had an instinctive knowledge of the approach of Indians, even at a considerable distance. My horse, "Joe Smith," famous afterward on the frontier as well for his intelligence, courage and docility as for fleetness of foot, snorted and showed signs of uneasiness. I therefore concluded that Indians were in the neighborhood. Quieting them and awaking my comrades gently, I whispered: "Get ready quick; I think the Indians are near." Then, seizing my gun, I sprang into the thicket. The Indians becoming alarmed at the growling of the dog and the noise, though slight, of our preparation for action, and presuming the whole party had discovered them, rushed out of the thicket through which they had been creeping up on the sleeping party and jumped into the dry bed of the creek and, to my surprise, suddenly disappeared from view. But for the intelligent, watchful dog, seconded by my no less faithful horse, they might have murdered us all in our beds. The Indian is of uncleanly habit and never bathes; his filthy body emits a rank, strong odor, and both dog and horse had smelt them afar and had given me timely warning of their approach.

An examination of this spot the next morning showed the whitish creek-bed against which the shadowy forms of the Indians had appeared for a moment in distinct relief, but the opposite bank, although low, was covered with a carpet of short, thick grass, and on this they had thrown themselves, lying still and, like all the hunted wild things of field and forest, secure in the knowledge that they would escape observation. Later on, during the night, they had silently slipped away. I learned a lesson from this experience which was most useful in my career in this frontier war and as scout and partisan ranger in the Civil War; it was this: In an uncertain light and with the protection of a suitable background, there was little chance of detection or recognition; if the enemy could thus elude me, so also I could deceive them by this and similar devices; and when afterward I had occasion to put this idea in practice, I always acted promptly and confidently, ever holding the conviction that the ruse resorted to, whatever it was, would succeed. And I may say here, in anticipation, that in no instance did this feeling of confidence desert me, nor did I at any time fail to accomplish the desired result.

The red men had by this time learned to respect the courage and strategy of the pale-faces in Burnet county and, unless they could secretly and furtively get as great an advantage in position as in numbers, would generally retreat to await a more favorable opportunity of slaying their antagonists without much risk to their own persons. Trained intelligence, coolness and courage make a combination that is nearly always superior to savage craftiness, ferocity and numbers, as has been frequently demonstrated.

We were soon on the march and moved rapidly forward, fearing bad news ahead. We reached the Overland Mail Route before night and found that the redskins had stripped several stations of their stock and killed all of my own oxen that had been kept for supplying the people of the several plains' stations. Knowing that unfortunate loss demanded prompt action, we drove the team night and day and reached our men in their little forts in time to relieve their necessities and re-establish our line. But being obliged to return speedily to the settlements, David Joy and I started thither on horseback. We made our way without incident to a camp about one hundred and fifty miles from the settlements known as " the mot "—a name applied to a small group of trees. One evening, just as we had finished supper and saddled our horses to continue the journey, we discovered a considerable body of Indians not far ahead. Drawing our horses into the brush, we remained in hiding until after dark, when we made a detour, eluding the savages while they were busy eating supper, their gormandizing habit perhaps blunting their naturally keen senses. The Indian habit is to stuff himself to repletion just short of bursting, when he can get food enough to meet the demands of his savage hunger, and then not to eat anything more for a day or two.

Our little party of two traveled on till midnight, when we came to a lone tree, beneath whose protecting arms we lay down to rest, after tethering our horses for the remainder of the night. Just before daybreak, the horses (almost as good sentinels as dogs) became uneasy at some noise, and they were brought up and tied close to the tree. A cold, wet spell, called a "norther," having blown up, we rolled ourselves in our Mexican blankets and waited for the rain to cease. In the morning when we unrolled ourselves, we found arrows sticking in our blankets and in the body of the tree where the horses were tied. Upon examining the ground, we found that

Indians on horseback .had been not very far from us, but had probably been scared off by the noise made by the horses and their riders just before it was light. Whether these savages were a few of the large band we had passed the evening before or some other Indians, we never ascertained.

A few weeks later, returning to the plains, accompanied by two men, while scouting ahead, I discovered a large body of Indians encamped at " the mot." The country being open, it required great care on our part to escape their observation, but, being well acquainted with the adjacent region, we managed, by circling around, to elude detection and reached our destination in safety.

Not long afterward, the Indians attacked the station at the head of the Concho and slew the station agent. A twelve-year-old boy, who was with the mules belonging to the station, was cut off from the house, but saved his life by his coolness and courage. They pursued him a long way and he perceived that when he rode over rough ground his pony, being well shod, forged ahead, leaving them further behind. So he sought out in his flight the rocky ridges and, by circling around the Indians, finally got in the rear and reached the house in safety.

The redskins next made a dash on the · station below, capturing all the stock. Pushing on hastily to the next station before the intelligence of their proximity could be communicated, they captured the stock there and came near taking old Bob Cavaness, well known on the plains, who saved his life by one of those daring acts which characterized many a frontiersman in those days of constant danger. The savages being between him and his house, which they probably intended to attack as soon as they had dispatched him, he determined to reach his family at all hazard and made a sudden, rapid rush through the line of Indians, striking right and left with the stock of his gun and reserving his fire for more desperate chances. The Indians on horseback would dodge him instead of shooting at him, thus fortunately leaving an opening for him, no doubt believing they could easily intercept him before he could get home; but by this bold and adroit stratagem and fleetness of foot he got away from them. His pursuers were not so anxious to get him as to risk their lives by charging in à body and bursting open the doors, so the heroic old fellow saved both himself and his family. The wily Indians rarely took any very dangerous chances, being more cruel than courageous.

The same band of Indians subsequently surrounded and attacked the station at Great Creek shooting the station agent, Pennington, through the face and breaking both jaws. The bravery of Elijah Helm, who was at the station, saved Pennington and his wife from being scalped. He told them to open the door and go as fast as possible to the dense thicket near at hand and, placing himself between them and the two foremost savages, kept the latter at bay until his friends had gained the jungle.

CHAPTER II.

The constant raids of this band of Indians, numbering about one hundred and fifty, on the Overland Mail Route, made it exceedingly dangerous and very difficult to obtain supplies. Johnson's Station on the plain was considered the most hazardous, as we had to haul water from a pool twenty-two miles distant; it was also a frequent resort of the Indians. They had captured and killed several of my ox-teams, but up to this time they had been unsuccessful in their attempts to slay my people. The station at the head of the Concho was the depot of supplies for both the plains and the Pecos and the water-pool lay ten miles above the station on the principal line running across the plains. My brother Thomas had gone one day in charge of the water-wagon with three men. They had just reached the little storehouse at the water-hole when one hundred and fifty Indians charged them unexpectedly. But, promptly covering the savages with their guns, they succeeded in getting into the house and barricading the doors. The Indians, disappointed in their first object, proceeded at once to round up the oxen, killed them in sight of the besieged, built up fires and went into regular camp. They coolly barbecued their stolen meat and engaged in a great feast. The stage going west came by after dark and carried the intelligence to Johnson's Station. As Johnson's Station depended on this water-hole for its supply, some plan had to be devised to drive away the redskins, for it was seventy miles to the next watering place and the station would have to be abandoned if the stock had to be driven so far.

I obtained a wagon that belonged to the mail line and, with several men, immediately started for the captured water-hole, determined to regain possession of it, if possible, but hoping that the marauders had left the neighborhood. It was dark when we reached a point that overlooked the spot. We perceived the camp-fires still burning bright, for the Indians were yet feasting as if they had been starved for a week.

I determined to make an effort at once to regain this valuable property. Indians are both superstitious and timorous when any strange, unusual expedient is employed to frighten them. As noiselessly as practicable we drove the team to within a few hundred yards of the feasting warriors, rioting in fancied security. I then had the men make a great uproar by shouting loudly and rattling the empty water barrels while driving at a gallop directly by their camp toward the storehouse.

Catching the sound of this unearthly hubbub largely multiplied, doubtless, by their excited imaginations, they became so much alarmed that they hastily smothered their camp-fires with wet blankets. Our little party soon reached the house. Ordering the noise to be kept up, I took one of the men and began skirmishing around their camp to produce the impression of numbers and make them believe they were to be attacked from various points. Before midnight they decamped, to tell to their squaws and papooses probably ever after miraculous stories of their mysterious night attack.

In a few days I returned to Burnet to attend to my official duties as county surveyor. I proceeded to survey some lands in the cedar hills of the county ten miles northward. While busily engaged in this work fifteen wandering Indians crossed the river and entered the timber where I was working with my assistants. They surprised and killed an old Scotchman named Robert Adams—the first man slain by savages in the county of Burnet.

I took up their trail and being reinforced by a party of citizens, followed it promptly, for in Texas, as in Kentucky in early days, it was deemed the best policy to follow up the Indians for reprisals whenever they made an attack on any one in the settlement. It was the custom to send riders toward all points of the compass, summoning horsemen to meet at some convenient rendezvous, and generally within twenty-four hours a large body of armed men were on the track of the savages, whom they followed hundreds of miles, if necessary. Only such prompt, decisive action could keep them

DOCTOR MOORE.

Early friend of Gen. Johnson and Southern sympathizer; arrested by Federals, confined in dungeon, and property confiscated with that of his son's.

within bounds at all. But this band by hard riding succeeded in eluding us. We found the body of Adams much mutilated and with head scalped. The Indians seemed to have amused themselves by filling his body full of arrows.

Soon after this event, a band of Indians was followed by a party of white men from Llano and San Saba to the west of Burnet. These savages crossed the river near where Adams had been killed. Early next morning a famous frontiersman, named John Jackson, came into Burnet and reported that the Indians were making their way toward the town and brought with him a number of arrows the redskins had wantonly used in killing colts. Immediately several parties left to intercept them. My horse was grazing out in the prairie and this caused me to be tardy in leaving the settlement, and I found but one man to accompany me, David Hunter, a young lawyer of the town. Believing that the Indians would keep in the brush on the Shin Oak ridges, I proposed to my companion that we should endeaver to head them off, and in advance of the parties who had left Burnet before us but who had taken more circuitous routes. Just as we had discovered the trail, John Moore, Dr. Jack McFarland, Captain McKee, Major Eubanks and a sixteen-year-old boy, by the name of William Magill, rode up to join us.

I was put in the lead and, pushing rapidly through the brush, in a short time we had reached the brow of a hill overlooking a broad prairie. Detecting that our foes had played their favorite trick of doubling on their trail, I called to those in the rear to look out for a branch-trail. This they readily discovered and soon we were upon the Indians, who at once fled, some dodging into the chaparral and the best-mounted of them galloping off across the prairie toward a high, bushy ridge about a mile away.

Our whole party dashed away in hot pursuit, but during the search for the branch-trail I had fallen to the rear and, to take a short cut, I jumped my horse off a high ledge of rock and expected, as I was riding a very fleet-footed animal, to soon overtake those who had gotten the start; but, to my chagrin and astonishment, I soon found that I was losing instead of gaining ground. I did not discover the cause of this mishap until my racer had reached the bottom of the ridge, and, leaping a stream, had started up the hill, when I ascertained that the saddle, slipping, had been too far forward on the withers of my unlucky steed, which was thus badly handicapped through no fault of his own.

The saddle being readjusted, like an arrow released from a bow-string, my spirited horse darted forward and quickly reached the head of the pursuing party.

Coming up with the savages on the top of the hill, I opened fire, killing one instantly. Rushing on, I was about to shoot another when I discovered it was a woman before me, as she raised her hands and exclaimed: "Me squaw!"

An instinctive repugnance to killing a woman caused me to lower my gun. But the boy, Billy Magill, suddenly fired and killed her, saying she had no business to be in the gang, carrying an extra supply of bows and arrows. Though I would not myself shoot her, I regarded her as one of the leaders of this band. Of course the very idea of slaying a woman is horrible, but the squaw unsexes herself in these raids, and will not only shoot, but mutilate victims; while in their camps and towns of huts, God pity the poor white captive brought in by the braves, as she and the children will take the greatest delight in torturing him slowly to death while they are dancing around him, abusing and deriding him like fiends as he begs for instant death.

The delay caused by this episode had given the third Indian, in our immediate vicinity, an opportunity to flee out of sight. But pursuing his trail, I soon tracked him to the brush. It required redoubled caution to follow on horseback a savage in the dense thicket, as much his natural element as water is that of a fish. The bravest Indian thinks it rash to fight in the clear if he has any chance to bushwhack or to draw his prey into cover. He does not expose his person if he can possibly accomplish his purpose otherwise. This friendly shelter gave the redskin a chance to glide away unobserved to another high, bushy knob. But I soon saw him, and circling around the glade, made an effort to cut him off. Hunter, having circled the first knob, and catching sight of him, made a rush straight for the Indian, who placed his back against the rocky ledge, and thus suddenly brought to bay, seemed determined to fight to the death.

Not waiting for his antagonist's fire, he began to shoot, with great rapidity, his arrows at Hunter, whose horse, sniffing the picric odor emanating from the savage's sweating body, became so unmanageable and pranced about at such a lively rate as to nullify his master's aim. The Indian perceiving me approaching, now sprang on top of the rock, whence he rained down arrows upon his new combatant, one of which struck me upon the nose, bringing "first blood," just as I fired. Receiving a number of buckshot in his leg and body he turned and plunged into the brush, absolutely disappearing in the dense woods, doubtless thinking it was unfair for his foe to fire so many missiles at one time while he could fire but one.

The next day's search found him in the thicket with his wounded leg buried in a hole which he had laboriously dug into the fresh earth to stop the flow of blood, an effective expedient his better educated antagonists would never have thought of, but which this unsophisticated child of Nature had probably been acquainted with from his babyhood.

Though the Indian has not the courage of the pale-face in battle, he is superior to him in stoical, quiet endurance of pain, and it is pathetic to think how patiently through the rest of the day on which he was wounded, and all through the long lonely hours of the night, clear to the time he was discovered in the morning, he had borne the pain of his wounds with the added mental torture through fear that he would be caught sooner or later in this trap, from which he well knew he could not extricate himself, if detected by his persistent foes.

The poor creature's apprehensions were realized; he asked for no quarter, but tried to shoot the whites as they came up; he was mercilessly "shot to pieces." To these pioneers, who were constantly attacked by the red devils, as they were denominated, this deed, which seems cruel to others, was a mere matter of course.

The frontier now seemed to be swarming with Indians, of whom the gang just mentioned was the advance-guard. Whole families were murdered and scalped; many of the settlers deserted the country, fleeing as from a pestilence; while others, to use a significant phrase of those exciting times, "forted up."

The people charged Governor Runnels with inefficiency and neglect.

Lieutenant Governor Lubbock, who had been elected at the same time, was making a campaign through these threatened regions and was traveling in a buggy with his wife. As he naturally desired some frontiersman to accompany him both as guard and guide, I volunteered my services; and from this association sprang a friendship that exists to the present time.

Dangerous as matters now were, it was nevertheless absolutely necessary to keep up the regular supplies on the plains; and so after this last adventure I started with a loaded wagon for the Overland Mail Line. Upon reaching the San Saba river and finding it had been greatly swollen by recent rains, and it being necessary to cross this turbulent tide, I fastened ropes around the wagon tongue and then to the horns of the saddles belonging to myself and my one companion and plunged into the rolling waters. When the wagon reached the main current it was swept down, and the strain upon the ropes broke the girths of our saddles and brought the riders to the ground upon the farther shore with a powerful concussion. Seizing one of the saddles from which a rope ran to the wagon I wound the rope securely around a tree; and soon succeeded in floating the vehicle near enough to the bank of the river to insure its safety. Carrying the contents of the wagon to the shore upon our horses we ere long had landed it also, but regretted to ascertain that one of the axles had been broken in the catastrophe. We cut down a sapling with the ax always carried upon expeditions, and quickly improvising another axle, rude but sufficient for the time, we were presently again on our way to the plains, having lost comparatively little time from what had seemed at first to be a very serious accident. On returning, I found that two of my men had been killed by the Indians at the water-hole and our team had been driven off.

The stage-drivers and old conductors of the mail line, always glad to have company when they had no regular customers, were in the habit of asking me to ride with them. By complying with their desires I acquired their confidence and friendship, and more than once these proved valuable.

Upon one occasion while making one of these trips, always more or less hazardous, a man by the name of McFarland being the driver, the conductor's name now forgotten, we had just reached Pecos river when we discovered a large band of Indians moving swiftly toward us. McFarland drew his team into one of the short horse-shoe bends so frequent on the Pecos river; I called to the conductor to close the curtains and to poke his gun out at one place and his pistol at another, and to make all the noise he could; I was sitting on the box with McFarland, both with gun in hand. When the savages were near enough, we ordered them to halt, which was done, and the old gray-headed chief, who was well known on the mail line, rode forward alone. McFarland, who spoke their language, pleasantly told him to send away his men, while I kept him covered with my gun and warned him not to stir till his men had left.

Seeing he had been neatly trapped (the conductor having played his role cleverly in making him believe there were several men inside), the chief complied with the demand, and waving his braves off, asked for powder and tobacco. McFarland refused him the powder but, giving him some tobacco, told him to follow his men. The temptation to shoot down this Indian was almost irresistible, for he was known to have murdered quite a number of men on the mail line, but recognizing our numerical weakness, we had to refrain, being glad to get to the station in safety in the face of such great odds.

There were two stations on the mail line known as Van Horn's Well and Eagle Springs at which the Indians were very troublesome in constantly stealing and killing stock. The superintendent solicited me to take charge of these stations, which I did and sent my brothers, Ben and Thomas, to occupy them.

Soon after, receiving a message from my brother Ben at Van Horn's Well as to the continual incursions of the Indians there, I took Captain Neil Helm and started for that station. While we were eating dinner at the mail station of Leon Water-hole, the Indians surrounded the herdsman, and would have killed him but for the prompt action of Captain Helm, who ran among them firing right and left with his six-shooter, killing a horse and wounding one of the Indians. A young chief rallied his braves and got between Helm and the station. Helm had but one load in his pistol now, but with his usual coolness, he reserved his fire, pushing toward the savages, pointing his weapon here and there, and thus keeping them at bay, until the chief, believing his revolver empty, made a rush at him, with uplifted spear. I and some of the station hands were near enough to open fire, and the chief falling, the other redskins fell back, but carried off the horses and mules belonging to the station.

Reaching Van Horn's Well the next evening late, my brother Ben and Helm and I went to work to surprise the Indians, if possible. Arranging some good dummies to show upon the walls of the corral, we left orders for one man to remain within and the others to take the stage stock out to graze just at sunrise. Then with Helm and my brother Ben, I climbed the mountain to a rocky ledge that overlooked the valley and the station. Secreting ourselves among the weeds, we rested there quietly till daylight should reveal the exact camping spot of the marauders. But carefully looking over the country next morning, we failed to discover the object of our search,

until the corral gate was opened and the stock had been turned out
to graze; when we detected seven savages immediately in front of
us. At the same time about sixteen more were seen crawling down
the mountain side on the other side of the station. To checkmate
this unexpected move prompt, decisive action was necessary, as the
men below were unconscious of their peril I instructed my brother
and Helm, who had rifles instead of shotguns, to each shoot an Indian, and then to follow me in a charge on the rest. At the report
of the rifles, followed by these two companions, I rushed upon the
Indians, and succeeded in getting close enough to wound one of the
redskins and to kill another, while Ben Johnson and Helm were
firing upon the fleeing Indians, and at the same time hurrying toward the station. The savages on the other side made a rapid retreat, probably thinking that they were threatened by a large force.
Three dead Indians were left upon the ground, and such a salutary
lesson was impressed upon the minds of the savages by this little
fight that no further demonstrations were ever again made upon
this station.

Returning to the Pecos river, where I had a contract
with a railroad company to sectionize four hundred sections (six hundred and forty acres each, hence 256,000 acres in the aggregate), I
now hoped to settle down to the work of my profession as a surveyor, especially as in this engagement my remuneration was to be
one-half, or two hundred sections of good land.

But I seem not to have been destined yet to a life of quietude and
work. While camping as Escondia Springs, I was joined one night
by two families that were on their way to California from old Virginia. They reported that they had seen a large body of Indians just
about sundown. Knowing that the band would visit the springs, a
common camping ground, in fact, I immediately removed my little
party to a rocky ridge that was at a convenient distance from this
watering place, and advised these travelers to do the same; but they
declined, declaring that they had several men in their party and
could defend their camp at the Springs, and doubtless thinking their
new acquaintances, the surveyors, were rather timorous. Just before day we heard firing in their direction, and taking with me my
right-hand man, Captain Neil Helm, I went to the aid of the travelers who had rejected my counsel. I soon discovered that the redskins had already captured one of the wagons and had wounded the
travelers. Although we estimated the Indians to be fifty strong Helm

and I determined to try the effect of a diversion on their rear. Cautiously creeping down a ravine, we came within gunshot before we had been observed by the savages who were deeply intent upon the murder and pillage of the travelers. Opening a rapid fire upon the attacking party, we soon killed three of them and wounded several others, when the Indians began a retreat, dismayed by the accurate, quick firing of their new, unseen enemy, whose numbers they must have greatly exaggerated. The spunky little Virginia party, emboldened by the action of the two surveyors, now made a quick dash upon the robbers and actually recaptured their wagon and horses.

A few days later while I was running a connecting line to Fort Lancaster, and had reached a point within a mile of the San Antonio and El Paso roads, I saw a train of freight wagons camped on the road, while a Mexican was herding their teams about half a mile away. One hundred and fifty Indians charged down on the train, while a part of them surrounded the herd and killed and scalped the Mexican and fired on the teamsters and drove them under the wagon. I was occupying a spot so elevated, though distant, that I witnessed all this exciting scene. I was in the open plain without any protection, but as it was a long way to Pecos river, and my team consisted of only one yoke of oxen and one horse, I knew I could not retreat with safety. Consequently I determined to move toward the Indians. Continuing to run my line, I instructed the driver to drop the tongue from the oxen and climb into the wagon, if the Indians attacked. I told him that by hanging the blankets over the side of the wagon I believed he could successfully defend himself. The savages, however, riding up and looking at us, and concluding that the booty was not sufficiently valuable for the risk involved, rode away without molesting us, leaving us with our little two-ox wagon. But they drove off over one hundred mules.

CHAPTER III.

It was in the spring of 1858 when Colonel John S. Ford, better known as "Old Rip," came into Burnet with his rangers on his way to the Wichita Mountains to fight Indians. I was then preparing to go on a surveying trip, but concluded to follow in their rear, as they would protect my party. Colonel Ford was very anxious for me to go with him, partly as a guide and also to strengthen his force, but I had work to do on the upper Colorado and across the Divide on the waters of the Brazos, in what is now known as Taylor county. I declined to accept the proposition. My party was composed of my brother Thomas, Neil Helm, Oscar Call and "Doc." Sullivan, and with these men I proceeded to Buffalo Gap, which was a famous crossing for both Indians and buffalo. Numerous signs were found of Indians moving in the same direction as our surveying party, and while it was hoped that the rangers had driven them from the country, every precaution was taken. We adopted the Indian mode of traveling on high ground so as to overlook the valleys, and just before Buffalo Gap was reached a fine herd of buffalo was discovered in the valley. Thomas Johnson and Helm were always ready for sport, and as fresh meat was needed, permission was given them to go down and try to kill some of the splendid animals. Selecting a thicket overlooking the valley, I and the others concealed ourselves so as to watch for the enemy and be able to give timely warning to the two men below. The hunters loaded their guns and took their way down a ravine on the windward side of the herd so that they would be able to approach them unperceived. Both young men were considered "crack shots" and felt fully confident that they would not come back empty-handed if they succeeded in getting within rifle-shot of the game. They stealthily approached until they were within a hundred yards of the herd, and then both guns spoke at once, the two shots bringing down a couple of the huge animals, which scrambled to their feet almost immediately and rushed away with the rest of the herd. The hunters were prepared for this and ran back to their horses that were close at hand, hurriedly mounted and were in hot pursuit of the madly stampeding herd before they could get beyond rifle range. The Texas ponies soon overtook them and the hunters spurring their steeds up alongside the wounded beasts, snatched out their pistols and quickly put fatal bullets in their bodies. "Doc." Sullivan had been standing in readiness with the pack mule and his own horse, watching the mad run of hunters and game in the valley below, and as soon as he was sure that the buffaloes were dead he took the mule down to bring up the meat. I had been an interested spectator of the hunt and while intently watching them, my attention was drawn to a clump of trees about a hundred yards west of where I was standing, and to my surprise three Indians were discovered. They were on their horses and were also enjoying the scene in the valley. Knowing the danger the hunters were in should these red men charge into the valley upon the unsuspecting whites, I called to Call and told him that I was going down to help my friends. Call grabbed his saddle, ran to his horse, pitched it upon his back, and hurriedly fastened the girths, but before he got the bridle on one of the Indians rode forward with hand up, calling to us, "Me good Injun; me friend; me Tonkawa." As he came nearer we knew by his paint and feathers that he was telling the truth. We learned from them that Ford's men would cross the Brazos that night, and that they had been sent to the Clear Forks of that river on a scouting expedition, and as they came stealthily through the country they had discovered a large band of Comanches camped near the Gap. They had passed them unperceived, and on coming upon the white men they had decided to wait until the hunt was finished and then warn them of their danger. The Tonkawa, in his original way, said to me: "Comanche see buffalo run. Know white man scare. Follow trail. Find dead buffalo. Find pale-face horse trail. Find pale-face camp."

"Pale-face find good camp over yonder," he said, pointing toward the Gap. I decided to see it for myself, and giving Call or-

ders to bring in the hunting crowd as soon as they had secured the
meat, followed the red guide's short distance to the place where
the Tonkawas had camped the night before. It was an ideal place
for safety—a small cove enclosing about two acres and near the
top of a hill, which was surrounded by a ledge of rock about four
feet high. At its mouth was a dense thicket that concealed the entrance to outsiders and served as a hiding place for all the horses.
I at once saw the advantage of having such a place to spend the
night, and dismounted, unsaddled my horse, tied him to a tree in
the thicket, and entered the cove to make any necessary improve-
ments that would add to our safety. It was not long before Call,
with the hunters and the other two Indians came in, bringing with
them an ample supply of meat. The Tonkawas had made their
usual fire the night before by digging a hole in the ground and
placing their sticks down in it so as to prevent its red light from
being seen by their foes and to keep the wind from blowing the coals
out into the grass while they slept. There was still a bed of red
coals in the hole, and one of the men was soon busy roasting buffalo
hump while Call and I cut out the undergrowth and placed it around
the outer edge to make our abode more secure. Neil Helm was
sent to a little hill that overlooked the valley to watch for the approach of the Comanches, while one of the Tonkawas was dispatched to the Gap as scout. The horses were turned loose in the
enclosure with their ropes on and everybody set to work to prepare for the expected attack of the savages. After I was satisfied that
we had succeeded in making this place one of concealment, the two
Indians who had been close observers of our movements said "Good.
Comanche no see now." In less than two hours the scout from the
Gap came in and told us that the Comanches were on our trail and
were fast approaching. The horses were secured, guns loaded, pistols examined, and all stood in readiness for the coming foe. Helm
was still on the hill near by, but on discovering their first entrance
into the valley he came into the cove to wait with his friends. As
the Tonkawas had said, as soon as the Comanches had discovered
the trail of the pale-faces they mounted and followed it. On locating
the camp of the whites they began to circle around it, getting nearer
each time. Those in the thicket counted twenty-seven braves, each
in his war paint and feathers, with their bows and arrows, and mounted upon horses that they had stolen from the settlers on one of
their many raids into the valley. Four or five gathered on a piece

of high ground about two hundred yards away and Helm bet the others he could hit one of them, a big, brawny brave with huge feathers in his warlock. The Tonkawa immediately exclaimed: "No shoot! No shoot!" But I told him to try his gun and see if he could bring him down. Call said he would try, too, and both shot, Helm's ball going straight to its mark while Call's took effect in a horse. The Comanches gave a yell of rage as one of their number fell, and instantly widened their circle and withdrew to the Gap, taking with them their dead comrade. They soon disappeared in the trees and on the fall of night the Tonkawas went in different directions to scout. It was midnight before they returned and reported the good news of the departure of the Comanches toward the Wichita. They had evidently received news from their main band of the advance of the rangers and had hurried to re-enforce their comrades.

As the country was now apparently clear of hostile tribes, I ran a line down on Elm creek in Runnel's county, surveyed the Burnet county school lands, and being out of supplies moved on to Fort Chadburn. On reaching there we learned of the fight of the rangers on Antelope Hills. As this was one of the most brilliant fights during the Indian times it is worthy of mention in this book, so that coming generations can read it and see what perils and privations existed along the Texas frontier in early days and what brave and loyal men their forefathers were.

The battle of Antelope Hills, fought in 1858, was probably one of the most splendid exhibitions of Indian warfare ever enacted on Texas soil. This was the immemorial home of a tribe of the Comanches; they had sought refuge here from their marauding expeditions into Texas and Mexico. Theirs was a veritable city of refuge, and should the daring rangers seek them they were sure to be encountered in full force. Pohebits Quasho (Iron Jacket) was the war chief of this place, and had gained his name from the queer coat of scale mail that he wore and that had doubtless been taken from the body of some unfortunate Spanish knight who had been slain perhaps a century before by some of this Indian chief's ancestors. He was a big medicine man and claimed to be invulnerable to the balls and shafts of his enemies, as by a few puffs of his breath he could divert them from their course and cause them to fall harmless at the feet. Peta Nacona, the young and daring husband of the white girl, Cynthia Ann Parker, who had been captured ten years before by a band of Comanches and never rescued, was in command of the braves.

About the first of May, 1858, Colonel Ford ("Old Rip"), at the head of one hundred Texas rangers, comprising such leaders as Captain S. P. Ross, W. A. Pitts, Preston, Tankersley, and a contingent of one hundred and eleven Tonkawa Indians, commanded by their celebrated chief Placido, so long the faithful and implicitly-trusted friend of the whites, marched against the marauding Comanches, determined to follow them up to their stronghold amid the hills of the Canadian river, and, if possible, surprise them and inflict a severe and lasting chastisement.

After a toilsome march of several days the Tonkawa scouts reported that they were in the immediate vicinity of the Comanche encampment. The Comanches, though noted for their sleepless vigilance, were unsuspicious of danger; and so unexpected was the approach of the rangers that on the day preceding the battle Colonel Ford and Captain Ross stood in the old road from Fort Smith to Santa Fe, north of Rio Negro, and watched through their glasses the Comanches running buffalo in the valley still more to the north. That night the Tonkawa spies completed the hazardous mission of locating definitely the position of the enemy's camp. The next morning (May 12th) the rangers and reserve, or friendly Indians, marched before sunrise to the attack.

Placido claimed for his red warriors the privilege of wreaking vengeance upon their hereditary foes. His request was granted and the Tonkawas effected a complete surprise of the village some miles south of the main encampment. The struggle was short, sharp and sanguinary. The women and children were made prisoners, but not a Comanche brave surrendered. Their savage pride preferred death to the restraints and humiliations of captivity. Not a single warrior escaped to bear the tidings of this destructive engagement to his people.

A short time after the sun had lighted the tops of the hills, the rangers came in full view of the hostile camp pitched in one of the picturesque valleys of the Canadian river, and on the opposite side of the stream in the immediate vicinity of the famous Antelope Hills. The panorama thus presented to the view of the rangers was beautiful in the extreme, and their enthusiasm found vent in a shout of exultation which was quickly suppressed by Colonel Ford. Just as this moment a solitary Comanche was discovered riding southward, evidently toward the village which Placido had so recently destroyed. He was wholly unconscious of the nearness of an enemy. Instant pursuit was made; he turned and fled full speed toward the main camp across the Canadian, closely followed by the rangers. He dashed across the stream, thus revealing to his pursuers the locality of a safe ford across the miry and almost impassable river. He rushed into the village beyond, sounding the notes of alarm, and soon the Comanche warriors presented a bold front of battle between their women and children and the advancing rangers. After a few moments occupied in forming line of battle both sides were arrayed in full force. The friendly Indians were placed on the right and thrown a little forward. Colonel Ford's object was to deceive the Comanches as to the character of the attacking party and as to the quality of arms they possessed.

Pohebits Quasho, arrayed in all the trappings of his war toggery—coat of mail, shield, bow, and lance, completed by a head dress decorated with feathers and long, red flannel streamers, and besmeared with war paint—gaily dashed about on his war horse midway of the opposing lines, delivering taunts and challenges to the whites. As the old chief rode to and fro, a number of rifles were discharged at him in point blank range without any effect whatever, which seeming immunity from death encouraged his warriors, and some of the rangers even asked themselves if old Iron Jacket really bore a charmed life. Followed by a few of his braves, he now bore down upon the rangers, described a few circles, gave a few puffs of his breath and let fly several arrows at Colonel Ford, Captain Ross and Chief Placido, receiving their fire without harm. But as he approached the line of Tonkawas, a rifle directed by the steady nerve and unerring eye of one of their number,[1] Jim Pockmark, brought the Big Medicine to the dust. The shot was a mortal one. The fallen chief was immediately surrounded by his braves, but the spirit of this conjuring Indian had taken flight to the happy hunting grounds.

These incidents occupied but a brief space of time, when the order to charge was given; and the rangers rushed to the assault. The enthusiastic shouts of the rangers and the triumphant yell of their red allies greeted the welcome order. It was responded to by the defiant " war whoop " of the Comanches. The shouts of the enraged combatants, the wails of women, the piteous cries of terrified children, the howling of frightened dogs, the deadly reports of rifle and revolver, constituted a discord of infernal noises.

The conflict was sharp and quick—a charge; a momentary exchange of rifle and arrow shots, and a heart-rending wail of discomfiture and dismay; and the beaten Comanches abandoned their lodges and camps to the victors, and began a disorderly retreat. But sufficient method was observed to take advantage of each grove of timber, each hill and ravine, to make a stand against their pursuers, and thus enable the women and children to escape. The noise of battle now diverged from a common center like the spokes of a wheel, and continued to greet the ear for several hours, gradually growing fainter as the pursuers disappeared in the distance.

But another division nuder the vigilant Peta Nacona was soon marching through the hills north of the Canadian to the rescue. Though ten miles distant, his quick ear caught the first sounds of battle, and soon he was riding, with Cynthia Ann by his side, at the head of five hundred warriors.

About one o'clock in the afternoon the last of the rangers returned from the pursuit of Pohebits Quasho's discomfited braves, just in time to anticipate this threatened attack.

Colonel Ford with two hundred and twenty-one men had fought and routed over four hundred Comanches and was now confronted by a much stronger force, just fresh from their villages. They had come to retake their horses, plunder, and prisoners, but did not fancy the defiant state of preparations awaiting them in the valley, and were only waiting to take advantage of any incautious movement of the rangers, when the wily Peta Nacona would spring upon them and with one combined desperate effort annihilate the whole force. But his antagonist was a soldier of too much sagacity to allow any advantage to a vigilant foe.

The two forces stood contemplating each other for over an hour—the Comanches challenging the Tonkawas to single combat; but few of them were accepted as they were more expert than the friendly Indians.

Colonel Ford now ordered Placido, with a part of his warriors, to advance in the direction of the enemy, and, if possible, draw them into the valley, so as to afford the rangers an opportunity to charge them. This had the desired effect, and the rangers were ready to deliver a charge, when it was discovered that the friendly

Indians had removed the white bandages from their heads because they served as targets for the Comanches; consequently, the rangers were unable to distinguish friend from foe. This necessitated the entire withdrawal of the Indians. The Comanches witnessed these preparations, and now commenced to recoil. The rangers advanced; the trot, the gallop, the headlong charge—all followed in rapid succession. Lieutenant Nelson made a skillful movement and struck the enemy's left flank. The Comanches' line was broken. A running fight for three or four miles ensued. The enemy was driven back wherever he made a stand. The most determined resistance was made in a timbered ravine. Here one of Placido's warriors was killed and one of the rangers wounded. The Comanches left some dead upon the spot, and had several more wounded. After routing them at this point, the rangers continued to pursue them for some distance, intent upon making the women and children prisoners; but Peta Nacona, by the exercise of those commanding qualities which had often before signalized his conduct on the field, succeeded in covering their retreat and thus allowing them to escape. It was now about four p. m. Both horses and men were entirely exhausted, and Colonel Ford ordered a halt, and returned to the village. Brave old Placido and his warriors fought like so many demons. It was difficult to restrain them, so anxious were they to wreak vengeance upon the Comanches. Seventy-five Comanches were killed, and only two rangers killed and five wounded.

The trophies of Pohebits Quasho, including his lance, bow, and his celebrated coat of scale mail, head dress and shield, were deposited in the State archives at Austin by Colonel Ford.

The brave old Chief Placido was assassinated by a party of Comanches at the reservation near Fort Sill in the latter part of the Civil War between the North and the South.

CHAPTER IV.

THE SURVEYORS.

After the battle of Antelope Hills the Indian incursions on our frontier seemed to be redoubled, and Major Van Dorn got permission from General Twiggs, who was then in command of the Texas department, to unite with Captain Ross and a hundred Caddos and pursue the Comanches to their headquarters on the Wichita. Both Ross and Van Dorn insisted on my going with them as a guide, but just at that time I made a contract to locate the school lands of Llano and San Saba, and declined to go with them. Again taking advantage of this expedition to shelter my party, I gathered my company, consisting of Oscar Call, Thomas Johnson, James O. Norred, "Doc" Sullivan, and one of the San Saba county commissioners named Hall, better known on the frontier as "Beardy" Hall, a name given by his friends on account of a huge black beard that flowed nearly to his waist. This little band, following in Van Dorn's rear, pushed on toward the plains, it being almost a duplicate of the expedition of a few months previous. When we reached the mail line, I left Norred there to take charge of the Mail Station and continued to journey to the North Concho and located the school lands in what is now known as Tom Green county, and almost in sight of the present town of San Angelo. We then moved on to Great Creek some fifteen miles further west, and worked on up that stream beyond its head. North Concho, Great Creek, and the Colorado River head westward, almost parallel with each other, and about fiften miles apart. We had about completed our work, by running a line about five

26

miles west, thence south two miles to the top of a tall peak, thence east on the south side of a divide between Great Creek and North Concho. While running down this east line, I discovered a large pool of water in a deep ravine at the foot of a hill about a half mile from our lines. As was my habit, I took a mental note of the conditions there and thought that it would be a good place to retreat to in case of danger. In running our closing line north to Great creek we found an error which made it necessary to go back and run the line over to the tall peak where we had made observation. It was about noon when Call and Neil Helm went west again to make the connection. The whole country here was without brush and open at that time.

I was figuring up my field notes preparatory to starting home, when some of the men saw Call coming back at full speed waving his hands above his head in a wild, excited way, and all knew that it meant some new danger, and hastily saddled their horses and held themselves in readiness to meet the emergency. As he came galloping up to the waiting group, Call cried excitedly that they had sighted a band of a hundred and fifty Indians—Sattanta's band, he thought—driving a number of mules and horses northward toward the Colorado River, and that they had discovered our " sign " where we were running our line toward the peak and had stopped and were examining it. He had left Helm to watch them and hurried back to report. We got everything together to move on a moment's notice, as we were in an open country without any protection. Shortly afterwards Helm came in and told us that a hundred of the Indians had taken our trail on the south side of the divide and were riding at full speed, and he thought they would reach our camp in about thirty minutes. Thomas Johnson, " Beardy " Hall and I were well mounted, but Call, Sullivan and Helm were riding animals that could not be depended on in a race. I at once determined to get to the " Big Pool " under the side of the hill, and gave Call, Sullivan and Helm orders to take our old trail westward directly toward the spot where the savages were first seen, and when they got to a certain flat rock to turn off to the left and make for the " Big Pool," while Hall, Thomas Johnson and I would follow the trail and cover their retreat. These three were riding large, well-shod horses, and I believed that we could outrun the Indians in case of pursuit, and by circling around until after dark we could throw the Indians off the trail and get into the draw or canyon of the "Big Pool" without discovery. The ruse succeeded; riding in advance, I saw, on reaching the top of the dividing ridge that the band of Indians left with the mules and horses had gone on toward the Colorado river, and far in the distance in the rear I could tell by the rising dust that the others were still rapidly following in the rear of our party. Turning again southward on our line toward the peak, which was now beaten to a plain path by the band of Indians that had passed over it a short time before, we continued our course to the peak, and as it was now thoroughly dark we climbed to the top of this rise without fear of discovery; then turning eastward on our line, we kept in until near the " Big Pool;" then dropping off one at a time, we made a circuit and had all come together at the " Big Pool " by nine o'clock. One man was placed on guard and the rest slept with their bridles in hand. Just at daylight I made a survey with my field glass and discovered an Indian on the peak. In a few minutes others appeared until there were eleven. These sharp-eyed men of the woods made a careful inspection of the country, and finding nothing to excite their suspicion, soon after sunrise took the trail northward to join their comrades.

With Hall and brother Thomas I returned to the line after breakfast to make the connection. Call, Helm and Sullivan went back to our old camp on the creek and we were all together again at noon, and preparations were made for our immediate return home.

This was one of the occasions in which quick decision and constant watchfulness had saved us from serious disaster. Had we undertaken to ride toward the Colorado, three of the little company would have been in great danger of being overtaken and murdered by the savages, as they were so poorly mounted, and as I would not have deserted my friends, it is probable that in trying to rescue them from the Indians the whole party would have been killed since the odds were so great against us.

James O. Norred is the only one that went out on that expedition with me who is now living. His present home is in Burnet county.

As Fort Chadburn was again in our route home, we stopped there and heard of the battle of Wichita, in which both Ross and Van Dorn were seriously wounded. There were several others in the fight who figured largely in the Civil War, prominent among whom was Lieutenant Majors, afterwards General Majors. Wallace says: " This was the battle of Wichita Mountains, a hotly contested and most desperate hand-to-hand fight in which the two gallant and dashing young officers, Ross and Van Dorn, were severely wounded. The loss of the whites was five killed and several wounded. The loss of the Comanches was eighty or ninety warriors killed, many wounded, and several captured, besides all their horses, camp equipage, supplies, etc. The return of this victorious little army was hailed with enthusiastic rejoicing and congratulation, and the Wichita fight, Van Dorn and Ross, were the themes of song and story for many years along the borders and in the halls and banqueting rooms of the cities, and the martial music of the 'Wichita March' resounded through the plains of Texas wherever the Second Cavalry encamped or rode off on scouts in after years."

We mention this battle as some of its principal participants were afterwards conspicuous figures in the Civil War. Van Dorn, Ross and Majors did honor to their country's cause as officers in the Confederate Army, and there were not three braver " wearers of the gray " in the whole army of the South than these young men who had so gallantly defended the homes and loved ones of the hardy pioneers along the Texas frontier, and so unselfishly risked life and limb in savage warfare where it took both brains and courage to outwit the stealthy raids of the Indians. " Though Texas's heraldic roll glows with the names of Houston, Rusk, Lamar, McCulloch, Hays and Chevellier, which illumine the pages of her history with an effulgence of glory, she never nurtured on her maternal bosom a son of more filial devotion, of more loyal patriotism, or indomitable will to do or dare, than S. L. Ross, afterwards governor of our Lone Star State."

In the summer of 1860 I had taken charge of two additional stations on the Overland Mail Route and was very closely confined to my work on the plains. The Indians seemed to have redoubled their desire for revenge upon the whites, and were making frequent incursions upon the settlements across the line as far down as Burnet county. Sattanta with a hundred and fifty Comanches was constantly passing to and fro between Mexico and the reservations.

I had received a letter from Captain S. L. Ross, who was stationed at Fort Belknap, not far from the mail line, requesting me to join him in an expedition against the Indians. I went at once to Fort Belknap to confer with Ross upon this matter, and after a discussion of the plans of the trip, had about decided to accompany him when

I learned that my team had been captured and two of my men killed by the savages at the Mustang Water-hole. This made my presence at the station upon the plains imperative, and I immediately returned to that place to replace my team and see to other affairs that demanded attention.

About this time one of the most critical and perilous incidents of frontier life occurred. I was at my mail station on the plains and had sent my ox team to the head of the Concho for supplies, when Charles Ranner, who kept the station of the Pecos, came to Johnson's Station on his way to the head of the Concho, also for supplies. He insisted upon my going with him very early the next morning so as to reach the Concho station before the other wagon left on its return trip. We started before day the next morning, Ranner riding a little Spanish mule and I my famous saddle horse, Joe Smith. When within about ten miles of our destination we discovered some horses in the road, and believing that the Indians had waylaid them, I advised making a detour so as to reach a high point that overlooked the road, where the savages had built a monument of stone. An agreement was made between us two that if the Indians attacked us we would fasten our animals together and fight it out at the monument, but on gaining the high point we saw the horses below us without saddles or bridles, although marks on their backs showed that they had been ridden. This convinced me that the savages were at the Mustang Water-hole, a short distance below, but I acted upon the rule, " Never to turn back until I was fully satisfied that it was necessary." Keeping up on the high ground we went on till we could overlook the valley where the water-hole was, and on discovering that there were no Indians there, we pushed rapidly forward on our journey. When within a mile and a half of the Concho station we met my wagon loaded and on the road. Turning the wagon back toward the station so as to get Ranner's supplies, we rode on in advance. Some half mile in front of us was a " mot " of timber covering a quarter of an acre, the road circling around it. The two mounted men had just passed on the opposite side of the wood in full view of the station when they heard shouts from the wagon. Fearing that something was the matter, we quickly turned back to see. As we came in sight of the wagon we discovered about fifty savages charging across the prairie toward it. It was one of those perilous positions that required immediate and prompt action to save the lives of the four teamsters, one of these being my brother Thomas. The way to the station was open and the horsemen could in all probability have escaped, but the thought never crossed my mind to abandon my brother under such circumstances; so calling to Ranner that we must charge the Indians, we jerked our guns from their holsters and dashed at the savages. As they passed the wagon I called to my brother to drive into the thicket. The team was composed of five yoke of young oxen, and could not be moved very rapidly. Had the Indians reached the wagon the oxen would have become totally unmanageable. The men with the wagon were cool and brave, and getting on each side of the oxen they coaxed them as fast as possible toward the thicket. During this time Ranner and I were rapidly advancing on the savages. It so happened that the old white-haired chief, who was about a hundred yards in front of his followers, was well known, as he had taken part in all the raids on the mail line. The fact that he would come in contact with the two pale-faces first caused him to halt and the whole band followed suit. I at once called to Ranner to ride back to the brush, and stopping my horse in front of the Indians determined to make a diversion in favor of Ranner should they attempt to charge on him. Instead of charging, however, the old chief began to move in a circle around me, his braves following close in his rear. I was compelled to move along with them in the inner circle. As I rode almost abreast with the old chief I remembered Cooper's story of the "Two Admirals," and wondered if I could play the same trick that Admiral Jervis did with the French, and rush by and fire at the old red man as he passed, feeling confident that my fleet-footed horse could circle and get to the thicket before the Indians could overtake me. Just about the time that I had fully determined to make the attempt loud cries came from the direction of the trees, and on turning, it seemed to me that the whole plain below the timber was covered with savages. On discovering the presence of these other Indians, it was perfectly clear to me that a trap had been laid for us. I wheeled my horse and galloped to the wagon. Dismounting, I gave orders for the blankets to be spread upon the sides and breastwork made of the flour and corn. This was quickly done, and feeling that a good fight could be made from this fortress, we calmly awaited events. The Indians circling from different directions, cencentrated their forces just out of gun-shot range and held a council. Neil Helm stepped out into the open, and, leaning his chin upon the muzzle of his long Kentucky rifle, calmly began counting them. The others sat in silence watching the young fellow. They were startled as he broke the stillness by exclaiming: " O, hell, there's not but a hundred and fifty-one of them." They asked him what he intended doing about it. "What am I going to do? Why kill the first damned red devil that gets close enough," he nonchalantly replied. The Indians, evidently concluding that it was best not to attack the wagon and its occupants, turned toward the northwest and rode into the woods. I was afraid that on leaving our shelter we would be subjected to another attack, so I rode to the top of a ridge where I could see the savages, and watched them until they were some miles away; then orders were given to start again for the station, which we reached safely. I always considered the little Louisiana creole, Charlie Ranner, as the hero of this occasion, as he had no interest in the wagon and was riding a little mule that could not have outrun the savages, and when he was ordered to charge them his black eyes flashed brightly and his face lit up with a determined look that showed a brave, courageous man. The next time I met this young fellow he was wearing a captain's uniform in Dick Taylor's army.

Ross' expedition against the Indians is so well and graphically written in Wallace's history that it is given here in detail for the purpose of showing the great dangers and trials that the whole of the Texas frontier was subjected to. Quite a number of people were killed in Burnett, Llano, San Saba, Brown and Lampasas counties:

" In the autumn of 1860 the indomitable and fearless Peta Nacona led a raiding party of Comanches through Parker county, committing great depredations as they passed through. The loud and clamorous cries of the settlers along the frontier for protection induced the government to organize and send out a regiment under Colonel M. T. Johnson to take the field for public defense. These efforts, however, proved of small service. The expedition, though of great expense to the State, failed to find an Indian, until returning the command was followed by the wily Comanches; their horses stampeded at night, and most of the men compelled to reach the settlements on foot, under great sufferings and exposure. Captain " Sul " Ross was commissioned a captain of rangers by Governor Sam Houston, and directed to organize a company of sixty men, with orders to repair to Fort Belknap, receive from Colonel Johnson all government property, as his regiment was disbanded, and take the field against the redoubtable Peta Nacona, and afford the frontier as much protection as possible with his small force. The necessity of vigorous measures soon became so pressing that Captain Ross determined to attempt to curb the insolence of these implacable foes of Texas by following them into their fastnesses and carrying the war into their own homes. General L. S. Ross says: 'As I could take but forty of my men from my post, I requested Captain N. G. Evans, in command of the United States troops at Camp Cooper, to send me a detachment of the Second Cavalry. As we had been previously intimately associated and were good friends, he at once sent me a sergeant and twenty well-mounted men. My force was still further augmented by some seventy volunteer citizens, under the command of the brave old frontiersman, Captain Jack Cureton, of Bosque county. These self-sacrificing patriots, without the hope of pay or reward, left their defenseless homes and families to avenge the sufferings of the frontier people. With pack-mules laden with supplies, the expedition started for the Indian country.

" ' On the eighteenth of December, 1860, while marching up Pease river, I had suspicions that Indians were in the vicinity, by reason of the buffalo that came running in great numbers from the north toward us, and while my command moved in the low ground, I visited all neighboring high points to make discoveries. On one of these sand hills I found four fresh pony tracks, and being satisfied that Indian videttes had just gone, I galloped forward about a mile to a higher point, and riding to the top, to my inexpressible surprise, found myself within two hundred yards of a Comanche village, located on a small stream winding around the base of a hill. It was a most happy circumstance that a piercing north wind was blowing, bearing with it clouds of sand, and my presence was unobserved and the surprise complete. By signalling my men as I stood concealed, they reached me without being discovered by the Indians, who were busy packing up, preparatory to a move. By this time the Indians mounted and moved off north across the level plain. My command, with the detachment of the Second Cavalry, had outmarched and became separated from the citizen command, which left me about sixty men. In making disposition for attack, the sergeant and his twenty men were sent at a gallop behind a chain of sand hills to encompass them in and cut off their retreat, while, with forty men, I charged. The attack was so sudden that a considerable number were killed before they could prepare for defense. They fled precipitately right into the sergeant and his men. Here they met with a warm reception, and finding themselves completely encompassed, every one fled his own way and was hotly pursued and hard pressed.

" ' The chief of the party, Peta Nacona, a noted warrior of great repute, with a young girl about fifteen years of age, mounted on his horse behind him, and Cynthia Ann Parker, with a girl of about two years of age in her arms, and mounted upon a fleet pony, fled together, while Lieutenant Tom Killiheir and I pursued them. After running about a mile Killiheir ran up beside Cynthia's horse, and was in the act of shooting when she held up her child and stopped. I kept on after the chief, and about a half a mile further, when in about twenty yards of him I fired my pistol, striking the girl (whom I supposed to be a man as she rode like one, and only her head was visible above the buffalo robe with which she was wrapped) near the heart, killing her instantly, and the same ball would have killed the chief but for his shield which hung down, covering his back. When the girl fell from the horse she pulled him off also, but he caught on his feet, and before steadying himself, my horse, running at full speed, was very nearly on the top of him, when he was struck with an arrow which caused him to fall to pitching, and it was with great difficulty that I kept my saddle, and in the meantime barely escaped a number of arrows coming from the chief's bow. Being at such disadvantage, he would have killed me in a few minutes but for a random shot from my pistol (while I was clinging to the pommel of my saddle with my left hand), which broke his right arm at the elbow, completely disabling him. My horse then became quiet and I shot the chief twice through the body, whereupon he deliberately walked to a small tree, the only one in sight, and leaning against it, began to sing a wild, weird song. At this time my Mexican servant, who had once been a captive with the Comanches and spoke their language as fluently as his mother tongue, came up, in company with two of my men. I then summoned the chief to surrender, but he promptly treated every overture with contempt and signalized this declaration with a savage attempt to thrust me with his lance which he held in his left hand. I could only look upon him with pity and admiration. For, deplorable as was his situation, with no chance of escape, his party wholly destroyed, his wife and child captured in his sight, he was undaunted by the fate that awaited him, and as he seemed to prefer death to life, I directed the Mexican to end his misery with a charge of buckshot from the gun which he carried.' "

So signal a victory had never before been gained over the fierce and warlike Comanches; and never since that fatal December day in 1860 have they made any military demonstrations at all commensurate with the fame of their proud campaigns in the past. The great Comanche confederacy was forever broken. The incessant and sanguinary war which had been waged for more than thirty years was now virtually at an end. The blow was a decisive one; as sudden and irresistible as a thunder bolt, and as remorseless and crushing as the hand of Fate. It was a short but desperate conflict. Victory trembled in the balance. A determined charge, accompanied by a simultaneeus fire from the solid phalanx of yelling rangers, and the Comanches beat a hasty retreat, leaving many dead and wounded upon the field. Espying the chief and a chosen few riding at full speed, and in a different direction from the other fugitives, Ross quickly pursued. The two chiefs engaged in personal encounter, in which one must fall. Peta Nacona fell. Most of the women and children with a few of the warriors escaped. The victory was an incalculable boon to Texas, as it put an end to the terrible ravages and murders of the savages, and once more restored peace and prosperity to the brave and noble frontiersmen on the Texas border.

Moving on as rapidly as possible toward home after my last expedition, I reached San Antonio just in time to get the earliest news of Lincoln's election, and that the whole country was in a fever-heat. Immediately upon arriving at Burnet, my home for so many years, I hastened arrangements to marry the young lady of my choice, and on the first day of January, 1861, I was united in the holy bonds of matrimony to Miss Josephine Eastland. My business on the plains requiring prompt attention, I and my brother Ben now went out together, making our way there unattended. Here I ascertained that the Overland Mail Route was to be removed from Texas. The drivers and conductors told me that the superintendent intended to leave and take all the property pertaining to the line without cancelling his pecuniary obligations to any one. A large sum of money was due me, and I determined to have a full, square, fair settlement with the gentleman "or know the reason why." And forthwith I proceeded to make proper preparations. My station-house was composed of heavy rock covered with earth, the main room being twenty by thirty feet, and the corral was attached to it. Upon the south, joining the larger room, was a smaller one which, with the corral, made an angle in which the gate opened; and the port-holes of the building covered this angle. With me were four men, upon whose fidelity and courage I could rely—my brothers Benjamin and Thomas, Neil Helm and John Barnet. Placing these men in the small room, I awaited in the large room the coming of the superintendent, who soon drove up, stepped out of his vehicle, and walked into this apartment, bringing a valise filled with money. He asked me for his account, pretended to examine it, and suddenly burst out with a big, round oath, swearing that he would not pay it. But the fellow did not know me. He simply regarded me as an Indian fighter.

Quietly, but firmly, I informed him I would not permit him to take the mules out of the corral until he had paid every cent he owed me.

"How do you intend to prevent it, sir?" he demanded; "I have got twenty times your number of men." "True," I responded as quietly and firmly as before, "but although you have the odds on the outside, I have the odds on the inside. You shall not leave the room until you have settled this account, which you know to be a just one."

The prisoner, for such he saw himself, turned pale, hesitated, wilted, then answered: "Well, I'll settle," and, counting out the money, he closed his grip-sack and pleasantly remarked: "Now, Johnson, I want to say that you have done the best work of any man on the line, and if you will go with me I'll give you the best station I have got."

I declined the proposition, the stock was given up, the over-landers going west and I and my men returning to the settlements.

The main purpose in chronicling the foregoing events is to show the school in which I was educated for the important part I was to play in a grander theater of action. And it should be noted that the majority of my conflicts with the wild, untamable savages took place far from the civilized parts of the State, away beyond the furthest settlements, and was waged always with vastly superior numbers, with absolutely no hope of coming assistance,

PHILIP B. MATHEWS.

and that I and my men were not soldiers, but peaceable citizens who were trying to work for an honest, modest living.

Of course, like many another adventurous young spirit, when I first made my home upon the very confines of civilization and barbarism, I rather enjoyed these perilous bouts with the Indian warriors; but it is certain that as soon as the novelty of such encounters wore off I would have been more than willing for the establishment of amicable relations between the whites and the reds in order that I, with my friends, might engage more earnestly and continuously in peaceful pursuits.

I should say that I never fired upon an Indian unless to save myself or others, or our property from these murderous, rapacious foes; and it is to-day a matter of pardonable and just pride that when I was personally present none of my men or stock was ever lost, and yet perhaps I was more frequently engaged in battle with the Indians than any other man upon the plains.

I may say, too, modestly enough, I trust, that I am the only man on the lengthy Over-mail Line that has found a place in Bancroft's "History of the Western Half of the Hemisphere." My faithful, intelligent, fearless, thoroughbred horse, Joe Smith, was equally well known along the route from Fort Worth to El Paso. At this time I was called by the Overlanders "The Young Colonel."

CHAPTER V.

When Texas seceded and military companies were forming to prevent the threatened invasion of the soil by the Northern soldiery, my brothers Ben and Thomas Johnson attached themselves to a battery, while my friends Helm and Barnet returned to their native States, all having plead with me to remain at home with my newly-wedded bride of sixteen summers.

I gave each of my friends a horse, but did not obey their injunction, and made preparations to make my wife comfortable and independent for a year at least, and started with Judge Edward Youtrease for Kentucky, leaving Ben first lieutenant and Thomas sergeant of Wilkes's battery.

I determined first to pay a visit to my father and mother, in Henderson. They were what is known as "Union people." Two of my brothers were in the Federal army, and Henderson was occupied by Northern troops. Upon my arrival in Bowling Green, Kentucky, I found quite a number of my old schoolmates and friends attached to Graves's battery, which afterward became famous. My former companions were delighted to see me after such a long absence, and begged me to cast my fortunes with theirs; but I declined to join them, and soon resumed my journey to Henderson.

At Hopkinsville I called upon Colonel Nathan B. Forrest, who was in command of the cavalry force at that place. He was in his private tent with his wife and child, a young boy. Colonel Forrest seemed to me to bear a close resemblance to my father. I saw at once that he was a man of great and prompt decision. His muscular, well-proportioned figure, over six feet in height, was indicative of extraordinary physical strength. But it struck me that his most wonderful feature was his piercing blue eye which flashed and changed so rapidly with every emotion that it was difficult to distinguish its true color. He was a man to catch the look and hold the attention of the most casual observer, and as we gazed on each other I felt that he was a born leader and one that I would be willing to follow.

As I entered he gave me a keen, searching glance and asked: " Well, sir, what do you want? "

" I want to join the cavalry," I replied.

" I have plenty of room for you and many more besides," he answered. " Where are you from," he asked.

" I am from Texas," I said.

" What have you been doing out there? "

" I have been surveying and fighting the Indians," I answered.

" Well, sir, I should like to have you with me," he exclaimed. " One of my companies is from Texas, and you may go in with it if you wish."

" I should like to make two conditions, Colonel," I said in answer to this statement.

" What are they? " he asked quickly.

" First, I should like to serve as a scout."

" Well, I have plenty of use for you in that line," he said. " What is the other condition? "

" I wish to go to Henderson, Kentucky," I responded.

" I want to go there, too, and we will go together," he said. " You can look around, then meet me here again promptly at two o'clock. I wish you to meet a young man who has just come from the front, where he has been killing Yankees. If you can equal him as a scout I will have a good team," he concluded, with a broad smile.

I departed for the headquarters of the Texas company. Captain Gould was absent, and Lieutenant Jamison was in command. He invited me to his quarters and offered me a place in his mess if I would join his company.

The whole command was very comfortably fixed with good floored tents and good beds, while their commissary department was most abundantly supplied. I got an excellent dinner. Every one was discussing the merits of Forrest's young scout. They told me that he had come in that morning with some Yankee caps, sabres, guns, etc.; that he said he had killed two Yankee pickets and these things belonged to their equipment. Few of the company believed the story, and some of them even thought he was a Yankee spy. Promptly at two o'clock I was at the Colonel's tent.

The young scout, Bob Martin, was already there; and I met for the first time a man who all through the war was to be my constant companion and with me in many perilous, personal adventures. He was over six feet in height, and although somewhat slender, possessed a well-knit figure. His hair was brown, his eyes a light blue, the pupils of which would greatly expand, thus enabling him to see pretty well in the dark. He had a genial, happy face withal, and a smile like sunshine. There was nothing in his outward appearance that bespoke the wonderful courage and daring that he continually displayed during the ensuing years of the war.

We scanned each other with a close scrutiny, and were mutually pleased. We had no time to parley, for Forrest gave us immediate work. Turning to Martin, he said: " Now, Bob, I want you to start at once for Greenville. Johnson will go with you; and if you learn anything he can come back and report. I'll not be very far behind you, and you'll find me on the main road. Go into camp now, get your rations and start right out."

In a short time we were on the road to Greenville. Martin's parents living in the vicinity, he determined to visit his home, and wanted me to accompany him. But I preferred to remain to meet Colonel Forrest if he came up. It was late in the afternoon, and I passed the remainder of the day in ascertaining where supplies for cavalry could be obtained, leaving the impression that they were for the Federal cavalry under Jackson. Next morning early Martin rejoined me and we started back, meeting Forrest in the road a few miles out. When informed that provisions and forage were to be had, and the country was clear of the enemy, Forrest determined to go into the town with his little force.

A long march over the rough, muddy roads required a short rest for the men and horses, but Martin and I were ordered to move down the road to Rumsey, ascertain the movements of the Federals, and report the results of our observations. Pushing forward, when we reached Rumsey we ascertained that the enemy had built a pontoon bridge and were crossing their cavalry. Thereupon, I returned to report to Colonel Forrest, while Martin remained in the vicinity to observe the movements of the enemy.

COLONEL ROBERT M. MARTIN.

I met Forrest on the road beyond the little town of Sacramento, and the Colonel hurried forward his regiment, determined to attack them. The news that the Federals were not far away, and that a combat was imminent seemed to send a thrill of pleasure through the entire command, for these young warriors already felt in anticipation " the rapture of the fight." When the order " Gallop! " was given, the men who rode the fleetest steeds impetuously crowded to the front. As I looked back at this confused body of riders, each rushing to meet the foe first, a fearful, sickening dread came over me which I well recall to this day, and I almost presumed to call Forrest's attention to this disorderly mass of men galloping pell mell at break-neck speed, when suddenly there came into view a young woman on a bare-back horse, wildly dashing up, frantically waving her hat, while her long hair was flying in the wind like a pennant, and her cheeks were afire with excitement as she exclaimed: " There the Yankees are! Right over there! " pointing back over the hill whence she had just galloped.

Forrest, not checking his horse in the least, shouted: " Johnson, go and see right where they are."

Letting my eager animal have the reins, I was soon up with the two advanced videttes of Forrest's regiment. They were fortunately riding good horses and at my word increased their speed. Observing a high point on one side of the road not far in advance, I rode up to its summit and spied just over the crest of the hill a large body of cavalry drawn up in a V-shape and a small platoon stationed in the road in advance of the main force.

I rode back rapidly to Colonel Forrest with this information; he was trying to persuade the brave girl, who was riding by his side, to retire.

I, of course, expected him to halt his disorderly men and order a proper formation to make battle. But this fiery leader, without checking his charger, galloped on until he had reached the videttes, whom I had left on the hill-top to watch the enemy, now quite close to them. Jerking his gun out of the hands of one of them, and without a moment's hesitation, he fired at the Federals. The Confederates in his rear gave " the wild Rebel yell," and the Yankee advance-guard fled back to their command. From his post of observation Forrest could plainly see the great odds which he was so eager to attack, but, undisturbed, he halted his men right in face of the enemy and ordered his captains to reform their companies. Under less serious circumstances this would have seemed

altogether ludicrous; as the captains rode to the right and the left
commanding their men to form around them, not one of them
succeeded in collecting more than a dozen or two men out of the confused mass, nearly every fellow seemingly " on his own hook." Just
at this juncture Captain Gould, of the Texas company, coming
up and hearing the order to form, dashed to the summit of the
hill immediately in the front of the astounded Federals, and shouted
in his deep sonorous voice: " All you Texas boys rally round
your leader."

Gould had more men to the front because his company had the
best horses, and as they rushed ahead to " rally round their leader,"
the Federals likely could see their peculiar saddles and so perhaps
concluded that not only Forrest's regiment was in their front, but
the entire regiment of the Texas rangers. At any rate, they began
to fall back in disorder, and Forrest throwing out flankers, both
right and left, adopting thus in his very first fight those tactics
which he afterwards made so formidable, swept down like an
avalanche upon the Federals now in almost as much disorder as
his men had lately been.

The Southerners, led by this impetuous chieftain, swooped down
upon their foes with such terrific yells and sturdy blows as might
have made them believe a whole army was on them, and turning
tail, they fled in the wildest terror a panic-stricken mass of men
and horses, Forrest's men mixed up with them, cutting and shooting
right and left, and Forrest himself in his fury ignoring all command
and always in the thickest of the melee. Never in any battle did
leader play a fiercer individual part than did Forrest on this day.
With his long arm and long sword, once during the fight and chase
he was some distance ahead of his men, making a pathway as he
cut and slashed on this side and on that, and the demoralized
Yankees, looking back and seeing a man whom their excited imaginations doubtless magnified into a veritable giant coming down
upon them, pressed to either side, thus widening his path into a
lane. Finally he came up with a man who had been a blacksmith,
as large as himself, muscular and powerful. While engaged in
combat with this man, another Federal was in the very act of
running his sword into Forrest's back, when a timely shot from
Lieutenant Lane felled this second antagonist. Forrest hewed the
big man to the ground by a mighty stroke.

Wildly onward rushed the fleeing and pursuing masses, all in the most disorderly manner, until again Forrest was engaged in an unequal contest with two Federal officers and a private, the latter shooting a ball through his collar, and Forrest quieting him with a pistol-shot just as the two officers made an attack upon him with their swords, which he eluded by bending his supple body forward, their weapons only grazing his shoulder. The impetus of his horse carrying him a few paces forward, he checked and drew him a little to one side and shot one of his antagonists as his horse galloped up, and thrust his saber into the other. Severely wounded, both of these officers fell from their steeds, which now uncontrolled, sharply collided with each other at full speed, falling together over the bottom of an abrupt hillock. Forrest, eager in the pursuit, inadvertently rode his horse over these two prostrate animals, causing him to fall and his rider to dart ten feet over his head. Seeing Forrest down, and fearing he had been shot, I leaped my horse over the fallen horses just in time to see him spring to his feet and call out: "Johnson, catch me a horse!" His own horse was badly crippled. Catching one that came plunging down the road, I handed him the bridle, but the saddle did not suit him, and while he was getting his own saddle his men gradually withdrew from the pursuit.

After the defeat of this cavalry force I was ordered forward to reconnoiter, and gathering up a few men on the way, I pushed forward to the top of the ridge where I could observe the road for some distance; finding it clear, I left the men there as a guard and rode back to Colonel Forrest. There I found Martin relating in high glee the role he had played in the late tragedy. He was leading a horse and had his belt full of pistols.

"Hello, Bob; what have you been doing?" I asked him as I rode up.

"I've been trying to get even with a fellow that stole my horse—old Beauregard," he replied laughingly, meaning the high-headed, slender-limbed gray horse he had lost.

"What success?"

"Well, here is his horse, this is his pistol, and this is his gun," he said as he smiled.

"What became of the Yank?" I inquired.

"I left him over yonder in that strip of woods you see to the left of that road," he replied.

Collecting the guns which the Federals had thrown away, Forrest returned to Hopkinsville.

CHAPTER VI.

Martin and I received peremptory orders to cross Green river and find out, if possible, the movements of the enemy. Saddling our horses, we were quickly on the road and that night reached John Coyle's, who was then sheriff of Hopkins county and was one of the truest and best Southern men in the country. We learned from him that all the boats on Green river had been destroyed except the ferry between Henderson and Owensboro, but that a negro had caught the hull of a ferry boat and had concealed it opposite Rudy's farm. I here found that my horse had not recovered from his hard ride from Henderson and exchanged with Coyle for a strong-limbed, high-bred but vicious mare that he could not work. I saddled her, and Martin and I again set out. Reaching the river, we found the negro and induced him to ferry us over. It was difficult work: the river was out of its banks and our two horses and ourselves made all the load the boat could bear. But we got over safe and arrived at Rudy's house just at dark. This was another good Southern man. We learned from him that Colonel Jim Jackson had passed down that evening to Owensboro and would return in the morning. There were five in the party, but Martin and I determined to try to kill or capture them. At the same time Rudy agreed to go to a neighbor, whose son was in the Federal army and was then at home, and ascertain whether they were expecting to move. All this was accomplished during the night and the negro was sent into Owensboro to watch Jackson's movements. It was nearly noon when the negro returned, and informed us that Jackson had returned to the army by a different road. Disappointed in

44

this scheme, we went over to little John McFarland's where there were two handsome girls, of whom Martin was very fond. While getting something to eat, they told us that a young man from Owensboro had captured one of Jackson's cavalry horses at Willis Field's, one of their neighbors, and had gone south, and that it had created a good deal of excitement in that neighborhood. Being informed at the same time that Jackson had a large number of horses at Field's, I took Martin aside and told him I thought we could play the same trick on Field that Sergeant McDonald played on the old Tory in South Carolina during the Revolutionary War. This delighted Martin, and going to the house I borrowed some paper from the young ladies and wrote out a requisition on Willis Field for six cavalry horses and signed it " Thos. Crittenden, Major-General Commanding." This looked so artistic when I finished it that I concluded to draw another one for twelve horses. Putting the requisitions in my pocket, Martin and I rode away in a different direction from Field's until we were out of sight, then skirted the farm and continued in a gallop until we reached his home. Martin had agreed to act as sergeant and I as Lieutenant Johnson, personating my brother who was with Crittenden. Leaving Martin to hold the horses, I entered the house, introduced myself and told my business, and learned that Mr. Field had gone to headquarters and expected to return soon with a squad of men to drive the horses over to camp. In the meantime Mrs. Field invited me to stay for supper, and if possible, to remain all night. I accepted the first invitation and told her I would have to ride all night under my orders. I then went out and explained matters to Martin, and we arranged to fight the party who came for the horses, but in the meantime I told Martin to get Field's son and negro boy and round up the horses, select twelve of the best and put them in the pen. This was all promptly done while I was playing Federal lieutenant and talking to the young lady, a very pretty girl of about eighteen. I had stationed myself near the window where I could see the lane. We had placed our guns convenient for use. It was not long before Mr. Field made his appearance, riding up the lane alone. I felt very much relieved, but Martin seemed disappointed, and I think he had rather had a fight than to have captured the horses. When Field reached the house I told him my mission, and after much persuasion I got him to let his boy and negro help us to the Henderson ferry. Thereupon, I made my requisition for the twelve horses. As our road would lie through the swamp, it was necessary to lead the horses, and how to do this was a problem. Miss Field, however, came to our relief and proposed that we take her bed down and use the cord. To this I demurred, but she insisted that she wanted to do something for the government. The cord was procured and the horses were all " tailed," as we call it in Texas, three to each one of the saddle horses; after which we were called to an elegant supper, Martin sitting on one side of the lady of the house and I on the other. When she said: "Lieutenant, don't you think one of those rascally rebels came here and stole one of these horses out of the pasture, and these Secesh around here say it was not stealing; it was only 'pressing!'" I remarked that it was not any more than she could expect from people who were trying to break up the government. Martin, in the meantime, was stuffing his mouth full of biscuit to keep from laughing. We hurried through supper, and mounting our horses, pushed for the ferry; we knew we had to get across before news of the capturing of the horses had reached that point. At early dawn we arrived at the river just below the ferry, and being very cold and hungry, we stopped long enough to get breakfast and feed the horses. We found there a young man who was a soldier in Jackson's cavalry and who recognized some of the horses that belonged to his company. He helped us to the ferry and across the river. Here Martin and I had to take charge of all the horses; placing him in front, I brought up the rear and drove the loose horses after him. In this way we reached Hopkinsville in safety. When General Clark heard of our exploit he ordered Major Servesson to pay us full value for the horses.

Next morning after we left Mr. Field's, Mrs. Field went over to Mrs. McFarland's to boast of our visit, and told the McFarland girls she wished they could have been over at her house that night so she could have introduced them to two of the nicest young men they ever saw, and that if the rebel army had two such young men in it she would have more respect for it. Two days later Mr. Field went to Crittenden's quarters and inquired of him if he had heard how they liked the horses that he had sent to Henderson. General Crittenden exclaimed: "What horses?" Field replied: "The horses that were sent to stand picket." Crittenden then asked his adjutant if he knew anything about such an order. He said he did not, and

did not think any such order had been given. Field exclaimed:
" Oh, yes; I have the requisition here in my pocket," pulling it
out and handing it to General Crittenden, who, as soon as he looked
at it, burst out laughing and told Field he had been sold out. Field
was much frightened, but the General laughed at him and restored
his good humor. But the story soon got abroad, and then Mrs.
McFarland had her inning. Meeting Mrs. Field, she asked her
what she thought of " the two nice young men," and was quickly
answered that " they were like all the rest of the rebel army—
nothing but a set of horse thieves."

As Forrest's horses were in such a condition that he could not
undertake the expedition to Henderson without a rest of two days,
and being too impatient to see my parents to brook such a delay,
I set out in a buggy with one of my old schoolmates who lived
there. When we arrived at a point about five miles from the town
we stopped at Mrs. Jordan's for dinner, and there I left my gun
and baggage, the family being old friends of mine and also strong
Southern sympathizers.

CHAPTER VII.

AT THE OLD HOME.

We entered Henderson without interruption, and after five or six years' absence, I was soon in the arms of my dear mother, whose loving heart no difference of political sentiment could estrange. Both my mother and sister shed tears of joy over my safe return, but their happiness was clouded by the alarm they began to feel for my safety, as there was a Federal force occupying the town. Assuring them that they need entertain no anxiety on my account, as I would be prudent, I left, telling them that I was going to pay my respects to Colonel Cruff, the commander of the military post. I thought I might succeed in gathering news of some importance at his headquarters.

Introducing myself as the son of Dr. Thomas Johnson, I informed Colonel Cruff that I had two brothers in the Federal army, General Crittenden's command, whom I was very anxious to see, as I had been living in Texas for some years, and asked him to aid me in meeting them.

Fortunately there happened to be several of my old schoolmates in the room, who corroborated my story by greeting me with a warm handshake and a hearty welcome.

The colonel was doubtless satisfied and had no suspicion of my being a Confederate, for soon these brothers procured a leave of absence and came to see me. We walked and slept and talked freely together, there being no concealment on my part as to my military connections, and there ensued a brotherly understanding that we would do all we could to protect each other during the war.

W. S. JOHNSON (brother of Gen. A. R. Johnson)

1st Lieut. 17th Ky. Vol., U. S. A.

Colonel Holloway, one of my old schoolmates, then in the Federal army, gave an entertainment to which I was invited, where I met a great many Yankee officers. Many of them were canal and flatboat men, and some of them rather tough characters, for the first time in their lives in "society." Even now at this distant date I am filled with indignation and disgust when I recall how such roughs were allowed to associate with the sisters of my old friends. For Colonel Holloway's family I entertained genuine affection, for I had spent under their hospitable roof many delightful days, and I was stung to the quick to see such fellows on familiar terms with his family. The swaggering braggadocio of some of these fellows inflamed me with a strong desire to meet them hand to hand upon the field of battle, and I determined to make that opportunity, if possible. Their blustering boasts of what they had done and would do to the rebels at the same time disgusted me.

Of course I could not very long live undisturbed under all the circumstances I encountered in Henderson; and ere long I ascertained that I had become an object of suspicion. I was informed by Mr. Phil Mathews (an old and true friend) that he had heard a conversation among some of the Union men in the town, and I would be placed under arrest if I did not depart.

Orders had been issued from military headquarters forbidding any one to leave the town of Henderson without procuring a pass, and nobody could go outside the lines without a guarantee of loyalty to the North.

The time had now come for me to go. The Ohio river being very high had flooded Canoe creek and encircled a large portion of the town, thus greatly increasing the difficulty of my secretly withdrawing, as all the bridges were guarded by soldiers. But I had hunted along the banks of this long, winding creek many a time in boyhood and well remembered that drifts of old logs, limbs of trees and trash used to form places strong enough to cross on; and one day went to see if such could still be found. A large body of the enemy was posted at the fair grounds in the vicinity of one of these old fortuitous bridges, and it was necessary to know exactly where their pickets were placed before I essayed escape at that point. In making this investigation I approached the spot where I had seen the guard standing the day before; but as they had been stationed further down the road I came upon the advanced videttes unexpectedly and dodged rapidly into the woods, flattering myself

I had been too alert and quick to attract their observation; but an order to halt undeceived me, and feeling sure I had been discovered, I ran as fast as I could to a place where I recollected such a crossing used to be. Swift of foot, I fancied I could easily outstrip any man under the weight of a heavy gun and accoutrements, especially in a long distance. So off I pushed confidently, but was soon surprised to hear the cry "Halt! Halt!" coming nearer and nearer. Wishing to avoid a fight, which even if favorable to me might result in capture by others, probably already on my trail, I redoubled my exertions, but observed to my great astonishment that my competitor in this novel foot-race was still gaining upon me gradually but surely. Knowing that the slow pace necessary to get over the loose, floating driftway would enable my foe to overtake me, I abandoned my original purpose, and seeing a large oak tree which had been torn up by the roots in a recent storm and thrown parallel with the creek, leaving a narrow passway, I sprang into this opening between the tree and the bluffs of the stream. A pendent branch of a dogwood tree at the mouth of this little alley compelled me to stoop as I entered. Here I determined to take the chance for life and liberty. The green curtain at the doorway of this little woodland court trembled in the breeze as if agitated at the immediate prospect of a human combat to the death; for nature seems often to sympathize with her children in their extremity. On followed the Yankee, and like a maddened bull with head down he burst into this closed arena, only to receive a pistol bullet into his skull. With a cry of pain and a leap into the air he sprang over the bluff into the surging waters.

I returned to the town immediately, believing that if the chase had been seen, I should be caught ere I had gone far, and so I resolved to put on a brave front.

It was dangerous to take either horn of the dilemma I was in. If the soldiers had tracked me and run me down after hearing my pistol shot, they would probably have found the body of their comrade and summarily riddled mine with bullets. If I had been suspected after my return and the corpse had been found, my Union family and friends, with a good lawyer, might have saved me from punishment on the plea of self-defense or lack of evidence, and finally might have effected my exchange, if indeed I had not profited by some opportunity to escape from prison.

The next day, Sunday, I accompanied my mother to church. I had always paid her this attention before going to the Lone Star State. On the route to church a part of the walkway was covered with a double row of broad planks. A number of ladies were in advance of us and a company of soldiers, coming from an opposite direction, marching by twos with locked arms, and keeping step to the call of " Hep, hep," forced these ladies off the narrow causeway into the mud. All the chivalry and gallantry of my nature and education as a Kentuckian rebelled at this indignity. I was so indignant that I resolved if they jostled my mother I would blaze away into the column with my revolver; but the leader just then seemed to recollect his politeness, and broke the ranks so that they could pass by in " Indian file " without compelling mother to step into the mud.

Still exasperated, I exclaimed: " See, mother, what kind of men this army is composed of. No Southern soldiers would ever have forced ladies off into the mud, and if they had jostled you I should certainly have hurt some of them."

" My goodness, how could you have done it? " she exclaimed. Pulling my coat open I displayed my revolver. " My son," she said, "you must leave this town to-night.

We went on to church, but neither of us probably was edified by the services. The moment we got out of the door mother again insisted that I must leave the place and go back to the Southern army.

Arriving at home, I observed Colonel Cruff's handsome dappled dun horse hitched at a church door immediately opposite the residence. Upon opening the gate, I told mother that I must bid her good bye then and there, for I had concluded to take her advice and was resolved to ride away on the Yankee colonel's beautiful charger. My prudent mother ran after me, and throwing her arms around my neck, implored me not to do such a rash thing, as I would be followed and killed. She was now joined by my sister, and together they detained me until the old colonel came out and mounted his horse.

But I made up my mind to leave that town mounted upon the best horse I could find, in order to distance pursuers and have a good animal to ride in Forrest's command. So I resolved to attack in the evening an orderly sergeant whom I had observed parading daily on the back of a splendid gray steed from the fair grounds to the hospital. Stationing myself near a deep cut in the road, I awaited the sergeant's coming. Stepping in front of him, I demanded his surrender. But the Yankee prized his fine horse too highly to give him up so easily, and turning the animal's head toward the bank he spurred him up and onward. The thought flashed across my mind that I would soon be surrounded and arrested if this man got away, and the next instant my pistol sent a bullet after the frightened, fleeing rider. But the gathering darkness defeated my aim, much to my surprise and chagrin. Convinced now that my departure could be delayed no longer, I returned home, got a horse from one of my brothers and rode rapidly out to Mrs. Jordan's, where I had left my things. After a bountiful supper I thanked warmly my kind hostess, and mounting my excellent steed (which I did not prize, however, as highly as if I had captured him), I started in a gallop for Hopkinsville, seventy miles away.

Reporting the military situation at Henderson to Forrest and offering to guide him there for its capture, he consented and ordered preparations to be made for the expedition.

But counter orders having been received from General Albert Sidney Johnston for Forrest to hold his command in readiness to move to Fort Donelson, I was greatly disappointed, for I had anticipated capturing the blue-coats or driving them out of my native town. Instead of this I was dispatched with Martin to go behind the enemy's lines across Green river with orders to report at Fort Donelson on Wednesday.

CHAPTER VIII.

Leaving Clarksville on the morning of the twelfth of February, one of those bright, balmy days which often heralds the advent of spring in this latitude, in the mere exuberance of animal spirits, I unconsciously rode my little mare at such a rapid gait that she manifested signs of distress by the time I arrived at the ferry at Dover. While waiting for the ferry boat to return to our side of the river, a young man came riding up on a stout, spirited white horse. I took a fancy to this horse and proposed an exchange, and after the usual dickering, the swap was made; a fortunate trade for me it soon proved. By the time the boat touched the other shore I heard rapid firing ahead and learned that Forrest was engaging the enemy beyond our earthworks. Putting spurs to my horse, I galloped off in the direction of Fort Henry and soon overtook Lieutenant Ed. Rankin, of Graves's battery, who, as we rode along together for a short distance, remarked the gaits and color of my strong, lively horse. Near where the road crossed our breastworks Rankin turned off toward Graves's battery while I pushed forward, and two miles further on found Forrest alone in the road, sitting upon his horse. He heartily welcomed me and said: "Johnson, I am glad you have come;" pointing to the right, he continued: "Ride over there and bring those fellows in; they are wasting powder." I galloped over to the detachment, which I found consisted of two companies of Gaunt's cavalry who were shooting at a body of Federal infantry out of range, but advancing rapidly. General Forrest's order was delivered, but I noticed that the head of the Federal column was marching obliquely across our front as if they intended to strike the bank of the river below our fortifications.

Observing a first-rate place to ambush the enemy as they passed, I persuaded the officer to dismount his men just behind a brushy ridge, and lie concealed till they got within a hundred yards of us, when I gave the command to fire a volley on them, causing them to fall back into the brush in confusion. We then mounted our horses and galloped over to where Forrest was still sitting on his horse, awaiting us, and talking with Bob Martin. Giving Martin and myself orders to watch the enemy, he took command of the cavalry and marched into the fortifications.

Martin told me he had been skirmishing with the enemy all day and showed me a beautiful Maynard rifle he had captured during a sharp skirmish that morning. He said he had been trying its range across an old field, and while lying down behind a stump and firing in his front, a body of infantry had got so nearly on him that he had to get up and run at the top of his speed, with the bullets pattering all around him. It was not long before we noticed the advance-guard of the enemy with a section of artillery moving up the road toward us. As soon as they saw us they wheeled one of the guns into position and fired a shell that burst almost directly over our heads and sent us galloping back toward the fort. When we were out of range we selected another point of observation, Martin on the hill side to the right of the road and I on the left. The Federal batteries were soon near us again, and I rode down the main road a hundred yards or so from the breastworks and was sitting on my horse waiting for Martin, when Captain Graves, seeing me and taking me for a Federal, trained one of his guns on me loaded with grapeshot, and was in the act of firing when Ed. Rankin, recognizing my white horse, called to him not to fire and told him who I was. Just at this time a shell from the enemy's gun exploded near Martin's horse, throwing rocks and dirt over us both, warning us it was time to seek cover; so we dashed away and were soon over the breastwork and out of danger.

We reached Forrest's tent about dark, and after feeding our horses and getting supper, he called us aside and said: " Now, boys, I want to know just what those fellows are doing. I shall go out here to the left while you can make your way in on the

right and find out just what we can depend on." Leaving Martin
at the tent, I rode to Graves's battery and showed him my orders
to pass through the lines, and left my horse at his quarters; he went
with me to the advanced vidette, who was walking his beat on the
bank of the river, and explained to him my mission, telling him
if he should leave before I came back to notify the relief that I
was out. I passed down the bank of the river and moved cautiously along until I came in sound of the Federal picket, and
then stealing along inch by inch, I came in sight of the Federal
advanced vidette, and finding a small ravine, or branch, I slipped into
it and lay there till I discovered it was the terminus of two .beats.
As the sentinels came together and started back I found the opportunity to glide in between them. I was wearing a large gray
traveling shawl, fastened at the throat and hanging low so as to
cover my shotgun, yet open in front in such a way that I could
easily use my gun. This was the same little English shotgun I
had carried on the plains of Texas and that had never failed me in
any encounter with the Indians, and I felt sure that if the picket
discovered me lying on the ground I would be able to get the
first shot, as being above me his person was clearly defined in the
skylight, while I was lying close under the bank of the little brook.
I felt I had every advantage, and as it was only a short distance
to the river bank, I could soon be out of danger and within our lines
in case of alarm. The little ravine ran in a diagonal direction and
carried me beyond their picket base. I felt secure and rose to my
feet and walked with confidence through the brush until I saw
the officers' tent with a fire in front; I made my way to within
a few feet of the rear of the tent, and screening myself in the
underbrush, I had a clear view of the surroundings. Many horses
were picketed in the vicinity which made me believe I was at some
important headquarters. Several officers coming out of that tent
and walking to the fire, I was confirmed in this impression, and others
riding up and dismounting and joining in the conversation, I was
satisfied I had found the right place. Pretty soon
some one coming hastily through the brush and walking up to where the officers were collected, exclaimed:
"Well, Colonel, I have found that the enemy's pickets
are a very little way this side of the abattis." A general
conversation ensued, and among other things, one of the officers
remarked: "If they don't do any better fighting than they did

at Fort Henry to-day we'll be in their breastworks before sunup."
Then the officer who seemed to be in command, whom I have
always supposed to be General Smith, asked if they had distributed
the ammunition as had been directed. Believing that I had now
obtained valuable information and that an assault was intended, I
made my way back as I had come, and getting my horse, I arrived
at Colonel's Forrest's quarters. He dressed instantly and we went
to report to General Pillow. I did not stop to reflect at that time
that it was strange Forrest should report these things to General
Pillow when Floyd was in command. When we returned to
camp it was daylight. Martin had already got in. Forrest had
several scouting parties ready to go out on the left, and taking
Martin and me along with him, he made an extended reconnoissance
all along the backwater. I was sent several times with messages
that day to Pillow.

In the meantime the assault on our right was made and repulsed
with heavy loss to the enemy. Some of our men were engaged
in strengthening the works, and others in watching the enemy as
they were closing in around us. That night I was required again
to go into the enemy's lines, and proceeded in the same manner as
before, but found that the Federals had doubled their pickets and
were far more on the alert; but I succeeded in reaching my former
station near General Smith's tent. Many were still engaged in
carrying off. their wounded. I learned that the enemy had been
reinforced and also that their gunboats were expected to attack us
in the morning. I again made my way back into our lines, and
having made my report to Forrest again, went with him to General
Pillow's quarters. I was fully impressed with the idea that there
would be a general assault the next morning, and I noticed as I
went along that our troops were moving out towards our left. As
soon as we had made our report Forrest started to the front and
required me to go on with him. It was intensely cold, for there had
been a regular blizzard during the night. As we galloped along we
met a courier from Captain Overton, who said he had found the
enemy in heavy force in the front. Captain Overton was in command of a Kentucky company which had been assigned to Forrest's
command. Forrest put spurs to his horse and rode to the advanced
videttes. He called Martin and me and directed us to go forward
with Lieutenant Ringold and find the exact position of the enemy.
When we reached the point where Overton's scouts thought they

had discovered the enemy, we found they had taken an old brush fence for a column of infantry, and pushing on some distance we came to an old field through which Ringold insisted on riding. There was a rather wide and deep ravine running down almost through the center of the field. Believing that the enemy was near, I rode close to the edge of the ravine, Martin to the left and Ringold to the right. Keeping a close lookout, we rode towards the far end of the field, and when about half way I heard the sharp report of a rifle and felt the force of a bullet as it passed through my coat at the top of my shoulder. I instantly put spurs to my horse and jumped him into the ravine. Bending low, it seemed that a thousand bullets passed over my head. Running down through the ravine till I found an opening towards the left and jumping my horse to the upper level again, I made my way towards the woods and caught a glimpse of Martin as he jumped his horse over the fence, and saw Ringold running back the way we came, leaning forward with his arms about his horse's neck. The whizzing of bullets about me warned me that I was still within range, and urging my horse to his full speed and leaping over the fence into the dense woods beyond, I found myself out of danger. Pressing on, I came up with Martin and was relieved to learn that he was not hurt. A little farther on we found Ringold lying on the ground and surrounded by a number of Confederate officers. He had three minie balls in him and was pronounced by the surgeon to be mortally wounded. I heard afterwards that he recovered, but I never again met him in the service.

Forrest in the meantime had hurried up his command, dismounted them and advancing as far as the field fence, opened fire on the enemy, although they were concealed in the dense woods opposite. It proved to be too long a range for our guns. One of our boys, more venturesome than the rest, crawled out into the field behind a stump and opened fire, and about the time he fired his second shot he received a ball in the head that killed him instantly. Another boy did the same thing, rolling his comrade's body out of the way, and soon himself met the same fate. A third boy—nothing daunted—started for the fatal spot, but Forrest coming up, in a stentorian voice ordered him back. Springing to his feet and running back to the fence, he was hit by a ball in the leg before he could get over. Forrest now made a flank movement and the enemy fell back to a strong position. About this time Forrest received orders to fall back.

Learning that the gunboats were coming up the river, Forrest determined to see the fight. There was a large two-story white house standing on the hill overlooking the river and he headed his horse toward it. I, however, turned mine into the low bottom and moved in the direction of the river. Forrest observing this, hallooed at me: "Johnson, why don't you come up here with me behind the house?" I told him I was afraid I should get full of splinters if I got behind the house. This apparently struck him as sensible, for he turned his horse and rode with me into the bottom where he could overlook the river and see everything. The sound of the heavy shells that soon began to shriek over us was enough to strain the nerves of the strongest man. And as the shriek would reach my ear I would unconsciously draw myself into as small a compass as possible, but did not dodge for fear I should make the wrong motion. Forrest noticing me, said: "Why don't you dodge?" I told him I was really afraid to do so. "I don't believe a word of it," he said, but such was the actual fact. Intense anxiety soon overcame all other feelings. We sat gazing intently at the boats, realizing that if they should pass the batteries we would be completely at their mercy, as the river was high enough to enable them to rake all the hollows and low ground around the fortifications. On, on they came, throwing their great round shot and shells against our works, many of them passing over the hills and dropping into our camps beyond. The leading boat was fairly abreast of us, and we believed that she would certainly pass, when we heard the crash of a shell against her side and saw the smoke of the explosion rise up and the confusion on board. Slowly turning with the current, she floated down stream amid the wild hurrahs and yells of the Confederates. Forrest himself stood straight in his stirrups and shouted with as much enthusiasm as any of us. The whole flotilla turned and followed in retreat. With great satisfaction we watched them all till they were out of sight. Then we returned to our camp.

Ever on the alert, Forrest sent Martin, myself and a young red-headed Missourian named Garner out on the left to see if the enemy were making advances in that direction. The earth was covered with a crust of frozen snow, so that we made much noise as we rode along. I suggested that we separate and advised each to ride a short distance and then stop and listen, Garner going to the right and Martin to the left. I took the central line, and carrying out my own suggestion, I galloped forward until I reached a point where I could see some distance down an open glade. Taking shelter beneath a large tree, I saw a column of cavalry crossing the glade some distance in my front, and while I was intently watching them I heard the crushing sound of a body of horsemen immediately in my rear and found myself inclosed between the two Federal columns. I was now in full view of the rear column, which was between me and our fortification. Knowing it would be almost impossible to escape by flight, and having my shawl around me so that no one could distinguish me, I turned my horse's head around and moved slowly along parallel with the column, or rather, gradually drawing nearer to them, but slowly falling to the rear and finally crossing between the rear guard and the column. I was slowly widening the distance between us, when quick firing in front caused the Federals to double-quick in that direction, and I was left to make my way to our lines without further molestation. On reaching camp, I found Garner and Martin had returned; all parties believed that I had either been killed or captured. Garner had got the first glimpse of the cavalry and had come in first and reported that we were both doubtless killed, as he had heard the firing. Martin had also got a sight of the cavalry, and taking a good position, waited till the advanced videttes got in close range; then, turning his double-barrel shotgun loose at them, brought down a man and horse. Some of the Federal troopers dashed at him and followed him close enough to our intrenchments to draw the fire of some of our infantry outposts, which turned them back.

We had time enough to feed our horses and get our suppers, when Forrest gave me orders to enter the lines again and ascertain, if possible, if the enemy were concentrating at any point to make an assault; he also wanted me to see the whole length of the line. Taking my usual route, I went to Captain Graves's quarters and he again went with me to the outposts and gave the same instructions as formerly, although I did not intend to return that way. Martin this time went with me as far as the battery, and taking my horse, led him over to our extreme left and there waited for me. Entering the line, I went up the ravine as formerly, but the night being extremely cold, I made very slow progress. It was necessary to keep my hands warm enough to handle my gun quickly if necessary. I had passed two lines of sentinels and was moving on with less caution, as I knew where the picket base was, and thought I could pass it without any trouble, but turning a sudden bend in the branch, I came upon the picket guard at their base, seated around a fire right where I had formerly passed; believing that I was discovered, a sudden inspiration came to me and I stepped briskly forward and ordered them to put out the fire, asking them why they had built it so near the guard line. All hands at once began kicking the wet snow and dirt over the fire, while I passed rapidly on towards Smith's headquarters. I am confident my Scotch shawl and peremptory order convinced them that I was a Federal officer. Reaching my station near Smith's headquarters, I waited patiently for something to turn up, and was soon rewarded by getting information from an aide of General Grant's, who came cantering up, and dismounting, was met at the front of the tent by General Smith, who asked hastily about the gunboats. The officer replied that some of them were so seriously damaged that they could not be repaired this side of Louisville. "And how is it about the reinforcements?" "We think they will reach here to-morrow evening, or, at the latest, Sunday morning."

Feeling the importance of this news and knowing that I had a long trip to make over a comparatively unknown country, and that every step I took carried me on much more dangerous ground with less chance of escape if discovered, I hurried away. The tangled brush and the deep ravines were in one sense a great protection, but in another it increased my danger, as I would frequently come suddenly upon a camp and had to make my way carefully around it. My danger was the greater, as there was a number of my schoolmates and two of my brothers scattered along this line. I determined not to be captured and intended to shoot any one, except, of course, my brothers, that should recognize me. I had the conceit to believe that I had a good chance of escape, as the country was a mass of tangled brush, and the woodcraft that I had learned while on the frontier of Texas would enable me to outwit untrained soldiers, let them be ever so numerous. Therefore, walking on rapidly, I reached the backwater, on which the extreme right of the Federals rested. I considered my situation here more desperate than at any other point, as I had to pass through the lines without any knowledge of the position of the Federal outposts. Working my way cautiously toward the front until I thought I was near their picket base, I turned squarely to the left, going back towards the river, hoping to find some ravine that cut their line which would enable me to slip through. I was not disappointed, and soon found myself in a ravine that led in the right direction; going down it and moving along with extreme care, as the crust of snow made it very difficult to move without noise, I proceeded some time when I found a fire had been kindled also in this ravine. There was a strong picket guard, some of them lying asleep, and others cooking and eating. My only chance was now to climb out of the ravine and manage to get back into it between the base and the videttes. It took me a long time to accomplish this. But I here got some information as I was passing along within earshot. I heard one of the men ask another if Crittenden's corps had searched the landing; I stopped and listened with intense interest and heard the others say " No, and will not till to-morrow evening, or Sunday morning." The other laughed and said: " This is already Saturday morning, for it's now four o'clock." The other said: " Well, no matter, they will not be here till this evening anyhow, and you had better go and relieve the guard, as it is now time." Knowing that 'I had but a short time to get out of the Federal lines and into our own, I moved along towards the front, the noise of waking the guard and getting them into line enabling me to escape notice and get to the edge of the ravine concealed by the undergrowth. I waited till the guard passed me towards the front and until the relieved guard returned. Then dropping into the ravine again, I moved down it to the front, and coming to a sudden turn, found that the pickets were on the hill and their beats only extended to the border of the ravine, which enabled me to easily pass their line. Continuing in the branch, I soon reached our videttes. Either I was less cautious or our sentinels were more alert, as I was halted and made to give the countersign over the point of a bayonet. I was taken quickly to the picket base, where I found Martin, who threw his arms around me and declared he had never passed a night of greater anxiety.

Mounting our horses, we rode rapidly to Forrest's headquarters, and thence to General Pillow's. Forrest quickly dismounted and went in, but soon coming out, mounted and rode with us back to his tent; then, telling us to go in and get something to eat, he turned his attention to having his command mounted and ready for moving. I now realized for the first time that everything had been prepared for some serious work. We were not half through eating, for we were very hungry, when Forrest returned and said: " If you are not through eating, fill your pockets, for we must go." It was very cold, and I persuaded Martin to wear my heavy overcoat. We were soon riding at the head of the column with Forrest. I now noticed that other troops were moving in the same direction. It was just about daybreak when we encountered the advanced videttes of the Federal forces. The pickets were quickly driven in on the main body, and then commenced the great battle of Fort Donelson. Forrest ordered me to report to General Pillow, and ask him to support him with a brigade of infantry, telling me where I would find the general, according to a previous agreement. Pillow was on horseback in a glade not far in the rear. After receiving my report, he said: " Tell Forrest to push forward; the infantry has been already ordered to his support." Galloping back, I was again with Forrest and the orders I brought seemed to fill him with delight. Onward we pressed, pushing the Federals back.

CHAPTER IX.

Wyeth, in his History of Forrest, gives the following vivid description of the movement:

"Forrest had worked his way well around the Federal right flank and in their rear. His quick eye caught the first break in Oglesby's ranks, and shouting 'Charge!' at the head of his men he rode into the wavering, yet gallant, Westerners. The pressure from the front and the rush of the horsemen on flank and rear were more than they could stand. Holding their empty cartridge-boxes up to tell why they yielded, they broke and fled the field. Panic was in the air, and to the mind of Forrest the crisis of the battle had come. Galloping at full speed to General Bushrod Johnson, he pleaded with this officer to order an advance all along the line, but the West Pointer would not presume. General Pillow was ever on the right, intent on urging Buckner to move out and attack, and the order for which Forrest was praying was not given. Observing a battery of the enemy comparatively unprotected, the lieutenant-colonel of cavalry, this time not asking for orders, put himself at the head of his command and rode the gunners down before they could escape. The battery of six pieces was his. For the first time in the war he was able to show what cavalry could do. General Pillow, in his official report, says: ' I found the command of General Buckner massed behind the ridge within the works, taking shelter from the enemy's artillery on the Wynn's Ferry road, having been forced to retire, as I learned from him. Our force was still slowly advancing, driving the enemy towards

the battery, and I directed General Buckner immediately to move
his command towards the rear of the battery, turning its left,
keeping in the hollow, and to attack and carry it. Before the
movement was executed, my force forming the attacking party
on the right, with Colonel Forresi's regiment of cavalry, had
reached the position of the battery. Colonel Forrest's cavalry gallantly charged a large body of infantry supporting the battery,
driving it and taking six pieces of artillery—four brass pieces and
two twenty-four-pounder iron pieces.' Here fell a number of his
men. His horse was shot, and that of his brother, Lieutenant Jeffrey
Forrest, was killed, and in falling badly crushed his rider.

"The lieutenant-colonel of cavalry did not rest upon this feat,
which won for him and his men the high commendation of his
chief. Leaving the guns to be taken from the field by others, and
under orders from General Pillow to leave Gaunt's battalion to
guard the left, he immediately moved his own regiment towards
Buckner's position at the Confederate center. As General Buckner
was advancing to the attack, General Pillow pointed out to Forrest
two guns of the enemy which were doing considerable damage
and greatly annoying the Confederate advance, and said: 'They
must be silenced; Forrest must do it.' Leading the squadron in
person, he asked General Pillow to give him the support of the
nearest infantry. Roger Hanson's 'Orphans,' the Second Kentucky Regiment, stripped for the fray and moved up for the work.
With sabres out and bayonets fixed, horse and foot plunged through
the tangled mass of undergrowth so thick that the infantry easily
kept pace with the mounted troopers until reaching the edge of
a narrow field or clearing. Here Hanson, shouting to his men,
'Hold your fire until at close quarters!' and calling for the cavalry
to go with him, rushed into the opening. With equal valor the
Federals stood their ground. They swept the field with bullets,
and crowds of Confederates went down. Riderless horses scurried
from the scene, while the troopers yet mounted, yelling like
demons, with guns discarded and pistols in hand, leaped over their
fallen friends and went right on. Like a canebrake on fire, the
Union muskets blazed and crackled right in the faces of the Southern men, and then it was hand to hand, bravely and briefly. Under
the pressure of this desperate onslaught the Federals finally gave
way. Forrest's men, charging with the infantry, were first on the

guns, but the glory was equally with the Kentuckians and their peerless leader, who, later on, at Murfreesboro, slept

'On Fame's eternal camping ground.' "

In this charge Forrest's horse, weakened by loss of blood from many wounds, fell under him, but instantly he was remounted on a horse tendered him by a young Baptist preacher, named Lansing Burroughs, who had been with him all day in the battle. This exchange caused but a momentary halt, and Forrest calling upon Martin and me to follow him, dashed off furiously after the retreating Federals; but was soon halted by the killing of this loaned horse by a cannon-shot. Disentangling himself, Forrest ordered me to push on again rapidly and ascertain what the beaten enemy was doing. After going some distance I got near enough to these retiring forces to see many of their officers strenuously striving to halt and reform them; which, however, they did not succeed in doing until reinforcements came up.

I then returned to report that the Federals had at last made another stand with greater numbers. I found Forrest with Pillow, Floyd and Buckner. As I rode up I heard General Buckner say: " The Wynn's Ferry road is open now, and if we intend to move according to the program we ought to do so at once."

" I am not in favor of retreating," General Pillow replied. " We can drive them into the Tennessee river." I gathered from this fragmentary conversation that Fort Donelson had been regarded as untenable and an evacuation had been anticipated. Buckner evidently thought the propitious hour had arrived; Pillow objected; Floyd was silent. They asked me what I had to report. I told them the Federals were again advancing and had been receiving reinforcements to a considerable extent. Just at this time heavy firing was heard upon our right, and General Floyd ordered the infantry to retire behind the entrenchments.

I received orders to go to the front again and keep a close eye upon the enemy's movements, reporting anything of importance that might occur; while Forrest received instructions to collect all the wounded and all arms and accoutrements he might find scattered about the battlefield.

Galloping forward, I soon came to a small farm not very far beyond the Wynn's Ferry road, where I discovered that the Yankees had turned the dwelling-house into a hospital. Coming around to the front of this house, I observed a young aid-de--camp sitting upon his horse, and could distinctly hear him order the surgeon to move all his wounded, that could possibly stand such treatment, to the rear. As he turned to ride off I commanded him to halt, but instead of heeding he drew his pistol and I was compelled to shoot him. I then caught the young lieutenant's horse, and telling the Federal surgeon that they were now within the Confederate lines, and that he must not stir from that spot, I rode on; but finding the captured horse a great impediment to my scouting, I tied him to a tree and proceeded toward the Federal lines, and soon got within range of some skirmishers advancing in line. I then retraced my route and was fortunate to find the captured horse where I had left him, and took him to camp, which I reached just as Forrest was preparing to go to headquarters. I found Burroughs with Forrest, and presented him with the captured steed, much to the joy of the unselfish young preacher.

Having reported to Forrest, he told me I had better eat my supper and go to bed in his tent, saying: " I know I have worked you pretty hard and you need some rest."

But Martin, weary and worn by the long and severe labors he had undergone, had already dropped to sleep in a bed of snow. His two best friends, Forrest and myself, fearing that he would suffer from this exposure, lifted him gently and laid him inside the tent, covering his unconscious form with warm blankets. In accordance with my habit, I first groomed and fed my faithful horse which I had ridden hard from early morn without food or rest; then proceeded to broil some bacon, the most savory and grateful meat a very hungry man can eat, which I ravenously devoured after making a sandwich of it between two pieces of hard tack. That meal of frugal fare after so long a fast made such an impression upon my mind that I remember it to this day as the most satisfying supper I ever partook of. I had been unceasingly employed ever since Wednesday morning, and had not once stopped to take much-needed repose from that morning until now, Saturday night. Still, under the excitement of the events of this day, I had passed beyond the desire to sleep and sat munching my cracker and bacon, and gazing thoughtfully into the camp-fire, when I was aroused from my reverie by the clatter of horses' feet upon the frozen road. It was Forrest, who dashed up and asked excitedly: "Johnson, where's Martin?"

"In the tent still asleep, General," was the reply.

"Rouse him up, for God's sake, rouse him up; there's work to be done," Forrest cried in the same excited tone.

I dropped the "hard tack" and sprang up and rushed into the tent where Martin was peacefully sleeping, having forgotten that there ever was such a disturbing element as Yankees. It was with much difficulty that he was aroused, and he was still sitting on the blanket rubbing his eyes when Forrest entered.

"Boys, these people are talking about surrendering, and I am going out of this place before they do, or bust hell wide open," he announced in his determined and expressive style.

Martin, now thoroughly awake, sat looking at the grim face of his leader in open-mouthed astonishment, while I stood straight and stiff with surprise. I had felt so confident that a great and decisive victory had been gained by the Confederates that the idea of surrendering had never once presented itself, but on Forrest's announcement I determined to make my escape also from that place before this plan was put into effect.

"That's what these damn fools intend to do, so you boys must go at once and find some way for my regiment to get out of here, for get out they must if I have to kill every Yankee picket to do it," the cavalry leader said.

"But, General, how are Martin and I to get through these lines when no countersign has been given and orders are to shoot any one who attempts to pass," I inquired, puzzled, but determined to do my best.

"I do not know how you are to get through, but all depends upon you and you simply must find a way or make one, for I am going to take my command out of here before daylight," was the stern rejoinder.

We were soon in the saddle and turned our horses' heads towards the Wynn's Ferry road. Our quickly-improvised plan was to assume the role of officers out with instructions to be doubly careful in letting any one through the lines. After searching for some time, we succeeded in finding a guard-line reaching the backwater of the much-swollen Cumberland river. A few paces from the picket base, out in the river, was a small strip of land completely surrounded by water and extending down into our lines. Riding a short distance back into the woods, we dismounted and tethered our horses to a tree: wishing to lessen the danger of being halted,

we decided it was best to pursue this course, as we were less likely
to be discovered on foot than on horseback. Slipping stealthily to
the bank, we noiselessly stepped into the water and waded out to
the small island; then dropping upon our bellies, we wiggled our way
carefully along until we had passed the pickets; then entered the
water again and waded back to the mainland. The ice-cold water
made our teeth chatter and cold chills chase in rapid succession
down our spines, but we set our jaws firmly with a great effort
to keep them still, and walked along lightly and rapidly until we
were in sight of the Federal picket-fires. A careful note was made
of their position, then we made our way back as we had come,
being fortunate enough to elude the eyes of the sentries as well
as to discover a fordable place in the backwater about a half mile
from the enemy's lines that could be easily crossed on horseback.

On reaching our horses we sprang into the saddles and rode at
full speed to the Confederate headquarters, where we found General
Forrest anxiously awaiting our return. He immediately conducted
us to the council chamber where Generals Floyd, Pillow and
Buckner were in earnest consultation over their dangerous situation
and their different views of policy. The supreme question of the
hour was already settled in Forrest's clear, decisive mind, for his
plan of action was fully mapped out. After hearing our report
these three Confederate leaders discussed the matter without reserve.
As Martin and I were almost frozen from our wade in the freezing
water and our wild gallop through the bitter wind, we hugged the
stove and listened attentively to the arguments of these generals.
We soon saw that they all somewhat doubted the feasibility of
escape in the night. Pillow strenuously opposed surrender;
Buckner believed that further resistance only involved a useless
sacrifice of life, while Floyd was non-committal. Floyd and Pillow,
while ranking Buckner, seemed desirous of shifting upon
his shoulders the responsibility of remaining and carrying out the
plans of surrender, while they would make an effort to escape. This
was the final conclusion of their heated discussion, and Forrest
gained consent to lead his command out before daylight. We
hastened to rouse the sleeping soldiers and get them under arms
and mounted for their hazardous nocturnal enterprise. These
fine fellows were completely worn out with their hard day's labor
in the bitter cold, and it was with great difficulty that Martin and
I succeeded in waking them; but we shook them and punched them

and yelled at them and rubbed snow in their faces and tried to make them understand the nature of the march before them. Almost all of them got into the saddle, but a few unfortunate ones were left behind and were afterwards found asleep in their blankets. Just as the regiment was moving off Forrest ordered Martin and me to return to headquarters. He had meantime arranged with Dr. J. W. Smith, a native citizen residing near, and familiar with the country, to guide him out by the route we described. Leaving our horses tied near the tent, we walked back to headquarters and were informed by Generals Pillow and Floyd that we were to be their guides as far as Nashville.

I must ask the reader to now pardon me for a slight digression from the main course of my narrative. The battle of Fort Donelson was one of the crises of the great Civil War. It produced the reverse effect of Manassas on our people—the one sent a thrill of joy, pride and confidence throughout the South; the other was followed by sorrow and dejection. Joseph E. Johnston and Beauregard were toasted as heroes; Albert Sidney Johnston, Floyd and Pillow had vials of wrath poured on their devoted heads, while a meed of praise was given to Buckner for staying with his men and sharing their fate. The veriest novice in the art of war, become critical, could see that Johnston could have destroyed Grant's army and then concentrating his victorious forces on Buell, have driven him from Kentucky; or, he could have retreated from Bowling Green with more safety before the battle of Fort Donelson than afterward. The fury of the people was expended on Albert Sidney Johnston for not availing himself of these opportunities. All the critics could see that Grant had made a great military blunder when he divided his forces at Fort Henry and marched to Donelson, he says, with only fifteen thousand men. Forrest always asserted that we could have beaten Grant between the rivers, had we marched out and given battle on Wednesday. The reason for this failure of Johnston is a matter of conjecture: Colonel William Preston Johnston has declared that Pillow's dispatches misled his father. If the question should be asked why Pillow was sending dispatches when General Floyd was the commanding officer, I give in answer my opinion that General Pillow had no confidence in the military ability of General Floyd, who was purely a " political general;" and, indeed, from what I saw of General Floyd, I think he had no confidence in himself; wherefore, General Pillow dóminated General Floyd and controlled affairs at Fort Donelson. I know this, that all the orders and reports I carried went to General Pillow; and as he refused to carry out the plan which, I take it, had been agreed upon,—to march the army out after uncovering the Wynn's Ferry road on the afternoon of the main battle when our victorious troops were in high spirits, as suggested by Buckner— I can not see why he should not be held responsible for the great disaster. Another thing that confirms the declaration of Colonel W. Preston Johnston, and indicates also the opinion of President Davis and his cabinet, is the fact that Pillow was relegated to the conscript department, and Buckner, after exchange as a prisoner of war, was promoted, and eventually became a lieutenant-general of the Confederate army. Buckner's kindness to me later on, while I was collecting the remnant of Morgan's command in his department, after the Indiana and Ohio raid, and his absolute refusal to issue the order to dismount Morgan's men at Chickamauga, as desired by Bragg, placed me under an obligation never to be forgotten. I have, therefore, a personal pleasure, as well as a soldier's sense of justice in presenting these views.

I was to go with Floyd and Martin with Pillow, but as all the boats had been burned, we set to work to improvise a raft to take the commands across the river, but while thus engaged a steamboat came down the stream. Pillow and Martin at once went aboard the boat and were landed across the river, and after some little deliberation Floyd mustered his Virginians in line and boarded the boat, taking me with him. For a few hours intense excitement reigned for fear the Federals would train their batteries on us, and the suspense kept all in a disagreeable state of confusion. This danger passed, I looked around for a place to get a nap, as I had for four days been deprived of both sleep and rest. My quest was in vain, as there was scarcely standing room upon the vessel. It was about noon, and accommodating myself to unavoidable circumstances, I was standing on deck watching the beautiful scenery on either shore of the Cumberland, when an orderly approached and told me that General Floyd desired my presence in his cabin. The general informed me that he wished to give me a commission upon his staff, but I very politely, but firmly, refused, giving as my reason for so doing that I felt it my duty to remain with Forrest, as that commander was very much in need of my services as scout, and I preferred that life to the duties of a staff officer.

As soon as Nashville was reached and the troops disembarked, having remained on board, I decided to make another effort for a refreshing sleep. First, taking my faithful steed to Floyd's headquarters and feeding him, I returned, slipped into a stateroom, locked the doors and stretched myself upon the berth to get, as I supposed, a long, refreshing sleep. After rolling and tossing for some time in a vain effort to woo slumber, I had just about reached the conclusion that my overwrought brain and nervous system had deprived me of the power to sleep, when I heard the captain giving orders to fire the boat. This put all thought of sleep far into the background, and springing out of my warm bed, I hastily drew on my clothes, opened the door and ran out upon the bank, where I stood alone and watched the burning of all the vessels to keep the Yankees from turning them into gunboats.

The whole city of Nashville was in an uncontrollable panic, people were rushing madly about with their most valuable possessions in their arms; every valuable vehicle was put into use to carry the fleeing crowd from the city, while thousands departed on foot, every individual intent upon getting away before the approach of the hostile army that was momentarily expected. I never saw such frantic apprehension any time during the war as I saw here; but it is not to be wondered at, because the fearful anticipation of the fate that befell so many towns was holding undisputed sway in the minds of the inhabitants, and self-preservation was their first thought. It was a supreme pandemonium. The ceaseless clamor of excited voices was almost deafening as the citizens rushed madly up and down the streets, their precious belongings hugged to their bosoms, trying to get a seat in some carriage to take them out of the town. Hysterical women, half laughing, half crying, dragged their children behind them, too much excited to know just what they were doing, but impelled by the nervous dread that if they did not move the Yankees would catch them.

This state of affairs continued until the arrival of General Forrest, whose reassuring presence soon impressed the restless crowd, and the orders given by him to the Texas rangers, who were now under his command, restored quiet.

Countermanding somebody's order for the burning of the railroad trains, Forrest detailed men to bring them in, and loaded them with valuable supplies of various kinds; also by impressment of all horses and mules and every available vehicle he organized wagon-trains, which were similarly used. Forrest had great common sense and a clear head for business and was a good quartermaster and commissary as well as soldier. His genius for turning small things to account was something wonderful, and his commanding air always inspired confidence and made people think that he knew what he was about. He had a clear preception of the duties of an officer of infantry or artillery as well as of cavalry.

CHAPTER X.

Martin and I met soon after my arrival in Nashville. Forrest imposed upon us the duty of taking charge of a railway train loaded with wounded men and delivering them at their various points of destination. But just after we had received orders to take charge of this train General Albert Sidney Johnston sent a messenger to Forrest requesting him to send him two reliable commissioned officers to take important dispatches to Texas. Wishing to confer a favor upon his two young scouts, he chose Martin and me, and obtained for us recruiting orders that would furnish us transportation and expense money. We purchased a horse and buggy as the only means of conveyance, and driving rapidly through the country, made the first stop at Shreveport, Louisiana, where I had left my favorite Texas horse, Joe Smith. Leaving Martin to care for the one we had driven, I went at once to look after this pet. On my approach the noble animal threw up his head and whinnied with joyful recognition. Anxious to reach the end of our journey, we soon had him hitched to the buggy and were again on the road. The intelligent animal seemed to know that he was homeward bound, and put his best foot foremost, bringing us into Austin in nine days after leaving Shreveport, a journey of over five hundred miles. The dispatches were delivered to Governor Lubbock, and we drove on to Burnet where my family was still residing. An attack of fever delayed me here for several days, but as soon as I was able to travel we set out on our return trip. Hoping to get transportation at New Orleans, we pushed directly for that place.

The high water still continued and both of us knew that it would be exceedingly difficult and dangerous to cross the river above that point; therefore, we indulged the hope that we should be fortunate enough to get passage upon one of the boats; but on reaching Bayou Teche in the evening, we learned that New Orleans had been surrendered that day. Flanking that city, we seized a small ferry boat manned by two negroes and proceeded up the Mississippi to a suitable landing on the eastern shore. Without further mishap we arrived at Corinth, reporting first at army headquarters, and then without delay to Forrest, by whom we were heartily greeted.

Just before our return to the army the great battle of Shiloh had been fought. General Forrest had again won great distinction, and although severely wounded, retained command until his condition necessitated more careful treatment. The enemy's lines still enclosed the late battle-ground. Our first orders were to go within these lines that night in search of information. We cautiously worked our way to General Lew Wallace's camp, lying along Owl creek, which, with Lick creek, embraced the sanguinary territory.

We entered the Federal lines at Grand Hill and gathered some very valuable information as to the number and character of the troops. Martin was sent back to report, and while riding quietly along the road, he spied two Federal soldiers ahead. Always ready for any daring exploit, he decided to capture both of the unsuspecting blue-coats and take them to headquarters with him. Putting spurs to his horse, he galloped up alongside of the astonished Yankees, and with his pistols pointed into their faces, demanded instant and unconditional surrender. He did not know whether they were stragglers or guards of a troop, but he quickly decided that the only way to find out was to capture them before they had discovered him or given the alarm. Both of the Federals were very willing to surrender when they looked into the determined face of their captor, and were soon mounted upon a horse that Martin was leading. The young Confederate proceeded rapidly upon his way until within a short distance of Grand Hill he came upon a farm house where he concluded to stop for the night. The owner of the house gave him permission to rest for the night, and putting his two prisoners in a small log cabin, he got a trundle-bed from the farmer, and placing it across the doorway, was soon fast asleep. Just about daylight one of the prisoners decided that Martin was so sound asleep that he could make his escape without pursuit. He

got to his feet noiselessly and crept cautiously to the door, guarded
by the slumbering jailer who was far in the land of dreams; he
jumped over Martin's prostrate form and took to his heels as if
the whole Confederate army was behind him.   Martin opened
his eyes just as the Federal made his flying exit from the log cabin.
The bright eyes of the Confederate scout were now entirely cleared
of drowsiness, and springing to his feet, he jumped out of the door
a short distance in the rear of the fleeing enemy.   Martin had
stripped for bed and had on only his underclothing; his tender bare
feet were very sensitive as they came in contact with the hard
ground; imagine, therefore, his dismay when his captive ran across
an old field filled with briars!   Martin hesitated for an instant, then
his teeth came to with a snap, and he was after the Federal as
fast as his legs could carry him.   He believed in pursuing as long
as there was any possible chance of overtaking his man, even if
it did lead him a wild chase through briars and thorns; but after
running half way across the field, his bare legs torn and scratched
severely, it suddenly flashed over him that the other prisoner also
might take "French leave," and get away if he did not hastily
return.   Martin stopped short as this idea presented itself, and looked
regretfully at the back of his fast-receding foe, being unwilling
to admit that he was far outstripped as a runner, and still confident that a Confederate ought to be as fleet-footed as a Yankee,
even if he were barefooted.   Martin was afraid to fire upon the
runaway, as he was so near the enemy's lines, but was almost
tempted to risk it when the aggravating fellow stopped for an
instant upon the edge of some trees and waved his hand tauntingly
at him, then turned and disappeared into the woods.   Martin had raised
his pistol to shoot, but thinking better of it, turned and began picking
his way back among the briars, laughing to himself over his breezy
chase in the cool air, and congratulating himself upon having had
no spectators.   But just at that moment he saw the flutter of a
dress in the door of the farmer's cabin, and his face reddened with
embarrassment as he thought that the ladies of the house had been
interested watchers of his run after the Yankee.   Springing hastily
behind a tree that was near at hand, he called to a boy to bring
him his shoes and clothes, thanking his stars that there was such
a friendly shelter for him while in this rather scanty "undress
uniform."   His toilet was made with much rapidity and Martin was
soon saddling his horses, impatient to be again upon his way.   The

other prisoner 'was safely conducted to the army headquarters at
Corinth. Martin had an inexhaustible flow of animal spirits and
was as delightful a companion in moments of relaxation as he was
the reliable soldier and steadfast comrade in times of peril. He
always hugely enjoyed his own adventures and escapades; and when,
on my return to camp, he told with infinite humor how the Yankee
got away from him, he laughed gleefully, like the big-hearted boy
he ever seemed.

In a few nights we were again near General Lew Wallace's camp.
We had with us a stalwart young fellow who had escaped from
"Island Number Ten" at its capture by the gunboats, and who had
a sweetheart just across the creek from the Federal camp. He
told us that his lassie's old father had taken the oath of allegiance
to the government of the United States, and had in his possession
some pistols and guns he had bought from the Yankees. I determined to have these arms, although the house of the owner was
within earshot of the enemy's guard-line. Martin grinned his ready
acceptance of the request to accompany me, and our new comrade
seemed equally willing. We reached the cabin about nine o'clock,
and Martin and the young soldier were placed as sentinels outside
with orders to rattle their guns just loud enough for the inmates
to hear them. I quietly opened the door without knocking and
stepped into the room, an unwelcome and unbidden guest, as a
Confederate soldier was the last person that this renegade Southerner wanted to see. My reluctant host was compelled to receive
his unbidden guest as he sat, half undressed upon his bed, his eyes
bulging with astonishment, if not fear. I strode up to the old
fellow, and looking at him sternly, said: "I have heard, sir, that
you have been buying some arms from my soldiers, and for such
an act it is my unpleasant duty to arrest you." With a trembling
voice, the old man rejoined: "Sir, I have' had nothing more to
do with your soldiers than I could help, for I have no use for
them. They came here after milk, and lounging around under
the trees left some pistols, sabres and spurs, which my little boy
brought into the house. I am not at all responsible for their carelessness, but I suppose that I will have to suffer for their wrongdoing
and be carried off to prison, like some of my old neighbors who
were put into your guard-house and kept there till they sickened
and died." Just as this moment his wife, followed by her daughter
and a little boy, came in. A black-eyed, resolute-looking woman

she was, and her would-be son-in-law had warned me that she was a genuine shrew; she certainly looked it as she marched right up to me, her dark eyes fairly blazing in her anger and fixed upon mine. But I met her glance squarely and said: "Madam, we may be able to arrange this matter so that no one will suffer any hurt, but if you give any trouble it will be the worse for you and all. If these arms are given up at once, and your husband will promise to report at headquarters in the morning, we may be able to find the owners of them before then, and he will be released instantly." But before she had time to answer the little boy came in dragging the coveted property, and said as he placed them before me: "This is all there is." I immediately opened the door just wide enough to pass them out and called: "Sergeant, take these arms and carry them to my tent at once." As Martin took them, I closed the door and turned again to meet the inquiring gaze of the lady of the house who had all the while been inspecting me inquisitively, and who now asked: "How do we know, sir, but what you are one of those villainous rebels?" I saw that the only way to do was to brave it out by assuming a very confident air and trying to allay suspicion until my comrades could reach a safe distance, so I answered: "Well, madam, if you are not satisfied with this arrangement and prefer to have your husband carried off to prison, all you have to do is to make a little disturbance and you will see what will be done." She became suddenly quiet, doubtless convinced that I would carry out my intentions to the letter. Believing that Martin was now far enough off, I opened the door, and without any adieus, stepped out into the night. I was soon up with my companions, and delighted the young soldier by giving him one of the captured pistols.

At another time we discovered a house about half a mile from the Federal camp, where some of the officers habitually breakfasted, drawn thither by the fresh milk and butter to be obtained. Selecting a suitable spot near the road, I put up what my friend Martin called "one of my Indian thickets," made by cutting brush wood and sticking it into the ground so that it formed a good natural-looking screen, behind which we could conceal ourselves and await the coming of our unsuspecting game. The material was rather short, but we believed that by lying flat it would hide us completely. Not entertaining a thought of danger, though so near the enemy's lines, we slept soundly until a boy turning the cows out to pasture awakened us. Among the lot was an obstinate old muley who refused to go in the direction that he wished to drive her, but came toward us, running at full speed. Just as she reached our hiding place, either seeing or scenting us, with a loud snort she leaped clear over the thicket. The little boy was following close in the rear of her nimble heels, and on discovering men with guns in their hands, stopped short, raised a loud cry of alarm, and ran into the house at fast as he could go. Knowing what discovery by the Yankees meant, we took to our heels and rushed into the woods. Remembering that I had seen a log on a hill overlooking the Federal camp, I led the way, still determined to carry out our plans. Another green thicket soon sprang up, and we were again behind an improvised shelter waiting for some luckless officer to pass. At last we were rewarded by seeing two leave the camp mounted upon fine, spirited horses and dressed in apparently new uniforms. They took the road leading by the screen, and when within twenty steps of the ambuscade, the girth of one of the saddles came loose and the rider stopped to readjust it. This threw them so wide apart that it was impossible to enclose them, and when Martin sprang out into the road with his gun presented, demanding instant surrender, the rear man whirled his horse to gallop back to camp. To prevent his giving the alarm which would have resulted in our speedy capture or death, I felt constrained to shoot him. Simultaneously, Martin had fired at his man, and turning, I saw the other horse running for the camp while Martin was pointing his double--barreled gun again at the Federal and demanding where he was shot. I heard him reply as he approached: "The fact is I am not hurt at all, sir." At this declaration both of us seized him and ran with him to the woods, disarmed him and gave him orders to keep up with us at double-quick, for the long-roll signal of alarm was now sounding in the camp as the riderless steed dashed up, and our safety demanded that we "stand not upon the order of our going."

Our partner in this adventure had been sent to the rear with the horses, a distance of about six miles, and orders had been given him to feed them and have them in readiness for instant travel. Knowing that the woods would be scoured for our apprehension, and if caught we should be hung as spies, we double-quicked nearly all the way, reaching the horses about noon, and finding to our great relief that the young fellow had all in readiness. Making

a circuitous route first toward Perdy and then toward Gravel.
Hill, we managed to pass all the picket-stands except the extreme
videttes. Coming upon the same house where Martin had lost his
prisoner, we decided to rest here all night. Before supper we put
the Yankee in a room were there was an old loom and tied his
hands behind him. Martin again secured his trundle-bed and put
it across the door and was soon where no disturbing element could
bother him. When I was sure that Martin was sound asleep, not wishing to be encumbered with a prisoner, I untied his hands and told
him as soon as everything was quiet to slip out through that hole
in the wall and get away; but the Federal believed that I only
wanted an excuse to shoot him, and was afraid to move, lying all
night without turning over. The next morning he told Martin that
I had invented a plan to kill him, but that he was too shrewd to
fall into the trap set for him; when the truth of the business was
that I really wanted him to escape, as I did not like to be encumbered with a captive, and, of course, would not kill him merely
to be rid of him.

The next morning by daylight our little party saddled up and
started upon our way. On reaching headquarters at Corinth, we
ascertained that our prisoner was a more important captive than we
had supposed, for he was a lieutenant of artillery of the Federal
army. The revolvers we had taken from him were presented with
our compliments to General Charles Clark, a gallant Confederate
officer, who had written us a note some days previous, requesting
us to get him a pair of navy sixes. General Clark had been the
good friend of both of us in the earlier part of the war at Hopkinsville; and it was pleasant to think that we were able to reciprocate
his kindness. We were also very much gratified at his eulogistic
note of thanks for our little present.

That night General Van Dorn sent a note to Forrest, asking him
to send him two commissioned officers to serve on his staff for one
day, emphasizing it by saying: "Send me men that you know can
be relied upon." He wished them to report to him at five o'clock
the next morning. Martin and I were quite proud to have been
selected for this service. Neither of us had ever been commissioned, although Forrest always held us as his aids and habitually
treated us as such. By early dawn we were at the headquarters of
General Van Dorn, who had recently come from the trans-Mississippi department where he had made a fine reputation in Missouri

and Arkansas. This was my first meeting with the General since he had left Texas some years ago, and he seemed glad to renew our frontier acquaintance. Ere long Van Dorn's command was engaged in resisting Pope's advance, and soon compelled him to fall back to a respectful distance from Farmington where they had met him. The General with his staff had pushed forward until they had actually gotten in the rear of the enemy's left flank, when the nearest Federal regiment broke and ran at "double quick." Their flag-bearer, who was carrying a huge banner, would turn every now and then and wave it tauntingly at the Confederates. The impetuous Martin could not stand this insolent challenge, and wishing to capture the beautiful ensign, decided that it should be his, and without even waiting to get permission to attempt such an extraordinary feat, put spurs to his horse and was off at full gallop after the fleeing Yankee. Coming up behind the Federal, Martin seized the flag and whirled his horse to gallop back with it, but the rich trophy was very heavy and drooped, unfortunately, within reach of the flag-bearer, who at once gathered its folds in his tenacious grasp while Martin swung to the staff with all his might. Each tugged away, and the result was that the cords that fastened the silk to the pole broke, leaving the flag in the hands of the Federal who made good his escape, while Martin rode back to his comrades bringing the finely polished staff surmounted by a golden eagle.

The Confederates had in their immediate front an open field of six or seven hundred yards, the south and east sides of which were bounded by heavy timber. General Van Dorn gave orders for his men to advance upon the enemy at double-quick, and went forward with his staff toward the southeast corner of the field, when a sudden, unexpected volley from the woods aimed at the little party caused them to seek a safer place. On looking back they discovered that one of their staff officers had fallen on the field, and a Federal soldier was riding toward him, evidently for the purpose of robbing him. The general ordered up a section of artillery to throw some shells at this pickpocket, but before they had gotten into position he had already reached his prey. Just as he dismounted there was a sharp report and his "itching palms" went up in the air as he fell backward, having fallen a victim to his miserable cupidity. As the smoke cleared away Martin came stalking out of the woods leading his horse behind him. He relieved the dead Yankee of his pistols, then mounted his horse and rode toward the group waiting for him, unmoved by the zip of the bullets that were sent at him. He reined in his steed by my side and asked, as a broad smile came over his merry countenance: " Say, partner, this is a cheaper way to get a dandy pair of navy sixes than to pay seventy-five dollars for them, isn't it?" His friends had all expected to see him fall at any minute, as a hundred shots had been fired at him, and I could not resist giving him a gentle reprimand, " Bob, you're very foolish to run such a risk for two pistols even if they are expensive, and I would not have endangered that fine horse of Forrest's for twenty such revolvers. If you had gotten him wounded you would have made no more attempts soon to capture pistols when you had once braved the general's wrath."

" Pshaw, Ad, I didn't get him hurt, so there's no use preaching over what's already done. I thought that you at least would be with me, old fellow, and could appreciate my love of fun, as you like such exploits as well as I. If a Yankee happens to show up just at the time I am in need of some of his property and I can get it by giving him a dose of gunpowder, why I consider myself in luck, and let him have it. One more to my list won't count against me in the hereafter. There now, don't you think that's so?" The gay, young fellow laughed audaciously as he put his hand on my arm and flashed a friendly glance from his gray eyes. Martin and I loved each other as brothers love, and neither would have hesitated a moment to risk his life for the other. We were perfectly happy when together and every one in camp remarked upon this yal friendship. So I didn't chide him further.

Bob Martin's feat was the finale of the famous battle of Farmington, as the Federals had hastily fled the field.

CHAPTER XI.

THE MESSAGE IN CIPHER.

The next day after the battle of Farmington Martin and I were bidden to Forrest's tent and notified that General Breckinridge had requested him to send him "the two young scouts." "Boys, you've made such a fine reputation I am afraid you will not be allowed to remain with me much longer," Forrest remarked after he had delivered his message. "It does not matter to whom we report, I am sure that we will never have a better commander, will we, Bob?" I asked, recalling the kindness of this noble-hearted officer. Forrest answered, smiling: " If you two boys will always do your duty as you have while with me, you will be sure to always have a good commander." When we reached General Breckinridge's headquarters he led us into his private room and began questioning us as to our nativity and rearing, ages, experience as scouts and spies, etc. He next informed us that he had need of two trusty, efficient men in our line to do special duty—two Kentuckians, and he believed that we were just the men he wanted, if reports he had heard of us were true. " In the meanwhile," he said, "you can go and enroll in my body-guard, where you can draw rations for yourselves and horses. There is room here in this house for you to stay, as whenever I move with my staff I wish you to be with me." That evening the general called me alone to his room and asked me if I had a brother Ben. "Yes, I had a brother Ben." "He was one of the best friends I ever had and possessed one of the most remarkable memories I ever knew; if you are as much like him in that respect as you are in face, I think you will suit me exactly," Breckinridge replied as he earnestly scanned my face. Evidently satisfied with his rigid examination, he continued: "I have some dispatches in cipher which I wish to send to two different men. They are too important to trust upon paper and risk capture. The first one reads thus: 'Number 7 to 11; number 21 back to 11 except 13;' the second like this: 'From 21 to 77 except 33, 41 and 56. Also figure 3 to 177 except 140, 50 and 60.' Now repeat these to me if you can," he finished, shooting a half-smiling, incredulous glance at me. The incredulous smile broke into one of astonishment as I repeated both dispatches word for word. "The time has not yet come for you to go on this mission, and any change in these figures would be fatal, so I wish you to repeat them to me until I am perfectly sure you have them thoroughly planted in your memory," the general said, much pleased at finding one to carry information for him and to do scouting in the enemy's lines. Every day I went to the commander's headquarters to repeat my lesson to him while Martin was sent through the lines on various missions. The day before the evacuation of Corinth an officer of Bragg's staff rode up to where we were sitting near the outworks, and calling General Breckinridge aside, engaged him in earnest conversation. As Breckinridge turned toward us we heard him say: "I'll find the men if you will show them what to do." He beckoned to Martin and me, and pointing at us, said: "These are your men, Major." Orders were given us to mount and come with him. We rode to a point from which we could see an open field, a railroad-cut and, immediately in their rear on a hill, a line of rifle-pits. "There is a road through the Federal lines which intersects that railroad-cut," said the major, as he pointed ahead. "It is very important that that road should be watched, and that little thicket on the brink of the cut is the only place from which you can have a good view of this road. You observe that you will have to traverse this field to reach that place. I have brought several men here who have attempted it but they have been either killed or wounded before they reached that fence. Do you young fellows think you can accomplish such a thing?" he asked, looking us over critically. I made no answer, but dismounted and throwing my bridle reins to Martin, proceeded to make a careful survey of the ground. About half way to the field I descried a ravine leading into the field. Crawling down this, I found that I could get into the field without

detection by removing a few pickets that served as a water gap.
Returning to the major, I informed him that I would make the
effort. "Remember that it is at the risk of your life, young man,"
the major warned me. I told the major that I wished both him
and Martin to remain on the outside until I reached the thicket, and
that I wanted him to send two men to take care of our horses
until we returned. Here my Indian education upon the plains of
Texas stood me in good stead, and cutting some bushes, I tied
them to my head and on my back so as to conceal my movements
as far as possible from the sharp eyes of the Yankees. On taking
another look at my path, I observed a low flat place just in front
where my bushes would not screen me, but seeing some weeds about
a foot high, I concluded that these with my bushes would enable
me to elude observation. Giving Martin a full explanation of my
plans, I entered the ravine and crawled slowly and cautiously along.
My progress was necessarily so slow and tedious that probably an
hour passed before I reached the thicket. The rapid firing of the
Federal sharpshooters caused me to believe that some movement
on the part of our army was being made, but I sat down to wait
for Martin. As soon as I was well upon my way, the quick-witted
Martin turned the plans over in his head and decided that it would be a
good idea to do something to attract the enemy's fire to this point,
as there would be less danger of their discovering his comrade; so
he at once set to work to make some dummies that would serve
as good targets for their fire. In a short time two grotesque figures
were standing in a not too conspicuous place, and no sooner were
they discovered than a rain of lead began to fall around them.
Martin chuckled to himself over their falling such ready victims to
his hoax, and arrayed himself in a coat of green boughs and started
in pursuit of his comrade when he saw him enter the thicket. This
heavy fusillade continued until Martin had reached the thicket, the
Yankees still unaware of the trick that had been played upon them
by the young scout. Once in the thicket, about one hundred yards
from the Union sharpshooters, we were comparatively safe, but
I made our place of refuge impervious to Federal eyes by cutting
and sticking bushes up to make a screen. Unfortunately Martin
was soon taken with a severe chill, followed by a high fever, and
the hours dragged heavily for both of us under such depressing
circumstances, particularly as all the water in our canteens had
been used to quench Martin's fevered thirst; he would have

D. R. BURBANK.

suffered greatly if his fever had not abated after several hours. We would have left this trying position at nightfall if we had not been under strict orders to remain until called in. Had the sharpshooters known of our concealment in the thicket we should have been riddled with bullets in very short notice. This was one of the most trying situations in which we had ever been placed. About ten o'clock the regular hoof-beats of a horse coming down the railroad reached our ears, and believing that he was ridden by an enemy, I slipped down near the cut, Martin close at my heels. When the rider had approached to within about thirty steps I called a halt. The man jerked his horse back on his haunches and cried in an imploring voice: "Don't shoot, for God's sake, don't shoot!" The voice was immediately recognized as that of Colonel Jils Johnson's man, Jackson, who took care of the colonel's horses, and was astride one of his fine Arabs. The good fellow's voice trembled with excitement as he cried to us: "Get out of here quick, boys; General Breckinridge wants you." Showing him the way through the cut, we hurried to our horses and finding them safe, mounted and galloped away with Jackson to Corinth College where we found the general anxiously awaiting us.

When Martin and I returned to General Breckinridge's camp he welcomed us both with much warmth and said regretfully: "Boys, I made a great mistake in letting you go over there at such risk of your lives, and should have sent some one else, as I had an important mission for you. Since you are back again in safety I am very thankful." Taking me aside, he asked me to repeat the cipher message, and on its being done correctly, said: "I shall now tell you the name of the man to whom this is to be delivered. It is our mutual friend David R. Burbank, of Henderson, Kentucky. The lives of many men depend upon your careful management of this affair and it will bring either good or evil to the Southern Confederacy." Calling Martin up, he said: "Now boys, I want you to flank this Federal army and bring out all the Kentuckians you can to serve as Southern soldiers. I wish you both to remember that you are commissioned officers on my staff, and if you bring out enough men you shall have the command of them. We are now the rear guard of the Confederate army, and I believe if there are any two men living that can and will carry out my orders you are the two." This encouraging talk from our leader gave us a new inspiration, and we resolved to deserve all the trust he had placed in us. The personal influence of General Breckinridge was wonderful. In fact, he possessed more magnetism than any one I ever knew. At that time he was the pride of Kentucky, the most striking-looking man in the whole army, and his mental powers far excelled his fine personal appearance. His power of expressing his opinions in such forcible language that a multitude was swayed by his convincing oratory was never equalled by any man in all the Southern army. Shaking hands with this splendid commander, so eminent both as statesman and soldier, his two new aids turned their faces toward Henderson, the fair city of my birth, and then the home of my aged parents.

We had traveled for twenty miles by daylight, when we reached a farm house on a by-road, where we found we could obtain food both for ourselves and steeds. As soon as we had gotten breakfast and food enough to last for two more meals, as well as forage for our horses, we were again upon the road and proceeded for some distance along this secluded way; then turning aside, we entered a convenient thicket, secured and fed our horses and stretched ourselves upon the grass for a long, refreshing sleep, of which we stood in great need. The sun was two hours high before we awoke, but hastily putting on our saddles, we started again upon our journey at a sharp trot. Just before dark we came upon another farm house, and ascertaining that feed would be furnished for our animals and supper for ourselves, we took the corn and led our horses into a field. Leaving Martin in charge, I went back for the supper. The master of the house had just returned from the hospital, where he had been nursed on account of the loss of an arm in the battle of Shiloh. He was suffering greatly from poison-oak on his face, and as I entered his wife was applying a poultice. I was helping in this soothing ministration when I was startled by hearing the tramp of horses' feet as the house was surrounded by Federals. I was much alarmed at being caught there in a trap, but a happy thought struck me, and I ran at once to the door and asked one of the soldiers where the commander was. The aid was already giving orders in the kitchen for the cooking of all the provisions there. As soon as I could find the major in command I asked in an alarmed voice if they had a surgeon.

"What in the world do you want with a surgeon?"

"Why, we have a sick Confederate soldier in the house and we are afraid that he has smallpox," I answered glibly.

"The thunder you say!" exclaimed the Yankee officer in a surprised tone. "Here, Doctor, you had better go in and look at the man," he said, turning to a middle-aged man near him. Calling the captain, he gave orders to have the place well guarded and see that not one of the men was allowed to enter the house. As the captain started to obey the orders of his commander, I ran back to the invalid and tearing the poultice from his face, told him to let it remain exposed to the medical man's examination and to stick his wounded arm out and moan and groan and say that his bones were breaking with fever. The Confederate soldier played this role to perfection, and when the doctor came in I held the candle to let him see what a terrible face he had. The poor fellow's face was swollen so that his eyes were entirely closed, his lips twice their ordinary size, while small portions of the poultice were smeared all over his distorted visage. No worse-looking countenance with confluent smallpox was ever presented to a visiting physician than the one now disclosed to the wondering eyes of this learned son of Esculapius, who solemnly pronounced it an undoubted case of smallpox in its worst form. I followed the doctor out of the room and into the presence of the major, who was ordering all of his men to mount, and now asked this supposititious nurse where he could get drinking-water. He was told that he could find it either up or down the creek, as there were farm houses all along the way. Commanding one of his staff to go back and inform those that were following, and ordering a yellow flag placed upon the gate, this Federal officer rode off ignorant of the ruse that had been played upon him and his duped command. As he rode off I heard him say: "I would take that fellow along to show us the way if he had not been so exposed to that case of smallpox." To reassure Martin, I ran to the back door and threw it open, standing in the light so that my comrade could see that I was still there and not in the custody of the Yankees, whom he had of course heard surrounding the house. It was well that I gave this signal to my friend, for as the last tramping of the enemy's horses was heard Martin stepped out from behind a tree, a revolver grasped in each hand. He had intended, in his bold, impetuous way, to attack the whole force if he found that I was a captive, trusting to the friendly dark and the confusion of the melee to give him an opportunity to escape. As Martin came up he asked, wonderingly: "Ad, what kind of a trick did you play on those foxy Yankees?" I told him what I had done, then took him in the room and showed him the terrifying face of our brother-in-arms. Martin broke into his usual great laugh when he was told of this effective hoax, and the others joined in the merriment.

Getting our cooked provisions and a new supply of forage for our horses, we again took a by-road and pushed on toward the Tennessee river. Nothing of consequence occurred upon our way and we crossed over and put at the ferry-house for the night. The host informed us that there was a Federal picket at the crossroads about a mile distant. We secured a buggy and placing our saddles under the seat, covering our guns with a shawl and using a blanket for a lap robe, we fancied we resembled peaceable citizens rather than soldiers. Learning from a girl that the picket was in the habit of stopping every man to examine him, and that there were several Federals at the picket house, a little log cabin at the crossroads, we decided to pass them as early as possible in the morning. We placed our arms so that we could handle them readily and went forward. If only two of the men came to examine us I was to hand the one next to me a paper and shoot him as he took it, while, simultaneously, Martin was to shoot the other, then whip the horses into a run. We reached the pickets just as the Federals were sitting down to breakfast, and one of them rose from the table and came to the door and scanned us closely for a moment, but as we were driving with apparent carelessness, slowly along, he seemed to think that we were two innocent country lads and did not halt us. I confess that I felt much relieved at their negligence, but Bob seemed actually sorry that we did not have a scrap with those Yankees. We met with no further obstacle, and in due time reached Union county and took dinner with Ignatius Spaulding, an old schoolmate of mine. He was astonished to see us in such perilous times, but gave us a warm welcome. I recall to this day the delightful dinner we sat down to as one of the best I ever ate, being doubly appreciated after our hard journey and short commons for so many days. Here we separated, temporarily, I going on to Henderson, while Martin rode to Slaughtersville. Upon reaching the farm of Mr. Charles Taylor near Highland creek, I met the very man to whom I was to deliver the ciphers, Mr. David R. Burbank, who was there on a visit to his father-in-law. Burbank was very glad to see me, and was carried away with excitement when the dispatches were repeated to him. The distinguished

Breckinridge was a warm personal friend of Burbank, who was a staunch, liberal friend to the South. Relieved now of the precious burden I had carried so long and anxiously in my mind, I enjoyed the hospitality of the Taylor family to the utmost, reposing the first night with a pleasant feeling of security not experienced in many a weary day. By daylight the next morning I was out of doors, breathing in with delight the fresh morning air of old Kentucky. I was soon joined in my early walk by my old friend, Mr. Burbank, who took me to a quiet spot, and pulling out of his pocket a small memorandum book, handed it to me, saying: " Look at these figures, my boy, and see if they are correct." Examining them, I read these figures and words, as cabalistic as those I had verbally delivered to Mr. Burbank, viz: " 7 to 11—Fine leaf," etc. They were written in his tobacco book (Burbank was a large dealer in tobacco), and each number was followed by a description of some kind of tobacco. The exceptions were all marked " trash," a term used by tobacconists to signify a very inferior quality. " If the Federals get hold of this they'll never get anything out of it," remarked Mr. Burbank with a very confident smile. " Now, Johnson, if you need any money you can get it," he said as he took a roll of bills out of his pocket, amounting to several hundred dollars. " Take this, and if you get a chance send it South to our old general, and if not, use it yourself, and when you want more let me know and you shall have it;" he smiled kindly into my face and gave me a friendly pat upon the shoulder. Any one who ever had the pleasure of the acquaintance of David R. Burbank will recognize this as a characteristic act of the big-hearted man, who, though but an adopted son of Kentucky, was truer to her in the bitter hour of her extremity than many of her native-born sons. " There are two other men in Henderson that you can trust, my boy," he continued, " your uncle, John Barrett, and Phil. Mathews. They will know of your arrival as soon as you reach Henderson, and you can place implicit confidence in both of them. Old Kentucky must go to the Confederacy. If they will only give us a half chance we'll put fifty thousand good soldiers in the field." The good man's face was alight with earnest feeling as he made this announcement, and after a few minutes he said, as he gave me a benign look: " I'll see that the messages you brought go straight. General Breckinridge will soon know that you've accomplished that part of your mission." I thanked him warmly for his great kindness to me as we went into breakfast. In an hour I was on my way to Tom Browder's, in Hopkins county. Martin was waiting for me and was rejoiced to hear that I had accomplished my mission safely and successfully. He informed me that ten or twelve men would meet us in the morning at Slaughtersville.

On reaching that place, we found all these men awaiting us, with Captain Andy Ray and Jake Bennett among the number. Ray seemed to be the leader as well as the spokesman, and at once demanded our business. I told them that we were trying to get the Confederate soldiers to their different commanders, and to get new recruits, etc. Ray looked me over intently, and then said: "You seem to be quite a young man for such a business. What we want in Kentucky is a leader, and when one comes I will be willing to follow him, and could bring a good company to back him." All the crowd seemed to endorse his opinion; so Martin and I, somewhat disappointed, left them. We agreed to separate and move on, Martin going to Daviess county and I to Henderson, and both to meet again on the Harpshead road on a certain day and at a point we both knew well. In the interval we each saw quite a number of Confederate soldiers, but Rosecrans's amnesty order and the seductive reception of these young fellows by charming young ladies, who elevated them all into heroes, made it very difficult for us to persuade them to accept permanently the hardships of a soldier's life in the field, far away from home and friends. Upon meeting at the appointed place, we found that our experience had been similar. As we discussed our failure, I said: "Well, old fellow, there are but two things for us to choose between. It is simply this, we will either have to return at once to our commands without recruits, or devise some way to make these soldiers leave here." Martin's eyes flashed as he met my gaze, and he said, hastily: "The latter is the best thing to do, and if you'll make the plans I'll work with you to the death." I was pleased with this new evidence of my friend's loyalty, and said: "The first thing for us to do is to settle this point, Bob. In all enterprises there must be a leader, and if you will accept that place there's no man in the army I would rather serve under than you."

"Well, Ad, I feel as you do about this matter, but you have a great many more influential friends than I have," Martin began, and as he saw the negative shake of his friend's head, he hastily added: "And you know I have already told all the boys that you are the captain and I the lieutenant."

I demurred for a moment, then said: "All right, Bob, I'll take the place with the condition that it matters not what circumstances arise, neither of us is to criticise the other's conduct, as it is necessary that we stand by each other through thick and thin and through good and evil report."

Martin readily accepted the condition, as he was heartily glad to get out of being placed in command of any of the men we happened to recruit, for at this time he was too fond of his free career to give it up for the confining duties of an officer. "Now my plan is to make the Yankees run these stay-at-home Confederate soldiers out of the country and to raise such a rumpus in this region that they will think all the boys are doing devilment," I said. Martin's face fairly shone with joy as he danced up and down to show his pleasure at the proposal; then he tossed his hat into the air and yelled with glee: "Hurrah for Dixie!"

Certainly this would seem a desperate policy for two lone men to adopt in a district thronged with numerous foes, both foreign and domestic, and most older men, even among our friends, would have shaken their heads in disapproval of an apparently reckless scheme which would put the country into turmoil and perhaps accomplish no useful results; but we did not count personal hardship or danger when there was work to be done that would gain fresh recruits for our hard-pressed army.

After some moments of reverie, I asked abruptly: "Martin, did you tell me that the provost guard was at Owensboro?" Being answered in the affirmative, I said: "We will go straight there and begin our work on them. If we can find a few men to go with us we will take them along, but if not, why we will go alone." Martin and I found but one recruit to help us in our enterprise, but he was a youth of mettle, brave and true and ready night or day: Frank Amplias Owen has since won a record that has endeared him to all his brothers-in-arms and gained their highest esteem.

I explained my plans to my little army as we three advanced upon the city of Owensboro. First, we must magnify our numbers in the vivid imaginations of our foes, who from this day on should never have a restful day or night. Owen, who had the distinguished honor of being the first recruit of these two aid-de-camps of the illustrious Breckinridge, would be left with the guns in the

thicket at the mouth of the lane on the Henderson road, while
Martin and I would take the more dangerous part of riding into
the town in broad daylight, where we ran a double risk—first, of
being shot as soldiers; second, of being hung as spies. Martin was
to cut the guy ropes of the flag flying in the frequented, central
courthouse square, and carry it out of town, while I acted as his
rear guard, to shoot down with revolver any man who interfered with us, fully confident that we could get our guns in the
thicket in time to kill the foremost of our pursuers, and escape
while others were organizing pursuit. Just as we reached the
thicket where Owen was to be left, a friend of Martin's, coming
out of Owensboro, informed us that the Federals had left for
Louisville, taking with them several prisoners. The reader may
smile at the small outcome of such a big scheme, but I beg
him to be patient.

While we were still discussing this fiasco, fortune, as if
pitying our keen chagrin, somewhat cheered our drooping spirits
by sending down the road Major Kimbly, of the Federal army,
who came dashing gaily along in a fine buggy drawn by a span
of splendid horses, and beside him the radiant and charming
Miss Georgia Shelby. We at once determined to capture the
gallant Yankee and make him descend from his place beside
his lovely companion. However ungallant this may seem, we
were in dead earnest about carrying out our plan of "kicking
up a rumpus," and to accomplish this we could not afford to
let young ladies stand in our way, however lovely and accomplished, for the South was greatly in need of her truant sons
and they must be driven out of their soft places at all hazards.
Not wishing to alarm the girl more than was necessary, and
to avoid, if possible, a wild chase after the Federal, Martin and
I made a detour and came to a point in the road where it ran
around a high hill. Martin stationed himself on one side where
he could easily catch the reins of the horse, and behind a tree,
which served to screen him from view, while I took position
on the other, concealed by a large maple; both waited silently
for the coming of "the foe." Just as the unsuspecting Major
was opposite us, Martin sprang out and seized the bridle,
while I covered him with my gun. The young lady gave a
slight scream at the sight of the two armed men, but I soon
quieted her fears by saying, "I know both you and your father,

Miss Shelby, and you shall not be hurt. We want only to see the Major's papers." The frightened Federal at once handed me his furlough which I read, and then requested him politely to get out of the buggy, which request was readily complied with, for the poor fellow did not know what next would happen to him, and as he looked into our faces he decided that the best thing for him to do was to do our bidding. I informed him that his papers were from the wrong side, and that as he was now "Down in Dixie" he would have to be held a prisoner. I then turned to Miss Shelby and said, as I lifted my hat, "It is now my pleasure, Miss Georgie, to furnish you a much better escort than the one I have been compelled to deprive you of, and one that will not give up his place to any three Yankees that might covet it. You can trust him to take you safe to your home, as blue coats inspire no fear in him and he will defend you from any danger that may arise; good evening." Miss Shelby made room for Martin upon the seat, and as he took the reins to drive off, she laughed a merry good-bye to me, and threw an amused glance at her forlorn-looking Yankee admirer, evidently perfectly willing to exchange a blue uniform for a gray. As Martin started off, with the intention of impressing upon the Federal officer's mind that I had a large force in reserve, I called out, "Tell Captain Ray to move his company up to the forks of the road, and Bennett to go at once to Slaughtersville." Martin's alert mind readily grasped the cue and he hallooed back, "All right! I'll deliver your orders; but what must Captain Sanders do?" "He is already on his way to our headquarters," was the reply, and Martin passed on down the road. He was scarcely out of sight when a man on horseback with a bell in his hand came in view, leading a drove of mules, while another rode in the rear. Owen, who had just approached, was stationed in the road, and I gave orders for a halt. The drover was asked if he had any arms, and replied in the negative, adding that if he had we would never have stopped him. I inquired what he intended doing with his mules, and he said that he was taking them to Evansville to sell to the government. He was informed that there was a closer market for them; and he told us that it did not make any difference where he sold them, just so he got his money. I offered him Confederate money, but he refused anything but greenbacks or gold.

Mounting the crestfallen drover upon Martin's horse, I made him take an oath that he would not attempt to escape, gave Owen orders to fall in the rear and shoot the first man that left the trail, and then led the way through the woods to Fisher's Tavern, where Martin was to meet us. A few hours later he rejoined us, after having deposited his fair charge safe and smiling at her home. Martin was directed to conduct the men and horses to Slaughtersville, while I drove with Major Kimbly in his own buggy to Green River, where I turned him loose; a steamboat soon picked up and conveyed him to Louisville, where he complained to General Boyle, who ordered the provost guard at Henderson to levy an assessment on my friends and relatives to reimburse Kimbly for the loss of his horses as well as to soothe his sensitive feelings.

CHAPTER XII.

A BAND OF THREE.

As soon as Martin, Owen and I heard of the arrival of the Federal provost guard, about eighty men, in Henderson, we determined to attack it. Having been born and reared in Henderson, I enjoyed the advantage of a thorough acquaintance with all its avenues, large and small.

Ascertaining that the Federal force was occupying a two-story brick house opposite Barrett's factory, where I had spent some years of my business-life, I knew the most favorable point from which to make a nocturnal attack. Some time after dark our band of three reached Alves's woodlawn, where we hitched our horses and proceeded on foot to the factory-lot immediately opposite the Federals' quarters, who had no pickets, never dreaming that a force of less than three or four hundred men would dare to attack them, and knowing that there was no Confederate command of any size within striking distance of them.

There was a plank fence sunken into an excavation on the side of the street opposite the Federal cantonment, and dropping into this ditch, behind the fence, we were completely hidden from the eyes of the guards. There was a street-lamp right in front of the double doors, which brought out in bold relief the forms of the Federal soldiers, but whose dim rays did not extend across the street. Two sentinels were parading up and down before the front door, to keep their comrades in rather than with any purpose of keeping danger out. The house was full of blue coats and quite a number were sitting on the edge of the sidewalk.

Captain Daily and Lieutenant Lyon were walking up and down the pavement, unconsciously tempting the markmanship of their antagonists, who felt indignant at the intended spoliation of their relatives and friends. I proposed to bring down the two officers with my shotgun, and Owen and Martin were to shoot the two sentinels, and then fire their other two barrels into the crowd.

My shot was to be the signal. I waited until the two officers were opposite the doorful of men, and then fired both barrels almost simultaneously, while Martin and Owen followed in quick succession, all the guns being leveled on the top of the fence. The confusion produced by these six reports was very great, and those who were unhurt scrambled over one another in their haste to get into the house.

Stepping behind a pile of barrel staves, we rapidly reloaded our guns and ran around the building, to get another shot; the Federals had carried in their wounded and barricaded the doors. We found a sentinel in the rear, whom Martin wounded with his pistol, when, with a wild cry he fled to the back door, which was quickly closed and bolted, but not before we poured through it another volley.

The Federals were too much demoralized to send out a scout to investigate. the numbers of their antagonists, but blindly fired out of the upper windows all night at imaginary foes. One of their random shots, it was discovered next morning by the citizens, struck an old sow, and as she moved about, here and there lying down, leaving blood all around, these fine marksmen claimed they had hit many a rebel, who, either dead or wounded had been taken off the sanguinary field by their comrades.

In the meantime, the assaulting army of three had remounted and ridden leisurely to Major Cragged Hatchett's farm, where we soundly slept till morning, having not the remotest idea we would be followed and disturbed. Here we remained until we could have the Evansville Journal brought to us, when we read the story of our adventure, introduced by the following headlines in bold-faced type:

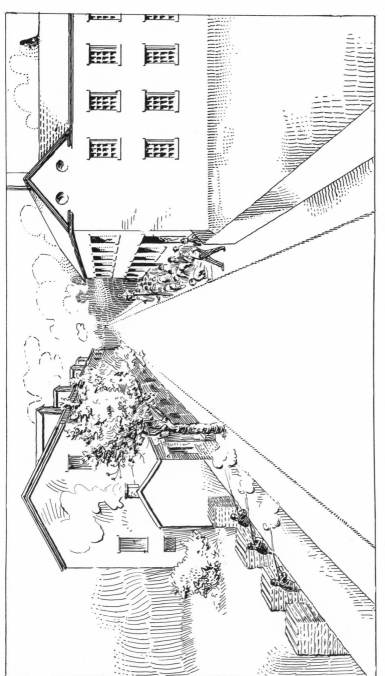

FIRST FIGHT OF "THE BRECKINRIDGE GUARDS," AT HENDERSON, KENTUCKY.

"BLOODY WAR ON THE BORDER!

Provost Guard Attacked by Three Hundred Guerrillas! After
a Desperate Resistance of over Nine Hours They Succeed in Driving the Enemy off with Heavy
Loss! Captain Daily, Lieutenant Lyon
and Nine Privates Wounded."

The Journal exaggerated the numbers of the attacking party
by 297 only!

Col. E. L. Starling, in his history of Henderson county, gives
the true account of the numbers, and adds, "Excitement in the
town became intense. A citizens' meeting was held in Barrett's
factory, at which resolutions strongly condemnatory of the course
of Johnson were passed. A short time after this, and when
Colonel Johnson had formed the nucleus of a regiment, he took
possession of Henderson, and by his words and orders greatly relieved
the anxiety of the people, especially those politically opposed to
him." Let me add, that at this public meeting, ex-Governor
Archibald Dixon was called to the chair and resolutions were
passed to this effect, "that the attack upon the provost-guard
was made by parties under no government; that they were guerrillas and outlaws, and all law-abiding citizens should aid in their
arrest and punishment." The document containing these resolutions
was signed by a number of Union men, among them Governor
Dixon and John Holloway. As soon as I read the resolutions
in the newspaper I saw that it was imperatively necessary for
the cause and policy I represented to adopt heroic measures.
So riding with Martin at once to a little meadow adjoining the
city of Henderson, on the 10th day of July, in the shade of some
haystacks, I addressed the following communication to the citizens
who had signed the offending resolutions:

"Hon. Archibald Dixon, John Holloway and others:

"Gentlemen:

"I observe in the last issue of the Henderson Reporter a
resolution signed by a number of your citizens, stating that the
attack on the provost-guard at Henderson was made by a band
of outlaws and guerrillas under the authority of no government,
and demanding that the citizens should aid in their capture and

punishment.   Now, I declare that every man on our side who
fired a gun upon that occasion was a Confederate soldier, and
had special orders not to interrupt in any way any citizen on
account of his politics.   And so I consider that every man who
signed that resolution has therefore placed himself outside the pale
of citizenship; that he has declared war against the Confederate
States and against us, and I inform you emphatically and plainly
that if that resolution is not rescinded in the next issue of the
paper, we will consider you as enemies and confiscate your
property.   Respectfully,

ADAM R. JOHNSON, Comdg., etc."

Henderson was full of soldiers, but Martin, with his characteristic, reckless daring, in company with William Hollis, who
lived there, and had just joined us, coolly rode into town and
delivered this written demand to Governor Dixon, in person.   He
then deliberately rode down to Quinn's livery stable and   put
up his horse, like the quiet country gentleman that he was!

Here the officers' horses were quartered, and Martin, as he told
me shortly after, intended to bring back the horse that best pleased
his fancy.

But he had other business to attend to first, and having no
more fear of a spy's noose than he had of Yankee guns, he
walked round to Dr. Thomas J. Johnson's residence.   Mr. Robert
Martin was entirely too punctilious a gentleman to enter the city
of his best friend's father and not to call to pay his respects to
the honored father.   True, he knew the doctor was an uncompromising Unionist, but   he knew him to be a man of t he
highest sense of honor, one who would cut off his good right
arm before he would betray such implicit, child-like confidence as
would be reposed in him.   Kentucky gentleman met Kentucky
gentleman, the Kentucky Unionist met the Kentucky Dis-Unionist
more than half way, for he insisted on his staying to dinner with
him, which polite invitation was gracefully accepted.

After dinner Martin walked to the parade grounds, took a seat
upon the fence and calmly watched the Federals go through with
their maneuvers, both infantry and artillery.   His next neighbor
on the fence was Robert Glass, whose brother Owen later joined
my force, and was one of our best and bravest men until he
was murdered after his capture near Morganfield.

Having counted the number of Federals, Martin told Hollis, whom he met on the parade-grounds, to meet him in an hour on the Knoblick road, he himself intending in the interim to go back to the livery stable and ride away with that beautiful steed. When he reached the building he felt a little chagrined at finding nobody there to afford him the pleasurable excitement of contesting for the animal; so he rather tamely began to saddle his prize, intending to ride him and to lead his own.

But at this moment, young Jimmie Quinn, a boy of eighteen years, appeared upon the stage. Being a youth of true Kentucky pluck, he did not allow his amazement to paralyze his action; he saw that his customer had made a mistake in the horse; Martin was mounted and just in the act of taking " French leave " of the establishment. Seizing the reins firmly, Jimmie demanded that he dismount at once, vowing that he shouldn't take that horse. Martin drew his revolver, stuck it into the boy's face and declared that if he did not immediately let go his bridle he would kill him. Quinn had no pistol with which to defend himself, but, looking Martin straight in the eye, he replied, " If you kill me, you will kill just as true a Confederate as you are; and if I let you take this horse, the Federals, who are aware of the political sentiments of our family, will think it was done with my connivance, and they will burn this stable, the only property of my father, an aged man. I'll die before you shall have the horse."

Martin was too gallant a soldier and too true a man not to be moved by this brave protest, and getting down he changed his saddle to his own horse, relinquishing the coveted prize. He frankly commended the young man's conduct; for he could but admire a youth who, unarmed, had dared resist him so strenuously.

Martin lost a splendid steed and at the same time an opportunity to emphasize the daring of his visit into Henderson by a brilliant finale, but he won the approval of his own conscience and gained a most excellent Confederate soldier, in addition, for not long subsequently Jimmie Quinn joined our band.

But Martin won another " feather in his cap," the complete success of his embassy to the Union leaders, for the very next issue of the Henderson Reporter contained a full retraction of the ill-advised pronunciamento which had denied that the men who had made the night attack on the provost guard were under the control of any government, and hence were guerrillas and outlaws!

Martin, Owen and I had now the satisfaction of reflecting that our nocturnal venture had resulted in magnifying most extravagantly our real numbers. We had vindicated ourselves, too, against the charge of outlawry; and however the Union element might declare that our assault, under cover of darkness, was a murderous affair, we felt fully justified under the rules and usage of warfare, which lend their sanction to one party slipping upon their antagonists in the dark, or in ambushing them night or day.

It might be added that with these advantages was the further fact that it gave us such a character for successful enterprise that many valuable recruits joined us at once. Among them were Captain Ray and Captain Bennett. Ray soon went to McLean county to gather other recruits, while Bennett and the men already enlisted remained with us at Slaughtersville, to which town we had proceeded on the conclusion of our affairs at Henderson.

I sent men into the counties of Henderson, Daviess and Union, with instructions to recruit men for the duty of picketing all the more important roads and demanding passports from citizens; thereby producing the impression that there were various, large, well-organized bodies scattered over that part of the State. From this time on almost every man that was seen in the woods was supposed to belong to my command, and the impression speedily spread that I commanded a large force.

A new and serious peril now threatened this section of the State. The authorities in Louisville sent a cavalry regiment to Madisonville with the loose and unwarrantable instructions to destroy by fire the houses of all the citizens that were giving aid to the Confederates. Of course the giving of a piece of bread or a glass of milk to a passing soldier could easily be construed into giving aid and comfort to the enemy. And the fact is, it was not necessary to prove such a charge as this, flimsy and insignificant as it was. All that was needed to have a comfortable home destroyed and its unfortunate inmates, old men, women and children, turned out into the street or woods, was for some Union foe to report such a charge, perhaps utterly false, against some one against whom he had either a political or private grudge: through envy, jealousy, or any base or petty motive, a

COURT HOUSE, MADISONVILLE, KENTUCKY.

Unionist could promote such incendiarism and cause great loss and suffering to Southern sympathizers.

The names of many of the most prominent men in and around Slaughtersville were on the black list, and it was terrible for me to contemplate the misery to which these good people would be subjected. I had at this moment six men to depend on; the others were scattered far and wide. I got these men around me and told them that we must do something to prevent this great calamity or we must leave the country at once. They promised to do whatever I said; so we repaired to an old briar-field near Madisonville, a place well suited for an ambuscade. It was full of gullies and small ravines thickly grown with blackberry vines and running back to the woods. We cut our way through the briars up to the road, divided the force into three little parties, Martin with two men on the right, and Bennett with two men on the left, while I stood in the middle ravine and was to fire the first gun. Bennett and I were to keep up the fire, while Martin was to make a circuit to the rear as soon as he had emptied his first guns. This was a small force to fight over three hundred men, but the desperate conditions required desperate measures. I knew from the looks of my men that they were sufficiently resolute, and their subsequent history proved that I was correct. Let me record their names: Robert M. Martin, Jake Bennett, F. A. Owen, Tom Gooch, John Conelly, and Marion Myers. We lay in our trenches all day, but for some reason the Federals did not come out. I told the boys at night that we would try to play Gideon of old on the enemy, and we mounted our horses and rode through the woods to the rear of their encampment. Here was woodlawn about a mile from Madisonville, from which a corn field extended nearly to the enemy's camp. Tying our horses, we proceeded through the corn field and got safe to the fence close to the camp. Each man was to take a corner of the fence, which was an old style rail or worm fence, and was to slip through and stand until I had disposed of the camp guard. There was a barn near where I was to cross the fence, and the beat of the guard was about thirty steps in front. Just as I dropped to the ground, the guard came walking hastily to the barn, and sat down in the door, throwing his gun across his lap. I stepped out with my gun to my shoulder and cleared my throat so as to attract his attention, but doubtless he thought I was one of his comrades trying to frighten him, for he sat still, and I lowered my gun a little and fired. He pitched forward, and there was then a mighty rush from the barn, which seemed to be full of sleeping soldiers. One of these fired a pistol so near me that the powder burnt my face, and I gave him a load of buckshot in the back as he ran. The rush of these men, followed by our yelling and shooting, carried terror and dismay into the camp, and the Federals fled wildly into the woods, leaving us in possession of the camp. Knowing that there was a heavy picket force a short distance away, and bearing in mind the smallness of our own force, we at once retreated to our horses and returned to our ambush on the road. The Federal officers, who, we afterward learned, were staying in Madisonville, had left the men without leaders, and when the soldiers reached town they exaggerated our numbers so that they remained there all night, and did not return to their camp until next morning.

On examining the corn field whence we had made the attack, and finding it full of tracks they themselves had made the day before, they gave us credit for a force of fifteen hundred men. Making a forced march to Henderson, they embarked for Louisville, leaving the country free and without burning a single house.

This proved to be a " glorious victory." The citizens were jubilant, and gave us the credit of saving their property, and all united to aid us in raising men. It was not an hour after the Federals had left Madisonville before I put scouts on their trail. By noon we had learned their destination, and having received some twenty recruits, I moved down in the vicinity of Henderson. I went into the town that night and had an interview with Uncle John Barrett and Phil. Mathews. I learned from them that the enemy had left on a steamboat. I told them I would march into town the next day. They notified the city officers and they came out to meet me on the road and surrender the city. The whole delegation was composed of true friends of the Confederacy. The mayor of the city, Ed. Hall, was afterwards one of my captains. The county judge, Luke Trafton, although he had but one arm, became one of my quartermasters. The Hon. John Young Brown, who was afterwards governor of the State, was one of the party. They all seemed astonished at the small number of men with me. They told me a gunboat was lying off the town on the river. I asked them if it would require more men than I had to take

JOHN H. BARRET.

the city. They assured me that there was going to be no fight, and I told them that I wanted only men enough to do a certain job, but if it took more I could soon gather them. They were anxious to know what would be my course toward the Union men. I told them that my letter to Governor Dixon would continue to be my policy. They said that a large number of the residents had gone across the river and would wait over there to hear from me. On learning my determination, they returned with Governor Dixon at their head. When I occupied the city, they all called on me at my quarters. I raised the Confederate flag over the court house, but in a few hours received notice from Captain Perkins of the gunboat that if it was not pulled down he would shell the city. This created a great alarm among the citizens, and they with the captain as envoy came to see me, and tried to get me to haul down my flag. I determined that the flag should float as long as I occupied the town, so I kept the envoy until I was ready to leave, then moved out just before dark with the flag flying at the head of my little army. The band of three had become a troop.

CHAPTER XIII.

THE CAPTURE OF NEWBURG.

While camped on the Soaper farm, where there was a cross-road leading toward Newburg, on the opposite bank of the Ohio, I was informed that there were hundred of stands of guns in the arsenal of this town, and immediately determined to make an effort to capture them. As soon as the men had eaten supper, I gave the command to saddle up, and soon the little troop of twenty-seven men were en route. We crossed Green river at the ferry near its mouth, and by ten o'clock next morning were opposite the little Hoosier city. I had learned that the guns were in a two-story brick house, the nearest house to the river. Halting the party, I went forward with Martin to reconnoiter, in the edge of the wood. The prize lay in plain view, being Colonel Bethel's storehouse full of guns, standing out in front of the town proper. I perceived that if, with two men in a small boat I should cross immediately in front of that building and get possession of it, we could hold it until Martin with his squad, crossing several squares above, could fight their way to me, should they meet with opposition. If Martin was opposed I was to set fire to the houses between us by shooting burning material into their shingled roofs. Our forces once united, the captured arms would be placed in skiffs that lay on the shore near by and rowed to the Kentucky shore under the protection of guns held by men in the house. Then these were to set fire to the arsenal and cross themselves.

When I had unfolded this scheme to Martin, instead of pro-

HOTEL, NEWBURG, INDIANA.

nouncing it impossible and foolhardy this daring spirit endorsed it at once. But the work must be accomplished quickly, if at all, for Newburg was connected by telegraph with Evansville, only twelve miles off, where was a large force of soldiers, with passports and gunboats. We went back to our little force, which was at once formed into line and dismounted; whereupon I informed the men that I contemplated undertaking a dangerous enterprise, but I desired no man whose hand and heart did not feel equal to the occasion. In my address, among other things, to put their mettle to the touch, I said: " Soldiers, as soon as you reach the other side of the Ohio, you will be standing upon a powder magazine, and cowardice would be the match to ignite it. All who are willing and confident take a step to the front." As one man the entire body made one step forward. I ordered the horses to be placed where they would make as big a show as possible to the people on the other side, and from two pairs of old wagon wheels, with their axles, and a stovepipe and a charred log, I soon had manufactured two of the most formidable-looking pieces of artillery into whose gaping mouths a scared people ever looked.

Martin, with his twenty-four men, moved quickly toward the ferryboat, while I, taking Felix Akin and Frank Amplias Owen, both of whom afterward became commissioned officers, directed my boat straight for the Bethel building; our guns lay in the bottom of the boat. As soon as we landed we secured our skiff, and in a few minutes reached the front of the house, the doors of which were standing open, with the prized guns in sight. Under the opinion that all the guns were in our grasp, and no guard about, we felt secure till Martin should come up; closing the doors, we began hastily to barricade them and the windows. While thus employed, I observed a number of unarmed men running into a hotel not far above this place, and concluded that I would go and quiet their fears. Martin had just landed and I was sure he would be at the Bethel house in a few moments. Just before reaching the hotel, I saw a man put his head out of one of its windows, holding in his hand a cartridge box. This made me uneasy, for I knew if these men were armed they might give me a severe fight, with the advantage of being inside of houses and not exposed, and if they were numerous, my chances of carrying off the guns might be small, particularly as the Bethel building commanded the river. By stepping forward quickly, I came to the large double doors of the hotel, and looked upon about eighty men, with their rifles cocked, all ready to fire. The muzzles of the cocked rifles of the front rank were in my face; hesitation meant failure and death. I did not halt. Commanding them in a loud voice not to fire a gun or snap a cap, I pushed aside the rifles of the front rank with my shotgun and walked right in among them, telling them if they put down their guns before my men came in not one of them should be hurt. At once they stacked their arms. Urging the whole crowd of them up the stairs, I drove them into the large dining-room at the head of the steps, and taking my place in the doorway with my gun in hand, I bid them keep quiet. Hardly had I done this when I heard footsteps on the rear stairs, and an officer burst into the room from the door on the opposite side. His whole face was blazing with excitement. " Where are our guns? " he asked excitedly, then catching sight of me he rushed towards me. When about twenty feet of me, I covered him with my gun and told him that if he came a step farther I would fill him with buckshot. Catching my eye and seeing I meant what I said, he froze to the spot, but his blazing eyes and foaming lips showed his anger. He was a superb specimen of manhood, and dressed in full uniform, he looked the typical soldier. He did not consent to surrender till some one called out, " They've got all the streets guarded, and are coming this way." His face then fell and he went reluctantly among his men. I told him to get his muster rolls and I would parole his men. As soon as Martin found out that I was at the hotel he came on the double-quick to my relief. I ordered wagons to be "pressed," and the arms loaded into them at once. Soon we had two wagonloads of arms on the way to Dixie. I was now notified that the home guards were forming to attack us, and their Colonel, Bethel, was pointed out standing on the bank of the river, near his store. The guards were represented as being two hundred and fifty strong. Our position, therefore, was still very perilous, and required prompt action. Leaving Martin to guard the prisoners, I walked down to where Colonel Bethel and several excited citizens were talking. I began the conversation abruptly by saying, " Gentlemen, I hear that there is a home guard near town that is about to attack me, and I must say that I came here to get these guns, I have them, and

I purpose to keep them; I want nothing more and do not intend to disturb any of the citizens or any of their property, but if I am hindered or fired on, I'll shell this town to the ground."

Addressing Colonel Bethel, I said, "I see, sir, that you have a field-glass and by looking across the river you can see that I am prepared to carry out my threat." I saw the captain glance at his house, and as it was the largest and most prominent building near the river, he probably reflected that it would be the first knocked down. Turning pale, he sent his runners at once to stop his men from coming in. Martin, with the last load of guns was soon crossing the river, and I, with my "body-guard" of two men, walked quickly down, and pushed off into the river, unmolested; we bent to our oars and made the water foam, being in a hurry, for we were hardly half way across the river when the whole town was swarming with the home guards. They shot down two of their own citizens, but never fired a shot at us, our terrible cannon keeping them in order. I now saw the black smoke of a gunboat around the bend, and that reminded me that we were still in a very perilous position, being on a long, narrow peninsula between the Ohio and Green rivers. The mouth of Green river was two miles below us, and if the Federals should run a force up that river they would have us cut off entirely. Resolving to make an effort to prevent this, as soon as I landed I took Jack Thompson, Julius George and John Patterson, and galloped down to the mouth of the river. By the time we got there both a gunboat and a transport were in sight. Placing George and Thompson on the extreme point that was covered with brush, I told them that, if the transport made an effort to come up the river, they must fire the first barrel of their shotguns at the soldiers, and if that did not stop the boat, to shoot the pilot. The channel ran right under this point, and thus the boat had to run very close to the shore. The steamboat, loaded with soldiers, came directly to the mouth of the river, and when about fifty yards from the point, my men fired as directed, and to my relief the captain reversed the wheel and turned back. Patterson, whom I had sent across Green river, in his delight at seeing the boat run off, fired his gun, and yelling with all his might, made them believe there was a force there also. The ruse succeeded to my intense satisfaction; the transport ran back until she got in the rear of the gunboat, and that boat lay to and shelled the point for several hours, giving us time to escape.

The employment of sham cannon at the capture of Newburg served to amuse our people, and some wag referred to me as " stovepipe Johnson "—a title which seemed to so tickle the fancy of the Southern sympathizers that they took it up and spread it far and wide throughout Kentucky and the South. This sobriquet, at first facetiously applied, has stuck to me, and I am distinguished by it to this day.

The effect of this little expedition was far-reaching. Troops were massed at all the principal towns on the Ohio river, and along the Louisville and Nashville railroad. Newburg was the first town captured north of Mason and Dixon's line. The Northern papers greatly magnified my force, and the London Times had a lengthy editorial upon the importance of the capture of Henderson and Newburg; and as Henderson was a great tobacco market, the price of that weed suddenly rose.

STOVE-PIPE BATTERY AT CAPTURE OF NEWBURG.

CHAPTER XIV.

THE BRECKINRIDGE GUARDS.

Our activity and appearance at points far distant, at short intervals, caused the Federal authorities to believe I had a large command, and this induced them to greatly increase their forces throughout a large section of Kentucky, thus preventing the augmentation of their armies in the South. And so it was that this swiftly moving little band accomplished results totally incommensurate with its size.

Moreover, the increasing fame of these rangers drew to them many kindred spirits. The band of three had now become a battalion, and was called " The Breckinridge Guards."

Another ruse now magnified in the minds of the Federals the numbers under my command, and that was my requiring recruiting officers in the different counties to picket the various roads, as if they had many military camps.

The people of Newburg were greatly chagrined and exasperated when they found that a mere handful of men had captured their town and guns without the loss of a man, or even having a shot fired at them, and Colonel Bethel determined to wipe out the disgrace. So mustering about one hundred mounted men and obtaining some three hundred infantry from the troops at Evansville, they were marched under his command to capture Slaughtersville which was then considered the headquarters of " the guerrillas," and also with the full determination to burn the houses of citizens in that vicinity, forgetting the forbearance of their chief antagonist when he had the town of Newburg at his mercy. The second night they camped at the Slaughter farm, about six miles from my headquarters. I had less than fifty men at this point, but, dividing them into four parties, I attacked the Yankee pickets on the different roads and drove them pell-mell upon the main body, who now fully believed that they were entirely surrounded. Captain Lorenzo Fisher, a gallant young officer, with a small force, ambushed this comparatively large force on their way toward Henderson, and wounded the colonel and several of his men, the command reaching the Ohio in a rather demoralized condition, and happy to get safe to the river. But they had managed in some way to capture John Patterson, one of our bravest soldiers, who in their wrath was shot through the head by a home guard, so it was said, and left for dead on the road. He did not die, but the ball destroyed his eyesight for life.

A month or so after this I decided to publish the following. proclamation:

"Headquarters Breckinridge Guards, August 11, 1862.

" Citizens of Kentucky:

" For the love of liberty, and the homes of those you hold dearer than all, will you stand still and inactive, while the enemies of your country are attempting to fetter your wrists and consign you to a slavery, compared with which, the most absolute despotism in Europe would soften to a mild and humane form of government? Can the infatuation of seeming peace and quiet in favored sections, where the insolent foe has never penetrated, but whose hands are red with ruin for the destruction of your rights, blink at the terrible ordeal through which you must pass, unless you raise your proud and strong arm to hurl back the blow, uplifted to immolate you? The Lincoln Government, while pretending protection, is despoiling you of your property, and robbing you of your liberty. Who has ever heard of a free people that were not allowed the right of suffrage at the ballot box? What other people but Kentuckians would tamely submit to being mobbed and driven from their rights by a horde of Northern vandals? Oh! Kentucky! you are indeed lost to your glory and sunk in your worth, degenerate sons of noble sires! You are now writing one of the most shameful pages of your country's history. You are entailing upon your offspring a shame that will follow them for generations. You must see that you are not allowed to remain neutral in this struggle. It can not

BARNEY SISK HILL,

Headquarters of 10th Ky. Partisan Rangers.

be that, serpent-like, you intend to sting the hand that warms you to life—that you will aid the Lincoln despot to rob your sister States of their property, when the same ruin that sweeps over the South will desolate Kentucky. Fellow citizens, I believe that Kentucky can rescue herself, if she will only make the effort. Already thousands of our gallant sons have armed themselves with the deadly shotgun and unerring rifle, and are determined to strike a blow for liberty. All such are branded by the Lincolnites as guerrillas. I can assure you, fellow citizens, that all who are now enrolled under me are recognized by the Confederate government. If those cowardly thieves beyond the Ohio river wish to be convinced, let them offer one of my men for exchange, then it will be time to doubt my authority. All those who disregard my parole will do so at their peril. No government has a right to force men into such a situation, but if they permit it I warn them that if caught, they shall be subjected to the penalty of their faithless violation. I now say to all persons who have been led to believe that they will be molested by me or by my men because they are Union men, that I have given strict orders against it and intend to enforce my orders. I have also given orders that from and after this date I will punish all citizens who aid Federal forces, and will treat them as I would treat a spy. All those who belong to the so called 'home guard,' that come forward and give up their arms and take an oath not to fight against us, shall, under no circumstances, be molested. All persons who were elected to office in those counties where the election was suppressed and who attempt to hold office will be treated as enemies. Any one levying or causing an execution to be levied on the property of any soldier under me, or in any department of the Confederate army, will be treated as an enemy to our cause and country. I challenge comparison between the acts of the so called guerrillas, and those protectors from Indiana who so recently claim to be guardians of your rights and property; I announce to those men who are engaged in robbing and murdering our citizens, and insulting our women, whose style of warfare is as merciless as any in the annals of Indian barbarities, that whenever and wherever found, my brave rangers will inflict the penalty that such offenders deserve.

"ADAM R. JOHNSON,
"Commanding Breckinridge Guards."

CHAPTER XV.

THE RANGERS' FLAG.

Our successful ventures brought recruits until the command now numbered three hundred men. I established headquarters in Union county where five or six companies were organizing. The arms that were captured at Newburg, Indiana, were distributed, but it became necessary to secure an additional number of guns. Understanding that a goodly store of them was in Hopkinsville, with two hundred men I made a forced march to this city. Arriving about daylight, we surprised the home guards and captured the place without firing a gun. We secured over one hundred stands of arms, but still being short of ammunition, I determined to make an effort to take Clarksville, Tennessee, where the Federals had a large depot of army supplies of all descriptions. In this undertaking Colonel Tom Woodward co-operated with about one hundred men. Leaving Hopkinsville just about dusk, we reached Clarksville at break of day. Learning that the commandant's sleeping apartment was in the city, and his military headquarters at the college in the suburbs, I made an arrangement with Colonel Woodward, that he should move the main force against the college, with the special understanding that he was to push the men right up to the breastworks and demand an immediate surrender of the enemy behind them. I hastened to the Federal colonel's room, but found that he had hurriedly escaped through the back way and had run to the college, reaching there just as Woodward was surrounding it. Following close in his wake, I came up on the side of the building opposite to Martin and

MRS. J. J. MASSIE, Fort Worth, Texas.

(Nee Miss Tennie Moore of Clarksville, Tenn.)

Woodward. Discovering that the enemy were parleying as to surrender, I decided to rush into the college, find the colonel and compel him to surrender. Giving Captain Fisher and the other captains orders to come immediately to me, if they heard firing within the building, I sprang over the picket fence, entered the house and ran up the stairs to Colonel Mason's room. There was but one sentinel on the upper floor, and leveling my pistol at him, I ordered him to open the door to the commandant's apartment. The command was obeyed, and on entering the room, I found the colonel in his night-clothes and four of his officers gathered around him. The Union commander was very pale and excited and decidedly in favor of surrender. Three of the captains sided with him, while the other fiercely opposed the proposition. Why these belligerents were not downstairs commanding and supporting their companies who were hesitating and wavering as to what course to pursue, I do not undertake to say.

But I had the drop on them, which gave me an advantage from which they could not recover, and the entire surrender was soon made without the firing of a gun inside or outside of the headquarters.

The beautiful little city of Clarksville, Tennessee, was one of the truest Southern towns, and her people had suffered many impositions at the hands of Colonel Mason and his men, and on the arrival of our little Confederate command, all of its inhabitants, old and young, turned out to joyfully welcome us as their deliverers from the hated " blue-coats." Their delight was shown to the boys in gray in the most extravagant ways, for these sons and daughters of the South were hilarious over being no longer virtually the prisoners of the Federals, under whose rule they had been unwilling subjects.

During the day, I received a polite notification that the ladies of Clarksville wished me to appear the next morning to receive in the name of our soldier boys a silk banner that had eluded the search of the Federals who had spent days in trying to find its hiding place, but found both the search and threats they had made of no avail. Now this precious bit of silk was to be presented to this Confederate command, and I felt deeply the honor to be conferred upon us. On reaching the appointed place I found a large and enthusiastic crowd gathered to witness the presentation of the flag, and my heart warmed toward these courageous townfolk who were braving the displeasure of the

Federals and risking imprisonment, fine and petty persecution at the hands of the enemy, for the sake of rewarding these soldiers of the South who were attempting to defend their rights and protect their homes and loved ones.

Miss Tennie Moore, one of Clarksville's most beautiful and attractive young ladies, stepped forth from the crowd and approached me, and with her fair face alight with enthusiasm and patriotism, and the pretty banner draped around her slender form, said in a clear, distinct voice:

"Colonel Johnson, this flag was made for a band of heroes who left this lovely little city to fight for their beloved country; but by the fortunes of war we have been cut off from communication with them, therefore it has been impossible for this symbol of the cause for which they are fighting to reach its destination. The Federal authorities have sought for this banner unceasingly and have heaped many indignities upon us, but through the love and fidelity of this old slave, we have been able to preserve it from the cowardly miscreants." (An old black mammy interrupted by stepping forward, her wrinkled, black face shining with pride, and patting herself proudly upon the breast as she bobbed her turbaned head, said, grinning broadly, "That's me.") "Now that another band of heroes has rescued us from the hateful bondage of these blue-coated Unionists, we wish to present, through you, this banner to your gallant boys, who, we feel, will never allow it to trail in the dust of defeat. (Moving forward, Miss Moore placed the flag in my hands, continuing): "Colonel Johnson, we place this banner of the stars and bars in your hands with the full assurance that its bright colors of red, white and red will be a beacon to light you and your brave followers to more glorious victories."

To this eloquent address, I replied: "Miss Moore, accepting this beautiful symbol of the Southern Cause from one of the fairest daughters of Tennessee, I feel the inspiration of the heroic sentiments expressed by you, and assure you that all that man can do to justify your confidence will be done by the brave men of my command. My heart is too full to express my appreciation of this great honor conferred by you, but knowing that it is deeds, not words, that must win the battle for the South, I promise you that we will try to prove on the battlefield that we will be loyal to your trust." I raised the flag, whose silken folds were to inspire us with nobler deeds of heroism for the South, and handed it to Colonel R. M. Martin.

In this loyal little town a company was raised by one of its principal citizens, Wm. Marr, and it joined the Partisan Rangers with him as captain. Aside from this valuable reinforcement, a more material and important advantage was won for the Confederates in this capture, as for some time Clarksville was an open passway from western Kentucky to the South, through which many needful supplies were conveyed to the Confederate army.

Colonel Woodward's command, a most efficient body, did especially good work in capturing and destroying Red River bridge, thus cutting off railroad communication between Nashville and the Federal army. The officers of this gallant little command were gentlemen of standing and all its men true sons of old Kentucky.

I paroled the three hundred and seventy prisoners and sent them to Fort Donelson, as I wished to be relieved of a great incumbrance and would not risk trying to send them South through the enemy's lines. Besides the capture of these men, we obtained five hundred guns, and a million dollars worth of army supplies, including several thousand wagons.

These five enterprises had followed in rapid succession: the attack upon the provost guard at Henderson, the capture of Newburg, the fight at Madisonville, and the taking of Hopkinsville and Clarksville, were accomplished without the loss of a man, a sufficiently satisfactory record when we add important later results, speedily ensuing, namely, the securing for the South some thousands of fine young soldiers and compelling the Federal military authorities to keep large forces scattered through western Kentucky—forces which otherwise would have strengthened their armies in their progress southward.

CHAPTER XVI.

THE PARTISAN RANGERS.

I now began to consider the capture of Fort Donelson. Encouraged by late successes, I felt sure my plans would not fail, and hurried matters to a finish. On the eve of starting, a dispatch was received from Madisonville bringing news of the advance of the Federal officer, Colonel John Foster, upon that town with a strong force. Entrusting the Fort Donelson expedition to Colonel Woodward, with one man I rode through to Madisonville that night. Captain Sam Taylor and Captain Al. Fowler, two most gallant and reliable officers, were sent, with about one hundred men, to ambush Foster and delay the Federals until I could move the captured Federal supplies out of town. This was accomplished. The cautious, dilatory, even timid manner of Foster's approach upon Madisonville convinced me that I had little to fear from this Yankee colonel; therefore the supplies were moved only about six miles, to a rough little mountain, Barney Sisk Hill.

As Colonel Foster had allowed less than a hundred men to hold his regiment in check and drive him back nearly a mile, I believed he could be kept in Madisonville until my command could arrive from Clarksville. Dividing my present force into three parties, one under Captain Sam Taylor, and the second under Captain Fowler, while the third was under my own direction, I attacked their pickets on the three main roads and drove them on the main body, making such a demonstration that our enemies were confident that it was my entire command so resolutely driving in their men. The next morning I picketed the main roads

LIEUTENANT COLONEL G. WASH. OWEN,

10th Ky., Partisan Rangers.

close up to Madisonville, and fired upon the Federal pickets repeatedly. Foster, believing that he was entirely surrounded by a superior force, started a negro to Henderson with dispatches asking for reinforcements, but the messenger was captured as he was trying to slip through the Confederate lines.

When I found that this little strategem had succeeded so well, I sent a courier to Martin with orders to take his command to a designated point between Madisonville and the Ohio River. I hastened to meet Martin at the appointed place (Given's Farm), and then with our reunited forces pushed on to Uniontown, where a Federal regiment was stationed, commanded by Colonel Farrow. It was my intention to surprise the Federals, but at nightfall a drizzling rain began to descend, making it so dark that it was impossible to see one's hand before one's face, and men were sent in advance to build fires so that we could proceed, but we were compelled to go so slowly that it was not until the next morning at ten o'clock that we reached our destination; we found the enemy in line of battle ready to dispute any further advance. I rapidly formed my men, placing a six-pounder on the right under the command of Lieutenant Cromwell, with instructions to keep it trained upon the front line. Young Cromwell proved a competent and courageous officer. Lieutenant Colonel Martin flanked the Federals on the right, while I led the center, myself. After a short fight, the enemy was driven back into the town, where a capture of the whole force was made. Immediately after the surrender I went to the Federal colonel's headquarters and found him much excited, as he had been told that he need expect no quarter, for the rebels were only a band of guerrillas intent upon butchery. He had told his men that they were sure to be slaughtered if they fell into the hands of this band, and they were anxious to know their fate. His relief, upon being told that they were not to be injured, but paroled and turned loose, was almost ludicrous.

Colonel Farrow, like his confrere, Mason, had committed many depredations upon the good people of Union county, and fearing just vengeance was anxious to put the Ohio River between himself and his victors, as he was afraid they would punish him for his cowardly treatment of the good citizens of the captured town. The waters of that river, however, could no more make clean his guilty fingers than could the waters of the sea take the blood from the hand of Macbeth. I found about fifty thousand dollars in bonds, which Farrow had extracted from the wealthy citizens of Union county and which I promptly burned. After paroling the Federals all the captured guns and camp supplies were loaded upon wagons and moved to Gieger's Lake.

As another illustration of the conduct of this unprincipled Union officer, I was shown a receipt for six thousand dollars which he had compelled the Union county people to surrender to him under the threat of instant imprisonment if they refused, alleging as a reason for so doing that some of the guerrillas had murdered one Hanks, a Federal soldier. These citizens, knowing that Hanks had been slain in fair warfare by some of my soldiers, were, nevertheless, forced to submit to these indignities.

At this time I contemplated attacking Henderson, but on ascertaining that more than half of our horses were unfit for the expedition, and that Shackleford and Foster, with a strong force, far outnumbering mine, were moving against me, I ordered my men to scatter through the country, to rendezvous at some future time and place. Retaining about sixty men, some of whom were on the sick list, I moved down to go into camp at Gieger's Lake. This was a beautiful sheet of water in the river bottom near the Burbank farm, in whose clear depths were many fine fish, and almost surrounded by trees, thus forming an ideal place for camping, hunting and fishing. Our tents had scarcely been pitched, when reliable information reached me that Shackelford was following me, having learned that I had all the arms and equipments captured the day before, and that my force was now small. I prepared to meet the enemy as best I could with such an inferior command. Martin, with less than fifty men, was placed on the main road to ambush the Federals, while I remained in camp with thirteen soldiers who were victims of chills and fever. A picket was placed on a by-road that was the only route accessible except the one on which Martin was lying in wait for the first advance of the enemy. I ordered the sick men to saddle their horses and hold themselves in readiness to move at any moment. Shackelford having been informed of the disposition of the Confederate troops made his approach by the by-road, thus avoiding Martin's ambuscade. The firing of the picket gave my little force timely warning, and instantly mounting, we galloped around the lake. The tardy movement of the

Federals gave us time to reach the other side of the lake, secrete ourselves and horses in the thick undergrowth, and wait behind the trees, Indian fashion, to fire upon the first foe that presented himself. It was about a hundred yards across this body of water to where our tents were pitched. The advance skirmishers, finding the camp abandoned, notified their commander, who ordered them to mount and galloped at their head into the deserted camp ground, and ascertaining the report to be true, formed his force on the bank of the lake. But a sudden concentrated fire from my band of thirteen sent them in disorder back into the woods. Shackelford ordered his men to dismount, and skirmishing behind the trees, returned the fire from across the water.

Martin, hearing the report of the guns, with his usual quickness comprehended the situation and at once started to the assistance of his comrades. His path led him through an old field well grown up with iron-weeds which completely concealed his movements from the foe, who were absorbed in their intention of capturing my squad. As was his custom, Lieutenant Colonel Martin, rode in advance of his men, his passion for scouting always having a strong hold upon him. Here, he again performed one of those daring, reckless feats that were characteristic of him, and which had won him a widespread reputation for bravery. Martin purposed to ascertain in person the exact number of the opposing force, and get them to turn their fire upon his soldiers that were concealed in the iron-weeds. Immediately in front of him were two small fields divided by a narrow lane, and he boldly took his way down this roadway as if he were out for a pleasure ride instead of for the purpose of attracting toward himself the fire of the Federal guns. Upon reaching the edge of a wood he looked back and observed that the Federals had thrown a body of men on either side of the lane for the evident purpose of intercepting him. Without a moment's hesitation he put his horse into a gallop and pursued his way down the road as confidently as if he were backed by a hundred of his gallant boys.

The Yankees at once turned their guns upon his mocking figure, shooting his hat off, piercing his clothes, and wounding his horse, but Martin seemed to be in his element, and only shook his fist at them and laughed in his loud, merry way, and wheeled his horse and sped back toward his command, the bullets nipping the air as they flew close about him. The Federals followed a short distance behind him. Upon reaching the iron-weed thicket where his trusty soldiers had stood watching with mingled admiration and wonder their heroic leader, he once more became the cool, calm commander, dropping all his defiant rashness and giving his attention to the rapid forming of his men to meet the charge of the fast approaching enemy. Unlimbering his little cannon, Martin loaded it to the muzzle with minie balls and stood ready to discharge it at the Federals when they were near enough for an effective fire. When within a hundred yards a rapid fire of small arms was poured into the advancing foe and Martin sent, with unerring aim, the contents of the noisy little cannon into the front ranks. This served to undo the Union soldiers as well as wound Shackelford in the foot, and the whole party beat a hasty retreat, leaving the Confederates in undisputed possession of their army supplies.

Several things occurred in this fight to add to Shackelford's discomfiture. Martin's cannon was drawn by two large mules, one of which a small boy rode, and on unlimbering this piece of artillery, the mules had become frightened at the firing and rushed out into the open, dragging the limber-box behind them. The brave little fellow gripped the reins tightly, and pulling with all his might at last got them back into the iron-weeds, but was unable to manage them, and this feat was repeated several times right in full view of the Federals, the limber-box still hitched to the snorting and terrified animals. This trivial circumstance operated in favor of the Confederates, as the frequent appearance of the mules and limber-box made the enemy believe that there were several cannons in the thicket; and the firing on their left flank from across the lake and Martin's ceaseless shooting in front caused them to suspect that I had again concentrated my whole force, which they thought several times greater than their number, and was surrounding them. This belief and the painful wound in his foot made Shackelford beat a retreat. Though the loss was small on both sides, the moral effect was greatly in our favor. One of our men, though very sick, had grimly held his post until a bullet ended his gallant career.

We had now accomplished more than we had reasonably hoped with such limited means, opposed often and threatened by so much larger forces than our own. We had captured

WOODSON, OR BROWNING SPRINGS.

Battle Ground: Fight between 9th Pa. Cav., Commanded by Col. Williams, and Capt. Adam R. Johnson with seven members of Breckinridge Guards.

garrisoned towns, routed the enemy in the field, saved various communities and districts from their tormentors, invited many young men to become regular Confederate soldiers and kept a great number of Federals following and watching us, who would otherwise have been at work in States further South. The capture of Clarksville and Hopkinsville had encouraged my troops as well as all the Southern sympathizers in western Kentucky while it had also served to dispirit the Federal forces as well as the Union sympathizers. My own conciliatory policy had a powerful influence for good and made the Unionists exert themselves to secure better treatment at the hands of the Federals for their Southern neighbors. My attack upon the provost guard at Henderson had multiplied my force of two men many hundred fold. My capture of Newburg, Indiana, had filled with dismay every river town on the north side of the Ohio and detained many hundreds of men from Southern battlefields, to protect these places; and my assault upon the strong force near Madisonville, who were utterly stampeded by seven men, had inspired new recruits with confidence and a spirit of emulation.

All of the papers were full of our doings, and the representation of our victories was so exaggerated that the mere mention of our names inspired fear in the heart of the Federals. The many epithets hurled at me individually by my foes did not disturb me in the least, but rather did for me work that it would have taken me months to accomplish, and the " River Robber " only smiled in his sleeve when exaggerated tales of the number of his soldiers were spread abroad by the unsuspicious Federals, who never for a moment dreamed that it was mainly to this end that I was laboring. When scouts returned to the Union lines and reported that " Old Stovepipe Johnson " was advancing upon them with his multitudinous band, preparations for resisting a small army would now be made by them, and when these Federals were confident that they had me in a trap, I would gather together my men, slip out of their clutches, and make a forced march to some town, and capture a score or two of their soldiers as well as their army supplies. Thus, I managed to hold large forces close in my track. The band of three had now become a regiment, and from the nature of the service, which all the men understood and appreciated, was designated " The Partisan Rangers of the Confederate Army "—a title highly relished by them.

The capture of Hopkinsville secured not only one hundred much needed guns, but made prisoners of many citizens who were carrying arms as home guards. Instead of sending them to prison and confiscating their property after the manner of the Federals, both themselves and their possessions were properly respected. One instance may be cited, the capture of John McGowan, who had been made prisoner after having tried to shoot me from the window of a brick house where the home guards were stationed. I not only spared his life, but his large stock of goods as well, which he afterwards was able to send South and disposed of with huge profit; which made of the would-be assassin a lasting friend.

The capture of Clarksville was of special importance, not only in the taking of the garrison and the immense supplies stored there for Grant's army, but in cutting the Federal railroad communications and burning the bridges, which so interrupted the plans of the Union leader, that he openly manifested his indignation.

CHAPTER XVII.

The time had now come when it was imperative that I should obtain commissions for my officers and file my muster-rolls in the war department at Richmond. The Federals had refused to recognize my men as Confederate soldiers and put Captain William Quinn, Paul Marrs and others in prison as criminals and guerrillas. Taking Captain Luke Trafton, my quartermaster, and a negro servant, I set out for the capital. Pushing rapidly southward on horseback, I learned, when near Springfield, Tennessee, that that town was full of Federal soldiers, and that Buell was moving his army into Kentucky. A stop for the night was made at Mr. —— Hutcheson's, near Springfield, the father, he told me, of the gallant Lieutant-Colonel Hutcheson of Morgan's command. Traveling incognito, Trafton and I were concealing our identity from friends as well as foes, but in some way our host discovered that we were from the Ohio River and began to question us about "Stove-pipe Johnson." Trafton, who greatly enjoyed the ridiculous, told his inquirer of a gray-headed, grizzly-bearded giant who cut a wide swath through the Yankee lines with a big fence rail, which he always used in place of a sword. Mr. Hutcheson was much pleased over this recital, as he was very anxious to hear facts from people who had seen this Confederate. The next morning when his guests were ready to depart, our host took me aside and told me that if I were a Southern man he thought that he was entitled to my confidence, and believing that it would further our mission and get us through the Federal lines quicker, I told him that I was the "Stove-pipe Johnson" that he had heard of through rumor. Hutcheson was greatly disappointed at this declaration, as he thought the young Confederate too youthful-looking to have that name, and mentally doubted its truth, but on being shown some papers, he went at once into the town to investigate the military outlook. It was not long before word was sent for us to go in, as the Federals had gone, and it would be several hours before any more would be there.

Following the guide, I soon reached the court house and found Mr. Hutcheson awaiting me.. I was taken by this old gentleman to a private upstairs room, in the neighborhood, where, to my great astonishment I found some sixty or seventy old gray-haired citizens to whom I was introduced. I was amazed to be ushered thus unexpectedly into the presence of such a large assemblage of venerable and unknown gentlemen. And I was disturbed, not knowing but that there might be in such a number of men some one who might betray me intentionally or otherwise, and be the cause of my arrest.

Of course I did not doubt Mr. Hutcheson's good motives in thus conspicuously publishing my name and destination, but I felt it was a very dangerous thing for so many, all absolute strangers to me, to know so much about me, although they all gave me a hearty, even enthusiastic reception, and I was assured that they had made arrangements all along the line for my accommodation and guidance from house to house.

Thanking then kindly, I excused myself and departed. Mounting our horses, we started rapidly down the road given, but with the caution of old soldiers, as soon as we were out of sight we turned towards Nashville, believing that if any one had betrayed us our enemies would be misled by this ruse, though we were going out of our proper course to accomplish it.

Upon reaching the city, I obtained a passport authorizing me to carry out some spun cotton to Lebanon. And when I found that this was on the line of march of Buell's main army, I moved along with them as far as Red Springs, and went into camp for the night with the Federals! That night Forrest came close enough to the camp to throw bursting bombshells into it. Feeling that it would be quite disagreeable to be killed by my friends in the enemies' camp, I concluded to part company with my protectors, and took the first crossroad that led to the Confederate lines; but as good luck would have it, had not proceeded more than a mile before I ran into Terry's Texas Rangers and was at once taken to the head of the column as a suspect, and delivered to my old commander. Forrest was riding with Governor Harris and Judge Ewing, of Tennessee. As soon as the general saw me, he exclaimed, "Why, hello, Johnson, where in the world did you come from?" I explained matters in short style, and both Forrest and Harris, thinking I possessed information of importance, insisted on my going at once with them to Bragg's headquarters, which they informed me would be at Glasgow, Barren county, Kentucky, that night.

Bragg recognized me as an old army scout and seemed delighted to receive all the information about Kentucky I gave him. He desired me to collect my regiment, concentrate them in the vicinity of Hopkinsville, and watch Buell's left flank, and, if possible, hinder his escape down Green River.

Though thus suddenly called on to change my plans, I readily obeyed this order, rejoicing that my native State at last had an opportunity of being freed from the thraldom that had so long been crushing the life and spirit out of her, and only too happy to be able to aid in her redemption. So I gladly took the printed circulars of Bragg and Harris, pledging the people of Kentucky that they had come to release her from captivity and to stay in their Commonwealth with a force sufficient to assist them to regain their liberties.

With such magnificent assurances I returned with Trafton to our old stamping-ground, and rode day and night till I had collected twelve hundred true and gallant troopers, with Camp Coleman, Todd county, Kentucky, between Russellville and Hopkinsville, as our rendezvous. I burned the Red River and Fishing Creek bridges, and fully carried out all of Bragg's instructions.

Old Kentucky quickly burst into a blaze of patriotic enthusiasm. Never, perhaps, during the entire war was recruiting so easy and rapid, never spontaneity of feeling and action so prevalent among what Sherman called the "vital population;" and I feel confident to this day that if Bragg had fought Buell at Green River, as he intended, or as he declared he intended, he could have crushed the Federal army, and with the aid of many thousand assured recruits could have held the State; here was the turning point of the war in the West.

The Confederates were never more anxious to fight. They

had heard all their lives that Kentucky was another Canaan for the good things of the earth, "a land flowing with milk and honey." Half-starved for so many months, full of enthusiasm over the great fields of golden grain and herds of fat cattle they saw everywhere, they were anxious to hold the fruitful territory. But Bragg's nerve failed him at the critical moment, and he allowed Buell to pass on to Louisville. Bragg veered off in the direction of Frankfort and Lexington and stayed in that region until his enemies had doubled their force, and although he got the advantage at the bloody battle of Perryville, he decided to evacuate Kentucky. The magnificent fight his men made there against superior forces demonstrated that they could easily have beaten Buell's army, which was in bad condition, at Green River.

I was left in an isolated, critical situation, overpowering forces were sent against me, ᴗd I was compelled to resort to my old tactics of disbanding my men to scatter all over the county.

CHAPTER XVIII.

Soon I received peremptory orders to report to the war department in Richmond, and taking Captain Trafton with me again, we pushed through the lines.

Upon reaching Murfreesboro, I received from General John C. Breckinridge and General Forrest letters of commendation addressed to Colonel William Preston Johnson, private secretary to President Davis, and a native of Louisville, Kentucky. Mr. Davis received me cordially and after reading the official report of my operations in Kentucky, expressed his pleasure and satisfaction.

That the readers of this history may understand the magnitude of the work accomplished by the Partisan Rangers up to this time, I append a synopsis of my first report to the war department, which I handed to Mr. Davis to read.

The full report, of which there is no copy extant, shows that Colonel Mason, Colonel Farrow and Colonel Olney, with their subordinate offices and men, were captured and paroled; Colonel Netter was killed at Owensboro; nine cities had been captured, two of them north of the Mason and Dixon line, over a million dollars worth of Federal stores had been destroyed, steamboats captured and streams rendered unsafe for transporting the munitions of war. That my command had occupied a territory not more than a hundred miles square and held it for many months, although this territory was surrounded by navigable streams and railroads, enabling the Federals to throw large forces to any point they pleased, secretly and quickly. While they employed thousands of men they were never able to surprise or capture the Partisan Rangers. During this occupation I lost fewer men, killed, wounded and captured than any other command of the same number in the Confederate service.

I had penetrated the Federal lines and begun an open warfare with a single recruit, and soon magnified the number so as to overawe the Federal forces that occupied the surrounding towns. The first three men by their attack on the provost guards in the city of Henderson were exaggerated into three hundred; seven men then attacked three hundred and fifty Pennsylvania cavalry, —it was at midnight, and the charge so scattered and demoralized them that they reported that they had been attacked by fifteen hundred guerrillas; next the city of Henderson surrendered to twenty-seven men while the gunboat "Brilliant" was lying opposite the town. These same twenty-seven men crossed the Ohio river in broad daylight, guarded one hundred and eighty prisoners, and carried away several hundred stands of arms. The main roads throughout the county were picketed, passports were demanded and the whole county was reported in the hands of the Partisan Rangers. These men were taught from the beginning to be minute men—to come promptly on call and never to be behind the appointed time. In this manner any small force of Federals was quickly routed and never allowed to ascertain the headquarters of the band of rangers. Early in the year 1904, I obtained the following transcript of the official records of the Civil War from Washington, which I present just as they were sent to me:

WAR DEPARTMENT.

Washington City, January 14, 1904.

Hon. James L. Slayden,

House of Representatives.

My Dear Sir:

In returning herewith the letter, received by your reference to-day, of General A. R. Johnson, of Burnet, Texas, who desires copies of reports made by him to the Confederate War Department about the first of November, 1862, and the first of August, 1862, also copies of his commission as brigadier-general and of the commissions of Colonel Chenoweth, Napier and Cunningham, I have the honor to transmit herewith copies of the two reports asked for by your correspondent.

Neither the original nor any copies of the commissions referred to by General Johnson are on file in the Confederate archives of this department, and consequently it is impossible to furnish him the copies desired. It is proper to remark, however, that they contain the following information relative to this portion of his inquiry:

Adam R. Johnson was appointed colonel, 10th Kentucky Cavalry, November 4, 1862, rank from August 13, 1862. He was promoted to be brigadier-general, C. S. A., September 4, 1864, to rank from June 1, 1864.

J. Q. Chenoweth and L. A. Sypert (not Cypret) were appointed colonels of cavalry September 6, 1864, to rank from the same date.

S. P. Cunningham and R. B. L. Soery were appointed lieutenant-colonels of cavalry September 6, 1864, to rank from the same date.

Thomas W. Napier was appointed lieutenant-colonel, 6th Kentucky Cavalry, September 18, 1863, to rank from September 2, 1862.   Very Respectfully,

F. E. ARMSTEAD,

Chief, Record and Pension Office.

Confederate States of America—War Department.

Richmond, Va., Nov. 1, 1862.

Hon. G. W. Randolph, Secretary of War.

Sir:—I submit to you the statements of Col. A. R. Johnson, of Partisan Rangers in Western Kentucky. He requests the companies of Captains Bennett, Fisher, Prow, Hammack, S. B. Taylor, Richardson, Marr, Chapman, Wall and J. N. Taylor to be organized into a regiment, and certifies that they were elected by their men.

He asks for commissions for himself as colonel, R. M. Martin as lieutenant-colonel, Philip Jones as adjutant, Dr. Geo. Porter as surgeon, Dr. Ben C. Redford, assistant surgeon, L. W. Trafton, assistant quartermaster, H. Garth as commissary, and W. G. Owen as major. As soon as his numbers are increased to sixty-four privates in each company he asks to be received into the line of the Provisional Army.

He asks that Lieutenant-Colonel Ben Anderson be authorized to organize a battalion of Partisan Rangers and when they reach ten companies of sixty-four (64) privates each, they shall also be received into the line of the Provisional Army to serve three years, and Colonel Anderson will be commissioned as Colonel.

Colonel Johnson asks that an artillery company be organized by him and directed to report to him for duty and that he be furnished with a battery of two light guns and the outfit for same. He asks that the irregularities of the organization of his regiment be overlooked and a disbursing officer be sent with funds to pay off his men from the date of their being sworn into the service.

He also asks for himself and Colonel Anderson full authority to swear in men for their respective regiments to serve for three years.   A. R. JOHNSON.

(Indorsement.)

A. G.:

Preserve the rolls of the regiment and commission the officers. Organize the battalion, commission the officers, authorize the increase to a regiment, and order Colonel Anderson to report to Colonel Johnson.

Authorize the conversion of both regiments to regiments of the line so soon as all the companies have at least sixty-four privates each.   The conversion to be with the consent of the regiments.

G. W. RANDOLPH,
Secretary of War.

Take him all in all, I think Mr. Davis was head and shoulders above all the great men of the country, North or South, who were conspicuous during the Civil War. He was an accomplished soldier, a statesman of the highest order, an accurate and profound scholar; .self-possessed and well-balanced; full of initiative, yet prudent; of strong and ready memory; of equal temper, wise and just; an orator and writer of the first class, and withal a man of action, alert, active, vigorous. This impression I had as we talked together, and to this day I believe he was the only man in the South who could have conducted the affairs of the Confederacy for more than four years; indeed, it is my conviction that we had no other man who could have piloted the new ship half so long. But this interview showed Mr. Davis in another aspect than that of the great president, namely, that of the man of refined sensibility, of tenderness and compassion and exquisite gentleness. After many sagacious questions, all of which I answered candidly and, appreciative of the importance of the time he was giving me, as briefly as possible, he asked me what I would do to protect my men when captured from maltreatment. I replied that "I had in the few cases calling for action on my part 'threatened' retaliation, which so far had answered [the reader will know that this was two years before the Burbridge and Payne atrocities in Kentucky], but this was a bluff, and I hardly know what I would do in an extreme case." Said he quickly: "Don't retaliate in kind, Johnson; think what it would lead to; the war is horrible enough as it is; what would it become if, when Federal officers were cruel and inhumane to prisoners of war and inflicted on them undue suffering or death, our officers should make reprisals? Only generals commanding an army should wield such terrible power, and even in such cases I shudder to contemplate the consequences. The war would become brutal and barbarous and sanguinary beyond conception; soon no mercy would be extended to prisoners and no respect paid to age or sex. No," he continued with great emotion, "never shall we come to this; let us win or lose with honor as Christian soldiers, without stain or reproach! Captured soldiers must be treated with consideration; non-combatants must not be harshly dealt with; private property must be respected; we make war against armed men only." More he said to the same effect. I assured him that I would obey his wishes; that was the kind of war any honorable soldier would want to see waged; thanked him for his courteous attention, and parted from him to meet him more than two years afterward, when he showed the same susceptibility.

Colonel Johnston next introduced me to General Cooper, adjutant general, who promptly accepted my papers and issued commissions to my officers. The necessary money to pay off my men was turned over to Captain Trafton, quartermaster.

I ascertained that Bragg, ever a thorn in the sides of Kentuckians, was insisting on all partisan rangers being called in, dismounted, and put in the infantry; but aided by my new friends at court, I succeeded in circumventing Bragg's designs, as far as my command was concerned, for the time being.

My next step was to obtain an order from the War Department

upon Bragg's ordnance officer for a battery of artillery; and with this I forthwith returned to Murfreesboro. But the obdurate old general flatly refused to honor the requisition until he could see, as he said, that I had men enough to need and take care of a battery, probably thinking mine was a "paper battalion." I sent for my command, and shortly four hundred manly fellows came riding in to confront him as a pledge for the care and protection of that battery.

BRIG. GENERAL JOHN H. MORGAN,

Commanding Division of Cavalry.

CHAPTER XIX.

ENTRAPPED BY BRAGG.

Bragg wanted my command to remain with the main army, and issued orders to conscript all soldiers that were not regularly enlisted and brigaded. We were entrapped. I was in a quandary, for I could not leave without disobeying the orders of the general commanding that department. So at the solicitation of General Morgan, who offered me the command of one of his two brigades, I united my force with his upon the understanding that General Morgan would divide his battery with me and allow me to return to my old department of Western Kentucky during the raid that he was then preparing to make into that State, known as the Christmas raid, as it was made in December.

Wishing to be freer to carry out this design than I would be if I commanded a brigade, I reported to Colonel Breckinridge, my junior in rank, who acted as the brigadier.

Our first important point of destination was Muldraugh's Hill, on the Louisville and Nashville Railroad, where we destroyed an extensive and costly piece of trestle-work in spite of a Federal regiment, strongly fortified, to protect it. We captured and paroled this force. We proceeded up the railroad, taking in small parties guarding it at several points.

Upon reaching Springfield, General Morgan ascertained that several heavy forces of Federals were converging upon him, and retreated southward. He found a strong force at Lebanon who were in a position to cut him off and seriously impede his movements. To me was given the office of holding the enemy in check till our body had passed. A heavy sleet was falling at the time and we experienced probably the most disagreeable night of the war, particularly as it was extremely dark, and we had to move slowly, suffering all the while from the cold and wet.

With three hundred men I proceeded against Lebanon. I attacked the Federals at three different places on different roads, di-. viding my force into equal sections, and easily drove the pickets into the town, for they did not suspect an assault on such a frightful night.

This attack on the·city of Lebanon made the Yankees believe that Morgan's whole force had beleaguered them, and while they were busily engaged in preparing for defense in anticipation of a general assault in the morning, I moved away quietly and headed for Burksville whither Morgan was marching. It was a weird sight when day dawned; all the men were sheeted in ice and looked like a ghostly army, as they moved silently through the woods.

No incident of interest happened until I rejoined Morgan at Burksville. While the command was crossing the river here General Morgan and his staff galloped ahead, but had not gone far when firing was heard in front, and the little party returned with the information that they had been ambushed by bush-whackers who were hidden on the mountain opposite the ford. I sent Colonel Martin and Neil Helm and five men forward to reconnoiter. Ere long I had brought up my regiment to support this squad, if necessary. But by the time I reached the spot Martin had charged on horseback into the dense bushes after these fellows, shot three of them, driven the rest of them into a cave, filled the mouth of it with dead wood and brush, and ignited the stuff, remarking that he supposed the fire would last long enough to keep the skulkers imprisoned till the command had passed.

I continued to be anxious to get back to my department of Western Kentucky, and as soon as we got far enough into Tennessee to send letters to Richmond I wrote Hon. Henry Burnett and Colonel William Preston Johnson, two Kentucky friends, and presented to them urgent reasons for my return to this special territory. In reply I·received very complimentary letters, notifying me that I was desired to go to Texas on a very important mission, and should hold myself in readiness for this expedition. In a few days I received dispatches to be delivered to General Magruder, together with a leave of absence for sixty days. Leaving the regiment under the command of Colonel Martin, near Woodbury,

Tennessee, I started upon a special mission to faraway Texas, for the second time since the beginning of the war.

Soon after I left, Lieutenant-Colonel Martin, with several hundred men, attacked a long wagon-train on the Lebanon and Murfreesboro turnpike, and although several thousand infantry were marching with it, he succeeded in capturing about one hundred wagons; but, unfortunately, owing to the breaking down of one of them, which blocked the narrow, rocky by-road, he had to destroy about seventy of them, but carried off thirty.

Not long subsequent to this episode an overwhelming force of Federals forced General Morgan to fall back, and Martin, with only a few companies of his regiment, tried to bluff and check the enemy, but was compelled to retire finally. Immediately in the rear of Martin was a low, open valley through which his men had to retreat. Seeing that the Yankees could reach a commanding hill with their batteries, he rode toward them waving his hat at them, then turned and rode slowly away toward the hill. The Federals suspecting that he was trying to entice them into some kind of an ambuscade, checked their march and threw forward a skirmish line to the foot of the hill. As soon as Martin thought sufficient time had elapsed for the passage of his men through the valley, he galloped away to overtake them, when the foe gave him a hearty parting salute of shot and shell.

But notwithstanding Colonel Martin saved his regiment from capture or annihilation by this ruse, he lost that day several valuable members of his command, among them Captain Sam Wall and Lieutenant George, both brave and excellent officers.

My journey to Texas being accomplished without incident, I delivered the dispatches from Richmond, and the gallant and urbane General Magruder was very complimentary at the expeditious way in which the lengthy, difficult journey had been performed.

Thomas Johnson, my brother, was serving in Wilkes's battery, and at my solicitation, the General seemed pleased to order that this young soldier should report to his brother.

Captain Neil Helm who had previously been sent back to Texas to procure recruits for his depleted company of scouts, sent me notice that he was for the present staying in Burnet, my old home, where my young wife was still living, and that it would be advisable for me to remove my family, as the Indians were committing many depredations in that neighborhood. Accordingly, I determined to take my wife across the Mississippi river and leave her at some place where she would have better protection and be nearer to me.

Upon arriving at Burnet, I found that Captain Helm had enlisted about a dozen recruits. Buying a carriage for my little family, I began the hardest journey of my life, rendered harder by anxiety. Intending to cross Red river at Shreveport, Louisiana, I sent forward Helm, in whom I had always placed great confidence from the time of our mutual Indian experience to the present.

When within about thirty miles of Shreveport, I met General Dick Taylor's command, falling back before Banks's large and well-appointed army. Taylor had issued orders for all privates and officers who were on leave of absence or furlough, to report to him immediately for duty; he was a fighting man, and was eager to engage Banks as soon as he could somewhat strengthen his comparatively small force.

Though exceedingly anxious to push ahead, I concluded not to dodge General Taylor or his military order, and proceeded to his headquarters at the crossing of old Caney on the river, and temporarily offered him my services and recruits. But after reading my papers, General Taylor kindly told me that I had better work my way through the country as rapidly as possible and rejoin my own command, a decision that delighted both Mrs. Johnson and myself.

The "Father of Waters" was then under full control of Yankee gunboats, which at this time had possession of almost every stream in the South, navigable or even unnavigable, for as President Lincoln once facetiously remarked, "his gunboats could make their way wherever there was any water, and often where the ground was only a little damp."

The Mississippi at this period was overflowing the country on both sides, so that it was dangerous to cross. I met quite a number of soldiers returning, who declared they had made efforts, but found it impossible to reach the other side. I saw General Polignac and staff just as we had come back again to the edge of the overflowed bottom, and learned from him that he had made an unsuccessful attempt, and that it would be absolutely impossible for me to take my carriage further, as the water had broken one of the levees and was passing through with such violence that the vehicle would be washed away. But as all my little party, including Mrs.

Johnson, were courageous and determined, I resolved to make a resolute trial, and drove for many miles with the water up to the hubs of the wheels. Upon arriving at the broken levee, after a careful inspection of the situation, I discovered a ridge of clay at the bottom of the break, and believing that I could keep the carriage from being carried away by straddling the ridge with its wheels, I succeeded in getting over, although the vehicle came very near upsetting.

Reaching Lake Concordia without further serious damage, I seized a flatboat with two negroes in it and reached the Mississippi proper late that night. The next morning while we were sitting in the carriage on the levee, opposite Natchez, a gunboat came up, puffing and blowing and running in close to shore, as if with the intention of examining the contents of the carriage; but after surveying us and concluding that we probably were only people from the neighborhood, it withdrew, much to our relief.

After this boat had got out of sight, the ferry-boat, which had been sunk to hide it from the Yankees, was raised, and we crossed over to Natchez.

Upon leaving the river, dangers on land threatened our little company, for we came very near running into General Grierson's command, just then making a raid through the country. Barely escaping capture, we slowly ploughed through the mud to Jackson, the capital of the State, reaching it just after Sherman had left it only an empty shell.

It was almost a day's journey from the old city of Jackson, or rather its remains, to the point at which the railroad was intact; and after having disposed of my horses and carriage, I took the railroad car and reached Marietta, Georgia, without further incident. Engaging rooms from Mrs. J. Stevens, we found that we were occupying the same chambers that the family of the great lamented General Albert Sidney Johnston had when he fell at Shiloh. The boot he was wearing when he received the fatal shot was now in the room as a sad souvenir, and was covered with blood-stains; a bullet-hole in it showed that he was struck in the calf of the leg.

Leaving Mrs. Johnson at Marietta, I went the next day to my command at McMinnville, Tennessee, and found that orders had been issued in my absence for me to reorganize my command, and that the rolls were in course of preparation.

Learning that the officers had agreed to have an election for a new lieutenant-colonel and major, I promptly sent in my resignation, and Colonel Martin and I began making preparations to go to the trans-Mississippi department. About twelve o'clock at night one of the captains came to me and declared that the regiment would disband forthwith if I failed to remain with them. To this complimentary expostulation I replied that there was but one condition on which I could remain with them, and that was that I should have the privilege of appointing the officers to be under me, and that the first two should be Lieutenant-Colonel Robert M. Martin and Major G. Wash Owen. I told the captain who was acting as ambassador for the regiment that as my demands were great and extraordinary, they were more than I had any right to expect or think would be granted by the regiment, and that I had no idea they would concede to me such privileges and power, but nevertheless upon no other terms would I consent to command them.

Martin and I were occupying at that time an old deserted cabin, and consumed the rest of the night in making arrangements to cross the Mississippi river, and discussing what we would do after our arrival in Texas, both being satisfied that the regiment would not accede to the demand. But to our surprise, the next morning before sunrise a petition addressed to me requested me to remain in command upon the conditions required, and upon examination, I saw that the paper was signed by every officer and man in the camp.

Both I and my old comrade-in-arms were much astonished, and I was very deeply moved by the unanimous and unconditional surrender of their rights by the men of the regiment and their wonderful devotion to me. I had the command mustered and made them an address, in which I told them that their remarkable deference to my will had excited my strongest emotions and completely disarmed me, so that I was now in such a mental condition that I must in turn surrender to them, and while appreciating their great confidence in my judgment and impartiality, I could not, even apparently, occupy the position of having taken advantage of their kindly feelings toward me, and that they could at once proceed to elect their own officers just as they pleased, explaining further that as my command was made up of seventeen companies, some here and some in Kentucky, it would be a very delicate and embarrassing duty to select the officers, for I would be obliged to leave out some of the best of my old and tried officers, men who had so long and faithfully devoted their lives and fortunes to the Confederacy; consequently, I would rather they should elect.

But even after this earnest argument, all the men and officers still insisted, and every commissioned officer on the spot handed in his resignation; and so I had nothing else to do than to proceed to make my appointments.

I was ordered to re-unite my regiment with Morgan's forces. Colonel St. Leger Grenfell, who had been an English cavalry officer, but who had the year before, thrown in his fortunes with those of the struggling Confederates, and was attached to Morgan's staff as assistant adjutant general, finding that I was the senior officer, determined, in spite of my opposition, that I should command the first brigade, and actually procured the appointment for me though I and all the other colonels thought that Colonel Duke ought to have it; and finally it was so decided. As I have previously said, I did not desire such an appointment anyhow, as I was very desirous to get back to my own military province of southwestern Kentucky.

Not only the commanders of regiments, but all the field and company officers and non-commissioned officers and privates alike joined in expressing the hope that Duke would be appointed to the command of the First Brigade, so universally popular was this brilliant young officer. Singularly enough, in date of commission he was the junior colonel of the division, for it happened that although he had commanded the Second Kentucky Cavalry for many months, while Morgan, with a colonel's commission, commanded the brigade, the application for commissions of neither of them had been forwarded to the war department or urged by General Bragg until after the battle of Hartsville in December, 1862. After that splendid achievement, the commissions were no longer withheld, but their date, instead of being fixed early in the year, was of the day of this battle. Pending the uncalled-for delay, other regiments had been recruited and organized during the summer and autumn of 1862, and commissions issued to their officers dated the day of their muster. Among other regiments whose colonels thus obtained commissions before Duke's came, were the Fifth and Sixth Kentucky Cavalry, commanded respectively by Colonels Howard Smith and Warren Grigsby, which had been recruited only a few months, and, at first attached to Buford's brigade, had by the disbandment of that body and through fear of being dismounted, applied for assignment to Morgan's command. They had reported to Morgan in February or March, 1863, just when the older regiments were all insisting, as I have said, that Duke should take command of the First Brigade; of course, they knew Duke's great ability and were familiar with his reputation for courage and conduct in the field, and would not have presumed to oppose his appointment as their commanding officer; so they, too, "waived rank" in Duke's favor and cheerfully ranged their regiments under him. The appointment of Duke under these circumstances to the command of the First Brigade put him as second in rank to Morgan and fixed the succession absolutely on him in the event of the disability or death of the famous cavalryman. Nor could Morgan's mantle have fallen on a worthier successor: an accomplished gentleman, a skillful tactician, ever successful in fight, I hold him to have been the ablest officer of his age in the Confederate army.

A few months after, when preparing for the great raid, General Morgan wished me to command the second brigade, lately completed, and we agreed to a compromise: I was to take command till we arrived at the Ohio river, where we were to cross into Indiana, and then was to be allowed to take my own command and proceed to Green river. But for the present Morgan's command had its attention turned to guarding the front, on the right of Bragg's army, whose headquarters were at Murfreesboro.

The Federals had strongly reinforced their cavalry, and there were frequent and heavy skirmishes between the horsemen. In one of these Lieutenant Colonel Hutcheson, of the Second Kentucky Cavalry Regiment, was killed, one of the most brilliant, efficient and beloved officers of the command.

The Union cavalry once broke through our lines and made a dash in force on General Morgan's headquarters at McMinnville, and would probably have captured him had it not been for the opportune appearance of Bob Martin, who, seeing the attack of the enemy, took his bridle in his teeth, and with pistol in one hand and sabre in the other, alone dashed in front of the charging enemy and held them in check until he was shot through the body. But sticking to his horse, he rode off to a farm house, where he was afterwards found and sent to the hospital. Profiting by the delay of the Federal squadron by Martin, Morgan soon arrived at his camp.

BRIGADIER GENERAL BASIL W. DUKE.

The loss of Martin to my command was almost irreparable, but his strong constitution sustained him and he was soon on the road to recovery.

Major G. Wash Owen succeeded to the command of the regiment. That I have not heretofore in the story of our enterprises in Kentucky referred to the services of this valuable officer more specifically demands an explanation: As he was the best drill-master in the command, he was invariably in charge of the camp wherever established; all of us considered this the post of danger. My general plan for protecting the camp was to scatter small scouting parties throughout the territory occupied, each commanded by officers who, with most of the men, were familiar with the neighborhood from boyhood; for instance, Bennett around Slaughtersville, Fisher near Henderson, Fowler at Madisonville, Sam Wall about Uniontown, while the camp would be at Sulphur Springs, Walnut Hill or Givens's farm. Martin and I perhaps would be operating in Daviess and Christian counties. Roads would be picketed for a short time by the several parties challenging all passengers and giving passports in my name, when they would be withdrawn, to reappear at other points. All kept in touch with Owen and through him with one another, and were promptly advised of any movement of the enemy. Through Owen the scattered detachments could be rallied at any point at a given hour, to unite for an expedition, under my command. I should say, furthermore, that no man was allowed to sleep in a house; the few instances of capture occurred in violation of this order. We thus held the territory, meeting with no surprise or defeat or loss. The success of my plans were largely dependent on Owen's promptness, and faithful and courageous always, he discharged his duties with marked ability and skill.

CHAPTER XX.

About the first of July, 1863, I received peremptory orders to take my command by way of Turkey Neck Bend, a point on the Cumberland river, and proceed toward Green 'river bridge, via Columbia, Kentucky. I sent Captain Helm with his company of scouts in advance to secure boats and reconnoiter the opposite side of the river and ascertain if possible the strength of the enemy, who was supposed to be in that vicinity in heavy force.

Reaching the river at McMillan's farm, we were received with real old Kentucky hospitality by Mr. McMillan, the father of the present governor of Tennessee. I found the river out of its banks, and no boats large enough to carry a horse. I swam my horses, carrying the saddles and clothes of the men across in boats, while many of the soldiers swam the swollen stream. The whole passage across was made with the loss of only three horses, and we were in the saddle by four o'clock on the morning of the third.

Captain Helm had returned and reported a large body of cavalry near Marrow Bone creek, with strong pickets on our road. I sent Captain Tipton's company of Cluke's regiment and Captain Bennett of Owen's regiment with Captain Helm's scouts, to attack the Federal pickets and drive them in on the main body. This was handsomely done, and my brigade, in column of fours, moved rapidly on the road, and passed the enemy without molestation; they believed from the spirited attack on their outposts that a general assault was intended, and took position on a heavily-wooded ridge and awaited our attack. A heavy fog covered our move-

142

ments and we were many miles on our road before they discovered our departure.

Leaving Captain Bennett and his men to watch the enemy, we moved on and by noon overtook Duke's brigade. Halting for an hour or so, my brigade took the advance, and by daylight on the morning of the fourth came in contact with the pickets of a force of about four hundred men that held the fortifications at Green river bridge.

After a close and careful examination, I found a short and heavy earthwork thrown up around an abattis, a deep ravine on one side and precipitous bluffs on the other, which prevented any approach except by the direct road to the bridge; the distance between the ravine and the bluff was not more than a hundred and fifty yards, and was so well and skillfully fortified that I deemed it impregnable against any dismounted cavalry, but believed we might use our artillery so as to induce a surrender. Bennett, who had now returned from the rear, was sent to the right to a point where he could enfilade the earthworks, and I sent Cluke with his regiment and the remainder of Owen's regiment, to cross the river at a ford below the bridge and make a demonstration on the rear. Bennett's enfilading fire soon drove the enemy from the earthworks in front of the abattis, and I was moving my artillery with the intention of opening fire upon the fortifications, when General Morgan joined me in the Federal earthworks, and gave orders not to use the artillery, and sent in a summons to surrender. The reply soon came back from Colonel Moore, saying: "The Fourth of July is a bad day for a Federal officer to surrender."

Morgan immediately ordered me to take the remnant of my brigade left on that side of the river, about four hundred strong, and storm the stronghold. I begged the general not to attempt it, as I had but seven rounds of ammunition and we could easily flank the place; but he insisted and I led my men to the charge. By the time we reached the abattis our ammunition was exhausted and about fifty of my men were killed and wounded, including the brave Colonel Chenault. Duke's charge on my right met a similar fate, he losing the gallant Brent and other valuable officers and men. Had the enemy's force in our rear used ordinary diligence, they could have given us trouble at this place.

We withdrew, and, flanking the bridge, moved on toward Lebanon, where we found Colonel Hanson posted with his regiment of infantry. We at once invested the town, Duke's on the right and my brigade on the left. After a sharp engagement, Hanson surrendered, and marching his command some miles on the road, they were paroled. This was another occasion on which an active foe could have done us serious harm.

Morgan with his usual skill, made demonstrations that misled the whole Federal force in Kentucky. The most important of these was a battalion of two companies placed under command of Major William J. Davis, at this time captain and adjutant general of the First Brigade, skilled in the conduct of scouting parties, to cut off communication between the forces at Camp Dick Robinson and Louisville, and to operate between Lexington and Louisville and along the Ohio river above Louisville. Among other results accomplished, this movement induced the moving of the gunboats above the falls of the Ohio, leaving the lower river unguarded.

At Garnettsville I dispatched Captains Sam Taylor and Clay Merriwether to Brandenburg for the purpose of capturing steamboats; and taking Captain Tipton with me, I went in person to a landing above Brandenburg to capture the regular packet that was due there at twelve o'clock that night. The packet came down within sight of the landing, but receiving some private signals, she ran off up the river. When I reached Brandenburg early next morning, I found that Taylor and Merriwether had captured two steamboats, and we were preparing to cross when a shell from the opposite side told us that we had enemies in our front. Bringing up my two pieces of artillery, under command of Lieutenant Lawrence, a few well-directed shots scattered the force and dismounted the gun. The crossing was begun and continued until the whole force was landed on the other side, which was done before daylight the next morning.

When we started on this raid with Morgan there was an agreement, as I have formerly said, that I should take command of the Second Brigade, and when we reached the Ohio river I should have my old command and two pieces of artillery with whatever boats we could capture; then I was to move down while he, with Duke's brigade and the other regiments of the Second Brigade, should move up the river.

When I crossed the river I was met by one of the staff who notified me that General Morgan wished to see me. As soon as I

MAJOR WILLIAM J. DAVIS,
(Photograph 1872)

reached him he told me that he was not willing that we should separate. I insisted upon his carrying out his agreement, telling him that he knew my runners had gone into my department, my men would be collected and subjected to capture and imprisonment; that the lower river was free from gunboats, and that I would capture Henderson, Owensboro, and Evansville, and thereby create such a diversion in his favor as would more than compensate for the loss to the regiment. Just then he pointed to the rear and said: " See, the boats are on fire; I gave orders to burn them." No bridegroom, suddenly separated from his bride on the day of his wedding, could have felt a more profound grief than I did when I saw the boats in flames, and felt that I was cut off from returning to my department. If there had been any consuming desire on the part of the Federals to capture us, no better opportunity ever presented itself than occurred during the crossing at Brandenburg. We were on the banks of the Ohio river more than thirty-six hours, and after I took up my march in advance on the morning of the 9th, my rear guard, which had been left on the bank of the river, reported that no attempt to cross the river had been made to that hour by the Federals. Had they closely followed us and attacked vigorously our divided force while crossing, it must have proven disastrous to us.

About 10 o'clock in the morning my advance guard came in contact with a heavy force of home guards, posted behind rail piles. Several of my men were wounded, among whom was Lieutenant Spencer Thorpe. A flank movement to the right and left, which was gallantly led by Duke's old regiment, the Second Kentucky, on the right and Ward's on the left, and a shot or two from Lawrence's Parrot guns caused the enemy to disperse in confusion. Passing on some eighteen miles, we encamped for a few hours.

Day after day we pursued our course, no resistance of any serious nature occurring. Sometimes forces doubly as large as our own would confront us, but a flank movement and few well-directed shots from the artillery invariably scattered them.

On the evening of the thirteenth, within a few miles of Cincinnati, General Morgan came up with me while I was riding with my advance guard. He asked me if I had any men in my command who were acquainted with the roads around Cincinnati. I told him I had two men who were reared in that city and that Captain Sam Taylor had passed much of his time there. He requested to have a conference with them. I immediately sent for Captain Taylor, with an order to bring one of his lieutenants, his cousin, with him. These two men were nephews of General Zachary Taylor and inherited the military characteristics of their family. I think it was Lieutenant John McLain that came with this captain, and General Morgan and myself, together with these men, fell back immediately in rear of the advance guard and conversed as we rode along. They gave him a minute description of Cincinnati and its surroundings, telling him that in the suburbs of the city was a high, flat ridge running parallel with the streets, that would help us to keep a direct course and give good ground to travel over. General Morgan expressed a desire to ascertain the strength and position of the enemy in Cincinnati, and both of these officers were to ride into the city and afterward report to us at a designated point, which was so clearly described that no difficulty could be found in recognizing it, although it was late at night. I remained here until my entire brigade passed, General Morgan going at the head of it. Colonel Cluke coming up to where I was standing, seemed to be perfectly exhausted, saying he would give a thousand dollars for an hour's sleep. I told him that I would hold his horse for him and he could sleep until my scouts came in. He at once assented and was soon fast asleep. It must have been two hours later, when Captain Taylor and Lieutenant McLain found me, and still Duke's brigade had not reached that point. Knowing the great danger of so wide a gap in our column, I sent Lieutenant McLain to find Duke and direct him to where he could find us, and in company with Colonel Cluke who had had his hour's sleep, we galloped forward until we found General Morgan, and gave him the information acquired. The scouts said that most of the town was in the utmost confusion and there was no appearance of any advance against us; they thought the whole city would surrender if the demand was made. General Morgan said that in a city the size of Cincinnati his little force would entirely disappear and he would never be able to collect them again. I halted my command on the outskirts of Cincinnati until Duke's advance communicated with my rear. Pushing forward, we passed Camp Denison and reached Williamsburg, where we went into camp for the night. We now felt that we had passed the real danger line, and nothing serious interposed between us and the Confederate lines except the Ohio river.

The next morning we took up our line of march, feeling a sense of security in our position. I think it was on the morning of the nineteenth, Duke's brigade being in the lead, with Morgan at its head, when I rode forward to get positive commands from General Morgan for crossing the Ohio, which was said to be but twenty-five miles ahead of us. I found him sitting on the gallery at a cross-roads store, where there was a fine well; the boys were filling their canteens from the pump. The General greeted me with his bright smile, asking me to get down and rest a little, remarking: " All our troubles are now over, the river is only twenty-five miles away, and to-morrow we will be on Southern soil." Resting awhile, we rode off together in the rear of Duke's advance guard.

Morgan had given orders for the advance guard to arrest or hold any one they met or overtook on the road. We had hardly traveled a mile when the advance guard picked up a man, old and gray-bearded, who had been riding toward us. Morgan at once began to question him about the crossing of the river. He assured us that Long Bottom was about twenty miles down the river, but the ford was much deeper. Morgan concluded to take the right-hand road, and this proved to be a disastrous mistake, as by turning in that direction we were advancing toward the gunboats. In spite of all this we might have crossed the river, but the night came on so dark we could not discern the horses in our immediate front, and fires had to built along the road to enable us to travel.

Nothing worth recording occurred until about three o'clock in the morning, when I found a broad right-hand road intercepting ours. Sending Captain Bennett and his company to scout the road, I was informed that there was a heavy body of cavalry advancing. I sent two other companies to support Bennett, with instructions to hold the enemy in check. This gallant officer had no superior in such tactics. As soon as the re-inforcements reached him he made such a spirited attack on the enemy's advance that they believed Morgan's whole force was on them, and instead of advancing they made preparations for defense, and Bennett was able to keep them in check until the day revealed the small force that was opposing them. In the meantime I had reached Long Bottom, examined the ground in person and found a high ridge immediately on our right, not more than four hundred yards from the river. I immediately dispatched my adjutant to Colonel Duke to ascertain if he had occupied the ridge. He soon returned and told me Duke had not, but would do so in a few minutes. The sharp rattle of musketry and the bursting of shells over us showed that the enemy had already occupied the ridge. I at once formed my command so as to support Duke, who was falling back before overwhelming numbers. At this juncture, Major Bullitt, in command of the Sixth Kentucky, threw his little force upon the advance of the enemy and held them in check, but this was only temporary. We were borne back by sheer force of numbers and Duke and myself were separated, he soon after being compelled to surrender, with the men still with him. I endeavored with the men gathered around me to stop the advance of the enemy. I did not succeed in doing this until I found Captain Shelton who had collected about twenty men, with a few rounds of ammunition left. Placing these few men with those about me in ambuscade, the first round arrested the pursuit, and we were not molested any more.

Here again the pursuing forces lost an opportunity of capturing our whole command, as our ammunition was exhausted and the men worn out and somewhat demoralized.

I soon received orders from General Morgan telling me to take my command to a ford some distance above, where he intended crossing, and I determined to cross at all hazards. Forming the men who were with me in column of fours, I appealed to them to keep their ranks and make a show at least of an organized force. There was hardly a company in the whole division that was not represented in this body of men. I assured them I would lead them across the river. Several of my staff had now joined me, and together with Captain Helm and a few of his men, we formed an advance-guard. We moved on toward the river and seeing the smoke of the gunboats coming up from below, I advised the men to push into the river as soon as we reached it. I took the lead and soon found myself in swimming water. Lieutenant Woodson, who could not swim, was by my side. He was riding one of those immense Norman horses, common to Ohio farms, which he had been using but a day, and I hoped it would be able to carry him safely across, but by the time we were half way over his horse turned on his side and floated against my mare. Seeing that this great weight would soon sink my horse, I jumped into the river and catching hold of the cantle of my saddle, and paddling along by the side of this noble animal, I urged and coaxed her until she actually dragged the heavy weight to the other side. My whole attention for the time being having been directed to saving Woodson, I had not observed what was going on in my rear. As I reached the shore, I directed Woodson to take my horse to the woods, and ordered all those who followed him to go to the same point. Already the gunboats were throwing shells on the Ohio shore, and, believing that they would soon turn their guns on us, I hurried the men forward, out of their range.

Looking across the river, I saw a number of hats floating on its surface, and knew that each represented the life of a brave and gallant Confederate, who had found a watery grave. Words are inadequate to express my desolation, and even wild thoughts of suicide flashed through my brain. Just then one of the hats was lifted out of the water, and a faint voice came to me, saying, "Oh, Colonel, can you do anything for me?" I recognized Captain Neil Helm, one of my truest friends and most faithful followers, one who had been with me on the plains of Texas and had never failed me when surrounded by the savage Comanches. I determined to rescue him or die. Seeing an old skiff on the bar, I rushed to it and shaking it from its sandy bed, I skimmed it over the ground as if it were a feather, and pushing it with a mighty force into the river, I sprang in and, jerking out one of the seats with superhuman effort, paddled to him just as he was about to sink. He had barely strength enough left to grasp and hold on to the stern of the boat.

By this time the gunboats were on us, and the soldiers gathered on the bow looked down on us with guns in hand. Helm, believing they were going to shoot, pleaded with me to jump into the river, but knowing the skiff would soon sink, I paddled with all my might toward shore. The skiff sank before we reached the bank, and I jumped into the water to assist Helm and found it shallow enough to wade. Seizing him I dragged him on the sandbar. All this time there was not a shot fired at us and not a single shell was thrown on that side of the river. This was an act of humanity I am glad to record. We were still in short range, and Helm, believing they would shoot, begged me to leave him. When I refused, he jumped to his feet and declared he would walk, and I supporting him, we reached the woods, where the men were now gathered, a little over three hundred.

Believing they would soon have a force in pursuit of us, I moved the men as rapidly as possible across the mountains, and traveling by unfrequented roads, we reached Green Briar county, Virginia.   When we first came in sight of fields of• harvested wheat and green, waving corn, I am sure each one of us felt as much pleasure as did Moses of old when he first viewed the Promised Land.

CHAPTER XXI.

MORGAN'S MEN REORGANIZED.

Leaving temporarily in Green Briar county, Virginia, the men I led from the Ohio river, with my adjutant, Captain S. P. Cunningham, I departed for Richmond.

I had hardly gained my room at the Spotswood Hotel, in the evening of August the first, when Senator E. M. Bruce asked admittance. He seemed to be very much agitated, and directly after his salutation, he said, " Colonel Johnson, I wish to have an interview with you before you make your report to the War Department, to ascertain how you stand in regard to General Morgan. I must tell you that General Bragg has been denouncing him as a disorganizer, and declaring that he had gone on this Indiana and Ohio raid against his orders. Colonel Grigsby, who escaped with you, has asked that the men be dismounted and turned over to him to aid in the formation of an infantry command he contemplates. Everything at present appears to be contrary to the interest of General Morgan and his men. But the entire Kentucky delegation are their friends. Our hopes are in you whom we know to be the ranking officer outside of prison, and I am here to know if we can count on you in this extremity."

I replied that I had a department of my own, and had come to Richmond to ask permission to return to it at once, that I had never regarded myself as permanently attached to Morgan's command, and believed that I could accomplish much more good for the Confederacy by recruiting and fighting in Kentucky than by connecting myself with the main army.

Mr. Bruce insisted that they must have my assistance in this emergency, that he felt sure that many of the best of Morgan's men would be lost to the Confederacy if forced to join the infantry, and that General Bragg would do all in his power to have General Morgan court-martialed.

To this my rejoinder was that I would take into consideration the proposition of reorganizing the command and would give my answer to-morrow morning before going to the War Department.

Mr. Bruce took his departure saying he would call at nine o'clock the next day, and that I had now the opportunity of doing a most generous act.

He had scarcely gotten out the door before Hon. Henry Burnett, Congressman Bradley, and several other representatives from Kentucky, made their appearance on a like errand, expressing similar sentiments and opinions. To all of them I gave the same reply, namely, that I would 'give them an answer at nine o'clock in the morning.

A perplexing problem confronted me, and I debated quickly with myself whether I should give up my own individuality and all my cherished plans for another expedition into western Kentucky or sacrifice all these in protecting an absent officer's interest and that of his men, not only outside but inside the prison, as the fate of the latter would almost certainly follow that of the former.

The latter considerations prevailed, and preserved Morgan's command in all probability, and in the morning, when almost all of the Kentucky delegation presented themselves at my room to receive answer, I gladdened the hearts of these patriotic men by informing them that I had decided to undertake the task of reorganizing the force, provided that it was to retain its original title "Morgan's Command," and to be mounted again as cavalry.

Colonel William Preston Johnson, with Bruce and Burnett, accompanied me to interview General Cooper, and the outcome of the matter was that I gained my point upon assuring him that if allowed to reorganize these men outside of General Bragg's department I would guarantee five hundred men mounted and ready for service in the space of ninety days, and in event of failure to fulfill this promise, I would turn all the men over to the War Department and accompany them wherever they were sent, no matter to what branch of service they were relegated. General Cooper, however, at first was incredulous, not believing the task could be performed, and replied, "Young man, you wish to undertake an impossibility; we are unable to obtain horses for our artillery, and half of our cavalry are horseless."

To this I answered, "General Cooper, this makes it more important that I should undertake this business. You have just said that the cavalry was a very important branch of the service and that half of them were without horses, hence ineffective. I know I am undertaking a difficult job, but the fact is our men are better able to mount themselves than any men in the Confederacy. They belong to the best families in Kentucky, and there is hardly one of these who has a dollar who will not aid them. Moreover, you say these men ought to be collected, and I assure you that the very best and quickest way is to make a call upon them to assemble at some convenient place for the purpose of reorganizing as cavalrymen."

At this juncture, Bruce stepped forward and said, "General Cooper, if you will permit General Johnson to take charge of these men, as he has requested, we Kentuckians will raise one hundred thousand dollars to assist him in his laudable and laborious task, if it be necessary." General Cooper replied, "Mr. Bruce, I will read General Johnson's report of the Indiana and Ohio raid and will then give you my answer."

When the callers had reached the anteroom, Senator Burnett, in his exultation said, "General Johnson, you have exceeded our expectations, and we believe that you can and will succeed in your enterprise. I advise you to go at once and see Colonel William Preston Johnston, and explain to him all your plan."

I immediately called at the executive department and explained everything so satisfactorily to Colonel Johnston that he directly took me to see President Davis, who questioned me closely about the great raid, which came so near being a magnificent and glorious success in its entirety, and which at any rate kept many thousands of Federals from their armies in the South, as they were completely broken down in the long continued chase; there was created a mighty uneasiness and alarm in all the border States of the North, which caused them to retain many thousand more men permanently, who otherwise would have gone South.

The President also inquired minutely how I proposed to collect so many men and horses. Like General Cooper, he thought the task impossible, but agreed that my method of assembling them was the most feasible.

At the end of the conversation, though Mr. Davis did not express his full approbation, I felt that I had won the victory, and so informed my friends.

I had a second interview with Colonel William Preston Johnston, and requested him to use his influence in my behalf, and permission gained, to get me the authority to report to General Buckner, hoping to obtain consent from him to take Morristown, Tennessee, as the place of rendezvous. A promise was given, with the happy result that the desired orders were issued, and a general order sent to all quartermasters and commissaries for transportation and rations to all men on their way to General Johnson's camp at Morristown. I advertised in the newspapers the order from the War Department for all Morgan's men to report at this place. A general order was also sent by the War Department, instructing all the officers in the army to send to Morristown any of those men who might be in their command.

One of these men, whose name is not given, furnished General Duke, for his " History of Morgan's Cavalry " an account of this camp, some extracts from which are here given. " On the — of August, 1863, Johnson issued orders, under instructions from General Buckner, for all men belonging to Morgan's command to report to him at Morristown, in East Tennessee. These orders were published in the Knoxville papers, and upon its being known that there was a place of rendezvous, every man who had been left behind when General Morgan started on the Ohio raid now pushed forward eagerly to the point designated. When that expedition was undertaken many had been sent back from Albany, Kentucky, as guards for returning trains, others because their horses were unserviceable. Many, too, had been left on account of sickness or disability from wounds. In a week or two General Johnson had collected between four and five hundred men, including those who had made their escape from Ohio. The general also issued an address to this effect: ' Members of General John H. Morgan's Command: Orders have been issued by the War Department for all officers and men of your old command to report at once at Morristown to be re-mounted and reorganized and held together in the name of your brave and unfortunate commander, General John H. Morgan, who is now suffering close confinement and unmilitary indignities in a Northern penitentiary. I appeal to you for the love you bear him, for the glory you have won under his command, and for the great and holy cause for which you have voluntarily left your homes, to come at once and join your comrades and be prepared to follow General Morgan again as soon as he has returned to the Confederacy.' "

Every train brought in some of these men until over twelve hundred had been collected inside of sixty days. Orders from the War Department were read, requiring the men to remain in camp except upon orders to leave, and to drill daily. They were told by their commander that they were expected to re-mount themselves. They devised every honest means to obtain horses. Many sold their watches for this purpose, others received aid from home through trusted men sent by me into Kentucky. Hon. E. M. Bruce notified me that all the men who needed money should have it, those who could to repay him, but nothing expected from those unable to do so. This generous, noble man used his money freely and even lavishly.

I notified the citizens in every direction that I would buy their horses and pay full value in cash. In less than sixty days I had more than seven hundred men mounted and ready for service and many more not yet equipped. General Buckner gave me all the assistance possible. In less than thirty days from the time I began my encampment I received orders from General Buckner to send a force into the mountains between Morristown, East Tennessee, and Asheville, North Carolina, to disperse some bush-whackers who were killing the men with forage trains. While this was a distasteful business, a hazardous service unattended by glory, I proceeded to execute the order. Sending for Colonel Bob Martin, I told him to select one hundred men, and placing twenty-five of them under Captain Neil Helm, and twenty-five under the command of Captain Quirk, to start toward Asheville; these two captains must protect his flanks, one on the right, the other on the left; he was to require every man under him to be ready to charge quickly to the spot whence a shot came. In this expedition, thirty bushwhackers were killed and fifty-six prisoners taken; thirty-seven serviceable horses also were brought in. Colonel Martin's loss was but one killed and five wounded. This was one of the most successful attacks upon bushwhackers ever accomplished.

After this Lieutenant J. B. Gathright also successfully conducted an anti-bushwhacking expedition in another direction, and these two well-planned and well-executed movements seemed to have exercised a salutary influence far and wide.

Colonel Martin led this entire body of Morgan's men now fairly equipped into the battle of Chickamauga, where they acted a conspicuous and brilliant part, notwithstanding the continued vexatious and harassing interference of General Bragg, which would have been more or less demoralizing to any command. Between Bragg and the other Kentucky troops, who had been longer under his command, there were much friction and bad feeling, and apparently the irascible old man extended his animosity to these men who had lately come under his command, because they came from the same State. For no sooner had I reported to him, as the commander of the department, than he at once began to make arrangements for dismounting these men, in accordance with his original determination to make infantry out of them. And had it not been for General Forrest, General Bragg would have spoilt in a few days the work of Generals Morgan, Duke and myself, a work which it had taken years to accomplish. General Forrest ran the risk of a trial by court-martial by refusing to carry out this policy of Bragg's. To ignore more decidedly this order to dismount the Morgan horse-men, General Forrest, as the immediate commander of all cavalry in this region, gave orders that I should establish my headquarters at Ringgold, Georgia, with one battalion, and Colonel Martin, with another battalion, should go to the right and guard the woods south from Chattanooga, while Captain Helm should have charge of the scouts. It was made the duty of these officers to keep General Forrest posted as to every movement of the enemy within their lines of observation.

But we had hardly been settled in our different quarters, when it was reported that General Bragg was still bent on carrying out his design of dismounting the Kentucky contingent, his animosity against the men in general from that State now seeming to culminate in an inimical feeling against me, because I had thwarted him at the war department in his machinations, and had it not been for the resolute action of Forrest, who again positively refused to execute his orders, Bragg might this time have succeeded. Whatever other things may be alleged as the cause of the breach between Forrest and Bragg, I think the real cause was Forrest's action in our behalf.

Immediately after the commencement of hostilities between the North and South, Forrest had hastened to Louisville and laid in a large quantity of war material; on this trip he secured as his first company a body of Kentuckians under Captain Frank Overton.

He had, all told, several thousand Kentuckians under him during the war. He well knew the fighting qualities of Kentucky's sons, and was always their friend and champion, and they in turn admired and loved him, and would have done anything he asked, no matter what the odds against them. But, notwithstanding Forrest's active championship upon this occasion Bragg separated from me my two mounted battalions which he never, so long as he was in command of the army, allowed to rejoin me or Morgan, and put me over the men I had not yet succeeded in mounting.

But Colonel Martin, with one of the battalions, was chosen to open in advance of our infantry the great battle of Chickamauga, on the right, and by their gallantry in charging and running out of their fortified position the Federal infantry, the Kentuckians attracted the attention of General Hill, who sought out General Forrest during the thickest of the fight and complimented him on their action. And subsequent to the battle it was again Martin, who with this battalion drove the defeated Federals out of their advanced works at Chattanooga. Then it was that the redoubtable Forrest begged and pleaded with the nervous Bragg, who ever acted after a battle as if he, and not the enemy, had been whipped, to move on to that city in close pursuit of the Federals who had just lost Chickamauga, and in their panic-stricken condition, were willing and ready to give up Chattanooga. But Bragg, as all the world knows, did not move. It is my conviction that had Bragg advanced, the Federals would have retrograded clear to Nashville, their only safe, fortified stopping-place in Tennessee, and all East Tennessee would have been in our hands again.

It was a memorable morning the next day after this brilliant feat of arms: Martin had formed our boys in the outskirts of Chattanooga, when General Forrest came riding down the line of the

Kentucky battalion, and taking off his hat in honor of the prowess they had shown, exclaimed, "Any man who says that Morgan's men are not good soldiers and fine fighters tells a damn lie." This characteristic speech of Forrest gave the boys more genuine delight than if he had made them the most eloquent and eulogistic address, for they recognized it as the natural, spontaneous outburst of the great cavalry chieftain. Whether or not it contained a barbed arrow for the breast of Bragg, they considered it a signal vindication on the part of their brave champion.

Bragg ordered me to move into East Tennessee, and Forrest, still fearing that Bragg wanted to dismount the Kentucky boys, in turn ordered me to take them along also, to get them as far as possible from "the old man's clutches."

Placed in command of Davidson's brigade of Forrest's division I pushed by forced marches towards Athens, Tennessee, and had a little skirmishing near that place with some Federals, who fell back in the direction of Chattanooga. Forrest, following, received orders to return, and to give me a chance to finally thwart Bragg's intentions, he ordered me to report to the War Department at Richmond.

I left as soon as possible, after securing letters of commendation from Buckner, Breckinridge and Forrest. These letters, together with the co-operation of the ever friendly Kentucky delegation, who nearly always worked as a unit, enabled me to obtain an order countermanding the order of Bragg for the dismounting of Morgan's cavalry. This nullification of the pet scheme of "the old man" greatly exasperated him, and he so far forgot his own dignity and that of the War Department as to telegraph an insulting message to this august branch of the government, and received, in his turn, a severe rebuke, which General Cooper informed me was the first ever administered by President Davis.

General Bragg was so careless, if not untruthful, as to state in his telegram that I had deserted my command while upon a dangerous expedition with General Wheeler. This he did not give as a report but made as a positive statement, as if he had official knowledge of the alleged fact. He asserted further that my men in large numbers had also deserted. This apparently malicious statement only strengthened my case with the war department, for they all knew that I had never gone on any such expedition with General Wheeler, and as to the desertion of some of my men, they knew also that Bragg was merely stating the condition I had warned the war department would follow if they allowed my men to be dismounted. General Bragg put himself in a very bad light by making this incorrect statement, if prevarication and falsehood are too strong terms to characterize his allegations. He simply ruined his case in court. I was fully authorized to extend notice that there would be, without delay, a second reorganization of Morgan's men. I was given carte blanche for transportation and supplies, and was informed that General Hardee would soon be in command of the army and that I would be allowed to select my own quarters in that department. General Cooper stated, moreover, that notwithstanding they thought it would be impossible for me to succeed in remounting so many horseless men it was resolved to allow me ninety days in which to make the effort, and if I could get five hundred horses in that time the command would be held intact, but if a failure should ensue they would all be mustered into the infantry. When I reported to General Hardee he laughed at the idea of my being able to mount that many men, while he himself had failed to find horses enough to supply a battery.

Selecting Decatur, Georgia, I went into camp with only my adjutant, and sent an advertisement to every important paper in the South, urging the men of Morgan's command to report at once to me, under special orders of Adjutant General Cooper. Soon I had a nucleus around which I expected at least several hundred to gather. Among the first to report were nine chaplains; these I sent to solicit supplies in the different States, and as I had been amply supplied with Confederate money, I offered to pay for everything and to pay the difference between serviceable horses and those in camp. I also arranged the quartermaster's department and began the manufacture of saddles, boots and shoes, placing Captain J. B. Gathright in charge of this work with Captain Paul Marrs as assistant. The enterprise, energy and intelligence of these two excellent officers enabled me to accomplish this purpose; and in less than sixty days I had over seven hundred horses fit for service, and had collected about seven hundred men, all of whom were well clothed and fed, and within the specified time I would have had the entire command mounted had not General Morgan, who had lately escaped from prison, returned to Tennessee and issued a proclamation countermanding my orders and plans, stating that the war department would give him all the supplies he needed.

But this statement he made upon the supposition that the government had an abundance of supplies, in which he soon found he was mistaken; and upon reaching Decatur, he had the candor and frankness to confess to me that he had sadly overestimated the ability of the government in this line. Surprised and apparently delighted with the work I had done in so short a time and in such a general scarcity of all things necessary to the rehabilitation of his command, he generously refused to supersede me, and ere long I had orders to take the men to Abingdon, Virginia. Soon thereafter I was ordered to report at Richmond, in person, for very important special service; whereupon General Morgan took command of his reorganized force, made up of fragments of his former different regiments. The majority of his men were still in Northern prisons, from which, however, so many were escaping through their daring ingenuity, that the commandant of one of these posts declared that the " authorities at Washington might as well turn all of Morgan's men out in a body, as they would all get out singly, anyhow."

I had been located in a district that both the Confederate government and General Hardee had declared entirely stripped of horses, and it is said that every official, even General Cooper who befriended me so kindly, was of the opinion that it would be a superhuman task to mount one hundred men, and that the idea of securing five hundred horses in ninety days was too preposterous to be seriously considered, although they allowed me to attempt it, since I was so confident and enthusiastic in my belief that I could accomplish it if allowed to try. Over seven hundred horses fit for service, and nearly five hundred dismounted men recently scattered all over the South, were in camp when General Morgan escaped from prison. Of course this work could not have been done had I not able and willing assistants. The men were in a good state of subordination and discipline, forming a body of efficient soldiers all ready to General Morgan's hands. Having had orders from the war department, as I have mentioned, to report at Richmond as soon as I had disposed of Morgan's reorganized command at Abingdon, Virginia, I obeyed the instructions, and arrived there about the first of May, 1864.

The authorities complimented me highly upon my success in

collecting and mounting, and supplying with the necessary war material so many men in such a short time, but informed me that they had now "a more important work for me to do, one that required not only extraordinary energy and enterprise, but extreme caution and excellent memory, too, since my orders could not be entrusted to writing, and that great secrecy and tact were requisite for the momentous enterprise in which I was to be engaged." This meant another trip into Kentucky and ·Tennessee. I was expected to co-operate with General Forrest and perhaps with the main army also, now in Georgia. Secret emissaries were to be sent into the disaffected portions of Indiana and Illinois to aid uprisings of citizens who were favorable, to the South or sick of the war. Instructions were to be given me through Colonel William Preston Johnston, who would give me daily lessons in his secret verbal code, reminding me of the confidential instructions given me in Mississippi several years before by General John C. Breckinridge, when about to send me to Henderson. The despatch of this business and my subsequent work in Kentucky were known at Richmond, and were perhaps the cause of my being selected for a somewhat similar expedition, but one of infinitely greater moment. I soon came to look upon this expedition as the forlorn hope of the Confederate States Government in its dire extremity.

CHAPTER XXII.

THE FORLORN HOPE.

Grant's policy of persistent attrition by pounding away at the dwindling army of Lee, after he found out he could not conquer it by strokes of arms, had gradually worn it into the historic "thin gray line" the Northern newspapers and military critics were so frequently mentioning.

Sherman was destroying not only the homes of the people in the central South but the granary upon which Lee relied to feed his army and was threatening to destroy railroad communications in the rear; conservative England, sympathizing with the South, but fearing the loss of Canada, had declined Louis Napoleon's proposition for simultaneous recognition of the Confederacy and active intervention by France and England jointly if necessary.

Something must be done soon, some coup de main performed, which would terrify the Northern heart or the South must succumb to the forces of Grant and Sherman, united in their brutal policy of non-exchange of prisoners. There was a very considerable contest between a Kentucky delegation, including General Breckinridge, and the opposition led by General Bragg. The day after the battle of Cold Harbor the Kentuckians called General Lee into their council; I learned from General Breckinridge that when Lee was asked his opinion, he said that it was absolutely necessary to make a demonstration in some direction to withdraw the forces that Grant had in his front, and if the conditions in Kentucky were as favorable as General Breckinridge thought they were, it was the most feasible and also the most vulnerable place within the Federal lines.

I was informed by Colonel William Preston Johnston that if my report as to the feeling of Kentucky should be favorable, General Joseph E. Johnston was to invade that State. If the people were still in sympathy with the South and necessary supplies for the sustenance of an army could be obtained, a strong enough force would be sent this time to hold the State. It was furthermore resolved that General Forrest, then in Mississippi, should go to Kentucky.

During one of my visits to General Cooper President Davis came into the room, and going to the wall took down a large map, and placed it on the table. He did not observe me. He ran his finger over the map for a minute or two and then asked General Cooper what was the full force that he could give General Lee. General Cooper answered that forty-six thousand men was the entire force, and that three thousand of these would have to be used to protect the Orangeburg road, and he believed that forty-two thousand would be the full number of the men that Lee could carry into action. Mr. Davis then inquired what was Cooper's information relative to the size of the Federal army. Cooper answered that Grant had over one hundred and twenty thousand of the best armed and equipped men that were ever mustered into service, and that they would be reinforced daily. Looking General Cooper steadily in the face, Mr. Davis asked, "Do you believe that General Lee will be able to sustain himself against this force?" "I believe that it will be impossible for him to do so," General Cooper replied.

The President hesitated a full minute, and then quietly but firmly responded, "I think that he will sustain himself, and I will not order the archives of the government to be removed." He then walked out of the room.

General Cooper turning to me, said, "Young man, you are now entrusted with a State secret that must not be divulged." I assured him that it would be held sacred by me, and asked to be sent to the front. But he reminded me that I had been reserved for special duty, and must wait until he was ready for me. The great battles that now followed from the Wilderness to Cold Harbor, I think constituted one of the greatest campaigns in all history.

After the battle of Cold Harbor and Grant's virtual retreat down the James river, seeking the protection of his gunboats, I received my order to go to Kentucky. I was authorized to take such supernumerary officers as I could depend upon, together with my adjutant, Captain Cunningham, Captain Marrs, my quartermaster, and T. J. Johnson, commissary. These were furnished with ample funds, and my orders were to move at once to my old department of West Tennessee and western Kentucky, where I must endeavor to make things lively enough to divert a threatened attack upon Saltville, Virginia, for which preparations were making in Kentucky. If possible, I was to co-operate in releasing the Confederate prisoners at Camp Morton, Indiana, and at Camp Douglas, near Chicago. I was assured that Forrest was expected to help me, and that our main army would flank Sherman and move also into Kentucky. As soon as General Joseph E. Johnston had executed this flank movement, I was to commence cutting the railroads in Sherman's rear, especially the Louisville and Nashville railroad beyond Nashville.

By the time I reached Atlanta, I had fifty men, including officers, but when I applied to General Joseph E. Johnston for munitions of war he replied that it was impossible for him to supply me with a gun or cartridge. This caused considerable delay. At last I appealed to Governor Brown, of Georgia, whose interest was at once enlisted, and he opened his State arsenal and gave me everything necessary for the expedition. Upon the morning of July 4th, I started upon my journey, going around the right wing of the Federal army, and heading for Mussel Shoals, Tennessee river. The Federals discovered my entrance into their lines, and put a considerable force on my trail. All roads were guarded, but I managed to elude the efforts to capture my little party. In north Alabama I met Rousseau's force of three thousand cavalry on their way to cut Johnston's lines in the rear of Atlanta. Dispatching a courier to inform the authorities of this raid, I prepared an ambuscade to endeavor to impede the movement. Placing my men in a ravine, I sent two men into the road to fire upon their advance-guard and then to retreat, through the intervening field, to the ravine. They executed their mission well, but while the ruse occasioned some confusion in the Federal force, they declined to follow our scouts, as if they feared some snare. We camped that night in the ravine, and sent out details to procure provisions, Captain Shanks having charge of one party, and Dick Stonestreet of another. Meeting in the dark, and each detail mistaking the other for the enemy, Stonestreet was seriously wounded by a load of buckshot fired into his breast. I never saw a man more distressed than Shanks when he discovered his great blunder. He carried the wounded man to a neighboring house, where the latter assured him that he had no cause to censure him, as he himself was just preparing to shoot a volley into the other party.

This was the only incident worthy of note until we reached the valley of the Tennessee near the Shoals, where we found several hundred of Dibrell's men encamped, the officer in charge not only supplying us with provisions, but guiding us in our passage of the river. The ford was very deep and dangerous, but we succeeded in crossing without loss.

There was hardly a day afterwards that we were not compelled to deviate from our course on account of parties of the enemy trying to intercept us. But by extra caution we managed to elude all of them and finally reached our destination in Union county, Kentucky, on the Ohio river, about the middle of July.

As soon as I could communicate with my friends in Henderson, I ascertained that the Federal General Burbridge had already collected in upper Kentucky a very strong force with the intention of capturing Saltville, Virginia, and cutting Lee's communication in that direction. As a diversion, I issued a proclamation, declaring that I had authority from the Confederate States' Government to conscript recruits from all over the State and should begin at once on a large scale. This paper was published everywhere, with the effect, as desired, of causing Burbridge to postpone his contemplated expedition, and giving me time to notify the Confederate authorities, who, when he finally made his raid had made preparations to meet him, resulting in a splendid victory gained by General John C. Breckinridge, who utterly routed and wildly stampeded the boastful Burbridge's much larger and in every way better equipped force.

Following is the proclamation:

Headquarters in the Field, August 14, 1864.

" Citizens of Kentucky:

" The alternative is now offered you of entering either the Federal or the Confederate army.

" All persons between the age of seventeen and forty-five, who are not lawfully exempt, will be required to go into service at once. You must now see that after the sacrifice of all that freemen should hold dear, to avoid the evil and save our property, the one has not been rendered secure, and you have not saved yourself from the other, even by the sacrifice of principle and honor.

"Your country has been overrun by lawless bands, whose depredations are only equalled by the outrages of large bands of the Federal army, who neither feel nor have any respect for the submissionists, and you are plundered and robbed and murdered with impunity. How long do you intend this to continue? To what depth of degradation and shame are you to be reduced before you will cut loose the bond of slavery and assert your rights as freemen of Kentucky?   Are you willing to see your families reduced to the level of your slaves?   Mothers, can you realize an affiliation of your daughters with the African?   Young men, can you expect to have any claim to manhood?   Can you hope to share the smile or claim the love of the bright-eyed daughters of this famed land of beauty, while those gentle beings are sub- jected to the insults of Yankee hirelings and negro troops?   If not, then seize the only way to bring you true liberty and honor. Too long have you listened to the siren song of the traitors to their country.   Already too much has been sacrificed to no advantage. Your only hope of peace is the success of the Southern armies.   Not alone your liberty, but your lives are involved in this issue. The moderate Union man, the Democrat of the North, as well as the Southern soldier, will all owe their lives and liberty to this result.

"I appeal to you again, as I did two years ago, to rally and strike a blow for the freedom of your country.

"A. R. JOHNSON,

"Colonel Commanding Confedrate Forces in Southern Kentucky."

Let the following extracts from the " History of Henderson county, Kentucky," written by Colonel E. L. Starling, formerly an officer in the Federal army, show our movements for the next few days:

"On Saturday, the thirteenth, Colonel Adam R. Johnson, with his command, arrived within three miles of the city, and great fear was entertained lest he should come in and the citizens be losers thereby, for the gunboat "Brilliant" was lying directly in front, anchored broadside, with her guns bearing upon the defenseless place. A committee of citizens waited upon Captain Perkins, of the "Brilliant," to ascertain if it was his design to fire upon the city. Captain Perkins stated that he had no desire to imperil the city by fire, and thereby render houseless the women and children and non-combatants, but that he had imperative orders to fire if it was occupied by rebel troops. The committee then went forthwith to see Col. Adam R. Johnson, but he was absent from his camp. A communication was left, and on Monday morning the following reply was received:

" ' Headquarters Dept. Southern Ky.
" ' August 13, 1864.
" ' To the Citizens of Henderson, Ky.:
" ' I am just in receipt of a communication to the effect that the Federal commander of the gunboat had notified the citizens of Henderson if any of my men came into Henderson that he would shell the town, and requesting me not to send any of my command to town. This request I can not comply with. So long as Henderson remains ungarrisoned I shall send my men into the town whenever I deem the interest of the Government requires it. The shelling of the Federal commander will be uncalled for unless an attack be made upon the gunboat. Whenever depredations are committed by men under my authority, you may rest assured I shall have them severely punished.
" ' Respectfully,
" ' A. R. JOHNSON,
" ' P. S.—I do not expect to occupy the place or use it as a garrison. A. R. J.
" ' Colonel Comm'g. C. S. Forces, Sou. Ky. '

"Colonel Johnson did not come into Henderson, but on that morning sent in a flag of truce, carried by officer Thomas Watson, of Henderson county, who held a consultation with Captain Perkins and Lieutenant Little, of the "Brilliant," at the Hancock House, in reference to two of the robbers who were with the invading party at the time Mr. James E. Rankin was shot. Colonel Johnson had captured these two men, calling themselves Captain R. Yates and

Captain Jones, and now offered to surrender them to the civil authorities. They were subsequently surrendered to D. N. Walden, sheriff of Henderson county, who took them before Judge C. W. Hutchen, who opened his court to give them a preliminary hearing upon the charge of robbery, and also as accessories to the shooting of Mr. Rankin. Captain Perkins, in command of ten marines, came into court and demanded the men in the name of the United States, when Judge Hutchen, very good naturedly, complied by directing the sheriff to turn them over. The men were then marched to the river in charge of the marines and taken aboard of the gunboat. A few days afterward Captain Perkins forwarded them to headquarters at Louisville, where they were imprisoned and subsequently shot.

" The News, of August 16th, said:

" ' Our city is nearly depopulated, particularly of the young men subject to conscript or draft. As for ourselves, we intend to remain till the last day of grace, believing that prudent council and patient endeavor can yet save Henderson from the flames.'

" Colonel Adam R. Johnson's conscript order was soon to be rigidly enforced; that is, it was so said, and every man who was of conscript age and unwilling to leave his home for the war in either army, was dodging around as best he could to avoid the conscript officers.

" The whole county surrounding Henderson was in a tumult of excitement, and intense anxiety was impressed upon every non-combatant's countenance.

" On the seventeenth Generals Hughes and Hovey, with six hundred of the Thirty-sixth, and three hundred of General Willich's brigade, all re-enlisted Indiana soldiers, with four twelve-pounders, left Evansville for Union county to intercept Johnson's recruits, and, if possible, to drive him from the country.

" Arriving at Mt. Vernon, the command was re-enforced by a large force of Warrick and Posey county home-guards, with three more cannon. Most of these troops were finely mounted, many of them on horses which had been sent to Evansville from Henderson for safe keeping, and, by the by, never returned to their owners. After marching through Union county, this body of troopers came into Henderson Saturday morning, the dirtiest looking set that had been seen, bringing with them a perfect army of cattle which they had captured, several captured buggies and their drivers, a great many captured teams and their drivers, a number of horses, fifty-seven negroes, two rebel prisoners, six or seven citizen prisoners and one wounded home-guard as relics of the raid. The Generals fixed their headquarters at the Hancock House, while the soldiers took possession, with the cattle and other evidences of military ardor, of the public square. A number of these scattered over the city, committing petty thefts and insulting citizens. The horses (many of them owned in Henderson) were quartered at the various livery stables and fed, while the citizens, with their accustomed hospitality, invited the tired soldiers to dine at their tables. In the evening all of the soldiery, with the exception of one hundred veterans of the Thirty-sixth Indiana, left by steamer for Evansville. Those remaining took possession of the court house. Next morning they were called to Evansville."

The day after publishing my "Proclamation," I forwarded to Richmond my second official report, which I append with its endorsement, as copied from the official records of the Civil War and sent to me by the War Department at Washington, D. C., in January, 1904:

"Headquarters Department Southern Kentucky,

" Union County, August 15, 1864.

" Hon. Secretary of War, Richmond, Va.

" Dear Sir:—When I came into this State under orders to rejoin my command (which was here when I started) I found that General Morgan had returned to Virginia, and believing it to be my duty to employ myself to the best advantage for the good of my country, I took the responsibility to remain here, where I found a large number of my old regiment (the Tenth Kentucky Cavalry) who had been captured and placed under heavy bonds. They were willing to fight, but anxious to be forced into service. I assumed the responsibility of selecting a department and enforcing the conscript law. In all these things I have been actuated but by one motive—the advancement of our cause, and am anxious to have your approval of my acts, and hope to receive it when I inform you of the present results and future expectations of my proceedings. Arriving in Kentucky August 1st, I commenced active hostilities and energetic recruiting. Up to to-day I have recruited, mounted, armed, and equipped 1,870 men, organized as follows:

Major Chenoweth's regiment, with Captain S. P. Cunningham, former assistant adjutant general of Morgan's command, as lieutenant-colonel; it numbers 587 men and will number at least 750 ere this reaches you. Captain Sypert's regiment, numbering 633 men, with Lieutenant R. B. Soery as lieutenant-colonel, and 320 of my old regiment under Lieutenant-Colonel Napier of the Sixth Kentucky Cavalry, with 320 men under an officer to whom I have given authority to raise a regiment. This recruiting has no parallel in the history of the war, and I am satisfied that by the 10th of September I will have 3,000 effective cavalry operating against the transportation by both river and rail to Sherman's army. We have killed 28 Federals, wounded 83, captured 147. We have captured and secured 28,000 pounds of bacon, 37,000 bushels of corn, 18,000 bushels of oats, 830 fat cattle, 43 boxes of army clothing, and 7 transports with supplies for the Yankee army. Have at present the Ohio river blockaded from Henderson, Ky., to Mound City, Ill., and hold undisputed possession of eight (8) counties in southern Kentucky. By obtaining immediate orders from the department to remain and operate on the Ohio river and the Louisville and Chattanooga lines of railroad I am satisfied that I can destroy Sherman's communications, relieve my department of Federals, and arm and equip an effective cavalry force of 2,500 men and an infantry brigade of 3,000. I therefore most respectfully ask that I be commissioned or appointed brigadier general of cavalry and assigned to duty in this department; that Major Chenoweth and Captain Cunningham be commissioned or appointed as colonel and lieutenant-colonel of the —— Kentucky Cavalry Regiment, my brigade, and Captain L. A. Sypert and Lieutenant R. B. Soery be commissioned or appointed colonel and lieutenant-colonel of the —— Kentucky Regiment of my brigade; also that some efficient Kentucky brigadier of infantry be sent into this department to take charge of the infantry brigade that I am conscripting. Should the department feel at a loss whom to send, I can recommend Captain Cunningham as a most reliable, efficient and energetic officer, well calculated to organibze, control and command said brigade.

"It is necessary to remind you that this is the golden moment for securing an army from Kentucky, and every day's delay is absolutely dangerous. For my capacity to command this department, I can only say that in '62 I recruited and brought into service twenty-two companies from southern Kentucky; since which time

I have commanded a brigade under General Morgan. But should you not feel disposed to have me promoted or accept of my recommendation of Captain Cunningham, I ask that others be selected and forwarded at once. I also desire to call your attention to the attempted correspondence between General Burbridge and myself, and urge that he be at once notified of my action having the sanction and approval of my government. I also forward with this my orders to go into Kentucky. The muster rolls of the regiments will be forwarded so soon as completed. With the hope that this brief report may prove satisfactory, and that my requests may meet the sanction and approbation of my government, I remain, with very much respect,   Your obedient servant,

"A. R. JOHNSON, Colonel."

(Indorsement.)
"Adjutant and Inspector General's Office,
"Sept. 6, 1864.

" Colonel Palfrey:

"The Secretary of War directs that Colonel A. R. Johnson be appointed brigadier general to rank from 1st June last; under the act authorizing appointments to recruit within the enemy's lines, appointments to continue for three months from present date. Also appointments under same act, and for same period, for J. Q. Chenoweth and L. A. Sypert as colonels of cavalry; and S. P. Cunningham and R. B. Soery as lieutenant colonels of cavalry.

"SAML. W. MELTON,
"Lieutenant-Colonel and Assistant Adjutant General."

This report was made under extremely difficult circumstances. We were virtually in the midst of the enemy's country, surrounded on all sides, and several hundred miles from the Confederate lines. The whole distance that would have to be traversed by any one carrying this report was occupied by strong detachments of the Federal army; several navigable streams would have to be crossed that were strongly picketed by gunboats. Consequently the bearer of these papers was liable to be captured. Under these conditions I had to word this report in such a manner that if the enemy should obtain them the papers would not expose the real object of our expedition into Kentucky. All the facts that were stated in this report the Federals already knew. The papers all over the country, especially the Louisville Journal, were urging the Federal government to send a force sufficient to drive us out of the country at once, or it would soon be beyond their power to do so. Knowing this, I did not hesitate to give the facts and figures as they were, but concealing all ideas of any movements of large forces to my assistance or any hope of support from the north side of the Ohio river. And this was the first time that any of my officers obtained any insight into my secret orders. , Colonel Cunningham was therefore entrusted with the fact that the Sons of Liberty would furnish us with fifteen thousand stands of arms and ten thousand men armed and equipped as soon as we had sufficient force in Kentucky to assure them that we would be able to hold the State, and that if Forrest and his cavalry were moved to my support the Sons of Liberty would join us at once, and if this could be done by the fifteenth of August that there would be a grand effort made to free the Confederate prisoners that were held in Indiana and Illinois, and with these trained and tried veteran soldiers maddened by their cruel treatment while in prison, we would be able not only to drive any Federal force out of Kentucky that could be brought against us, but be able to capture Louisville and Cincinnati, which would necessarily compel Grant to withdraw his forces from Virginia and perhaps induce the Federal government to cease the war and acknowledge the Confederacy. The orders that I returned with these papers were given me when I left Richmond and were so worded that they would give no clue to our real design. As all these facts were well known to both Mr. Davis and General Cooper I knew that no explanation would be necessary, and the fact that my commission was dated back to the day that I left Richmond and that every request that I made was granted without hesitation, is conclusive evidence that they fully comprehended my report and remembered all the arrangements that were made with me before I left Virginia.

My success in recruiting was phenomenal. In the palmiest days of the Confederacy no man ever received recruits more rapidly. I had brought with me soldiers from many counties in Kentucky, and sent them to their respective counties to collect men and to picket all the important roads, thus giving the appearance of my having a large force in the State. Soon I had four regiments in the process of formation, forty men having been commissioned, each to raise a company.

Colonel J. Q. Chenoweth was to be colonel of the First Regiment, Captain S. P. Cunningham, lieutenant colonel; Captain Napier, colonel of the Second Regiment, Captain Shanks, lieutenant-colonel; Captain Lee Sypert, colonel of the Third Regiment, Soery, lieutenant-colonel; Wm. Hollis, colonel of the Fourth Regiment.

About this time I received a communication from the Sons of Liberty in Indiana, through Captain McLean, who commanded a steamboat running from Henderson. They proposed to furnish to the Confederacy ten thousand men and fifteen thousand stands of arms from Indiana, Illinois and Ohio. The guns were to be sent up Green river on steamboats, and I was to use the steamboats to transport my men across the Ohio. It was expected we would co-operate with the organized forces who were prepared to free the Confederate prisoners at Camp Morton and at Camp Douglas.

So far everything seemed to be working exactly as had been planned. Colonel Cunningham was sent back immediately to Richmond with my report, as I have said, to transmit dispatches to Forrest that it was time for him to come up with his command, and also to General Joseph E. Johnston.

The time was appointed for the delivery of the arms and the concentration of the ten thousand men at Newburg, Indiana, and it was believed that the contemplated freeing of the prisoners would be promptly made. We intended to capture Evansville and the necessary railroads so as to co-operate effectually with forces in Indianapolis and Chicago. But our plans were frustrated by counter-moves of the Federals against Forrest and Johnston, and by the divulging of our schemes through spies in Indiana and Illinois, and lastly by the movement of General Hobson against my men with an overwhelming force. His rapid and unexpected movement compelled me to move on toward the Cumberland river, and as it was the intention to draw the Federal force after me I moved my main body under Colonels Chenoweth and Napier in the direction of Canton, on the Cumberland, and sent runners to each of my stations to concentrate their men and be prepared to harass Hobson's rear. On the evening of the twentieth of August I learned that a force of Federals about three or four hundred strong were occupying what was known as Grubb's Crossroads. I made my arrangements to capture them. Dividing my force into three parties, I

sent Colonel Napier to the rear, and moving at the head of Colonel
Chenoweth's regiment, I charged their camp just at dawn. The
Federals running toward a thicket, I dashed in front of forty or
fifty and called to them to surrender, which they did. I ordered
them to face about and move toward the command which was now
coming up on the opposite side; these seeing Federals with guns
in their hands, opened fire on them; one of the balls struck me in
the right eye, and coming out at the left temple, cut out both eyes.
As soon as my misfortune was discovered, great confusion ensued,
and when I ordered my horse to be led to the rear, a portion of
the prisoners taking advantage of the confusion, escaped to their
companions in the thicket. Learning that I had been shot, the
Federals made arrangements to fight. Captain Shanks coming up
with a small body of men, was wounded, together with several of
his men, and fell into their hands. All of this happened at daybreak,
and there was a very heavy fog making everything quite indistinct.

Some very daring feats were performed on this occasion. Captain
Paul Marrs, quartermaster, having sent his horse across the river
the evening before, undertook to swim the river with his clothes
on, the Federals firing on him, and finding that he was about to
sink, he turned back, and getting behind a big rock near the water,
stripped off his clothes, tying his money in his shirt, put his
clothes on his head, and again dashed into the river, succeeding
this time in getting across, although under a heavy fire of the enemy.
To his chagrin he found that his horse had been carried off, but
being a man of wonderful resources and courage he slipped on his
underclothes and at once went to work to find a way out of the dilemma. Hunting through the brush, he found a loose mule with
a rope on. Catching the animal and improvising a halter out of
the rope, he mounted and soon overtook the little party that had
crossed the river the evening before. Recovering his horse and procuring a suit of clothes, he and Captain T. J. Johnson, the commissary, persuaded the party to return and help Colonel Chenoweth to cross the river. This was accomplished in good style
by constructing rafts. I consider it one of the most daring feats of
the expedition.

Colonel Chenoweth had sent a part of his men across a bridge,
and going that way to join them, ran into the Federals and was
captured. They were marching with him along the river bank when
Johnson and Marrs, who had returned to the opposite shore with a

portion of Napier's regiment, opened fire across the river, and the gallant Colonel, taking advantage of the confusion caused by the fire, dashed his horse into the river and made his escape without further damage, although the water foamed with Federal bullets. He gave Napier's men credit for his rescue. They afterwards succeeded in getting the remainder of the men across the river.

CHAPTER XXIII.

The story of the events in southwestern Kentucky after I lost my eyes and until the war ended is told in this chapter by Colonel James Q. Chenoweth:

In the summer of 1864, while General Johnston's "Army of the Tennessee" was resting upon its arms at Marietta, Georgia, I received orders to go to Kentucky and organize and take command of a regiment of recruits, which, in broken commands, were scattered through the western portion of that State and desirous of joining the army of the South.

Learning from General Wheeler that General Adam R. Johnson, with orders from the War Department, was at that time preparing to march into Kentucky with about fifty of his old officers, and that he was ordered to take command there and organize a department on the Ohio river and execute a certain important mission with which he was specially charged, I reported to him near Atlanta, Georgia, having with me Lieutenant John Spalding, who had been specially detailed to accompany me.

General Adam Johnson's command took up its march and proceeded immediately to the field of operations in Kentucky. We met with no special incident en route before crossing the Cumberland river, except that in northern Alabama, not far from the Tennessee river we came near running into Rousseau's cavalry, which was just entering Alabama, bent upon a desperate and destructive raid through the State. Our advance vidette, however, being under cover, was not observed by the raiders. Returning to Johnson's

COLONEL JAMES Q. CHENOWETH.

column, he reported what he had observed. General Johnson ordered me to go to the front and make reconnoissance. Taking with me Lieutenant-Colonel Napier, Captain Quinn and Lieutenant Spalding, I stealthily approached the road over which Rousseau's command was moving. To secure a proper place for observation we were compelled to cross a branch swollen by recent rains and which luckily proved to be, in our hasty retreat, our salvation. Noiselessly nearing the road, we concealed ourselves in the thicket not twenty feet from the clattering column, as it dragged along stretched out with artillery and wagon train, miles in length. We crouched in our hiding place for quite an hour and until we believed the whole of the Yankee raiders had passed—rear guard and all. In this we were deceived. Just as we had risen upon our feet and were about to beat a retreat, we heard voices on the road and two officers appeared in sight, riding leisurely abreast. Realizing that we were discovered, we fired upon the horsemen, and in all haste broke for the rear. Before we reached the swollen branch we heard the sound of the enemy's bugle, and, deploying through the woods the enemy's rear guard, for such it was, came in a sweeping gallop almost upon us. The high banks of the creek were all that saved us, and I think the leap I made across from bank to bank would have done full justice to almost any modern university athlete. Rejoining General Johnson's little command, we re-mounted our horses and the general, appreciating the situation, stood not upon the order of putting as great a distance, and as rapidly as possible, between himself and the enemy. We hastened on to the Cumberland river, crossing that stream by swimming our horses in the manner understood and practiced by most Kentucky scouts. A Kentucky newspaper, falling into my hands a few days after arriving in the State, discovered to our party that two U. S. commissaries riding in the rear of Rousseau's raiders had been " bush-whacked" and killed in North Alabama. The incident was as described.

General Johnson arrived in Morganfield, Kentucky, on the ——day of————1864. We were received by the people with every demonstration of enthusiasm, and the brave sons of Kentucky hastened by the hundreds to join our standard. Captain Anderson's company of cavalry, recruited in that neighborhood, had been organized and was all ready for service. By special order the company reported to me and constituted Company " A " of my regiment.

Colonel Sypert with several organized companies was in that neighborhood, and in a very few days reported to General Johnson. Through western Kentucky General Johnson was well known and admired, having early in the war recruited there his first regiment and won for himself and command a great reputation for brilliant and romantic achievements. The people were unanimously and enthusiastically Confederate in their sympathies, and our stay in their midst, as I dream of it and remember it now, was a spring-time picnic amidst all my varied war experiences. We not only carried about with us the blessings of all the people of that section, but particularly did we enjoy the smiles and enthusiastic cheers of those supremely brave and beautiful women who supplied us with all necessary information and made useless our commissary. My mouth fairly twitches to this day with the delightful recollections of the sweet and luscious dainties with which our camps were laden during the campaign.

General Johnson's book describes all the details of the campaign. I will only say that about the middle of July our muster roll contained more than one thousand seven hundred men. With these rolls, under special order from the General, Captain S. P. Cunningham, afterwards lieutenant-colonel of my regiment, proceeded to Richmond to confer with the Confederate War Department. Before Colonel Cunningham had returned to the command in August with commissions and special orders from the President and the Military authorities at Richmond a terrible deathly blow had fallen upon our command.

General Johnson, learning that a Federal regiment was camped at Grubbs' Crossroads near Cerulean Springs, determined forthwith to give them battle, and, by defeating and capturing them, secure arms and necessary supplies for his recruits. Marching nearly all night we reached the neighborhood of the enemy's camp just before daylight. Without many preliminaries Colonel Napier was directed to take all the men who had arms, pass around to the rear and fire upon the camp. I was directed, after the first volley fired, at the head of the unarmed horsemen, to charge. These orders were faithfully executed, but the charge I led, was, of course, "all sound and fury signifying nothing" except the fright it was expected to occasion. To my great amazement and surprise when I had reached the camp the enemy were crowding across the main road opposite, firing as they retreated. My horse was killed and while I was securing another of the number that were galloping about the woods, ı officer of the staff rode up to me and informed me that General Johnson was fatally shot. I was dumfounded and heart-broken. I was not so greatly upset by the confusion and demoralization around me, but the information that our leader had fallen quite extinguished the sun of every hope I had entertained. After stripping my good charger of his harness and saddling the steed I had captured I rode with the officer to that part of the field where I found the wounded chieftain. The officers of his immediate staff had placed him in an ambulance where I found him as cool, dispassionate and self-possessed as he was on the starless night before, when he gave me his orders for the charge. I sat down beside him, myself speechless with distress at the unutterable calamity which had befallen us. But the wounded general, with a bullet hole through his temples, blind and suffering, lay calm and apparently unconcerned except for the fate of his little army. He quietly bade me assume command and as rapidly as possible make my way across the Cumberland and Tennessee rivers. On our way to the Cumberland river over the Cadiz pike we left the general at the residence of Colonel Fenton Simms, a noble, generous Kentucky gentleman. When we next heard of the general his wounds had healed, but he was blind and in a Federal prison.

An incident occurred at Grubbs' Crossroads which to this day excites my wonder and doubtless will be accepted with incredulity. As I was transferring my cavalry appointments from my wounded horse to the back of another, I saw one of my captains lying by the roadside, as I believed, shot to death. I had no time to emphasize my deep emotion or place the body in a more secluded and less exposed position, but as I passed by, my hands and arms being occupied with my cavalry saddle and trappings, I turned the body quite over with my foot and gazed for a moment in the pale face of the stark and breathless form of my dead soldier friend. About five weeks afterwards, as I was seated in front of my headquarters in the suburbs of Paris, Tennessee, on a beautiful moonlight night that I will always remember, I saw coming up the path what I could not for a moment doubt was the incarnated spirit of the late Captain John Shanks, who had fallen in the battle of Grubbs' Crossroads. But the captain, although he had received a gunshot wound through the liver and kidneys, was before me alive in the flesh. He had been rescued from the battlefield by good Samaritans, and nursed to life by that noble mother of the Confederacy, Mrs. Dr. Nick Gaither, of Cerulean Springs. Captain Shanks after a short respite took command of his company, commanded it through the following desperate winter campaign in Kentucky and survived it all to become, after the war, a most useful citizen of his State and father of a noble family.

I can not recall the terrible incidents of Grubbs' Crossroads without especially remembering that it was here I lost my faithful, able and chivalrous adjutant, Waller O. Bullock. I believed him to have been killed until after I had arrived in Paris, Tennessee. There I ascertained that he had been wounded and captured. He was at this time in Paducah in the blood-red hands of the brutal General Payne, of vile memory. The information came to me that he was confined in a dungeon and doomed to be shot. A lady of Paris, of strong Union sympathies, having expressed a desire to visit Paducah, I agreed to pass her through my lines if she would bear to General Payne a letter from my hand. To this she readily consented. I first sent the lady under the guard of a staff officer to a building in Paris, where I had confined several Federal prisoners whom we had captured, en route to Paris, on the Tennessee river. I gave the lady the opportunity of communicating with these Federal prisoners and then trusted to her the letter to be delivered to Payne. In the letter I informed that brutal commander that I held these soldiers of the Union army as hostages for the personal safety of Adjutant Bullock and that if he was brought to harm in any way and treated otherwise than as an honorable prisoner of war I would cause them to be shot to death in retaliation. This letter was delivered, and the lady on her return informed me that shortly after Payne received it Adjutant Bullock made his escape. The truth is that Bullock's noble old grandmother from Lexington, Kentucky, made a pilgrimage to Paducah, upon learning that her brave boy was held there as a prisoner, and succeeded in purchasing his liberty from Payne himself with gold. Just before our winter raid into Kentucky, at the instance and earnest request of two old Kentucky people from near Midway, situated between Paris and Paducah, I released a young boy who had enlisted in one of my companies. They were his grandparents and had freely given up their older children to the defense of the South, and, pleading for their Benjamin, begged for his return. I have forgotten the names, but the residents of the locality who are still living will remember the cruel incident. The old people were returning with their boy to their desolate home near Midway, and fearing trouble from Yankee scouting parties, hid the boy under a quilt in their wagon. This miserable brute, General Payne, on his return from Midway to Paducah, met the old people on the road, the boy was discovered, dragged out from his hiding-place and cruelly and in cold blood shot to death. Oh, if I could have captured the old scoundrel, Payne, I am sure I would have greatly enjoyed swinging him to a limb! Just prior to the time of my surrender I met General Meredith under " flag of truce " at Paducah. He had succeeded Payne in his command. I was informed by that grand old Federal general, he of the Iron Brigade, that I would have been morally justified in executing my threats; that Payne was an outlaw and should have been hung. His foul memory is a blot on the pages of American history.

From Grubbs' Crossroads I marched the command by the Cadiz turnpike to. Canton on the Cumberland river. Gathering such plank skiffs as could be found on the river, we proceeded immediately to cross over, the men seated in the frail boats and leading their horses swimming alongside. I did not doubt but that with the dawn of the morning I would be attacked by the enemy. As the last loaded boats were shoving from the shore I started to relieve the pickets who were under the command of the sturdy brave officer, Lieutenant Spalding. Before I could communicate with him I heard the blast of the enemy's bugles and the clatter of their charging horses. Putting spurs to. my own steed, I sought to reach the bridge over Little river that, at this point, empties into the Cumberland. At the far end of the bridge I was halted by the Yankee guard who had just reached that point, and taken prisoner. The Federal picket-guard were dismounted and I yielded to them without resistance. The officer, whom I presumed to be a sergeant exercising command, seized one of my bridle-reins and one of his soldiers seized hold of the other. Strangely enough, I was disarmed but not dismounted. As the guard led my horse off the bridge, and along the road skirting the swollen river, I noticed that the banks from recent rains had broken away into the road. Coming to one of these narrow places in the road the. soldier, holding the rein on the right of the horse, turned it loose and hied himself to the off side; without previous thought, but inspired I suppose by immediate conditions and the little confusion which was occasioned, I dug my spurs into the sides of the spirited mare I was riding and we plunged into the river. Colonel Napier's men, who had crossed the river during the night and were posted on the banks immediately opposite and evidently on the lookout, almost instantly opened fire on the Yankee guardians, who broke hurriedly for cover. I succeeded in getting across the river, the Yankees from the trees beyond the road not being able to fire upon me until I was nearly on the other side on account of the height of the river banks at that point.

Having thus passed over the Cumberland we proceeded through the Coalings to Paris, landing on the Tennessee where we crossed about the first of September, and proceeded to the neighborhood of the city of Paris.

I was myself in a desperate condition, suffering mostly from nervous prostration. I directed my surgeon, Dr. Netherton, a very young man just out of the medical schools, to invite into consultation with himself the best medical assistance in Paris. After inquiry the doctor informed me that one Dr. Mathewson was regarded as the leading physician in the city but was a "very strong Union man." I bade my surgeon not to regard Dr. Mathewson's political sentiments, if he possessed the confidence of his neighbors as a man of integrity. Dr. Mathewson visited me, and after a careful examination had me transferred to his own house. With his good wife and beautiful daughter aiding him, he nursed me back to health, perhaps saved my life. His family, those who have survived him, will remember that this noble conduct of the brave and generous old doctor was not unrequited. However we may have differed with reference to our duty to our country, I beg leave to testify that no nobler or more generous gentleman ever passed the threshold of a sick chamber than this grand old Scotchman. He might well have sat for the picture of Barrie's hero doctor in "Under the Bonnie Briar Bush." It was in camp near Paris that Lieutenant Colonel Cunningham reported on returning from his official journey to Richmond. He had with him my commission and orders from the Confederate War Department. Just prior to his departure from Richmond the authorities there received intelligence of the desperate wounding of General Adam R. Johnson and the Secretary of War, upon consideration designated General H. B. Lyon, then with General Forrest, as the commander of the department of western Kentucky.

Lieutenant Colonel Cunningham informed me that General Lyon with his staff and escort would reach Paris about the 1st of October. I received further information that the general would first make a reconnoissance into Kentucky and that he would be at a certain date in the neighborhood of Eddyville, Kentucky. My health was now reasonably good; youth, a sound body and Confederate enthusiasm being a great health restorer. I had long known General Lyon and had previously served under him and for him personally entertained a great admiration. He was under all circumstances as cool and self-contained as Adam Johnson and considered by army men in the Confederacy amongst the bravest of the brave.

I determined to organize a scouting party and meet General Lyon in Kentucky. I selected one hundred brave and well armed and mounted men and proceeded across the river. While crossing the Tennessee river at Paris, I was joined by one Captain Phillips with about thirty men, all of whom I was assured were soldiers of the Confederate army and had made their escape from prison. They were seasoned, stalwart men of dare-devil appearance and I readily accepted their proffered services. I continued on in the direction of the Cumberland river and down that stream in the direction of old Fort Donelson. When within a few miles of the fort my advance vidette reported the road filled with negro soldiers proving to be a regiment returning to the fort after a foraging foray. I made my dispositions immediately for an attack.

The enemy being negro infantry, I disregarded their numbers. Riding rapidly to the front I could see from an elevated position the moving column and many loaded wagons. About a mile off on the Fort Donelson road I saw a farm house, and what I afterwards understood to be tobacco barns. I ordered Phillips with his men to dash rapidly around and secure the buildings. They were situated immediately on and commanding the road over which the enemy were marching. Throwing my command into column by fours and giving Phillips all reasonable time to reach and seize the buildings, I ordered the charge. There was not a laggard in my little column and with enthusiastic shouts we bore down upon the rear of the enemy who, in dismay and fright broke into disorder and crowded the road in their efforts to escape. We drove them about a mile strewing the road with their dead until the advance squadron had reached the farm house and barns, when, to my amazement a deadly fire was poured out from these buildings upon us. The advance companies of the Federal negro regiment, in the meantime, being rallied and formed upon the opposite side of the road from these buildings, were now blazing away upon us with deadly execution. I was compelled to withdraw my command, not, however, until the lieutenant-colonel of Sypert's regiment, Captain Gist and eight other brave cavalrymen had been killed. I believe there were twelve other men wounded. I was enabled to remount those who had lost their horses from the many wagon teams I captured. The wagons were burned. The sudden change in our fortunes was brought about by the man Phillips, whom I trusted with his command to capture and hold the buildings on the Fort Donelson road. After the fight I found this man Phillips lurking in the rear and ordered him to report to General Lyon in Paris under arrest. His excuse was that he was prevented from reaching the objective point to which he was ordered, where he could seize and hold the buildings in the main road, by a large ravine that he could not cross. If he and his men had been soldiers, they would have reached and held the buildings which were so absolutely necessary to the consummation of our victory. Phillips and his men proved to be only perfect types of the element which infested the country at that time between the opposing armies and from which they had slouched and afterwards organized for plunder. We ever afterwards regarded them as enemies, outside the pale of all military consideration. After burning the captured wagon-train, we continued down the river to a point near Eddyville, on the Cumberland, and soon were in communication with General Lyon, to whom I reported.

Having enjoyed the rest and luxury of camp life for one day, we were ordered by the General, who had accomplished his mission in Kentucky, to join him at a certain crossing on the Cumberland river, from which point we were ordered to return to our command near Paris, Tennessee. During the scout to Kentucky, Colonel Malone reported to me with his regiment and Major Housely with his battalion, both of which commands had been recruited for General Adam Johnson's department. I brought them safely with me across the Tennessee and Cumberland rivers into the camp, of which General Lyon continued me in command until the reorganization of all the forces into two brigades preparatory to a contemplated raid into Kentucky. Immediately after General Lyon arrived in Paris and assumed command of the department of western Kentucky, he proceeded on an official visit to the headquarters of General Forrest then somewhere in North Mississippi. His purpose was to arrange plans for a movement which would co-operate with those of General Hood, who had already taken up his march for the Tennessee campaign, which embraced the bloody and unnecessary battle of Franklin and the disastrous siege of Nashville and gathered the clouds which foreran the fall of the Confederacy.

General Lyon returned to the headquarters of the department about the 20th of November, bringing with him, besides other troops, a battery of light artillery composed of two guns. A number of Confederates who had escaped from Northern prisons had made their way to our camp at Paris, and these all reported to General Lyon for temporary duty.

General Lyon having assigned me to the command of the brigade composed almost entirely of Adam Johnson's Kentucky recruits, I proceeded to organize the same and appoint my staff mostly from escaped officers who were with us whom I had well known in the early days of the war. I was most fortunate in securing the official services of Captains D. W. Thornton and Frank Chinn of the Sixth Kentucky Cavalry as assistant adjutant general and aid-de-camp, and if I had had the rank and file of the Confederate army to select from I could not possibly have secured for the purpose in hand two more efficient or more chivalrous young gentlemen. Captain Jeff. Rodgers, who reported to me as a volunteer aid, had served by my side for three years in the First Kentucky Cavalry. He won his spurs and advancement from service in the ranks to company commander and was of that sort of stuff out of which the true soldier is made. No braver or better officer served the cause of the South. Captain Steedman, my inspector, had joined me early in the Adam Johnson occupation of western Kentucky and was with me constantly and faithfully until just after the brigade's organization. I sent him on a secret mission to Kentucky, and at Morganfield he was captured and brutally shot to death. He was an accomplished gentleman and officer, and I mourned the loss of his capable services and his comradeship as a soldier and faithful friend. My surgeon was Dr. Netherton, of whom I have previously written. He remained by my side faithfully, through every struggle and hardship until the sad end of all. He was my guardian and protector, and if not my guide, was "my philosopher and friend." My quartermaster and commissary were appointed by the general commanding but their services were hardly in requisition, for in such campaigns as that we contemplated, every soldier becomes his own quartermaster and commissary. Will I be pardoned, or rather could I be forgiven if I failed to mention in this connection my faithful body servant, Box? The other negro servants were proud to call him "Major." He was ugly as original sin and wonderfully formed; he possessed a hunchback and legs of enormous length, he could ride a zebra, was not afraid of Satan, and could bum rations for his hungry master on a desert plain.

I was ordered about the 21st of November to proceed with my brigade in advance of the main column to the Tennessee river, and to gather boats to be used in crossing that stream.

An incident occurred here which I beg to narrate. When the advance guard had reached the banks of the river a flag of truce was displayed from the other shore. Upon reaching the landing place myself, I ascertained that Phillips's guerrillas were desirous of communicating with my command. My former experience with these outlaws had excited my hostility, and General Lyon had issued an order that these men were not to be received within our lines. During General Lyon's trip to General Forrest's headquarters one of these men had been caught within our camps; he was denounced and I caused him forthwith to be drum-headed and shot. While Phillips was being informed that he and his men were under a Confederate ban and that I would hold no conference with them, I noticed that a man was advancing rapidly steering a canoe to the shore where I was standing. I ordered him at the risk of his life not to land. He disregarded my warning and came boldly on. As he approached I ordered a file of soldiers to take position, and, at my order, be ready to fire. I was amazed at the boldness of this man who so defied my threats. He spoke not a word and his only protest was to steer steadily and boldly for the shore. He presented a most picturesque appearance, and as he came nearer to view, I noticed he was stalwart and handsome, and only a boy in years. I bade the guard .to ground their carbines. It was not in my heart to fire upon this young man, possessed of such splendid courage, without first giving ear to his message. He landed, looked me squarely in the face and at once declared "I am not a guerrilla, I am a Southern soldier." It was thus I met Bob Gillaspie. He was a lieutenant in Wheeler's escort company. He had been captured at Farmington during Wheeler's raid through Tennessee, and had made his escape from prison. On his way South he had "come up" with Phillips's men, whom he soon measured for what they were worth and "shook them" when an opportunity offered. Lieutenant Gillaspie was assigned to duty and remained near me, bravely and faithfully, to the end. Having executed orders with reference to crossing the Tennessee river as soon as General Lyon arrived, we expected comparatively easy passage and the column pressed on to the Cumberland near Dover. Early next morning the advance guard were fortunate in capturing two Federal transports on their way to Fort Donelson, which, having served the purpose of ferry boats were burned to the water's edge. In a very few hours Lyon's entire division was in line for the winter's raid in Kentucky. By forced marches and through a driving snow storm we reached Hopkinsville. Here General Lyon concluded to rest until he could receive definite information concerning Hood's army of the Tennessee, which had fought the disastrous but glorious battle at Franklin on the 30th day of November, and was now investing the city of Nashville. At Hopkinsville a large number of furloughs was granted, and, after a day's rest, the general with Turner's brigade and one gun of the battery, left upon a reconnoissance, designating to me the places to which couriers could be dispatched from time to time. There was no enemy of which we could hear nearer than Russellville, where Johnson's negro brigade was reported, but this gave us no concern. Johnson was held in great contempt. On the second night after the departure of Lyon the officers of my command were being entertained at the hotel by the "beauty and chivalry" of Hopkinsville at a grand ball. The dancing and festivities had continued until the small hours of the morning, as it was in Belgium's capital the night before Waterloo, and "joy was unconfined." " But hush! hark! a deep sound strikes like a rising knell." Scouts reported to me that the enemy were approaching Hopkinsville in large numbers and were in the neighborhood of the lunatic asylum.

I quietly left the scene of festivities and dispatched orders for "boots and saddles." Relying implicitly upon the careful soldiership of one Colonel Ross, a West Point graduate and former United States officer of experience, who had but recently reported to me by order of General Lyon, I sent him with a company to make careful reconnoissance, satisfied that the enemy, whoever they were, would not make attack until daylight. In due time Colonel Ross returned and reported that Johnson's negro cavalry were in force just beyond the asylum. It was still some time before daylight, intensely cold and very dark. I moved my column, less than four hundred (many had been furloughed) and one gun of the battery which had been left with me, out on the Russellville pike and took a good position, my command deployed across the pike road west and south of the asylum grounds. With the first streaks of the morning light I could see faintly the maneuvering of the enemy and catch some idea of the position they occupied. I had begun to believe that I had been deceived about the enemy with whom I was fronted and that it was not Johnson's negroes after all. To satisfy myself I ordered a flag of truce to the front with a certain polite request. When the staff officer bearing the same returned, I readily gleaned from his haste and bulging eyes that I was in the midst of a fix. My aid informed me that the flag was received by General ————— who I understood was commanding a brigade in McCook's cavalry division. Skirmishing had now commenced and the dismounted enemy were rapidly closing upon my front. On my left a large body of cavalry was passing to my rear. It looked as if my command would soon be surrounded and overwhelmed, possibly destroyed, certainly captured. With me was a soldier guide who understood the topographical surroundings. As best and as fast as I could, I dismantled my piece of artillery, mounted my men and with my guide by my side led the column to a creek some distance on my right. It had been swollen by recent rains and snow, was sheeted with thin ice and was not at all inviting. With my staff I leaped in and crossed, swimming some distance and breaking the ice. Only a few of the men forded readily, they mostly were huddling on the bank. This was only for a moment, however, for the Federal cavalry now put in their savage appearance and were seen charging down upon them. It was a dilemma—sabre or water. Suffice it to say, most of my men reported on my

side. The Yankees did not follow. I went up the creek to a
ford where we crossed and returning down the creek directed our
course by the asylum, where I halted long enough to interview
Dr. Rodman, the noble and humane superintendent. I ascertained
that two of my men had been killed and some ten or twelve
wounded. All of these the doctor promised faithfully to look
after, to bury the dead and see that proper attention was given
to the wounded. Dr. Rodman informed me that the Federals
claimed to have captured many prisoners. My reports showed
twenty officers and men missing. I continued my march, passing
around Hopkinsville within a mile of that city now occupied by
the Federals. I calculated where I would find Lyon and about
daylight rode into his camp. After a short " blow " for our horses,
the general started in the direction of Green river, arriving at
Ashbyburg late the next evening, resting in the meanwhile only
long enough to wind and feed the horses. Green river, if not
very wide, is deep, swift and forbidding at this point. We procured what boats could be had, the citizens about here very
generally sympathizing with us and aiding us to the extent of their
ability. By daylight the command had all crossed over, including
the remaining piece of artillery, except General Lyon and his staff
and escort company and myself. I was consulting the general
at his headquarters at the little hotel before crossing, when a vidette
galloped up with the information that a flag of truce was approaching. The turnpike here was level and perfectly straight,
enabling us to see a great distance. We observed the flag fluttering nearly a mile away. Lyon, with whom I rode, followed by
his staff and escort, rode out to meet it. It was in the hands
of an old West Point officer with whom Lyon was well acquainted.
They were cordial in their greetings and after the passage of
compliments Lyon's unconditional surrender was demanded in the
name of General McCook. " Go tell McCook " replied Lyon,
" that he knows me well enough to know that I will not surrender
without a fight." The flag of truce was not out of sight before
General Lyon and the rest of us were crossing the river, and when
safely on the other side we heard the booming cannon shelling the
woods before the " final assault." The morning following we
entered the town of Hartford, garrisoned by a battalion of Federal
troops who, on our approach, took shelter in the court house.
They were speedily surrounded, captured and paroled and the

court house burned.   Just here I beg to remark that all the court
houses burned by General Lyon on this raid through Kentucky
were in every case used as Federal garrisons or prison-houses for
our Southern friends.   It was early in December that we passed
through what was called " Devil's Gulch," in Grayson county, Kentucky.   The surrounding hills had furnished a safe harbor for
that murderous and thieving class known as " bushwhackers."   We
had hardly passed under the shades of these unsavory hills before
a vidette had been shot and murdered from behind a projecting
rock.   It was necessary to send out on the flanks of the column
dismounted scouts and our progress was very slow.   In a short
time one of the leaders of the gang infesting these hills was
captured.   He was put under guard and given a seat in the ammunition wagon.   The wife of this miscreant coming out on the
road, at her request, was given a seat by his side.   The column
halting for a while, one of the guards brought a live coal from a
cabin by the roadside and proceeded to light his pipe for a smoke.
The prisoner begged for the privilege of a smoke, and, when fire
for that purpose was given him, he deliberately dropped it through
the hole in the powder keg from which he had already extracted
the wooden stopper.   Wagon, mules and driver and the wife of
the prisoner were instantly killed.   One of the guards standing
not far away was seriously injured.   The prisoner himself was
blown some ten or twelve feet and was still alive when the guard
who had not been hurt by the explosion ran up to him and
emptied his loaded gun into his head.   Our column reached the
Louisville and Nashville railroad at Nolin's bridge in Marion county,
Kentucky, about the 20th of December.   It was now some hours
in the night.   We had already set fire to the bridge and were tearing
up the rails of the road, when a train of cars laden with Federal
infantry plunged into the cut not far from the burning bridge.   One
shot from our remaining six pounder was sufficient to induce the
Federal commander to display the white flag.   We paroled the
soldiers by the light of our camp fires, burned and destroyed the
train, and by early morning took up our line of march for
Columbia.   General Lyon here learning of Hood's defeat on the
16th of December in front of Nashville, determined, the purpose
of his raid having been accomplished as far as possible, to march
his army back across the rivers by the most practicable route, to
some point within the Southern lines.   Resting at Columbia for a

few hours, we proceeded to Burksville on the Cumberland. The
river was high with winter rains and angry with floating ice. The
enemy were, however, in such proximity that it was necessary to
make immediate arrangements for crossing. As it was in
Columbia so was it at Burksville and other county seats through
which we were compelled to pass considered by General Lyon " a
military necessity " to destroy the court house. These court
houses were no longer needed by the citizens of Kentucky as
houses of law and temples of justice, but as military barracks and
stockades for Federal soldiers and prison-houses for unoffending
Kentuckians who dared to entertain any sympathy for the Southern
cause. The writer of this some years after the war, being a
Kentucky legislator, was placed in rather an awkward but amusing
position by being required to report from his committee in the
State senate a bill to relieve Cumberland county of all State taxes for
a period of ten years, in order to enable the county to rebuild their
court house.

It was necessary, considering the constant and incessant pressure
from the rear, to keep our transportation outfit in as good order
as possible and this necessitated frequent " horse swappings " en
route, and occasionally it happened sadly enough, that no consideration but good will was returned to the owner for his property.
Recently meeting a distinguished physician, who had in late years
removed from Burksville to Texas, I was informed by him that
he had been anxious to meet me for nearly forty years; that he
desired to thank me for returning his horse, from which a soldier
of my command had unceremoniously dismounted him. I accepted the courteous doctor's thanks, but did not think proper to
tell him that had I known him at the time to be a major surgeon
in the Yankee army at home on furlough, he might have considered
himself lucky to have gotten off himself.

We succeeded in getting across the Cumberland and had almost
finished the work of destroying our frail boats when the advance
vidette of our friends, the enemy, hove in sight on the other shore.
Waving them a fond farewell we took up our march by the most
practicable route to the Tennessee river. We were delayed
many hours at the swollen and angry little Obie, but succeeded in
passing over, and hurried on. The line of march was by the
way of Tullahoma and through the old camp grounds and by the
dismantled fortifications of Bragg's army. I rested my command

almost upon the identical spot I had occupied with the First Kentucky Cavalry during that great campaign. One of my "bread detail," as they were called, which, by the way, was our only means of supplying our commissariat, returning to camp, brought to me a handsome wolf-skin robe, which I had left at a farmhouse more than fifteen months previously.

We reached the Tennessee river about the last of December in a blizzard, which, it seems, would have been more at home on the bleak coasts of New England. A "block house," one of those pestiferous interferences which had interrupted our peaceful progress throughout our extended raid, frowned upon us from an elevated point on the river bank and challenged our passage. To wipe this little nuisance from our path expeditiously, General Lyon was compelled to resort to the same means which all along proved so persuasive. One shot from the little six-pounder brought a surrender, but it brought something else, in the shape of an ugly gunboat which, before our crossing was completely effected, nearly consummated our ruin. Commencing with the shadows of night, General Lyon had crossed all of Turner's brigade, and, in sections, his remaining gun. Of my brigade there had crossed over all but about one hundred men. General Lyon was himself safe on the Southern side, when the black smoke down the river and the warning puff of overstrained boilers told me only too plainly that I was cut off from the main command. I furthermore very sorely realized that the Federal prisoners from the block house, whom we had paroled, would carry information to the nearest post that would bring upon me "the dogs of war." This was near about midnight, and I rode away from the landing with my men and sought the wooded bottoms near the river. The next day I induced a denizen of the neighborhood, an old resident, to bear a note to the general, which informed him where and at what hour of the following night I would make an effort to cross. At the appointed hour and place I plunged into the icy stream with my faithful one hundred. The gunboat, coming up, was engaged by General Lyon. I succeeded with eighty-three others in making a landing on the Southern side but in as woeful a condition as men ever found themselves. I landed on the "other" shore, dripping and famished. Dr. Netherton (who with the rest of my staff and couriers passed over the night before) met me on the banks and conducted me to my headquarters which had been provided in a small farmhouse near by. He stripped from off my bruised body my bedraggled and icy clothing; cut off my sodden boots, doctored my bruises, and, after giving me something to satisfy my hunger, put me to bed, wrapped in one of the good old farm wife's night dresses. It was not necessary to sing to me a lullaby, for I was asleep and dreaming of heavenly things before the puffing folds of the old fashioned feather bed had closed about me. I was harshly awakened. I was only partially awake when I was dragged out of bed. I heard continuous firing over at what was afterwards explained as Lyon's headquarters, half a mile away. I was rapidly jammed into my clothing, belted with my side arms, and hurried, still half asleep, out of doors. My negro boy, the faithful Box, was holding my horse at the gate, and, as I mounted, a company of Federal cavalry galloped up and evidently taking me for one of their own number excitedly cried out " Where are they? " Just then some of my staff and couriers galloped out into the road, possibly twenty paces in advance. " There they go," I shouted, and the Yankees and myself took after them. Half a mile beyond this point was General Lyon's headquarters, and intermediate was a county road crossing the main road and running up on quite a little mountain, which, as I remember, was known as " Snow Hill." At the forks of the roads there had been stationed a dismounted squad in position to bag General Lyon and myself, with our staff and escorts, as we were driven from our respective headquarters into this cul de sac. It was too dark to distinguish friend from foe. I was now, however, wide awake and charging with the Yankee cavalry in the wake of my own flying friends. We all came together in an undistinguishable mass, while shouting, cursing and shooting swelled the din. I could recognize the fierce voice of Lieutenant Bob Gillaspie, and, finding myself near him, we rode together away from the scene on the Snow Hill road, not, however, until our pistols were emptied. Good luck rode with us, and we found ourselves not entirely alone when we had reached the plain which spread out on the little mountain. Dr. Netherton, badly winded, and others of my personal staff had arrived. Most of my men who had slipped out of the clutches of the enemy were gathering here. It was quite daylight when General Lyon in a " Georgia cavalry uniform " of drawers and boots came in on foot with his terribly wounded staff officer, Major Rankin. Lyon, and his staff and escort had been surrounded by the enemy at his headquarters and most of them were taken prisoners. The general and Rankin were occupying a bed together and were " taken in " asleep. Lyon was granted permission to put on his uniform but his side arms were demanded. Taking down his belt from the bedpost and, as if in the act of handing it to one of the guards, he drew his pistol and fired. In the desperate struggle which ensued, Major Rankin was terribly wounded through the thigh and two of the guards were killed. Taking his wounded officer and friend in his arms the general leaped from the window and made his escape. We secured a horse for the general, but I do not remember how we succeeded in clothing his body—hardly, however, after any recognized military style.

Gathering what he could of the remnants of his command, General Lyon now directed his march South on a course which would lead into the lines of Forrest's command, making his first objective point Tuscaloosa, Alabama. This beautiful Southern city was reached some time late in February. The bruised and battered relics of that splendid band of rangers who had bravely ridden out with Lyon from Paris, Tennessee, in November, and who had passed through the hardships of a long, fierce winter campaign inside the enemies' lines, realized indeed that they were home again. Most of the command were properly housed in hospitals. General Lyon and myself with our personal staffs were entertained at the hostelry presided over by that true Southern lady and typical Southern hostess, the late most admirable Mrs. Street. After a few days I took my only furlough, and later on joined General Lyon at Forrest's headquarters at Columbus, Mississippi. From here General Lyon directed that I should accompany him back to Paris, Tennessee, and gather up the men who had doubtless returned to the old camp there. We were not dreaming that the death rattle was even then in the throat of the Confederacy. We arrived in Paris on the 6th day of April, and being entirely without information of the true status of the war, selected a few men and scouted in the direction of the Ohio river. At Humboldt, Tennessee, from a Memphis newspaper we read, sorrowfully read, of the surrender of General Lee.

" It's all over, Chenoweth," said the general, after a moment's reflection, " I shall go to Mexico and cast my fortunes with Maximilian." I almost immediately bade my noble friend, the general,

good-bye and returned to Paris. I found there in camp about
three hundred men.

I called together at my headquarters the officers of the several
squads and, without informing them of my intentions, directed
that a detail be made of the best mounted, best armed and uni-
formed men, and that they be in readiness to report to me on
call. In a few days all my plans were completed. I had learned
that Payne, the villainous old thief and assassin, had been superseded
at Paducah by General Meredith and I determined to go to
Meredith. Captain Jeff. Rogers and Dr. Netherton were still with
me. I required that every officer and man in the detail escort
should be well mounted, his uniform and toilet be in first class
order and his arms burnished. I provided myself with the linen
for a flag and saw to it that a bugler was at command. By easy
stages we arrived in the suburbs of the city on the morning of the
15th of April. Lieutenant Gee was riding well advanced, with the
white flag streaming from his saber point. There were no advanced
outposts, and camp sentinels were performing only perfunctory
duties. So perfect was their faith that " the cruel war " was over,
that they hardly concerned themselves enough with my advancing
column as to demand " Who comes there? " Without any bugle
call for parley, we were soon in communication with the " officer
of the day," who immediately and politely agreed to send word to
the general commanding. I was not detained unduly, when there
came galloping out to meet us, in all the " pomp and circumstance
of glorious war," General Meredith himself, his numerous staff and
escort.

No son, not even the prodigal of Biblical renown, was ever
received more graciously. " The war is over, my dear boy,"
happily spoke the handsome old Federal chief. " Come with me
to town and talk it over."

My horses and men were ordered to be taken care of by the
quartermaster. With several officers of my staff I was taken to
the general's headquarters. Before the appearance of General
Meredith I had learned from the soldiers on duty on the guard
line that President Lincoln had been assassinated the night previous
to my coming. Had I known of this I should have hesitated
before entering Paducah. Every courtesy and kindness, however,
was shown me by General Meredith and his staff, and amongst
the number I was astonished and gratified to find Captain Clay

Gooding, an old college chum.   We were feasted all day and
given over without restraint to the noble and beautiful Confederate
daughters of Paducah.   During the day General Meredith had
arranged for my surrender on most generous terms with General
Thomas, department commander at Nashville, who was to send
a command to Paris, where our paroles were to be executed;
a steamboat was also to be sent to Paris landing to carry the men
to a certain landing in Kentucky on the Ohio river.   I would have
been base, indeed, had I failed properly to appreciate the magnanimous and soldierly generosity of General Solomon Meredith.
He had been a great soldier in war; he was naturally great in
heart and mind and body.   General Meredith fearing an ambush
from some of the excited negro troops camped about Paducah,
if I returned without an escort, ordered out Colonel Hoskins's
Tennessee regiment of cavalry and instructed them to accompany
me for a stage on my return march.   A few miles from the
city, we went into a common camp.   At a nearby farm house
Colonel Hoskins and his adjutant and myself, Captain Rogers and
Dr. Netherton, spent pleasantly the night.   To complete the new
order of things Colonel Hoskins and myself slept in the same bed
—our side arms and belts hanging from opposite bed posts.

The day after returning to Paris, Colonel Shephard, of the United
States army, arrived with his regiment, and after arranging for
the parole and transportation of the men, accompanied me and
such officers as I selected to Nashville.   Here I met with old
college friends, soldiers wearing the blue uniform of the Federal
army, who soon convinced me that they were my friends even
though they had been my enemies.   On all sides the " glad
hand " was extended, and I thought that now the " bone " of particular contention having been destroyed it would soon be made
apparent to every patriotic eye that the war was indeed over.   I
was too mentally blind to see that I had only played a small part
in the first act of a great drama.   Terrible, cheerless and wasting
years were to pass before the bell was to ring down the curtain
upon the final scene of what was to be, and has been, the
Nation's Tragedy.

CHAPTER XXIV.

I resume my narrative: After being wounded and left at the hospitable home of Garland Simms, tenderly nursed by his noble wife and kind son, Richard, I was visited by Dr. Gaither and several of the physicians of the neighborhood, all of whom believed that I was mortally wounded. That night Colonel Sam Johnson surrounded the house with his regiment, but he was so exceedingly nervous that when one of his men accidentally discharged his gun he rushed off, carrying his men with him. General Hobson soon after arrived, and accompanied by his staff came to my room. He treated me with the utmost consideration, leaving papers there to protect me from any intrusion from Federal soldiers. A day or so later, Mrs. John Green and her accomplished niece, Miss Bettie Nelson, came to see me, with the intention of conveying me to their home. Finding this impossible, Miss Bettie remained with the family to assist in nursing me. My brother William, who was living at Henderson, as soon as he heard of my misfortune, came through the country in search of me, and remained also. No one ever had better care or more excellent nursing. The whole neighborhood brought everything they thought would give me comfort or pleasure. Then my mother came and relieved Miss Bettie Nelson, whose sweet and gentle manners had won the hearts of all with whom she came in contact. Dick Simms had lain upon my bed night after night, bathing my wounds, and was as kind and as tender as a woman. The kind nursing I received tided me over, and, strange as it may seem, this was one of the most pleasant episodes in my life. I learned a lesson then that I shall never forget; that is, that human affection is the sweetest thing in life. As soon as I could be removed I was conveyed to Eddyville, and thence by steamboat to Henderson. The Federal colonel who commanded the negro regiment, who occupied the town, becoming jealous of the respect and attention his negro soldiers showed me, demanded that I should be sent away; consequently, I was first sent to Louisville, and afterwards to prison at Fort Warren, Boston Harbor. I wish to record here that the Speed family, through their relative, James Speed, the attorney general, applied to Mr. Lincoln to have me released, but after canvassing the matter with Governor Powell and Mr. Speed, Mr. Lincoln said he thought I was worth swapping, but required them to send me papers to sign in the form of a petition to the Confederate government to exchange some Federal officer for me. These I refused to accept, and remained in prison until the following February. During this time I had the misfortune to fall into the basement of the prison and was seriously crippled.

On being finally exchanged I was sent around by way of New York and Fortress Monroe and thence to Richmond, Virginia. At the exchange boat I was met by Governor Lubbock, of Texas, and taken by him to the Spotswood Hotel.

At Fort Warren there were about four hundred Confederates confined; there were nine general officers in our barracks—Generals Trimble, of Maryland; Ed. Johnson, Cabell and Jones, of Virginia; Marmaduke, of Missouri; Henry Jackson, of Georgia; G. W. Gordon and Smith, of Tennessee. Smith was captured at Nashville and had been severely wounded, after he had surrendered, by a Federal colonel, who cut him over the head with his sword several times, and so injured his brain that he never recovered. My prison life was not altogether unpleasant. We had eleven ounces of bread and about the same amount of cold beef issued to us daily, with an abundance of pure, clear water. Provisions of all kinds were sent to us from our friends within the lines, and many of the citizens of Boston made efforts to supply us; but all these were refused and we were not allowed to receive anything except the rations issued, and one mess suffered severely from hunger until after my fall in prison, when the doctor authorized me to purchase vegetables, butter, eggs, etc., as a diet, which enabled us to live fairly well. All these officers were exceedingly kind to me, General

Gordon especially, rendering cheerfully every service necessary to health, comfort and cleanliness, which in my comparatively helpless condition I could not myself perform.

After I arrived in Richmond and had been made comfortable at the Spotswood Hotel, Governor Lubbock went at once to the War Department and secured my retiring papers; he brought them for me to sign, but I refused to sign them and told him if he would get me orders to take command of my department again I would accept that. I believe the governor thought I had lost my mind. Soon after, President Davis and Colonel Johnson came to my room. The President seemed much affected by my condition, and, like Governor Lubbock, tried to persuade me to take my retiring papers, I thanked him for his courtesy, and begged him not to be disturbed; " my wounds were the fortune of war, and were honorable, since they befell in the service of my country and in fighting for all that I held dear and loved best; many had given their lives to the cause, and others had been worse maimed than I; all our people had made great sacrifices, and the dark shadow of war lay at every threshold; let us not grieve, then, over individual affliction, nor repine: all will be well, if our cause triumphs." " Yes," he replied, " we live for our children; freedom for them will well be worth the price we pay for it;" and pressing my hand warmly, he bade me goodbye. Shortly after he left General Breckinridge came and insisted on my taking my retiring papers and going to rejoin my wife, who was then in Virginia. On my refusal to follow his advice he lost his temper and asked me if I thought any man would be damn fool enough to go with me. I told him that if he would give me my orders and the men refused to go with me I would be willing to quit. I received the necessary orders, with transportation for me and my men.

Major Theophilus Steele, who had come around with me from Fortress Monroe, went with me to Fincastle, where my wife was, and we all started to north Mississippi, where my men were stationed. My old friend and comrade Captain Neil Helm was here, and soon after William Hamby joined us. Captain Helm was killed at Chester, South Carolina: he was riding on top of the car, and the train running under a low stone bridge spanning the track, he was struck on the head and instantly killed. We buried him there, and with heavy hearts continued our journey. Being compelled to travel by private conveyance from this point, as the railroad tracks had all been torn up, at Mount Pleasant, about twelve miles from Montgomery, Alabama, we met Generals Buford and Adams with their commands, falling back before Wilson. They insisted that it would be impossible for us to go any further in that direction, but procuring a two-horse wagon, and in company with Captain William Moore, of Forrest's command, Colonel S. P. Cunningham, of my command, and Lieutenant Ferguson, of Arkansas, we started on a flank movement, making directly for the ferry across the Alabama river, near the State penitentiary. By the time we reached the river and secured the boat, the Federal bullets were flying thick over our heads, but we reached the opposite shore in safety, and having the river between us and Wilson's raiders, we flanked them, and getting in their rear, made our way to Selma, Alabama. We found the railroad tracks torn up and the town in ruins, but we succeeded in getting transportation and proceeded to our destination, Macon, Mississippi. Here I found about one hundred and fifty of my men under command of Captain Shanks. These men received me with enthusiasm, and declared themselves ready to go with me into Kentucky. We went to work at once to prepare for our trip, but before we were quite ready the sad intelligence of Lee's surrender reached us. Now for the first time I collapsed; in all my life I think this was the blackest day. General Dick Taylor soon notified me that he intended to surrender. Wherefore, seeing that all was over, I bade farewell to my men and pursued my way to Texas. We went directly to Big Black river, where the Federals had established an exchange station. Here we met Mrs. General Bowen, who, by her pluck and courage, had obtained permission to take supplies to our sick and wounded. She was one of the most elegant ladies I ever met, and was particularly kind to us; through her we found good quarters in Vicksburg with true friends. We met with kind treatment from the Federal General Smith, who was in command at Vicksburg. He gave us transportation to New Orleans. Arriving at that place, I found a letter from one of my officers in Kentucky stating that a large number of my men had been arrested, charged with horse-stealing, etc., and it would require my evidence to keep them from being sent to the penitentiary; at the same time they advised me not to come back as I might myself receive rough treatment. I determined to go and share the fate of my men. Taking passage on a steamboat, my wife and I returned to Henderson, and on my making affidavit that my men were regularly enlisted in the Confederate army and had orders from me to impress horses if they could not otherwise procure them, all the cases were dismissed. It was here that I received another evidence of the love and affection of my men: they made arrangements to buy one of the finest farms in that part of Kentucky, known as the Samuels, or Slaughter, farm, and sent a delegation to me to say if I would come and live on it they would have it deeded to me, and would guarantee that it should be cultivated for me without any expense on my part as long as I lived. It would be impossible for me to express my appreciation of this generous offer. I know I had the truest and best body of men that ever belonged to any command; their lives since the great war bear me out in this assertion. I declined this kind offer, telling my men that it might happily fall to my lot to have a family of children, and I could not bear the thought of having them reared on the bounty of others. My two brothers who had been in the Federal army insisted on giving me a home at Henderson, but this was declined for the same reason. Uncle John Barrett, Mr. Burbank and others insisted on providing for me—all seeming to think it impossible for me to make a living. Having confidence in the great resources of Texas, I determined to return to my home in that State.

Before concluding this chapter I wish to say a few words in justice to one of the greatest and best men of this country. My interviews with him in Richmond show that President Davis, beneath a dignified and calm exterior, dominated by an iron will, had a kind and tender heart; in every order or advice I ever received he exhibited the greatest consideration for non-combatants who were Union men, and never at any time did I receive any instructions that would permit me to seize, confiscate or destroy private property, or to rob or plunder any one of money or goods on account or his politics. After reading the sketch of Major Walker Taylor, hereinafter published, which includes a letter from President Davis and an account of an interview between Mr. Davis and Major Walker Taylor, the most skeptical will be convinced that President Davis never had any knowledge of the assassination of Mr. Lincoln before it happened; those who knew Mr. Davis intimately, or even casually, know that his whole life gave the lie to such an outrageous accusation. The South has long since learned that Mr. Lincoln was a good-hearted man. His idol was the Union. " The Union " was his war-cry. It enabled him to use every means to attain his end. He could declare martial law and suspend the writ of habeas corpus; these extraordinary powers are essential to success in a civil war. The Northern States were consolidated and unified under one Federal head. On the other hand, Mr. Davis, by his doctrine of " States' rights," was hampered from the start. The Southern States retained their " reserved powers " and exercised them. The Confederate Government was merely their agent. Constitutional freedom could not be restrained by it. Each State demanded protection, and thus scattered the armies that might have been concentrated and launched at once into Northern territory. Mr. Davis's inaugural address foreshadowed this policy when he said if there must be war it is Northern homes and Northern fire-sides that shall feel it. But the policy was not executed; it was constrained by the principle.

CHAPTER XXV.

THE NEW HOME.

In September, 1865, I returned to the Texas frontier, but deprived of sight, temporarily crippled, stripped of all my property, in debt, health shattered by continued exposure, and confronted by the duty of making a living for self and family. The conditions were generally bad. Many of the citizens were without the common necessities of life, there being no money in the country. The Indians often made raids on the scattered settlements, stealing from their small herds, sometimes taking the last cow or horse. Wishing to relieve my neighbors to some extent and to earn my own livelihood, I set up a small store and took as partner John Moore, a Confederate soldier and a most excellent man. This business was fairly successful, but it was very hard to carry on, as the nearest market was at Austin, a fifty-mile journey, and only to be made on horseback, since the roads were very rough and the trip could be made quicker by this mode of travel. Possessing a good horse, I often made this trip in a day, with only a small boy as companion.

The first election for governor of the State was about this time and Mr. Throckmorton and Colonel G. W. Jones, both of whom were my personal friends, respectively were elected governor and lieutenant governor, but " reconstruction " measures being enforced, they were ejected from office, and confusion reigned all over the State. Many citizens were thrown into prison; among them were my partner, John Moore, and his father. The irritation of constant contact with the agents of this new organization determined me to move further west. I much preferred to face the dangers of Indian raids rather than the meanness and rapacity of the reconstructionists; so securing the former homestead of the Reverend Jonas Dancer, who had been killed some time before by the Indians, I took my wife and child and settled in Llano county.

This home was situated in the beautiful and romantic " Honey Creek Cove," right in the heart of the loveliest and richest part of the county. A range of mountains rose in the distance, while broad, fertile valleys, flanked by gently rolling hills, stretched to their base. The landscape was brightened and the air rendered fragrant by a multitude of wild flowers that covered the virgin soil. A hundred springs burst from the mountain side, and leaping down their rocky beds, winded their way through the valleys.

One of these lovely streams flowed through the wide valley to the " Cove," where the old Dancer home was situated. Here in a bit of forest land many song birds and birds of brilliant plumage found shelter; deer roamed in its recesses, and bears and wolves, both black and gray, made their lairs in these solitudes, where they were often pursued by hunters. Enormous quantities of delicious honey were found in many old trees in this forest, which the settlers prized as well for its rare flavor as for the pleasant addition it made to their frugal fare. That is why they named the place " Honey Creek Cove." Mr. Dancer had chosen this spot on account of its beauty and fertility; others came and soon the ring of the ax and hammer resounded through the wilderness. While the new comers were building their cabins Mr. Dancer, who was of the Methodist persuasion, was engaged in erecting and forming a large church. Within this building the gospel was first preached to the mountaineers of this border country. ˙For several years these brave people lived in peace and happiness, pursuing their various vocations. But at last their quiet was rudely broken.

On the twenty-third day of May, 1859, Mr. Dancer and others were to meet at a certain point to cut out a new road from Llano to the city of Austin. Always punctual in his appointments, Mr. Dancer, tools in hand, repaired to the spot. From some cause the others failed to come. Dancer had a couple of horses which he hoppled, and thinking the others would soon arrive, he began work by himself. While he was thus engaged a party of five or six Indians stole up and attacked him. Being unarmed, Dancer fled to a deep ravine, closely pursued by the savages, who made several attempts to rope him with their lariats, but failed. He reached the bed of the ravine unhurt, but the Indians rushed up on the bluffs.

RESIDENCE OF GENERAL ADAM R. JOHNSON,

Burnet, Texas, 1884.

overlooking this place and began pouring showers of arrows down upon the unfortunate old man. A number of the poisoned missiles took effect, and being weak from the loss of blood, he walked around a projecting rock in the bluff, and seating himself on a stone bench, soon expired. The Comanches then came down from their station on the bluff and scalped, as well as mutilated their victim. On the following morning a searching party found their faithful counsellor and friend as the savages had left him, and standing around his bier each of his neighbors took an oath of vengeance against the red devils who had murdered him.

Ten years after this tragedy I took possession of Dancer's old home. It had been sadly neglected during this interval. The roof had fallen in, and wild vines ran in undisturbed confusion in and out among the crevices of its framework. The whole place had a desolate air.

Such was the condition of the Dancer house when I arrived with my family; but stretching a wagon-sheet over the decayed roof, we began repairs at once and soon were comfortably housed. Two Brazeal boys were with us, and the sound of their hammers could be heard from morning till night as the shingles were put in place. One day the last shingle was nailed on just as the sun sank in the west; both men hurried to get the horses corralled in the lot near the house so that they could retire immediately after supper, as they were very tired from their hard day's labor. It was a bright moonlight night, and while the inmates of the Dancer home were peacefully sleeping a band of Indians crept up to the corral, and silently opening the gate, drove all my horses out into a herd they had stolen from neighboring settlers. No one dreamed of the nearness of foes, and the Brazeal boys were greatly surprised when in the early dawn they ran upon them camped upon the other side of the creek. The white boys gave chase, but the wily savages escaped with three of my finest horses.

CHAPTER XXVI.

INDIAN RAIDS.

Early in the spring of '67 one of the Miller and one of the Morrow boys loaded a wagon with corn and set out on a thirty-mile trip to mill. They reached their destination safe, and after getting their corn ground, started on their return. They were crossing the valley of Brady creek, when a body of Indians on foot suddenly rushed out from a dense thicket near the road side and fiercely attacked them. The two men in the wagon seeing the great odds against them, whipped their horses, and dashed down a steep, rocky hill, the jolting of the wagon causing Miller's pistol to fall out of the holster into the road. One of the foremost Indians snatched it up and emptied its contents at him, but luckily no shot took effect. The white men had but one six-shooter left, but as the savages rushed upon the wagon using their bows and arrows, Miller and Morrow took turn about and made every shot tell. While some of the Indians were trying to shoot them with arrows or spear them others endeavored to stop the wagon by throwing large stones in front of the wheels. In this manner the running fight continued for some time, when Morrow succeeded in killing another Indian with his last shot. This made them fall back temporarily, and seizing the opportunity the men cut loose one of the best horses from the harness, mounted him and fled to a thicket near by. Finding it impossible to enter it on horseback, they dismounted and went in on foot, secreting themselves in the thickest brush they could find. The red men came up, took the horse, but did not· venture into the brush.

During the fight Miller had received twenty-seven wounds and Morrow twenty-one. The fact that none of these were mortal was on account of the drizzling rain which was falling, and which slackened the bow strings so that it was impossible to send the arrows with much force. The red men returned to the wagon, emptied the meal into the road, took all the horses, and disappeared in the woods.

The two wounded men suffered terribly for water, and as soon as they were sure the Indians were gone, Morrow, who was not so badly hurt as his companion, crawled to a creek that fortunately was near, and after slaking his own thirst, he pulled off one of his boots, filled it with water, and with the greatest difficulty and the most intense pain managed to carry it to where he had left Miller, thus saving the poor fellow's life.

Miller and Morrow not reaching home at the time they were expected, a party went out to look for them, and found them in a most terrible condition. They were unable to walk and their clothes were stiff with clotted blood. After reaching home and having good attention paid their wounds, they recovered.

Captain Morrow lived for many years at Marble Falls, Texas, where he died recently.

Miller is living in the Indian Territory, and the last time he was heard from was doing well.

It was not long after this that another raid was made upon the settlement of " Honey Creek Cove." It was almost twilight—a cool, peaceful evening, and no one had a thought that Indians were near. Mrs. Johnson went down to turn in the cattle—some sixty head— into the lot near the house, while with my child on my shoulder I stood guard, my gun in hand. I never went out without my shotgun, which, loaded with buckshot, could do full execution even in the hands of a blind man, who was practiced in its use. While we were thus occupied two boys who had been gathering cattle rode up, dismounted, hoppled the horses and turned them into the adjoining pasture, and then went off down to the field to gather corn for the morning feed. The field was only a half mile away and they were gone only a short time. On their return they found the Indians had stolen all the horses. These two boys had hardly got out of sight when a band of eleven Indians sneaked up, unhoppled the horses and drove them out of the pasture. They were out of my hearing and out of Mrs. Johnson's sight, and probably my lack of sight saved me, for the red men seeing me with a gun had planned to kill me if I interfered with them and had placed an ambush for that purpose. They had made their escape by the time the boys got back, and this time took all the horses. This band of savages had gone down the river, and coming upon old man Smith at the Fort Mason crossing, killed and scalped him; then passing on through Burnet, made their way northward, taking my fine lot of horses with them.

In the summer of 1868 a party of eight Indians came into the settlement on the waters of the Leon, in Hamilton county. The first house they approached was that of a Mr. Pickett. They sent one of their number as a spy ahead, who took his position on the top of a hill near Pickett's house. In his eagerness to spy out the land he advanced too far out of the brush and was discovered by one of Pickett's children. The child reported the fact to its father. Pickett, knowing well the cunning of an Indian, walked in his yard for some time, carelessly showing himself as if unaware of the Indian's proximity, then entered his house. When he came out he was accompanied by another man, each with a blanket wrapped around his shoulders, and with a bucket in his hand; they took their way toward a spring a short distance off, as if for the purpose of getting water. The blankets were worn to prevent the savage from seeing their guns. As soon as they were out of the Indian's sight they dropped their blankets, slipped around to the opposite side of the hill, then cautiously crawled up to within a few yards of the place where the Indian was watching for them to return from the spring with their buckets of water. Pickett and his companion both fired at him at the same time, and he fell dead, pierced with two bullets. They then hastily concealed themselves in the bushes near by and reloaded their guns and stood in readiness for the advance of his comrades. They had not long to wait, for the other eight Indians hearing the shots came rushing up to see what was the matter. When they were in close gunshot the two men in ambuscade fired upon them and killed two more. The remaining five turned and fled, but unfortunately for them, they had gone but a short distance when they met Captain Crawfield. This gallant officer at once charged them, killed three of the band and wounded a fourth, the fifth making good his escape. The wounded Indian was disabled entirely and died soon after the fight occurred; that

PUBLIC SCHOOL, BURNET, TEXAS.

night the one who had escaped returned to the place and buried him. Only one of these eight Indians survived.

In the fall of this same year it was even harder to live than it had been in the summer, as food for both man and beast was scarcer, and there was more work to do, as wood had to be cut and brought in, and plowing had to be done; but all the settlers were resolved to stay in this wild country and risk the monthly raids of the Indians and make for themselves homes in the fertile valleys of the Texas frontier. Provisions of all kind except beef and pork were very high in price, and as money was scarce their trials and tribulations were many. Though both cattle and hogs were cheap, there was hardly any sale for them, as the owners generally would not venture out to find a market for them for fear of the Indians. But not having the fear of the red men before me, I decided to take a herd of cattle and find a market for them. Employing two cowboys, I had them gather together all my spare stock, and inviting my neighbors to put in as many as they desired, I started on the journey. Fortunately, we were not molested by the savages, and on reaching Fort Worth, which then was only a small village, 127 acres of land was offered me for the herd. Had it been my own individual property I would have made the deal, for I realized that at some distant day that very piece of land would prove a fortune: the small town I foresaw would in a few years be quite the splendid city that it now is, and the land would be very valuable. Remembering, however, the wants of my neighbors, I looked for a cash market, and disposing of the herd, returned home with money and provisions.

On the fifth of February, 1868, while Mrs. Friend, the owner of a home in Legion Valley, about fifteen miles from Llano, and a less distance from Honey Creek Cove, in company with two or three ladies and a lot of children, was at the cow pen, situated about one hundred yards from the house, engaged in milking, they were startled at the sight of some fifteen Indians passing by. The women, with the children, fled to the house and barred the door. The savages seeing no men around the place, turned their course toward the house also. At the time of attack the inmates of the house were: Mrs. Friend, Mrs. Samantha Johnson, Mrs. Rebecca Johnson, Miss Amanda Townsend, a little girl, Malinda Cordle, Lee Temple Friend, a lad of eight years, and the two babies of the Mrs. Johnsons. The house was made of pickets, and when the Indians found that the door had been barred, they pulled out a couple of pickets. The only resistance made was by Mrs. Friend, who insisted upon the other ladies joining her in the defense of the place, but they counselled conservatism, thinking that the Indians would not bother them if they submitted quietly. There were two guns in the house, and Mrs. Friend, seeing an Indian about to enter through the aperture made by pulling out the pickets, seized one of the weapons and attempted to shoot, but the gun was wrested from her hands by an Indian buck, who doubtless would have shot her had not another Indian (possibly fearing an alarm would be given by the report of the gun) snatched it from him. The savage who had attempted to shoot was then struck by Mrs. Friend with a smoothing iron. The blow almost knocked him down, but he recovered himself, fitted an arrow to his bow and shot Mrs. Friend in the side; a second arrow passed through her arm, while a third struck her in the breast. After receiving the third wound, being unable to make further resistance; she seated herself upon the bed and leaned her head against one of its posts. Thinking she was dead, one of the brutes began to scalp her. This gave her so much pain she threw up her hand and caught the knife. The Indian drew it fiercely through her hand, cutting it severely. Attempting to seize it a second time, the savage dealt her three hard blows which completely disabled her. The brute then finished his fiendish operation of scalping her at his leisure, and left the poor woman for dead. One of these fiends incarnate, thinking possibly she was not quite dead, returned and gave the arrow sticking in her breast several severe jerks backward and forward to see if she would flinch. Mrs. Friend, seeing the savage coming back, placed herself in exactly the same position she was in while being scalped and remained as if lifeless during all this painful torture. Satisfying himself that she was dead, the red devil left.

All the others who were in the house when it was attacked were taken prisoners, and Mrs. Friend, hearing their cries as they were led off, arose and tried to walk to the window to get a farewell look at her friends, but being very weak from the loss of blood, she was unable to stand, and with great difficulty managed to crawl to the opening in the side of the house to take the last look at them. When the Indians were out of sight the poor wounded woman bound a cloth around her head and shutting her teeth together with determination, went out of the house, put the few things the savages had left back in the room, shut the door, and started on foot to Mr. Bradford's, about a mile and a half away. It was about sundown when this brave woman started on her painful journey, but it was not until eight o'clock that she reached her destination. On her way she slaked her burning thirst with snow. As she approached the house the dogs began barking fiercely, and Bradford came out to see what was disturbing them. When he saw the bloody figure the moonlight revealed it frightened him so he ran back into the house. Mrs. Friend called to him and told him who she was, then he came out and took her in. At her request he extracted all the arrows from her body, then fled with his family, as he feared the Indians would return. Bloody, faint from wounds, scalped and still bleeding, Mrs. Friend was left alone, these heartless people not even taking time to dress her wounds or remove her bloody clothing. They did, however, make a fire and set a bucket of water by her, but then deserted the helpless woman.

The next morning two widows living in Legion Valley came to her relief. The cloth on her head had dried and stuck so fast to the wound that it could only be removed by the use of hot water, and her body was so swollen from the arrow wounds that it was with great difficulty that her clothing was gotten off These kind ladies did all they could for her, but it was not till late in the evening that a doctor arrived. It was almost a year before this heroic woman recovered, but finally she regained her health and removed to Kansas.

During the night of the same day a runner arrived in the town of Llano and announced the sad tragedy. Early next morning ten or twelve armed citizens rode to Legion Valley. Arriving upon the ground, their examination showed that the Indians had gone in a southerly direction. "When about a mile and a half from the house (says Mr. D. L. Luce, of Hayes county) we found on a large rock six or eight feet high Mrs. Johnson's baby with its brains knocked out. Four miles further on the trail, on the top of a mountain, we found where they had stopped, built a fire, roasted their meat, and from impressions on the ground we suppose their stay here had been for some time. At this place a trail was found leading out from the camp to a thicket about a hundred yards distant. Following the trail to this point we found the mangled body of Miss Townsend, Mrs. Johnson's eighteen-year-old sister. She had been tied down on the snow-covered ground and from all appearances had been brutally outraged, then killed and her body mutilated almost beyond recognition. Continuing the pursuit some three miles further off the mountain and down into the valley, not far from the J. C. Talley place, we found the body of Mrs. Johnson, stripped of nearly all her clothing, and nearly eaten up by the hogs. At this point our party divided, a portion continuing the pursuit of the Indians and their remaining captives, while the others stayed behind to bury the dead. I, with six or seven others, still followed the trail. The Indians, after winding through the mountains and collecting about thirty head of horses, turned due west. We followed these red skins for five days, often traveling at night when the trail could be seen. From the little tracks seen around the water-holes where the savages had stopped to drink we knew they still had the little eight-year-old son of Mrs. Friend. Our determination to follow and overtake them was much strengthened on discovering this fact, and we continued the pursuit to near Devil's river, and were but a short distance behind them when, for want of food, our horses gave out and left us afoot."

The little girl, Malinda Cordle, was carried off with the little Friend boy, and remained a captive for about eight months, when she was recovered by a body of United States dragoons and sent to Fort Leavenworth, Kansas, from there to Fort Arbuckle, and then returned to her relatives in Texas. The little boy was held by the Indians for nearly five years, but was finally recovered by his grandfather, L. S. Friend. At the time of his reclamation he could speak nothing but Indian dialect and had learned all the customs of the savages.

These Indians who had been guilty of this horrible crime, as well as many similar ones all along the Texas frontier, were the proteges of the government, fed and clothed by it, and its agents and traders who knew nothing of their fiendish nature furnished them with guns and ammunition. The Northern people were secure from all danger of savage warfare and perhaps knew nothing of the crimes committed monthly by the Comanches. With hearts overflowing with sympathy, they wrote and spoke at their clubs and societies of the tribulations of the poor red man, but were his accomplices all the same in the outrages he committed, as they furnished him the weapons necessary for their accomplishment. Could they have been witnesses of such deeds as the Friend case, all their misplaced sympathy with the Indian would have been swept away,

RESIDENCE OF GENERAL JOHNSON.

and they would have shuddered with horror at the thought of their having helped in bloody wars against women and children.

As each month, during the light of the moon, a raid was made by the Comanches and more horrible deeds were committed, I determined to get the frontier people together and make an appeal to the government to put a stop to their incursions. I interviewed Judge John Hancock and Governor E. M. Pease and got them to enter immediately upon the work. These two men did all they could, but the misrepresentations of the sutlers and Indian traders and misled philanthropists retarded this movement, and murders, thefts, and raids continued. Companies of minute-men were formed by the settlers and the different passes in the mountains guarded, but the wily savages managed to elude these men and come down into the valleys and kill and steal as before.

Many of the frontier men organized to go into the Indian country and retaliate by making war against them and fighting it out on their own ground. Captain Buck Roberts, commander of the minute-men, fell upon the trail of a band of marauding Indians, chased them to Packsaddle mountain, ran them off down to Honey creek, and killed and wounded several, but most of them escaped. The feeling of insecurity among the settlers increased, and many people left the frontier.

The counties of Denton and Cook at this time were sparsely settled, and large game of all kinds roamed over its prairies. In these counties frequent incursions were made by the wild Indian tribes of the upper Red river valley, from the early settlements as late as 1868, when the last raid was made by a band of Comanches, estimated at three hundred strong.

On the fifth of January began this memorable raid in which more than three hundred painted warriors took part. The attack was unexpected, and the citizens were unprepared to resist the over-whelming numbers. Among the first settlers that came into this part of the country was D. G. Menasco. Mr. Menasco and his brother-in-law were absent from home that day, and his two oldest children were visiting their aunt, Mrs. Shegog, whose home was a mile away. Hearing that the Indians were in the country, Mrs. Menasco's father went to Mrs. Shegog's to bring her and his grand-children over to Menasco's for better protection. While returning the Comanches came upon and surrounded the party, killing the grandfather and making captives of the others. The weather for that time of the year was warm, and they were thinly clad. The capture occurred about four o'clock on Sunday afternoon. The captives were Mrs. Shegog and her eighteen-month-old baby and Lizzie and May Menasco, six and four years old respectively. The Indians then crossed over the creek and surrounded Mr. Menasco's dwelling. They approached with the usual demoniacal yells and whoops, threatening each moment to enter the house and capture the inmates, while Mrs. Menasco, with courage born of a mother's love and with gun in hand, defended her fireside. At the same time she saw with horror that they had her two oldest children. Maintaining a threatening attitude for some time, the Indians finally withdrew, taking with them the horses found in the lot. They went about a mile in an easterly direction, then stopped and dashed Mrs. Shegog's baby's brains out against a tree while she stood looking on, powerless to defend her child. The savages then went on through Gainesville to a point six miles east of that town, then retraced their way and went into camp one mile west. They waited for daylight, as the moon had gone down and the latter part of the night was dark. During the night a freezing norther blew up and just before day Mrs. Shegog made her escape and found her way, though almost frozen, to a settler's house, where she was kindly received. At daybreak the Indians started on westward. After going seven or eight miles west of Gainesville they left the Menasco children. One month afterward the remains of one was found and the other three months later. It was supposed they had frozen to death.

Soon after this the Shegog and Menasco families removed to Pilot Point, where they have since resided. .

We give this story in detail as it is an illustration of many that happened about that time. The whole of the Texas frontier from the Red river to the Rio Grande had been raided during the year 1868. Meetings of the pioneers were held all along the line, their object being to devise ways and means to protect their homes. Another factor in the trouble and danger of the citizens of Llano and Burnet counties was a so-called military company raised under commission from Governor Pease. They proposed to aid the civil government in arresting and bringing to justice criminals who they claimed had committed crimes during the civil war. In this company were men who joined it for the purpose of wreaking their private spite or for plunder. Many citizens determined not to be arrested by this band, and armed themselves and took to the woods for protection. This was a desperate state of affairs; these hardy pioneers had not only the Indians to fight, but a band of white maurauders as well. The whole country was in a state of agitation and alarm. I was appealed to and took decisive measures to rid the land of this military company. I first obtained a pledge from the citizens that they would report to the district court as soon as it convened, then interviewed the district judge and attorney, both of whom were strong partisans as well as appointees of the governor, but were honorable men and good friends of mine. They gave me a written statement that the military company was altogether unnecessary and that the civil law could be enforced. Taking these statements to the Governor, I secured an order for the disbandment of the company. Having accomplished this, and finding that the neighborhood was again in great want, as many of the cattle buyers were unwilling to come into this territory, I gathered another herd of cattle, drove them to Houston, disposed of them and again brought back supplies.

The organization of minute-men during the year 1869 proved to be of great value; this year closed with the advantage greatly in favor of the white men. Some ten or fifteen settlers on Squaw creek recaptured about two hundred head of horses and killed the entire band of thieving Indians. Colonel Dalrymple and the gold hunters in their fight on Wichita mountain succeeded in driving off a large body of Indians that had surrounded them, killing and wounding a number of them. The colonel himself was so seriously wounded that he could not follow up his advantage, but a company of soldiers near at hand followed their trail and killed twenty of them while twice that number was wounded.

The killing of Hazelwood, in Stevens county, was followed by one of the most daring and desperate fights of this year, which deserves to be mentioned.

Early in the autumn of 1869 two young men named Dillard and Dorrell arrived in Texas from Louisville, Kentucky. They were very anxious to see the wild West generally and set to improving a place yet known as Fort Davis. Dillard planted the farm in watermelons, and raising a large crop, he and his little brother started with a load of them in a two-horse wagon for Fort Griffin. On their way home a party of thirty Indians attacked them. The savages were mounted, painted, and in full war costume. Both of the boys jumped from the wagon, Henry with a repeating rifle.

After running a short distance, Henry halted and fired upon the foremost Indian, but his shot flew wide of the mark and the only effect it had was a temporary check. Taking advantage of their halt, the two boys ran for some timber on a creek until they were compelled to stop again and confront their pursuers. The second shot from Henry's rifle only stopped them for a moment. The third ball brought down both a horse and its rider. Seeing their comrade fall, the other Indians gave a yell and rushed upon the boys. One of the savages seized Willie and was in the act of setting him in front of him in the saddle when Henry put a bullet through him. The boys then made for the thicket as fast as they could go. Just as they were within a few feet of the brush Henry stumbled and fell, but quickly regaining his feet, he shot the Indian that was dismounting, scalping knife in hand, to scalp him, thinking no doubt that he was dead. In another moment the boys reached the timber and the unequal contest came to an end, for the savages had been so roughly handled they dared not follow them further. These daring white boys came out of the fight without a scratch and the Indians on their return to Fort Sill reported that they had a fight with a "heap damn big captain and his little boy" and that "their medicine" was too strong for them. The boys stayed that night at a farm house and next day went to Fort Griffin and reported to an officer, who sent out a detachment of dragoons at once in pursuit of the Comanches. It was found that the Dillard brothers had killed and wounded eleven Indians besides several horses.

COLLEGE, MARBLE FALLS, TEXAS,
Built by Gen. A. R Johnson in 1890.

CHAPTER XXVII.

INDIAN RAIDS. (CONTINUED.)

Burnet county is traversed by a broad, heavy ridge running from northwest to the southeast corner, and is covered with a dense growth of cedar timber and a short scrubby oak brush called shin oak, almost impenetrable in many places. When I first knew it it was the home of the bear, panther, wolf and the fiercer Mexican lion. It was also a retreat for deer, wild turkey and smaller game. This ridge is the divide between the Colorado and Brazos rivers, and the source of many a clear, sparkling spring, making an ideal hiding place for the Indian in his raids upon our settlements, which sprinkled the beautiful valleys that lay along its base. From its summits the Indians could spy out the settlers, and descending, murder them when off their guard. It was along this ridge that Van Hook, Skaggs, Jackson and several others were killed. And it was here that my wife, her sister, Mrs. Hammond, and Miss Luce were hunting dewberries, when Mrs. Hammond, seeing some ripe ones, insisted on getting down to gather them, while Mrs. Johnson urged her not to do so. Miss Luce also begged Mrs. Hammond to remain on her horse, saying she saw an Indian, and pointing up the road, exclaimed: "There is an Indian!" Mrs. Hammond becoming frightened endeavored to mount her horse. All three of the animals seemed to be disturbed, but at last Mrs. Johnson, catching the bridle, succeeded in holding Mrs. Hammond's horse until she could get into the saddle. Mrs. Johnson knew her horse could leap the shin oak bushes, so she gave her whip to Miss Luce, and telling the others to follow her, that she was not going back by the road, she settled herself in the saddle, determined to put her horse to his best gait, and looked back to see what the Indian was doing. To her terror she saw another Indian standing calmly in the road by the other. Mrs. Johnson did not give a second look at these red men, but shook her bridle reins and called to her companions to come on. " Joe Smith " tossed his head as if he knew the danger his mistress was in and started away straight through the brush, taking the bushes as they came. He needed no spur or whip to urge him on, but kept his pace nobly through the rough country, speeding over stock and stone as nimbly as a deer. Mrs. Hammond allowed her horse to have the rein and kept close in her sister's rear, while Miss Luce laid whip to her little pony and managed to keep up with them in their mad race. The three frightened women did not stop until they reached the town and told some of the men of the presence of the Indians. A party of the citizens went at once in search of them, but failed to find them.

Soon after this a large party of savages raided down through Honey Creek Cove, in the vicinity of Packsaddle mountain, crossed the Llano river at the mouth of Honey creek, and came upon Mr. Whitlock, who was ploughing in his field. His little three-year-old boy was playing in the road near by. They captured him, laid down the fence, and rushing in upon Mr. Whitlock, killed and scalped him, then moved up to the Whitlock home on the side of Long mountain. Mrs. Whitlock seized a gun and tried to defend herself, but the Indians shot her and tied her body between two of the beds, took the other children into the yard and dashed their brains out against a tree, covered their little bodies with sheets, set fire to the house and then pursued their way, carrying off the little boy. This home was right on the public road between Llano and Burnet, and not far from the town, but the savages were so stealthy and cunning in their movement no one knew of the terrible deed until the brothers of the murdered family reached the house as the roof was falling in.

District court was in session and a number of people were in the town of Llano. Court was suspended and parties of men were sent in pursuit of the Indians, but they escaped with their captive— the little Whitlock boy—and he was never recovered.

During the war between the States there lived in Young county on " Peter's Colony " Moses Johnson, and with him a shining black, good-natured negro, named Brit. Brit had a wife and four children, all of whom he dearly loved. Brit's master, Moses Johnson, depended in part upon his strong arm to defend his family and the neighborhood from the bands of hostile Indians. On the thirteenth day of October, 1864, while Brit Johnson was absent in Parker county after supplies for his master's family, one thousand Comanche warriors swept through the neighborhood, carrying death and destruction to every hearth-stone. They killed Brit's son, Jim, Joel Meyers, Doctor T. J. Wilson, James McCoy and his son, Miles, the widow Durgan and five out of fifteen Texas rangers, and wounded many others. They carried off as captives the widow Patrick, two daughters of the slain widow Durgan, and the negro's wife, and those of his children whom they had not murdered. When Brit returned home he was not paralyzed by his great grief, but determined to have back his wife and children or perish in the effort to release them. Under the generous treatment of his master he had become the owner of a number of horses and cattle, and when the war was over and he was given his freedom he tried every way to recover his lost ones. He visited the forts in the Indian Territory, and offered as ransom all he had. He made inquiries at every Indian agency, but could find no trace of his family. He returned home and tried to resume his work, but could not stand the thought of his wife being the slave of the red men; so mounting his favorite black horse, he started out alone across the Panhandle of Texas, a part of the State, hundreds of miles wide, filled with hostile tribes, to find the tribe that held his wife in bondage. One evening, when he was almost worn out from his hard journey, he discovered upon a mountain peak some Indian pickets. They discovered him at about the same time. Brit signaled them as a friend, approached, and informed them that his purposes were friendly and that he wanted to find his wife and become one of the tribe. After being held by the pickets for three days he was taken to the main village, where he was received very kindly; his wife and children were restored to him, and he disarmed suspicion by becoming a member of the tribe. It was the custom of the Indians when hunting for game to scatter out over the plains in small squads to kill and cure their meat. The negro took advantage of this custom, got his wife and children and one of the captured Durgan girls in his hunting party, and under the friendly shades of night, set out with his party on horseback for his Texas home, which he finally reached in safety, guided by the stars and his general knowledge of the country. The Indians never forgot or forgave what they deemed his treachery to their tribe. In the latter part of January, 1871, while returning from Weatherford with a couple of negroes who were to assist him in gathering in his stock, they camped over night on the road. Unknown to them a wagon freight train was camped on the same road about one mile further west. Early the next morning while " the freighters " were rounding in their stock, about twenty-five mounted warriors suddenly appeared and began hostile maneuvers, but at the same time rapid and continual firing began at Brit's camp, to which this party of warriors hastened. A large band of painted Indians, once the friends, but now the deadly enemies of Brit, had surrounded him and his two companions. Brit's companions fell early in the action, but though he knew his time had come he determined to sell his life dearly to his foes. He cut his horse's throat and made a breastwork of his body. Armed with his own and the weapons of his comrades, Brit fought with a skill and strength almost preternatural, killing and wounding many of his assailants before he was killed. The savage demons cut off his ears, one of his arms, disemboweled him, then killed and thrust in his little pet dog. This negro had made a brave fight; one hundred and seventy three empty cartridge shells were found lying around his dead body.

This was only one of these red fiends' deeds. The whole frontier was stirred up again and determined to find a way to put a stop to this awful slaughter. In the movement to obtain protection I joined, and addressed several letters to prominent citizens in Austin, requesting their aid and assistance. Among these were John Hancock, Governor E. M. Pease and L. S. Ross, from whom I received the following replies:

" Austin, Texas, June 3, 1871.

" General A. R. Johnson,

" Llano, Texas.

" My Dear Friend:—I am just in receipt of your letter and assure you that I am in deepest sympathy with you and the frontier people, and have written the President about the matter. I have a promise from him that an investigation will be made.

"I have some hopes of being a member of Congress, and if these things are not adjusted by that time, I pledge you that my first and best efforts will be to induce the government to give protection to our frontier. With best wishes for your safety, I am

" Your friend,

" JOHN HANCOCK."

ROCKY REST,
First Home of Adam R. Johnson, Burnet, Texas, 1860.

"Austin, Texas, June 10 1871.

"A. R. Johnson,

"Llano, Texas.

"Dear Sir:—In reply to your letter will say that I have strong assurances that the government will at once take steps to investigate our frontier troubles. Your statement that up to this time you have never known a white man killed in Indian disguise has caused me to look into that matter, and I find no reason to believe the stories circulated to that effect are true. It is very difficult, however, to remove that impression from the U. S. Government, as they have the testimony of the sutlers and Indian traders that vicious white men are using that disguise to effect murders and thefts upon our people; therefore, you will have to be patient and await the investigation that is promised. Yours truly,

"E. M. PEASE."

"Waco, Texas, June 19, 1871.

"General A. R. Johnson,

"Llano, Texas.

"Dear Friend:—I have had many letters from prominent men along the frontier, urging me, as you do, to aid them in their great extremity. I am ready and willing to serve those people to the very best of my ability, under the circumstances; however, I am really not competent to advise what is best to be done. I have interviewed our representative and senator, and they assure me that as soon as the Legislature meets they will urge the formation of State troops for frontier protection. This, perhaps, is the best thing to be done, and I am willing to meet you and any others of our frontier people on that occasion and aid, if possible, in this matter.

"Truly your friend,

"L. S. ROSS."

I showed these letters to my friends and bade them be patient until they saw what the government would do for their protection, and if it failed to help them, then they could act for themselves and form troops and try to stay on or leave the frontier, whichever they thought best. The excitement grew less and they decided to take my advice.

Early in the summer of 1874 General W. T. Sherman, making a tour of inspection along the Texas frontier, arrived at Fort Sill.

It happened that Sattanta, Big Tree and Satank, Kiowa chiefs, had come to the fort at the same time to draw rations, for as "wards of the nation" they and their tribe were fed by the government in the intervals of their incursions. Sattanta, in a talk with the agent, said, boastingly, that with one hundred warriors he and the two chiefs then present had recently made an attack upon the trains between Fort Richardson and Belknap, killing seven teamsters and driving off forty-one mules. The agent reported this to General Sherman, who ordered the Indians to be brought before him. Sattanta attempted to prevaricate, but finally admitted that the statement made to the agent was true, whereupon Sherman ordered the arrest of the whole party; but subsequently releasing the privates, he held the chiefs as prisoners with the view of having them tried for their offenses by the civil authorities of Texas. On the way to Jacksboro, Satank, attempting to escape, was killed by the escort, but Sattanta and Big Tree were landed in jail, heavily ironed. A day in July, at the term of the court ensuing, was fixed for their trial before Judge Seward, of the Thirtieth Judicial District at Weatherford. They were the first and only Indian chiefs ever tried before a civil court in America. While they were vigorously prosecuted by the district attorney, the prisoners were ably defended by two prominent lawyers who were faithful to their clients. The jury rendered a verdict of "guilty of murder in the first degree," and fixed their punishment at death. The sentence was commuted to imprisonment for life; and in 1873, the reconstruction governor of Texas, upon recommendation of the President of the United States, set them at liberty upon parole, and had them escorted to their reservation. As was expected by the frontiersmen, who knew the Indian character, they soon violated their paroles. Sattanta was rearrested and returned to the penitentiary, where, in a few years, he died. Big Tree was not recaptured.

The object of rehearsing these Indian raids and murders on the frontier of Texas at this time is to emphasize the dangers that existed there, and to show that it required true courage, both of men and women to remain in their homes in this section; also that posterity may comprehend the hardships and trials that their forefathers had to encounter.

The trial and punishment of Sattanta and Big Tree did not restrain the Indians, but seemed to influence them to greater deeds of cruelty. The political conditions of our State were such that we could not hope for any protection from what we called the Reconstruction Administration; as they seemed to be much more inclined to elevate and protect the negro in his so-called " rights," than to care for the lives of the white people along the frontier. The whole State was now aroused and determined to throw off this yoke. A convention was held at Corsicana, and Richard Coke was nominated for governor. He was elected by an overwhelming majority.

The convening of the fourteenth Legislature and the effort of the reconstruction Governor Davis to hold over, and the rush of thousands of prominent men to Austin, resolved to seat Governor Coke at all hazards; the seizure of the arsenal and the filling of the lower story of the capital with armed negroes by Davis—was one of the most intensely exciting periods in the history of the Lone Star State.

I was present on this occasion, and going to the capital with Colonel G. W. Jones, both of us carrying our old army six-shooters, we took our stand at the head of the stairs so that we could fire down into the basement where the armed negroes were gathered, but the conservative men, headed by Coke and Ireland, kept the peace, and Judge George Clake, of Waco, forcing his way through the negroes to the executive department where Davis was, showed him that the course he was pursuing would bring destruction to the negroes and he would share their fate. These representations induced him to give up the contest. Coke was installed, and the Legislature passed a bill authorizing the raising of a frontier battalion, and Major J. B. Jones was placed in command and sent at once to the border.

The settlers were encouraged and made arrangements to aid in beating back the Indians. The experience of General Sherman while reviewing the different posts among the Indians, and his narrow escapes from death from the hands of these treacherous savages, did much to aid our congressmen in obtaining protection for our frontier. The Indians were ordered not to cross Red river. Many small bands disobeying these orders were met by Major Jones, and in some nineteen engagements lost many of their best warriors.

CHAPTER XXVIII.

PEACE.

Peace at last smiled upon these determined men and women of the border who had so valiantly fought for their homes, and many who had left returned, bringing with them numbers of others to settle in these fertile valleys. Now, where the wigwams of the savages had been pitched, cozy little homes of the pale-faces were built, and the vast herds of buffalo were replaced by hundreds of cattle, prosperity and quiet reigning where destruction and war had been predominant.

I disposed of my ranch and cattle and returned to Burnet, where I reopened a land office. My knowledge of the land not only here but all over western Texas enabled me to do a good business.

The frontier and reconstruction troubles had seriously affected Burnet. The town was depleted; there were only two small stores, which sold goods at such high prices that the settlers began to take their wagons and go to Austin to make purchases. I resolved to stop this extortion, and traded for a stock of goods. Employing two young men as clerks, I instructed them to sell goods at such reasonable prices that people would trade in Burnet instead of making a fifty-mile journey for supplies.

A school, too, being much needed, I raised a subscription, built a stone schoolhouse and employed teachers. Both the school and the store proved a success, and the town soon showed marked improvement. A paper known as the " Western Texas Advertiser " was added to the list of my undertakings, and through the columns of this paper the healthfulness and resources of Burnet were made

COTTON FACTORY, MARBLE FALLS, TEXAS.

known. Recognizing the great value of the granite in Burnet county, I got Dr. Burleson, of Waco, a man of learning, to come down and examine Granite mountain. His report drew attention to the value of the stone. To utilize the stone for building and other purposes a railroad was absolutely necessary. I succeeded in interesting a party of capitalists, and although my own means were limited, I became the largest cash subscriber in the county and donated seven miles of right of way to the railroad company. The building of this railroad enabled the Capitol Commission later to use this stone in the construction of the beautiful capitol building now at Austin.

Being a part owner in the property at Marble Falls, I resolved to open it up and in that way develop the resources of the county. I attribute much of the success in this Marble Falls undertaking to the public spirit and energy of my associates:

B. Badger was a Confederate soldier, a member of Wall's Legion, and served under Van Dorn and Sol Ross in north Mississippi.

F. H. Holloway was also a Confederate soldier in the same department.

S. E. Holland was a Mexican war veteran, in Jack Hayes's band of Texas rangers. He settled in Texas in 1848, and has lived in Burnet county longer than any of its citizens.

W. H. Badger is in business with his father and is one of the leading merchants in the county.

J. A. Ramsdale was a " Copper Head," or " Son of Liberty," and moved from Illinois to Texas soon after the war. His former home had been in the immediate neighborhood of General Payne, and he often tells of the elegant furniture, silverware and bric-a-brac that that notorious Federal general had stolen from the homes of the Southern people.

Marble Falls is located in the central part of Texas, on the Colorado river, forty miles from Austin. The town is laid out on an elevated plateau that gradually rises from the river bank to the height of several hundred feet. Commencing at Marble Falls and extending northwest for over fifteen miles is Backbone valley, the largest valley north of Austin for a hundred miles, and as fertile as any spot in the State; while south and southwestward extends a beautiful and picturesque country composed of low hills, covered with groves of post oak, live oak and mountain cedar, and growing an abundance of mesquite grass, the best and most nutritious wild grass native to the State. The rich and well-watered valleys form the finest grazing land in the State, as well as fine farming and ranch country, while, perhaps, the best water power in the South is found in the great Marble Falls, Burnet county, Texas, where the Colorado river delivers itself from a beautiful, romantic lake two miles long, over immense granite ledges that span the entire river. The first three of these give a fall of twenty-one feet and furnish five thousand horse power at an average stage of water; fourteen other falls within a mile and a quarter aggregate fifty feet. All along on either side of the river are lovely situations for 'manufactories, so that the power can be reproduced time and again, as neither freshets, droughts nor freezes can affect it. Among the other important resources of Marble Falls are its granite, red and gray, variegated marbles, steatite and lithographic stone, red and gray sand-stone, which are found within a few miles of the town in vast quantities. The town is rapidly growing and can boast of a two-story granite bank, a college building, also of granite, M. H. Reed's large two-story store, Evans's two-story steel front hardware store, Badger's steel and glass front mercantile house, a large stone hotel, and last, but far from least, a two-story cotton-mill building, of which the town is very proud. The "Little Gem City" does more business than any other town of its size in the State, for it is blessed with a few public-spirited and enterprising men who have succeeded in keeping business going in the gloomiest times by utilizing the abundant growth of fine cedar along the banks of the Colorado; the railroad is kept busy supplying cars to ship out these posts, while tents are pitched in the brakes and wagons are continually on the road; the ring of numberless axes can be heard from morning till night as the trees are felled and prepared for shipment.

In this busy little town, founded by me, and largely built by my efforts, in the declining years of a life tempered by danger and sweetened by the uses of adversity, I am living with my family in happiness and in peace.

MRS. ADAM R. JOHNSON.

THE PARTISAN RANGERS.

PART II.

Sketches, Incidents and Adventures: Contributions by Confederate and Federal Officers.

ROSTER OF THE RANGERS.

BRIGADIER GENERAL ADAM R. JOHNSON.

Field Officers of the Partisan Rangers.

GENERAL ADAM R. JOHNSON.

By E. L. Starling (Colonel Regiment, Federal Army).

My affectionate regard for the distinguished man whose name will be observed at the beginning of this brief sketch was not in the least diminished by the overthrow of the great cause for which he fought and contributed the better part of his life. Without concern for his own comfort or personal safety, he dared every danger, and in the brief period allotted him, achieved a reputation for intelligent and valued daring in the interest of the cause of the Southland, than many, more fortunately situated than he, ever attained throughout the whole sanguinary conflict of arms. On the contrary the interest felt in his exploits by those who labored and suffered with him and those who knew him in his childhood days is yet a living evidence of his consummate genius and prowess. My knowledge of General Johnson from his boyhood days to the present time constitutes the motive I have for supplying this exordium, and this I trust will subserve to place at rest the very natural question what right or what purpose I may have to claim qualification for the task I have assumed. The task has been one of my own seeking, simply a desire to portray and vindicate, as far as I am able, his military record, that his countrymen may cherish it as a yet living recollection of a life fraught with dangers at all times and a daring unsurpassed by any. I am fully aware of the undertaking and its multiplied difficulties. I am further aware that perfection was never the privilege of any man in any of his work; therefore, I am prepared to learn from criticisms of others that my work has not been wholly successful. Especially would I declare that in relating the share borne by the subject of this sketch in his campaigns in this particular portion of Kentucky, I am actuated alone by a cordial and friendly desire, not only to do simple justice, but to align myself closely with one of his most prominent characteristics—" scrupulous truthfulness." It has often been said that contemporaries can not write impartial histories because of their too partial sympathy for the passions which governed and agitated the actors. This I shall not undertake to deny, but when it is known that I was never a military comrade of General Johnson, but wore the blue and fought beneath the graceful folds of the stars and stripes it may—and will no doubt—be thought strange by many that I should undertake the work of contributing to a history intended to do justice to a noble man, a true friend, and a military chieftan with but few peers.

It was my pleasure years ago to tax my limited and undisciplined capacity in the preparation of a history covering the entire life of General Johnson, but adverse circumstances confronted and prevented its appearance in book form. This great disappointment is, in a measure, appeased by the opportunity now offered to contribute briefly my testimony to a friend who has been the victim of abuse from many who owed him much for the protecting influence it was his pleasure to throw around them during a period in the history of this section of the country that tried men's souls to the utmost limit.

Adam R. Johnson's mother, Juliet Rankin Johnson, was a native of Henderson, having been born in 1800. She grew up among the pioneers and was notedly one of the purest and most popular women of her day. She impressed upon her son the noble characteristics that so, adorned her life, and he would have proven himself a strange offspring indeed had he strayed away from the teachings of this truly holy mother in the exciting scenes of frontier life in Texas, or in the even more strenuous times of the war in which he took so conspicuous a part. While he was throughout his military career a thorough-going partisan, fully determined upon doing his duty to his beloved Southland, detesting her enemies as he conceived them to be, he yet held in reverence the impressions made by his saintly mother, and as far as in his power, endeavored to impress the same characteristics upon the men under his command. He abhorred the mistreatment of a non-combatant citizen, and only when dire necessity demanded did he ever give them reason to criticise his acts harshly. In the collection of supplies he oftentimes made levy upon his friends and the true friends of the Southern cause rather than impose upon those who held allegiance to the Union. Hundreds of instances in this particular section of the country can be cited to bear evidence to the truthfulness of the statement. Notwithstanding the many outrages committed by commands in the service of the enemy, General Johnson did not consider their acts a justification of a similar retaliation upon the part of his command upon Union sympathizers who had no part in the acts committed by troops in the service of the Federal government. He gloried in a fight and was never known to shirk one, even when the odds were greatly against him. He was never known to shun a duty, no matter how dangerous or daring, and in numerous instances he was known to undertake the most dangerous escapades rather than impose the duty upon an under officer or soldier of his command. His object appeared to be to make friends rather than enemies, and though positive and determined in his every act or order, he leaned to the humane side if the situation in the least justified it. It was far from his purpose to punish an inoffensive, non-combatant Union sympathizer for the act or acts of some satrap in the ranks of the Union army. Many outrages were committed by outlaws, and the effort was as frequently made to impress communities with the belief that Johnson and his command were the real offenders, but investigation by his non-combatant enemies, as well as by his friends, proved him innocent. He was known to punish offenders within his own command and other so-called Confederate commands, with as much severity as he did those of the opposing commands.

Incidents in his military career about Henderson and contiguous territory fully bear out this statement, notably, the influence he exerted in the capture and turning over to the Federal authorities men captured and charged with some outrage while claiming to have been in the Confederate service and acting under authority. He detested guerrilla service, and those known as guerrillas, and to his active and well-known opposition this country owes a debt of gratitude for much that was never done, but would have been done but for his interference and his well-known opposition. Much of his time was given to the ridding of the country of such characters and placing the service of the Confederacy upon a high plane, and yet the acts of many bad men claiming to be Federals and others claiming to be Confederates were most cruelly and without decency charged by Union newspapers and some Union men to him and his command, when the slightest investigation on their part would have proved him not only innocent, but as much opposed to the outrages committed as they themselves could have been. He was not of the class who claimed that all things are fair in war; on the contrary (unless compelled by attending conditions), he believed in fair dealing with non-combatants. He held the man or men in uniform and gun in hand in a totally different light from the non-combatant as bitterly opposed to him as the soldier in the service. He knew the price that was put upon his life, and he well knew what would be the result were he surprised by the enemy. He knew the opinion had of him, and how unjustly and undeservedly the enemy had been taught to consider him. Newspapers with no regard for the truth had misrepresented him; they had created the impression that he was a roaming guerrilla, with no end in view but murder, rapine and theft, and had lost no opportunity in the endeavor to impress this most false and unworthy impression upon the minds of every one not acquainted with the nobler attributes of his nature. Their course was calculated to drive a far less chivalrous nature to deeds of horrid violence. Their determined pursuit of his character as well as his person was in every way calculated to drive him mad and make of him a demon rather than the true soldier that he was. He was upon his native heath, the home of his nativity, among the friends of his childhood. He felt that he had a right to be here. His purpose was to recruit men into the service, and to do this quietly and without doing harm to any one. It was not his purpose to involve his country or his friends in a war, but to transact his work quietly, and decamp. But this course was denied him by meddlers and mischief-makers who persisted in giving him a false name and his mission an altogether false impression. To this end, therefore, the Government was appealed to and hundreds of troops commanded by men little caring what they did, and with no regard for the higher or nobler attributes of manhood, were sent to the State to hunt him as they would a wild beast bent on devouring the land. His command, in a very large measure, was composed of young Kentuckians like himself—young men who had been correctly

CAPTAIN JOHN BROOKS,
Aid-de-camp General Johnson's Staff.

reared and total strangers to any act that would smack of inhumanity to man or the wholesale robbery of their friends and acquaintances. They were men like himself, who enjoyed the countenance and esteem of the communities in which they were reared, and yet, notwithstanding all this, Johnson and his command were given the credit for all that was done by interlopers and bad men who had associated together without authority from any source save that emanating from their own wicked desires. The opportunity for theft in many ways was great, and bad men stood ready to take advantage of the situation, and for the acts of all such, Johnson's command was given much of the odium attaching to such conduct. Thus it was, he was not only forced to fight his own battles, but compelled to withstand or else combat the influence of combines who were thieving and committing other outlawries under the pretense of being members of his command. Thus it will be seen that his time spent in Kentucky was hedged in on all sides by a .multitude of opposing conditions well calculated to drive a commanding officer to extremes and yet through it all he exercised the most complete control of his temper, and when wounded and incapacitated for further service, was in the zenith of his glory, commanding not alone the admiration of Confederates in the highest authority, but the people of that portion of Kentucky through which he had campaigned.

At the age of twenty General Johnson's disposition for wild adventure induced him to give up his Kentucky home and go to Texas, where he settled in what was then known as Hamilton valley, at that time the extreme frontier settlement. He soon after associated himself with a surveying party, and in the pursuit of his duties became engaged in frequent rencounters with the Indians, who were then in large numbers. He was compelled to exercise the greatest care, precaution and strategy to preserve not only the safety of his companions, but his own life also. The keenest vigilance which he found so absolutely essential soon became a second nature with him, and it was in this school that he learned the lesson which in the days of the great war between the States proved so valuable to him while acting in the capacity of scout or partisan ranger. His entire frontier life up to and including a part of the war was replete with the wildest and most daring adventure, showing him to have been a man of great intelligence and unlimited nerve and courage.

General Johnson was of the greatest service at the battle of Fort

Donelson and the Corinth Campaign subsequent to the battle of
Shiloh; commanded a brigade with Morgan in his Indiana and Ohio
raid and escaped at Buffington Island by swimming the Ohio river,
while a large majority of Morgan's men, including that chieftain,
were captured. On coming to this immediate section of Kentucky,
in the effort to increase the depleted ranks of the Confederate army,
he necessarily created much excitement among the Union men, and
they, of course, left no stone unturned to have him driven from the
country. He fought a number of battles of minor importance, and
was generally successful in carrying his point. The Indiana border
was aroused to a pitch of absolute fright, possibly never known by
any community. Evansville, a city of twenty-five or thirty thousand
population, was kept guarded by soldiery and gunboats, and notwithstanding Johnson had but a handful of men to contend with
this superior force backed by the Government, the Evansville newspapers displayed at all times an alarm that was amazing.

The capture of Newburg by Johnson and a dozen or more men
set the Indiana border from Evansville to New Albany afire with
excitement. At Newburg the Confederates crossed the Ohio river
in midday by the use of skiffs, scows and old boats, in the face of
a population of fifteen hundred citizens, including one hundred and
eighty soldiers in hospital, a majority of whom were able for light
duty. Johnson, with one or two men, captured the hospital, paroled
the soldiers, and removed one hundred or more stand of arms to the
river, and had them successfully ferried across to the Kentucky side.
Steamboats loaded with soldiers and conveyed by a gunboat were
hurried from Evansville to Newburg to reinforce a command of
home guards rushed in from the country to drive away or capture
Johnson and a dozen or more men who had recrossed the river
and were lying in wait at the mouth of Green river for the transports and gunboats. It was the first time the great State of Indiana
had been invaded by the enemy, and the disgrace was well nigh
unbearable; especially so when it was discovered that a community
of fifteen hundred or more, together with near two hundred soldiers
splendidly armed, had unconditionally surrendered to General Adam
Johnson and a couple of dozen men armed with shotguns, and required to cross and recross the Ohio river in broad daylight in skiffs and
ill-conditioned little boats. The little band of Confederate braves had
scarcely recrossed the Ohio when a mountain of dust rising from
the main thoroughfares leading into the town of Newburg indicated

the appearance of a hastily-organized army of countrymen armed to the teeth en route to drive Johnson and his men from Indiana's sacred soil. They quickly arrived in the town and were soon upon the river bank, but the birds had flown and it was left them to wreak their vengeance upon a few non-combatants who were accused of meeting the Confederates with an approving smile and aiding them in the work they had done. How different was the treatment of these men as compared with that of Union men and soldiers by Johnson and his men! Johnson treated the citizens with the utmost civility, and yet he knew that the greatest precaution must be exercised for there were non-combatants around and about who would have assassinated him and his men in a moment but for the fear they had of impending consequences. These men were known, but were civilly treated, and yet after his departure and the arrival of the motley aggregation from the country into the town, two men who had been pressed into service by Johnon were brutally shot down in the streets while a number of others were arrested and transported to Evansville as prisoners of war. This treatment of men accused of being rebel sympathizers was declared to be all right by the Republican newspapers, but the action of Johnson and his men for invading the State was denounced in the most brutal language to be employed. They were denominated thieves, marauders, murderers, assassins, and a regiment was sent forth-with to capture or kill the last one of them.

Just prior to the capture of Newburg General Johnson had received the surrender of Henderson, and for a day had control of the city. It was during this time, by his words and orders the anxiety of the citizens were greatly relieved; especially were those who were politically opposed to him. He assured a committee of citizens who had gone out from the city to meet him that his orders were positive as to the treatment of citizens. He had not come to wage war upon non-combatants because of their political opinions, but only upon those who were combatant enemies of the cause for which he had left his home-circle and sacrificed his business. He proposed to disturb none but those who were in actual warfare against the Confederacy. He entered the city and faithfully kept every promise he had made the citizens' committee. He stood upon his native heath a conqueror, bold and fearless, and it was for him alone to indicate by word and order what his policy should be. His spirit lost none of that grand and resplendent evidence of honest blood and noble purpose imparted by his sainted mother, and it was not for him to violate any of those teachings so sacred to his heart. His orders were conciliatory, temperate and just, and upon his assurances many professed Union men, who, dreading his approach, had fled to Indiana, recrossed the river and admitted him to be a soldier of liberal, congenial, honest, humane motives instead of the wild uncultured, heartless desperado pictured by Republican newspapers and others who could not find it within the limit of their narrow consciences to do him even partial justice. Governor Archibald Dixon and other leading and influential citizens, unflinching in their adhesion to the Union, and unqualifiedly in favor of the suppression of the rebellion, were callers at his headquarters, and were received by him with the utmost cordiality and treated as though they were among his warmest and most trusted political friends. As a sample of the fairness accorded him by the Republican newspapers, the following, printed in the columns of the Evansville Journal at the time, is here reproduced:

"THE REBEL FLAG IN HENDERSON.

" By the arrival of two citizens from Henderson yesterday noon, we have reliable information that the guerrillas entered that place yesterday morning in considerable force and hoisted the rebel flag on the court house and hotel. It was stated that they had thrown pickets across the river, but this is doubted. One thing is certain— that the people of Indiana will not allow our State to be invaded for a moment. Later—A gentleman arrived from Henderson last evening and says the town is occupied by about forty guerrillas who seem to be enjoying themselves very greatly. He says the citizens of Henderson cheered them as they entered the town, and they were treated with great consideration by many citizens. At latest account Honorable Arch. Dixon and others were negotiating with Colonel Johnson to have the guerrillas withdrawn from the town."

It will be observed that the command was denominated as guer-rillas; nevertheless, it was a regular authorized body of Confederates. On reading the foregoing article in the Evansville paper, Colonel Johnson was impressed with the force of the following sentence: " One thing is certain—that the people of Indiana will not allow our State to be invaded for a moment." He thereupon determined upon the Newburg raid, and for the inception of that daring visitation, the Evansville paper is entitled to all of the credit.

In passing out of Henderson en route to Newburg, the evening of the first night was spent in camp on the farm of Mr. William Soaper, a mile or more out on the Owensboro road. Adjoining Mr. Soaper was the farm of E. W. Worsham. Mr. Soaper was known as a conservative Union man, while Mr. Worsham was regarded as a conservative sympathizer with the South. It was necessary to feed the horses of the command, and upon that a question presented itself that was decided in keeping with all that Colonel Johnson had promised. By the decision additional evidence of the integrity and honesty of purpose on the part of Colonel Johnson was made still more manifest. The camp had been pitched upon Mr. Soaper's farm and its owner was a man of great wealth for those days. He was not a Confederate sympathizer, and with most commanding officers it would have been decided to impress what was needed from the Soaper farm to feed the men and stock; but not so. So anxious was Colonel Johnson to do the fair thing, to do nothing that might be construed into a disposition to oppress or inflict punishment upon one who differed honestly in his political opinions from him and the cause represented by him, he requested Mr. Worsham, at whose house he was making his headquarters for the time being, to call upon Mr. Soaper the next morning and obtain from him a statement of the provender taken from his farm and to remunerate him in any amount that might be agreed on between the two, and then to report his acts to him. Mr. Worsham did as requested, and, as might have been expected, Mr. Soaper declined to make any charge for the provender required.

There are hundreds of instances of honest dealing and fair treatment of citizens by Colonel Johnson, and yet no man was more unjustly abused by his enemies, and that, too, in the face of evidence easily attained, but not desired, because of the injury it would have been to the purposes in view in maligning him. He was held responsible for the acts of unauthorized and irresponsible bands of men, many of whom were known to have been deserters from the Federal army, and more afraid of Johnson than they were of the army they had deserted, and whose acts would have been visited by the severest punishment had they been captured. No officer was ever more unfairly treated by his enemies, non-combatant and in regular line.

THE NEWBURG VICTORY.

The fruits of the victory achieved at Newburg when summed up showed the capture and paroling of one hundred and eighty prisoners, the capture of three hundred stand of arms, an immense supply of medical stores and ammunition, to which was added the prestige of being the first Confederate command that ever dared to invade the free soil of a State north of the Ohio river. Insignificant as this brilliant achievement may now appear, it nevertheless at the time made a very decided impression upon the press of this as well as foreign lands. The London Times, in a lengthy article, acknowledged the capture of the great tobacco port of Henderson, Kentucky, the subsequent capture of an important town north of the Ohio river—in all, conceded to be a very decided Confederate success. The following account of the capture of Newburg appeared in the Evansville Journal of July 18, 1862, which gives a fair idea of the intense excitement produced by Colonel Johnson and his handful of men in the capture of the Indiana town:

"GUERRILLA RAID INTO INDIANA.

"A. R. Johnson's Cavalry.   The Hospital Plundered.
The Legion Under Arms.   Great
Excitement.

"About three o'clock yesterday afternoon our city was thrown into great excitement by the arrival of a messenger from Newburg with the intelligence that a squad of forty of A. R. Johnson's marauders had crossed the river at Newburg and plundered the hospital at that place. The signal of danger was at once given, and in less than one hour one thousand men were under arms, and cannon went rattling through our streets. The city, which has been in a lamentable state of torpor for months was thoroughly aroused, and every man who could get a musket, rifle, shotgun or revolver was at once under arms, and hundreds more were eagerly seeking weapons for aggression or for defense. The alacrity with which the citizens responded gave most cheering evidence that when convinced of danger our people are equal to any emergency. A company of infantry, together with a squad of artillery, with two guns, were taken on board the steamboat 'Eugene' at 6:30 o'clock for the scene of the trouble. Captain Dexter had the steamer 'Courier' fired up with all possible dispatch, and having armed his crew, and with a squad of infantry, steamed off up the river. He was fearfully in earnest and declared his determination to prevent the rebels from recrossing the river if they were found on this side, and to use the ' Courier ' as a ram in case of need. The saucy little steamer went out flying light and running for glory. The' Eugene ' made excellent time also, and with guns on each guard and decks crowded with men, made a formidable appearance. We learn that the chivalrous horde who make war on sick soldiers in unguarded hospitals, did not tarry long in Newburg, but skulked back across the river after they had stolen what they could. A Union soldier arrived from Newburg and says the rebels number thirty-two men. They stole all the arms and equipments to be found, a lot of provisions, paroled all of the Union soldiers in the hospital, stole a wagon and two horses, and then recrossed the river. Two men, residents of Newburg, who were notorious secesh sympathizers and who came over the river with the guerrillas and remained when the latter returned, were shot down and killed by a citizen. Their names were Carney and Mefford. The ' Courier ' returned at nine o'clock and reported that she proceeded to the mouth of Green river, where she found the boat in which the marauders had crossed the river, and which they took possession of. A man on the point dressed in a red shirt stepped out of the brush and fired on the boat with a shotgun, wounding one of the hands on the boat slightly. The boys on the boat fired into the brush, but with what effect is not known. They took one man prisoner, whom they handed over to the ' Eugene.' The ' Courier ' having performed her mission, returned to the city. The ' Eugene ' proceeded on to Newburg. It is said that the rebels had four pieces of artillery planted on the Kentucky shore. If this is so and they remain there until the ' Eugene ' arrived, there would be somebody hurt, sure, as our boys went up to rid the world of all such cowardly thieves as those who rob hospitals.

" Several reports of artillery were heard about eight o'clock, since which time all has been quiet. Evansville is full of armed men, and an earnest spirit prevails. It is supposed the guerrillas got some two hundred guns and paroled about eighty-five sick soldiers. They occupied the town some three or four hours. The citizens watched the guerrillas crossing the river and, strange as it may seem, offered not the slightest resistance.

" By the steamer ' Eugene,' which returned from Newburg Saturday morning about two o'clock, we gather the following particulars in addition to those published in Saturday's Journal: The steamer 'Eugene,' with two companies of convalescent soldiers and a section of the Union artillery, left, as stated in Saturday's Journal, about 5:30 o'clock, preceded by the 'Courier' and 'Commercial.' On coming in sight of Green river, the 'Courier' and 'Commercial' were discovered 'lying to' and soon a jet of smoke from a little swivel on the 'Courier's' forecastle indicated that she was firing at some object on shore. The 'Eugene' ran up Green river about a mile and landed one of the companies, who were deployed across the narrow peninsula between the two rivers as skirmishers, but the birds had flown. The ferryman, whose wife informed our boys that he was a 'States rights' man, was arrested, and his flats, etc., placed in charge of the 'Courier,' which returned to the city, while the 'Eugene' went on to Newburg. On arriving at Newburg, it was found to be nearly filled with well-armed, resolute men, who had flocked in from the surrounding country to drive the marauders from the State. Colonel John W. Foster, after a short consultation with some of the citizens who had been robbed by the marauders, immediately passed over the river with the 'Eugene' and took possession of all the flats and skiffs that he could discover on the Kentucky side. Some were scuttled and others brought to Newburg. We then made careful inquiry of several of the citizens of the town, who gave us the particulars of their humiliation, as follows:

"Several citizens of the town, it is supposed have been in communication with the guerrillas for many days. Indeed, five men heretofore living in Newburg are known to have joined the rebels. Their names are Robt. Slaughter, Wm. Lukin, Andy Mefford, Jim O'Connell, Chas. Applegate. They are outlaws, and every citizen is justifiable is shooting them down wherever and whenever he comes across them. The guerrillas were thoroughly posted, both as to the defenseless condition of the town and the carelessness of its inhabitants. On Thursday one of the two men who was shot (we think it was Mefford), who had been absent for several days, returned. On Friday he went across the river and held a consultation with Johnson and his pirate gang. About noon on Friday, when most of the citizens were away from the landing and at their dinners, the marauders placed themselves in the ferry boat, concealing themselves as well as possible, and rowed rapidly across the river. On landing in Newburg, a dash was made for the hospital, and the arms found there secured. Pickets and guards were thrown out in every direction, and the citizens given to understand that their only chance of safety was in keeping quiet. Johnson, the leader of the precious pack of thieves, informed the citizens that he had a battery planted on the opposite side of the river, and if any resistance was made to his demands he would immediately shell and destroy the place. The fellow is as proficient in lying as well as stealing. With cool audacity, the leader of the gang of 'free-booters' then made out paroles of honor for all the soldiers in the hospital which he signed as 'A. R. Johnson, C. S. A.' Meanwhile his men, guided by some of the citizens of the town, commenced pillaging. Horses were taken out of their stables, dwellings entered and searched, the hospital was ransacked and everything calculated to be of any service to them was appropriated. The doors of the dwelling of Mr. Union Bethel were broken open and the whole house ransacked. The horses of several from the country were pointed out and taken. In one stable the free-booters were on the point of taking all the horses, when one was pointed out to them as the property of Jesse Fuller, of Boonville, which was passed, the scoundrels remarking that 'Jesse was all right.' Several of the citizens of the town mingled freely with Johnson and his gang, drank with them, and seemed highly gratified in having made their acquaintance. As some of these men are under arrest, it may be proper not to criticise their conduct too severely just at present. After remaining in the town four or five hours the free-booters departed with their ill-gotten gains. Andrew Huston, a resident of Newburg, helped to ferry the scoundrels across the river, and was very busy in carrying arms that they had stolen from the hospital to the boat. He was arrested by Colonel Foster and brought to this city.

"After the robbers had departed, two of the citizens, H. H. Carney and Elliott Mefford, who had been particularly active in pointing out property for seizure, were attacked by some of the citizens. Carney was shot dead in the street and left lying there for several hours. He afterwards was thrown into a wagon. Mefford was shot and bayoneted, but not killed. We learn that he was shot again on Saturday morning and killed. One or two others who were suspected of sympathizing with the rebels to the extent of giving them aid and comfort, narrowly escaped with their lives from the exasperated citizens. Old Warrick county was ablaze;

from every part of the county the yeomanry came pouring into the town, and by nine o'clock in the evening six hundred or seven hundred armed men had arrived. The 'Eugene' left at twelve o'clock, having on board the following prisoners: Andrew Huston, Sol. Koker, John Husk, Wm. Lee, Joseph Fuller and Geo. Wayes. These men will be disposed of as Governor Morton may direct."

The Evansville Journal of July 21, 1862, contained the following very remakable editorial production:

"WAR ON THE BORDER.

"The cowardly raid committed by A. R. Johnson, who is ashamed to append his title to his signature, and his gang of thieves upon the hospital at Newburg has aroused our people to a degree never equalled. The sturdy yeomanry of Warrick county, as soon as they heard of the cowardly thieving operations of this bold proclaimer, who sedulously avoids meeting armed men, rushed to arms with an impetuosity that manifested how ready Indianians were to meet and resent an insult or an outrage, and we much mistake the temper of our citizens and of the people at large if the most terrible retribution is not speedily wreaked upon the bandit horde. Even savages and barbarians would scorn to make war on sick and defenseless men and rob hospitals, but this vapid boaster and chief of hospital robbers seems to have no stomach but for such barbarous deeds. Why don't he come to Evansville? He knows he would meet such a reception as would send his soul reeking with murder and robbery to the regions of the arch fiend, his master. His name and that of his gang are in the possession of the people, and unless they beget themselves speedily to a safe place far beyond the borders of Kentucky or Tennessee, they may as well make their wills and take farewells of their families.

"The decree has gone forth in Indiana that the cowardly outrage at Newburg must be wiped out with traitors' blood. The Hoosiers are aroused and their vengeance is terrible."

The humiliation experienced by the people of Indiana over the capture of Newburg was more than terrible, and may have offered the Evansville Journal and other Union newspapers an excuse for indulging in the vitriolic language, the foregoing of which is a fair sample. General Johnson and a dozen more men in midday crossed the Ohio river in badly conditioned skiffs and little boats of one kind and another, captured a town containing a citizenship of fully one thousand men, together with eighty-five or more sick and convalescent soldiers splendidly armed, and two hundred stand of arms and an abundance of ammunition close by without firing a gun. The battery of artillery planted on the Kentucky shore, its gun pointed at the town and threatening its destruction, was nothing more nor less than an old charred log placed on the wheels of a dilapidated two-horse wagon and a stovepipe similarly mounted. As an evidence of the fright under which the Indianians labored at the sight of Johnson's battery, it may be cited that there was not one who even thought of bringing to bear an opera or spyglass, by the use of which the genuineness of the battery could have been established in ten seconds, and the real strength of the command exposed. In the face of all the facts associated with this, the most courageously daring and utter disregard of the safety of himself and his little band of fearless troopers, Colonel Johnson and his men were denounced as cowards by the Evansville Journal and other mediums for the dissemination of news, while citizens, home guards and Colonel John W. Foster, with three steamboats and soldiers convoyed by a gunboat with abundant artillery sent to whip twenty or more men armed with shot guns, were lauded to the skies as courageous heroes, totally ignorant of fear.

Johnson was denounced as a heartless knave, a thief, a poltroon, a robber of the sick, because, forsooth, taking his life in hand he went in person to a hospital filled with Federal soldiers, a majority of whom were amply able to load a gun and fire, and reload and fire again, with hundreds of guns and ammunition in great abundance close at hand, and demand their surrender together with all of the government supplies in store in the building. For three or four hours his men were engaged in removing the captured guns and government supplies to his little boats at the river, and never an effort was made to prevent. The mounted wooden cannon on the Kentucky bank had demoralized the whole town for four or five hours and no effort was made to discover its character or the possible damage it might inflict. Not a citizen or non-combatant in Newburg on that day was subjected to insult or personal injury by Johnson or his men, but in return for his kindly and most conservative course, he had scarcely recrossed Green river and out of hearing of the Comanche yells of the approaching home guards rushing in from the country contiguous to Newburg, men who had been impressed into service by Colonel Johnson were spotted, denounced as rebel sympathizers, and two were shot and killed most brutally, while a number of others were placed under arrest and forcibly carried from their homes prisoners of war.   Patriots, model heroes, courageous hearts were these men, while Colonel Johnson who had executed a deed of daring unparalleled throughout the war was denounced as a coward, a thief, a poltroon, a robber, and so on, ad infinitum, and that, too, in face of the pronounced fact that the war he made was upon combatants and government property and not upon private citizens and what they possessed.   I have dwelt at a greater extent, perhaps, than the demands require in the matter of the capture of Newburg, but it was done to conserve the purpose of showing how mercilessly and unjustly Colonel Johnson and his men were abused by non-combatant enemies who owed him better treatment. He was never immune to that character of misrepresentation and abuse, no matter how honestly he observed the announcements made by him on his visit into Kentucky, concerning his treatment of those people, in order that the present and following generation may know more accurately of his object and aim in coming into Kentucky so early after the outbreaking of the rebellion. When it is considered that Colonel Johnson, at the time of the capture of Newburg was only twenty-six years of age and had for several years been engaged in fighting Indians on the Texas frontier, it was very greatly to his credit that he retained such excellent control of himself. Especially is this true when we consider the relentless fury with which he was hunted and pursued, and the bitter and most determined abuse, misrepresentation and other unwarranted treatment he and his command were subjected to by those opposing him.   It is more of a wonder that he had not been driven to a condition of desperation and had determined upon a war with the black flag as his emblem.   Contrary, however, while secreted in the chaparral of a farm near Henderson, he wrote a conciliatory proclamation which had no difficulty in getting into print.

ANOTHER EXCITING INCIDENT.

One of the most exciting and at the same time most overdrawn and unreliable statements of the conditions connected with it, was the attack made on the last Sunday night in June, 1862, by Colonel Johnson, Bob Martin and Amplias Owen, calling themselves "The Breckinridge Guards," on what was then known as the

Central Hotel, a double brick house located on the east side of Main street between Fourth and Fifth and occupied by a company of soldiers under command of Captain Daly. These troops had been sent to Henderson a few days prior to the attack made, for a purpose, it is needless to mention just now. Johnson, Martin and Owen at that time were endeavoring to increase their numbers and were in the vicinity of Slaughtersville where information was sent them of the arrival in Henderson of Captain Daly's command. A council of war was held and the three men determined to proceed with all possible dispatch to Henderson and make a night attack with their shotguns upon the troops camped in the hotel. This they did, firing from the opposite side of the street into the soldiers sitting about on the front pavement and inside the building. At the first fire there was a rush made by those on the outside for the inside of the house and the doors and windows were immediately fastened. The three Confederates then moved to the old cemetery in the rear of the hotel, and finding the soldiers safely housed they returned to their horses and galloped out of town. The following account of the attack made by the three men named appeared in the Evansville Journal of July 1st, the day following the attack, and shows what reckless disregard newspaper writers of that day and time had for the truthful statement of facts so easily to have been secured. The Journal's report, headlines and all, is here reproduced:

"WAR ON THE BORDER,

Bloody Fight at Henderson, Ky. Guerrillas Attack the Provost Guards. Federal Loss, One Killed, Eleven Wounded. Rebel Loss Not Ascertained. The Guerrillas Driven Off.

" At ten o'clock on Sunday night, an attack was made on a company of provost guards stationed in Henderson under command of Captain Daly, by a party of guerrillas supposed to number one hundred and fifty men. On Sunday the provost guard had arrested a notorious rebel guerrilla, named Griffin, and had him confined in the National Hotel which was occupied as quarters by Captain Daly and his company. An attack was anticipated and Captain Daly was keeping a careful lookout for it. A short time before the attack was made the captain with one of his men made a reconnoissance, when they discovered men skulking up back alleys and behind board fences armed with shotguns. Captain Daly then returned to the hotel, aroused his men and ordered them to lie on their arms ready to resist an attack, and then sat down in the door to watch the movements of the rebels. He had scarcely seated himself when a volley was fired and the captain and one or two other men were wounded. The fight at once became warm. Captain Daly sprang to his feet to rally and encourage his men when he received a second wound and a third. His men fought well and to the best advantage they could under the circumstances, and finally succeeded in driving the guerrillas off. During the fight Captain Daly received three ugly wounds, seven buckshot striking him in his left leg below the knee, three balls passing through and four lodging in his leg. He also received two or three balls in his right leg and one in his arm, Lieutenant Tyler, second in command, was pierced by six balls and died in about half an hour. Second Lieutenant Daly, brother to the captain, received an ugly wound in his right leg below the knee. Nine others of the provost guard were wounded more or less severely. The loss of the rebels can not be ascertained. Numbers were seen to fall and one was heard to exclaim that he was killed. Several pools of blood were found and evidence manifest where killed or wounded men had been dragged away. It is thought that four or five of the guerrillas were killed and several wounded. A number of convalescent soldiers of the hospital were sent to reinforce Captain Daly, and further reinforcements are on the way. We think it would be proper to send a company of a hundred men from this city to assist the provost guard until reinforcements can reach Henderson from Louisville. A large company might be made up from citizens and convalescent soldiers now in the city. The war is coming close to our doors and Evansville may soon need defenders. The officers of the Legion should rally their men and be ready for any emergency. The guerrillas are growing more bold every day and if not speedily checked may cause great trouble and damage along our border. The property holders in this city and in all the border towns of Indiana are interested.

"Will they look to their interests or will they sleep on?"

This article, on being read by the three men who had caused all of the excitement, was greatly enjoyed, especially that part of it reciting that a number of dead rebels had been dragged away from the scene of the conflict. The citizens of Henderson were very much excited and the day after the attack a public meeting of the citizens was held and resolutions reflecting upon the action of the three Confederates were passed. The resolutions were printed in the town papers and of course fell into the hands of the Confederates. They were considerably exercised at the time and determined on visiting Henderson again, and having an explanation. With this view of the situaton, Johnson and Martin came to the Barrett farm near the town and there, in secret, Colonel Johnson addressed the following letter to ex-Governor A. Dixon, Colonel James Shackelford, John G. Holloway, James B. Lyne, and others whose names were attached to the resolutions passed at the meeting of citizens.

JOHNSON'S LETTER.

Headquarters Breckinridge Guards, July 6, 1862.

Gentlemen:

Noticing in one of the Henderson papers a series of resolutions condoling with the Federal troops on their loss in a recent attack made on them, and denouncing the attacking party as thieves, murderers and robbers and declaring war on those who made that attack, I wish to thoroughly understand the position you occupy. As it was a portion of my command that made that attack and every man engaged being a sworn Confederate soldier, I conclude that your declaration is against my government. My orders when I was sent to this department were imperative regarding citizens and their property. I was charged not to molest them in any manner unless they were engaged in war upon us. Now, gentlemen, you perceive why I wish to have a definite answer upon this point. If you are fully resolved to war against us, we will necessarily be compelled to fight you. I have repeatedly said to Union men who are now living in Henderson that I did not intend to molest any citizen on account of his politics. I have written to the same effect, and I now repeat it, but I contend that each and every one who signed those resolutions have placed themselves without the pale, and I await an answer to this to show you what it really means to be an enemy to us. I deprecate civil war and have used my best endeavors to avoid coming in contact with citizens, and here I reiterate a piece of advice given to Mr.

Delano, viz., for citzens to let soldiers fight their own battles. If they do not wish to see and hear the din of war in their midst, let them have their town cleared of bluecoats and I will guarantee that no one of them will be molested by Confederate soldiers.

I want all persons to know that we are at war with the Federal soldiers and if they will shut themselves up in houses will sometimes give them a little fight just for recreation. Attached to this is a list of names signed to those resolutions, all of whom I consider as having declared war against the Confederate States and each name that I do not find appended to an article denying that to be their intention, I shall hold him as an enemy, and his property subject to confiscation. The said article must be published in the Reporter by Thursday the 17th of July, 1862. All those so appearing shall not be in any manner molested by my men. I have sent a copy of the resolutions to the army.

A. R. JOHNSON, C. S. A.

List of names—Rev. Joel Lambert, Col. J. M. Shackelford, Hon. A. Dixon, Peter Semonin, John G. Holloway, Jas. B. Lyne, C. W. Hutchen, James H. Holloway.

This letter was intrusted to Colonel Bob Martin, a comrade of Colonel Johnson, to be delivered to Governor Dixon in person. The privilege of undertaking this dangerous venture was greatly appreciated by Colonel Martin, a man who, like his commander, knew no fear. Accompanied by a comrade named Hollis, a recruit of the day previous, Martin started on his journey to Henderson and to Governor Dixon's residence. The town at the time was garrisoned by a company of Federal troops and every road leading out of it was closely guarded by pickets. The story of Martin's entry and how he employed his time during his stay of three or four hours will be found elsewhere in this history and is intensely interesting. Replies to Colonel Johnson's letter were received by him from C. W. Hutchen, Rev. Joel Lambert, Peter Semonin and Governor Dixon, all named in Colonel Johnson's letter to Governor Dixon.

C. W. HUTCHEN'S REPLY.

Henderson, July 16, 1862.

Henderson Reporter:

On yesterday I received a letter from A. R. Johnson to Governor Dixon, myself and others. I have only this reply to make. No man of common sense could or would construe the action

of the citizens' meeting in question as a declaration of war against
the so-called Confederate States.   I had no such intention nor
do I suppose any one of the large meeting dreamed of anything of
the sort.

C. W. HUTCHEN.

LAMBERT AND SEMONIN'S REPLY.

Henderson Reporter:

In answer to the letter of A. R. Johnson we have to reply that
we are now and have ever been Union men, but never have
joined nor do we expect to join the army, but are now and expect
to hold ourselves ready at all times to join with any law and order
citizens to put down bands of marauders and robbers, but we do
not class as such regular bodies of organized troops carrying on
war in a legitimate manner and under the authority of a regular
organized government and we did not intend in the resolution to
make war upon the forces of the Confederate Government, nor
can we understand how any man of ordinary intellect could so
construe them.

JOEL LAMBERT,
PETER SEMONIN.

GOVERNOR DIXON'S REPLY.

Henderson, July 13, 1862.

A. R. Johnson, C. S. A.:

Sir: In response to interrogatories contained in a letter addressed
by you to myself and others, I have only to say that the resolutions
adopted by the meeting referred to were not as I understand them,
a declaration either of myself or the citizens of Henderson to do
anything but assist in putting down a band of lawless men who,
as we learned, were unauthorized by either the Federal Government
or the Southern Confederacy, and who are engaged in robbing and
plundering the honest citizens of Henderson county, both Union and
Southern Rights.

That band is condemned by all honorable men here whether
of Union or Southern Rights proclivities and who are determined to put it down at whatever hazard or sacrifice.   I am glad
to learn that you do not countenance and that the Confederate
Government does not authorize it.   Whatever may be the merits
of the rebellion, this predatory warfare surely has nothing to redeem it in the estimation of those who would not upheave the
foundations of society and scourge with fire and sword the fairest

portions of Kentucky.   I can not speak with certainty of the
object of the other members of the committee—I think we had a
common purpose—but for myself I disclaim all intention of declaring war against the Confederate States or of making myself a
belligerent in the present unhappy contest between the sections and
agree with you that it is better that the citizens should take no
part in it, and that if it must be settled by the sword that the
armies alone should fight the battles, and as your orders are not
to interfere with private persons or property, but to protect them,
may not the people of Henderson rely on your aid in suppressing
the lawless bands who are committing so many wrongs throughout the country?   To me the declaration in your letter that your
orders are not to interfere with private property or persons on
account of their Union principles is very gratifying.   These orders
are right and strictly conformable to the rules of warfare established by all civilized nations and you must be greatly changed
since I knew you if you do not as a man of honor `comply
with them in letter and spirit.   To seize and confiscate the
property of Union men on account of a difference in politics would
be not only to provoke retaliation on their part but on the part of
the Federal Government, which is bound to protect them, and in
this way all, both Southern Rights and Union men, would be
involved in indiscriminate and general ruin.   So horrible has this
war seemed to me from the beginning that I have had no heart
to take part in it.   It has been a war in Kentucky of father against
son and son against father, a war that has broken the ties of
friendship, severed the sacred bonds that bound brother to brother,
destroyed the relation between the citizen and his government, and
left him almost ready to exclaim in the desponding language of
the ruined and banished Bertram, 'I have no country; that name
comprises dear kindred, kind friends, protecting laws; all that binds
man to man, but none of these are mine.'   That there may be
no misunderstanding, I will have your letter published with this,
my reply.   I have the honor to be

Your obedient servant, etc.,

ARCHIBALD DIXON.

Colonel Johnson's letter served its purpose and the replies proved
to be most satisfactory.   The fact that they denied any intention
of making war upon him or the Confederate States Government
was a pleasing announcement.   It will be observed that Governor

CAPTAIN WM. DIMMETT,

1st Capt. afterwards 2d Chaplain of Co. H, 10th Ky., P. R.

Dixon referred most touchingly to the days he knew Colonel Johnson and his high honor. When it was learned that it was his command that had made the attack and that he was a regularly enrolled Confederate soldier, the previous estimate became greatly changed and all hands were ready to combine with him, or rather to accept his aid in ridding the country of predatory bands of men such as had been ignorantly credited to him. Knowing him and his honorable character, rabid Union shriekers settled down under a feeling of security in the fact that he was as bitter an enemy of the bands to be feared as they were themselves. Shortly after or about the time of the passage of the letters between Colonel Johnson and the citizens' committee, the Colonel caused the following proclamation to be given prominent publication throughout this section of Kentucky, setting forth more fully his object and aims in invading the State.

COLONEL JOHNSON'S PROCLAMATION.

Citizens of Kentucky:

It has gone forth to the world that you are a subjugated people, that the iron heel of despotism has destroyed all spirit of resistance and crushed out the last spark of patriotism. This idea has gone through the North and they look upon you with contempt and send their hirelings to rule over you. It has crossed the Atlantic, and the eyes of all Europe have been looking at the position of Kentucky with wonder and astonishment. Down in the Sunny South amongst those who ought to be your brothers you have become a byword and a scoff. The Kentucky army have turned their anxious eyes to their native State and at each new outrage would listen for the tocsin of war, but they have listened and hoped against hope until the last ray has expired. The Confederate Cabinet and Congress have looked for some movement indicating a desire for freedom, but they have looked in vain and think Kentucky lost. But there is one man who has never despaired; that man is John C. Breckinridge, the hero, the statesman and the patriot. With the same never despairing love that a mother bears to her offspring, does he regard Kentucky, with the same anxious case has he watched her. He has asked his government and the world to suspend public opinion until his State shall have one more opportunity to redeem her character and now, citizens of Kentucky, the opportunity has presented itself, and for the sake of your former fame and glory—for your country—for your liberties which ought to be dearer to you than life itself, come to the field. Rally to your country's call, rise in your majesty and might and drive from your midst this monster of oppression.

Then prepare now to meet the enemy; send the young men to the field, let them retrieve the character of this once proud and noble State. Circulate through the country that the Confederate Government does not war against the citizens of the country. Can you, with the example set by the people of the South tamely submit? They have with heroic devotion applied the torch to their property and with unparalleled unanimity have they battled for their country.

Will you not risk as much as they to achieve your freedom and independence?   A. R. JOHNSON, C. S. A."

The Breckinridge Guards at that time numbered four men, but their daring not only attracted the attention of the young men of the State, but appealed to their love of the South and the Southern people to such an extent recruits began to rapidly pour in and a very dangerous command was beginning to manifest and make itself felt. Colonel Johnson was idolized by his men, in fact, there was none other to be compared with him. At the time of the terrible wounding inflicted upon him he was in the zenith of his greatness, and men were flocking to him in such numbers that George D. Prentice, in the Louisville Journal, warned the Government that unless an army sufficiently strong to drive them out of the State was sent on his trail, he would become so strong it would be a most costly and difficult matter to rid the State of him and his unparalleled influence in behalf of the Southern army.

In this brief contribution to a life and character of a truly great and deserving Kentuckian, I have endeavored to place him correctly before the present age. He was unmercifully abused and with little genuine reason for it. His conduct since the total loss of his eyesight has rendered his life beautiful, and if possible has endeared him to his old comrades with a force and affectionate regard and admiration never approximated even in the days when with sword in hand he led his heroic braves on and on in an unequal contest in which victory perched upon their waving banners. He fought numerous battles in which he was largely outnumbered, but that did not deter him, and on he rode to victory until his brightest and most earnest hopes had been well nigh realized, when,

COLONEL JAS. H. HOLLOWAY, U. S. A.

at an unguarded moment Fate called a halt, and his usefulness as a leader of men in mortal combat was brought to speedy and everlasting end. Nothing daunted by becoming in his young manhood a physical wreck, he returned to his adopted State, and by the exercise of a rare intelligence accumulated a handsome competency and reared a most charming family of splendid children. He is nearing the twilight of his life and yet retains much of the energy and vigor that characterized his younger years.

ADAM R. JOHNSON.

A Characteristic Sketch, by James R. Holloway (Colonel Battalion of Cavalry, Crittenden's Division, Federal Army).

General Adam R. Johnson and myself were both born in Henderson city, Henderson county, Kentucky, about the same year, 1835, and our early lives were paralleled along very much the same lines: congenial spirits in many respects, attending the same schools, engaging in the same sports; our experiences, very like, both getting good or bad marks for lessons at school, the same switch and ferule left more less their imprint on us. Our sports and frolics night or day partook much the same direction and Adam Johnson, possessed of self-reliance and adroitness and natural strenuosity, led, and I, a good second, followed.

He was ever characterized by a genius in designing and a boldness in executing, and as a leader among the boys, got us into and out of many scrapes. If we be-hoys wanted a holiday Adam knew how best to barricade the school-house doors and lock out the teacher, knew best how to tease the old William Goat and give the unwary boy the hardest butting; to place across a puddle of water a plank with the cracked side turned down and catch an unlucky pedestrian. Could reverse more saddles, change more doctors' and merchants' signs, put more gates and bars in the wrong place, rig up the queerest vehicles. In fact an all-around, strenuous be-hoy, running fastest, jumping highest and longest and throwing the straightest and truest ball, and batting hardest of most of us. Could catch more fish, kill more game, hunt more indefatigably and fish withal more patiently than any of us.

In attempting to write the varied incidents in the life of and give the salient points in the character of such an one who has, by his own individuality, lifted himself above the majority of his

ιℓllows, I find it difficult after a lapse of half a century and more
to recall to memory except in a general way, and select such incidents. Among the many of those I would like to insert, Adam
Johnson and I were always the warmest friends and most closely
associated of perhaps any two, and almost every Saturday at
early morn found us with fish lines, etc., and salt and pepper, fat
meat and crackers and biscuits in our pockets and game bags and
guns on our shoulders Trudging for and equipped for different
kinds of game to a point about three miles below Henderson
opposite an island in the Ohio river, where we usually secured
both fish and game, which we prepared; the fish, by removing the
entrails and salt and pepper and fat meat placed inside and
roasting in hot ashes and when done and the paper removed,
all the scales came off with it; the birds and squirrels were roasted
on spits and with melons and fruits foraged from nearby neighbors,
made a feast fit for a lord.

Occasionally accidents occurred. Our skiff would overturn and
planks on which we sometimes paddled over to the island would
sink and give us a ducking, but what cared we boys? One
incident I recollect while hunting ducks on the Indiana side of the
Ohio river. Adam, to get a better position for a shot, walked out
about forty feet on a large rotten log that had fallen into the
water and raising his gun to fire, the log gave way and down
he fell in water about three feet deep; a rather amusing scene
occurred as he made effort to save his gun from a wetting. As he
lifted his arm aloft with his gun, his body went under the water and
after some struggles he and gun finally got to shore, wet and
muddy; and as we returned home he proposed we would take
a wash in the Ohio, and though the 12th day of November we both
went in and took a good swim and wash. I could relate other
incidents of his boyhood days, but let this suffice, as such gives, I
think, an insight into his boyhood years and characteristics. When
about twenty years of age his adventurous spirit led him to leave
his Kentucky home and go alone to Texas and settle in a comparatively unknown and unexplored region, and thought by those
of his old Kentucky chums a very risky and in many respects a
foolhardy trip, and especially so when he wrote and related his
encounters with wild animals and wilder and more savage Indians
who made raids on his ranch, stealing his horses and cattle. We
kept up a correspondence that to me was a great pleasure for years,

and he was my hero of a man and I frequently dreaded to learn next of him for fear of some disaster to his ribs or scalp.

Thus passed the years till mail communication was broken off between the two sections of the country by the unhappy and dreadful Civil War, which divided families and embittered friends, especially in the border States like Maryland, Kentucky and Missouri; fathers against sons and brothers in different armies. In General Johnson's case, himself and two brothers were in the Southern army and two in the Northern army, the latter two in my command. For reasons I will not enumerate, I enlisted a company of infantry and joined the U. S. army, and after the battle of Shiloh the regiment to which I belonged, being much depleted, was consolidated with another Kentucky regiment and I resigned and raised a battalion of cavalry. But while engaged in infantry service and encamped at Calhoun, Kentucky, in General Tom Crittenden's division before January, 1862, I had frequently wondered what had become of my friend, Adam Johnson. No news of or from him, and he away down South in Dixie land. My bold hero and courageous friend, resting quietly on his oars and a tremendous conflict on hand! It was no conjecture or room for doubt with me as to which side my friend would draw sword, when he buckled on his armor, for was he not from the extreme South and he an adopted son of the Lone Star State with all his sympathies and interests there? Though I took sides against him and his section, I always loved and honored him for his manly courage. When I had a forty-eight hours leave of absence from camp at Calhoun, Kentucky, and visited at Henderson the 1st of January, 1862, I met Adam at a reception given me at my father's house that January eve, and when we parted that night at twelve o'clock (I to return to camp and he, as I hinted to him, to the Confederate camp) pledged a life long friendship for the future as of the past and though he gave no hint of what he really intended, except a visit to an old father and mother, yet I guessed I'd hear again from him, and did sooner than I expected, for on the third, sometime during the darkness of the night Colonel Johnson, who had a commission to raise a regiment of Kentuckians, with Lieutenant Colonel Robt. Martin, made a sly visit into Colonel Jim Jackson's cavalry camp at Calhoun, Kentucky, and took without leave or license a number of said Jackson's horses and arms of his sleeping soldiers, made off safely with them, and never to my knowledge did they return said property. And to crown it all, Colonel Johnson had the assurance to send me a sassy message, stating that since he had met me a few nights before he had joined the Confederate army, and as they needed horses and guns, and these were more accessible, please return his compliments to Colonel Jackson for the loan of same. From that time on for months he and his lieutenant colonel, Robt. Martin, made matters very lively in the Green river country as well as dangerous for those who were opposed to them, and I, as his old friend, was compelled, when visiting or prospecting that section, to take with me for safety a number of soldiers, his old neighbors and friends in ye olden time. His and mine were independent cavalry commands in the country between the Green and Cumberland rivers, and when out trying to establish order and protect the peace of its good citizens, and be as watchful and careful as I tried, would have some of his command unexpectedly and unceremoniously pounce down upon me and thus many a skirmish we had. Without going into detail, I will say that 'twas the general opinion of the military authorities of Kentucky, especially of those of us who had charge and operated in western Kentucky, that General Johnson and his command gave us more trouble and did more execution than any other. I tried to keep him down and regulate him so long as I had to meet his forces, but after following him across the borders of Kentucky, through Indiana and Ohio in General John Morgan's great raid, in which raid Colonel Johnson commanded a brigade, I returned to Kentucky, and in September, 1863, I was mustered out of service and did not again enlist. Colonel Johnson, however, after the Morgan raid, again returned to the Green river section of Kentucky and was most actively and successfully engaged with his command. Seemingly ubiquitous, pushing his successes in every direction, capturing towns and cities and many soldiers, with many a hard-fought skirmish.

Time has passed, and we have both about reached the allotted age, but time can not dim or efface the lustre of such a life as his; and when he does surrender, may the dear Lord of us all give him that rest that remains to His people.

JAS. H. HOLLOWAY.

REV. J. S. SCOBEE,
1st Chaplain 10th Ky., P. R.

GENERAL ADAM R. JOHNSON'S COMMAND.

By Colonel E. L. Starling.

I have stated elsewhere in the brief sketch of General Johnson that his command was largely composed of young Kentuckians like himself—young men reared in this immediate section of the State. The majority of them were sons of esteemed and most deserving fathers and mothers; parents, in fact, who enjoyed the confidence of the communities in which they resided to a very large degree. These men had received liberal common school educations, many of them having graduated from well-known colleges throughout the country. They had been properly trained and were as well versed in all of the noble characteristics of true Southern manhood as any to be found throughout the length and breadth of their much-loved Southland. They had inherited from association and large reading an affection for the South that amounted largely to an infatuation or worship. They believed their country to be the garden spot of the universe and the Southern people the beau ideals of all human kind. Their sympathies were all with the South and an impetuosity of determined purpose actuated and guided their every movement in life. Born horsemen and active, they would mount the most dangerously wild or unbroken animal with a spirit altogether a stranger to fear. They were active, full of life and snap, healthy and robust; therefore, qualified to become the very flower of the cavalry service.

Such men in the main constituted General Johnson's little army of bold riders, who feared no foe and would shirk no duty imposed upon them. The General knew his men and they knew what confidence he placed in them in the times when the services of the courageous were most needed.' As I have said before, his men loved him with a confident devotion that amounted to an infatuation, and though now in the twilight of life, that devotion with those yet living has not diminished in the least degree. With such a command and such men associated with him it would be an impossible undertaking to convince those now living that they would or could be induced to practice the many crimes that were charged to them by non-combatant enemies and Republican newspapers published at that time. Very many of General Johnson's soldiers survived the war and returned to their homes bereft of their property and required to begin life anew without a dollar they could call their own. With the same impetuosity and determined purpose that governed their actions on joining the army they applied themselves to the peaceful pursuits of life, and to their credit be it said many of them have been conspicuously successful and are to-day numbered among the most valued and progressive citizens of the Commonwealth. Those now living are among our foremost citizens, exerting an honorable influence wherever known, not exceeded by any communities of people on earth. Such I am proud to say was the character of men who largely composed the ranks of General Johnson's command. I submit sketches of two officers of this command: Colonel E. G. Hall and Major G. Wash Owen.

COLONEL E. G. HALL.

Edwin G. Hall, who was promoted to a Colonel in General Johnson's command, was born at West Point, on Salt river, Kentucky, seventy-four years ago and came to Henderson when a boy. He had a number of relatives in the then town and county of Henderson with whom he passed his time until becoming of sufficient age to launch out in life for himself. He worked upon a farm, and tobacco being the leading staple cultivated, became an expert judge of its qualities and was therefore qualified to be of great service to any one of the large firms then doing business in the town of Henderson. His intelligent foresight and strong judgment, his energy and general efficiency attracted the attention of the firm of Hugh Kerr, Clark & Co., then one of the largest in the town, and he was employed to do business for them. He became the head bookkeeper of the firm and largely assisted in the general management of the firm's business up to the outbreak of the Civil War. A year or two prior to the war he had been elected mayor of the city of Henderson, having defeated one of the most popular and worthy old men of the city at that time. Henderson being on the border, was continuously annoyed by Federal troops, and the frequent clash of authority between them and Mayor Hall greatly exasperated' the mayor and rendered his position one rather to be shunned than sought by him. The object of the soldiery seemed to be to force Mayor Hall to decide with the Union and to do things altogether revolting to his high and honorable manhood. He was persistently pursued in one way and another, and finally an obnoxious oath altogether out of the regular line was prepared, and he was required to subscribe his name to it or be arrested and transported to some bastile far away from his home. Being a man of the highest honor and thoroughly detesting the acts of those in command, he determined on casting his lot with the Confederacy, and between two suns and without tendering his resignation, he departed from the city, and in a day or two reported at Bowling Green, Kentucky, where General Albert Sidney Johnston was in command of a large army confronting General D. C. Buell, who, with an equally large army, was moving in the direction of Nashville. Subsequently Colonel Hall became a soldier of General Adam R. Johnson's command and proved to be one of his most valued soldiers and advisers. Colonel Hall was active in recruiting and during the time was engaged in a number of skirmishes calculated to test his courage as well as his military ability. Failing to recruit his regiment to the standard, and being otherwise dissatisfied, he resigned his commission and soon after went north, spending a good portion of his time in Canada in business. He afterward engaged in business at Chicago and Detroit, Michigan, and was quite successful. At the close of the war he returned to Henderson and again associated himself with Kerr, Clark & Co., with whom he remained up to the dissolution of the firm.

During the great California gold excitement of 1849 Colonel Hall, in company with ten or a dozen more, made the trip overland from Henderson to the Golden State, and for quite a while engaged in mining. Becoming wearied of this venture, he returned to Kentucky at the age of seventeen years. At one time he was engaged in the dry goods business in Henderson with his cousin Alvan Jones and subsequently with David Hart. He married Miss Elizabeth Alten of Harrodsburg, Kentucky. Some time during the seventies Colonel Hall moved to Louisville, and under the form of Hall & Hayward carried on an extensive manufacture of crackers and all kinds of candies. In this as in all other engagements he was most fortunate in adding greatly to his already comfortable fortune. No man in Louisville was held in greater esteem, and the greatest regret was manifest when it was learned that he had sold out and would locate in California. This he did, however, and has continued to reside in that State to the present time. Wherever he has lived he secured to himself a friendship most to be desired, the foremost men in the communities becoming endeared to him with a devotion seldom approximated by any one. Colonel Hall is to-day an old man, quite wealthy and living a life of comparative ease.

MAJOR G. WASH OWEN.

The subject of this sketch was another of General Johnson's most valued officers. Major Owen came to Henderson during the year 1859 or 1860 from the State of Maryland, and engaged with relatives as prescriptionist in one of the leading drug stores of that day and time. He was an expert compounder of medicines, and altogether a young man of much brilliance. He was a great favorite in the social circle and enjoyed the esteem of a host of friends in the largest degree. He was a young man of studious habits, highly educated and was possessed of unquestioned courage. Among the first to respond to the call of the South, he went to Bowling Green along with Colonel Hall and others, and was subsequently assigned to General Johnson's command in western Kentucky. In the early part of the war, knowing that there were one hundred stands of the finest rifles and a six-pound brass cannon stored in an armory of the Kentucky State Guard at Henderson, he planned a midnight raid into that place for the purpose of seizing the arms and transporting them South. The way was absolutely clear for him, and no difficulty was experienced in getting possession of the coveted arms. There were no Union soldiers in the town at that time, and a large majority of the company in charge of the guns and cannon were pleased at the opportunity of having them seized and turned over to the Confederates. The next morning when it was learned that Owen had seized the State Guard arms and fled in all haste for the South, Honorable Robert T. Glass, who was a very strong Southern sympathizer, in company with several others, mounted on horseback, started in pursuit of Owen for the purpose of having the arms returned to Henderson. This course on the part of Mr. Glass was thought very strange until it was learned that he and the others with him were security on the bond executed to the State for the safe-keeping and safe return to the State of all the arms upon the abandonment of the company. Some fifteen thousand dollars were involved, and the bond was perfectly plain and positive. The military board then in authority in Kentucky was composed of uncompromising Union men, and they would have held the securities for the payment of every cent of the State's loss. Glass and his friends knew that to be true; hence the effort to regain the lost property. Hurrying on as fast as their horses could withstand, they succeeded in overtaking Major Owen at a point in Webster, the adjoining county, some seventeen miles out of Henderson, in camp, taking a much-needed rest. Mr. Glass being the spokesman, approached Major Owen and explained the situation to him in its most forcible light. The major listened attentively to their every plea and appeared much interested. He knew the party to be composed of his friends and friends of the Confederacy. He knew also that he was safe from attack, and that the way to the South was clear to him, but yet his honor and former friendship was at stake. To seize what appeared to be the property of his friends and perhaps financially ruin most of them was a matter for his consideration. He recognized the further fact that while his friends were in no way responsible for his acts there was yet an opportunity for involving them in great trouble with the State if not the Federal Government. Taking into earnest and honorable consideration the questions at issue, the young major was put to a severe test as to what he should do. He knew that his country needed the arms he had seized and that his act of seizure and safe transportation to the South would be applauded from one end of the Confederacy to the other and tend, in all probability, to his promotion, and yet his high sense of honor caused him to consider in deep earnestness his duty to his country and his non-combatant friends. He knew or believed no doubt that nine officers or soldiers out of ten would hold on to the arms and turn them over to the army regardless of consequences, but for him to do so appeared as a proposition too monstrous and one that would punish his conscience for all time to come. He weighed the appeals of his friends in one scale and his duty to his country in another, and without the toss of a copper his decision was rendered and the seized property restored to his friends. The wagons were immediately wheeled around and started on their return journey to Henderson, where they arrived in safety during the evening, and were a few days after turned over to an authorized agent of Kentucky and his relinquishment of the bond received.

Such was the character of Major Wash Owen, who subsequently became a dashing, daring cavalrymen, admired for his courage and high honor by all who knew him or came within the zone of his sunshiny disposition. Major Owen continued his residence in the Southland at the close of the war and became one of the foremost and most respected physicians and surgeons in Atlanta, where he died several years ago.

I could extend my contribution to General Johnson's book to an indefinite length in contributing to the honor, capacity and high character of officers and men whose acquaintance I enjoyed and whose friendship I shared.

COLONEL LEONIDAS ARMSTEAD SYPERT.

By M. D. Sypert.

Colonel Leonidas Armstead Sypert was born in Lebanon, Tennessee, December 15, 1832, a son of H. A. and Ann S. Sypert, of German-English descent. He acquired a finished education and was a graduate of Lebanon, Tennessee, Law College. He located at Hopkinsville, Kentucky, where he engaged in the practice of his profession several years before the Civil War.

When the war broke out he was among the first to respond, and during these four years of colossal warfare won an enviable name upon the battlefield. Colonel Sypert first joined Green's Cumberland Battery in 1861, which was ordered to Fort Donelson and did gallant service up to the surrender of the fort. Both Sypert and Green made their escape. The former followed up the retreating army under Albert Sidney Johnston, overtaking them at Shelbyville, Tennessee, where they had a considerable battle with the Federal forces. From this place he was ordered to Huntsville, Alabama, and thence to Corinth, Mississippi, where Johnston was concentrating his forces. He then engaged in the battle of Shiloh and was put in charge of fifty prisoners whom he conducted back to Corinth, ranking at that time as captain.

The summer of 1863 he was commissioned colonel and given authority to raise a regiment. The original has been preserved by Mrs. Sypert and reads as follows:

CONFEDERATE STATES OF AMERICA.

WAR DEPARTMENT..

Adjutant and Inspector General's Office.
Richmond, Va., August 26, 1863.

Authority is hereby granted to Captain L. A. Sypert to raise a regiment of cavalry for the Provisional Army Confederate States of America. The companies will elect their officers and will be mustered into service of the Confederate States for the war. If the companies are mustered into service as a regiment the field officers will be elected; and if mustered as independent companies the field

COLONEL L. A. SYPERT.

officers will be appointed by the President. Copies of the muster roll and elective certificates should be forwarded to this office for file.
By command of the Secretary of War,

ED. A. PALFREY,
Lt. Col. and A. A. G.

CAPTAIN L. A. SYPERT, RICHMOND, VA.

On his return from Richmond, Virginia, the train was captured by the enemy, and by jumping from the fast moving train Colonel Sypert succeeded in making his escape through North Carolina to the nearest railway, on which he returned via Atlanta to Dalton, Georgia. Here he found his old command and remained with them until after the battle of Chickamauga, participating in this hard-contested victory. Shortly after this the regiment was attached to General Wheeler, with whom they made a successful raid into Tennessee, capturing Shelbyville and other points and doing much damage to the enemy.

In the spring of 1864 he returned to Kentucky and succeeded in raising a regiment of cavalry, recruiting principally from the counties of Union, Henderson and Webster. With this force of raw recruits he first encountered Colonel Sam Johnson in Crittenden county at Bell's Mines and next day at Blue Lake, whom he completely routed and drove from the country.

Shortly after this Mr. J. E. Rankin, a Union man, was shot by a party of guerrillas, falsely called Southern soldiers. In retaliation two innocent Confederate prisoners were brought to Henderson and shot. The next day Colonel Sypert attacked Henderson and drove the Federal army out of the city. The Union citizens fearing revenge upon themselves, the city was thrown into the wildest consternation, but were promptly reassured by Colonel Sypert who issued the following proclamation:

"TO THE CITIZENS OF HENDERSON.‘

" On yesterday two Confederate soldiers were shot to death in the streets of your city. They condemned, their whole command condemned, as earnestly as any citizen of Kentucky, the shooting of Mr. James E. Rankin and the plundering of your city. But they are gone and their murder is another crime added to the damnable catalogue of the despotism that rules you. We are Confederate soldiers. We fight for the liberty our sires bequeathed us. We have not made nor will we make war upon citizens and women. Let not your people be excited by any further apprehension that we will disturb the peace of your community by the arrest of Union men or any interference with them, unless they place themselves in the attitude of combatants; such conduct would be cowardly and we scorn it. We are in arms to meet and battle with soldiers, not to tyrannize over citizens and frighten women and children.

"We move with our lives in our hands. We are fighting not for booty but for liberty; to disenthrall our loved Southern land from the horrible despotism under which it has bled and suffered so much. We know our duty and will do it as soldiers and men.

"Even if what are denominated as 'Southern sympathizers' be arrested by the tyrants that lord it over you, we would scorn to retaliate by arresting Union men who had no complicity in the matter, but our retaliation will be upon soldiers. Let not the noncombatants of your community be further excited by any fear that we will disturb them; all Union men who may have left home on our account may safely return. In war soldiers should do the fighting.

"L. A. SYPERT,
"Col. Commanding, C. S. A.
"R. B. L. SOERY,
"Lieut.-Col., C. S. A.
"J. WALKER TAYLOR,
"Major, C. S. A."

To this brave utterance the Henderson News thus responded:

"Colonel Sypert has been known in peace and war as a thoroughly brave man and a gentleman. When he entered this city he issued this proclamation which speaks for itself. No eulogy could add to the honor it sheds upon the man. Everything here at the time was absolutely as his mercy, but he refused a temptation to plunder and an opportunity for vengeance upon the citizens not in arms. His words composed our people who were in a fearful state of excitement. They were grateful to him and admire him for his manly and soldierly conduct."

After this incident Colonel Sypert removed his command to Sulphur Springs, Union county, and shortly after with about five hundred men attached himself to General Adam Johnson, who had come into the State to recruit a brigade. His command followed the fortunes of this able officer and was near him when he was wounded.

Colonel Sypert's command was then transferred to General Lyon, with whom he remained until the close of the war, when he surrendered to the Federal General, Wilson, at Columbus, Mississippi.

JOSEPH WEAK,

Co. I, 10th Ky., P. R.   Confidential Scout for General Johnson.

When the war was ended he returned to Hopkinsville, Kentucky, and resumed the practice of law. He rose rapidly in his profession, and in a few years stood among the first of the bar; he also took an active part in politics.

On June 30, 1868, he was married to Miss Martha Douglas Henry, whose ancestors date back to the Douglas of Scotland and days of Cromwell and later of Colonial prominence, a lady of many graces and much wealth, daughter of Colonel R. W. Henry of Confederate note. His union was blessed by the advent of six daughters and two sons: Mrs. Annie Sypert Russell, of Oklahoma; Mrs. Margaret Sypert Mason, of Oklahoma; Mrs. Sadie Sypert Patton, of Alabama; Mrs. Lee Sypert Cleveland, of Tennessee; Mrs. Susan Sypert Johnson, of Kentucky; Mattie Lee, Douglas Wilkins and Robert William Henry Sypert. These three last-named died in infancy.

Colonel L. A. Sypert died of pneumonia in Hopkinsville, Kentucky, March 23, 1892, at the age of sixty years.

He was a brave soldier, a dashing, daring officer, unflinching in duty, a strategist, lawyer and politician, a leader in war and in peace.

ADDITIONAL SKETCH OF COLONEL L. A. SYPERT.

By C. G. Duke.

My acquaintance with Colonel Lee A. Sypert began early in the spring of 1864. I had made up my mind to recruit a company of men, if possible, for the Confederate army, and had succeeded in getting ten or twelve of our neighbor boys and acquaintances together for that purpose, when I learned that Captain Sypert, of Colonel Woodward's regiment was at that time in Christian county with a commission to raise a regiment of men for the Confederate service. I sent word to him that if his commission was all right I believed that I could be of some benefit to him. He came to Caldwell county at my request, and after being being associated with us a short while, our little band concluded that he was a leader that we could follow with confidence. We at once decided to cast our lot with him, and so we took the oath of allegiance to the Confederate cause. About this time it became very warm for us in Caldwell county, as there was a regiment of Union soldiers stationed there at Princeton, the county seat. We made our way across the Cumberland and Tennessee rivers and remained three weeks, and as we did not recruit very fast there we decided to return to Union and Hopkins counties and remain until we recruited a body of men sufficiently large to constitute a regiment. We were so few in numbers that we made slow headway recruiting, but the people in those counties received us with open arms and hearts, fed our men and horses in many instances. The ladies of Union county would bring large baskets of provisions to us themselves, some on horseback and some in buggies. We boys thought they were the noblest creatures that the sun ever shone upon.

About this time Colonel Sam Johnson, who was located at Hopkinsville at the time, heard of our whereabouts and declared that he would come over to Morganfield and stay until every rebel was killed or captured.

We had men on the watch who notified us that the Yankees were on their way to Morganfield. They arrived about sundown.. We were camped at Blue Pond, about six miles from town. About dark Colonel Sypert came up smiling and said: "I want four or five men for a particular purpose to-night." We asked what was up and he told us he wanted some fun out of "Old Sam;" so five men volunteered and they proceeded forthwith to Morganfield and captured the pickets and fired on the command as they were in the houseyard cooking supper. They made a break for the court house in a hurry and the citizens told us that they forgot to eat the supper they were cooking when we fired upon them. The next day Johnson came out to our camp, as he had said, to annihilate us. We heard them forming a line of battle in the underbrush and we did not wait for them to rush upon us, but instead we were ordered to charge that army of three or four hundred men. We did so with about twenty-five men and to our surprise they fell back in confusion; we pursued and completely routed them. The road on either side was thickly covered with timber and every now and then we would fire into this column with small squads upon either side until they thought the woods were full of us. Johnson declared when he got back to Hopkinsville that he believed every tree in Union county had a rebel behind it.

After this the men became bolder and we recruited more men rapidly. Some of Morgan's men who had escaped from prison joined us and we had skirmishes every once in a while. We got our encampments as a result of these skirmishes. Shortly afterward we attacked a camp at Bell Mines and took quite a number of prisoners, guns and ammunition, then we surprised a camp at

Old Salem, took the pickets and other prisoners and killed and wounded several men and horses. About this time General Adam R. Johnson came upon the stage of action. We then began making preparations to go South where we were to go into regular service. We had by this time five hundred raw recruits and only about one-third of them were armed; we heard of a company of Federals it Grubb's Crossroads and we decided to pass that way in our course out of Kentucky and surprise and capture the men and secure arms to equip our men. This we accomplished, but unfortunately General Johnson received the wound that caused the loss of his eyesight.

By this time a large force of Federal troops were following us by land and by the river in gunboats. A constant firing was kept up between the Federals and the Confederates from near Canton on the Cumberland river on through Steward county, Tennessee, and in crossing the river there we were shelled by the gunboats which cut off about one-third of our men, and between the Cumberland and Tennessee rivers our command encountered a large force of negro troops. In that fight we lost two gallant officers, namely, Lieutenant Colonel Robt. Soery and Captain Presly H. Garr, and on reaching Paris, Tennessee, we found General H. B. Lyon there in camp quarters. Our command having been reduced in numbers we were consolidated with the Eighth Kentucky.

I was never with the command after the shelling of the woods at the river in Steward county, Tennessee, as my colonel gave me orders to go back to Union county and collect the men who had been cut off and bring them out in squads of six or eight at a time, and as I was making an effort to cross with the last remaining squad of men left in Kentucky I was captured and sent to Johnson's Island, Ohio, where I remained until the close of the war.

There are many little reminiscences that I could mention in a funny way that I do not attach much importance to, so I will refrain from making any mention of them.

MAJOR J. WALKER TAYLOR.

Major J. Walker Taylor was born in Jefferson county, Kentucky, February, 1825, and died October, 1889. He was reared on a farm near Louisville, and was a brother of Captain Samuel Burk Taylor. He reported to me for duty a few days after I arrived in Union county and was assigned to Sypert's regiment as major. He bore

information from General Forrest that he would join me as soon
as possible after learning the conditions and results of my expeditions. He was sent with Colonel Cunningham as guide on account
of his knowledge of the country and the positions of the Federals;
as soon as he reached the lines he was to report to General Forrest,
while Colonel Cunningham was to proceed directly to Richmond.
All this was well executed, and he joined Colonel Cunningham on
his return to Kentucky. Learning that I had been wounded, Colonel
Cunningham reported to Colonel Chenoweth's headquarters near
Tennessee. Major Taylor came on to where I was staying, at the
home of Garland Simms, and stated that Forrest had received
peremptory orders to hold his department and check the expeditions
that were formed against him, but if we could induce the Federals
who were following me to cross the Tennessee river that he would
in some way join me and clean them up. Of course, this information was of no service to me, but it showed the indefatigable
courage and determination of Major Taylor. I had known him
since my first expedition into Kentucky and considered him one of
the best secret service men in the Confederacy.

Upon a memorable occasion he went into Louisville and interviewed Colonel Henry Dent, the provost marshal of the city, who
had offered a large reward for his apprehension. Dressed as a
poor old countryman, he introduced himself under a fictitious name
and talked a long time to the colonel, even mentioning Walker Taylor
himself; certainly a bold piece of business, the penalty for which
rashness, if detected, would have been a drum-head court martial
and speedy death by hanging. But fortunately he escaped.

The following is reprinted from the Confederate Veteran of April,
1903:

A PROPOSED ABDUCTION OF LINCOLN.

Henry T. Louthan, Adjutant Magruder-Ewell Camp, U. C. V.,
Williamsburg, Va.:

"Springfields," six miles east of Louisville, is surrounded by
sloping hills, crystal streams, picturesque woodlands and bluegrass
fields. The house was built about 1785 by Colonel Richard Taylor,
the father of President Zachary Taylor, and remained in the family
until the reconstruction days of 1865-70, when, like so many other
homesteads of the South, it passed into the hands of strangers.

In the old family burying ground, now overgrown with
myrtle and inclosed by a crumbling limestone wall,

sleep heroes from the Taylor family of four American wars. In the center rises a snow-white marble shaft, upon the top of which stands a figure of General Zachary Taylor, the hero of Fort Harrison, Black Hawk, Okechobee, Palo Alto, Resaca de la Palma and Buena Vista. Beneath the monument lie the ashes of the general's father, Colonel Richard Taylor, of Revolutionary fame; of his brother, Hancock Taylor, of the Indian wars waged in the West; and of his nephew, Major Joseph Walker Taylor, of the army of the Confederate States. "Springfields" was the boyhood home of President Taylor, but at the death of his father it fell to the latter's eldest son, Hancock Taylor, the father of Major Joseph Walker Taylor, one of the central figures of this sketch. Major Taylor died at his home, near Louisville, in October, 1889, and a few weeks before his death received the following letter from Jefferson Davis:

"Beauvoir, Miss., August 31, 1889.

"Major Walker Taylor.

"My Dear Sir:—Your attention has, no doubt, been sometimes attracted to the revived, though baseless, accusation against me as having been connected with attempts to assassinate President Lincoln. As you were the only man who ever talked to me on the subject of his capture, or at least the only one who I believed intended to do what he proposed, and that was carefully guarded against any design to kill, the purpose being to get the advantage of possession alive, I thought I would write to you for such recollection as you retain of your proposition to capture and my declining to entertain it on the ground that the attempt would probably involve the killing instead of bringing away the captive alive. It has been so long since I saw you that I may as well ask how you are and how fares it with you. I am, as ever, affectionately yours,

"JEFFERSON DAVIS."

The original of this letter is in the possession of Miss Virginia Taylor, of Louisville, Ky. She is a daughter of Major Walker Taylor, and gave the writer the main facts for this paper.

Mrs. Jefferson Davis, in some notes to the writer concerning the above letter, says: "I was my husband's amanuensis, and he could not tell my handwriting from his own. He occasionally wrote during his whole life, though not often, as I both wrote and signed his checks and letters. The letter you sent me was dictated to me by Mr. Davis and is in my hand, every word, and the signature as well. Mr. Davis rarely ever signed anything I wrote. In the last years of his life he disliked very much using a pen."

Major Taylor was a first cousin of General Taylor's daughter, Miss Sarah Knox Taylor, who was the first wife of Jefferson Davis. In this way Walker Taylor, as he was known by his friends, came to be upon familiar terms with the Confederate chieftain. Walker Taylor was a small man; but, like his uncle, " Old Rough and Ready," nothing but brave and daring blood ran in his veins. During the first year of the war he was on the staff of General Simon Bolivar Buckner, of Kentucky, and gave his special attention to the secret service. This training made him the man to propose and carry into successful execution the capture of President Lincoln. If Taylor had obtained the consent of Davis to carry out the proposed abduction there is not the least doubt in the minds of those who knew the brave Kentuckian but that the civilized world would have awaked one morning in 1862 wondering at the mysterious disappearance of the President of the United States.

In February, 1862, Major Taylor was severely wounded in the cheek and throat at the storming of Fort Donelson. He escaped capture, and after becoming well enough to travel, donned a citizen's suit and boarded a train bound for Louisville. He sat by a Federal officer, with two others facing him. He wore a muffler around his neck and a plaster over the hole in his cheek. One of the officers said to him: " Friend, is that a cancer on your face? " Taylor carelessly replied: " The doctors disagree about that," and nothing more was said about the wound. He reached Louisville without being molested, and though the place was held by Union troops, he spent some days with his family at his home, just east of the city.

While recuperating Taylor conceived the plan of abducting Lincoln. From Louisville he went directly to Washington City. He had two brothers in the Union army, while he and another brother had cast their lot with the Confederacy. He had some kinsmen in high Government positions in Washington, but he knew they would not betray him, as they had no idea of his real mission in the city. He stayed while there with his uncle, General Joseph Taylor, of the Federal army; and the old general was quite uneasy while his reckless nephew was at the capital. Taylor had quite an extended conversation with one of the President's secretaries, and a few days later boldly went to the White House, and at a public reception had himself introduced as "Mr. Taylor, of Kentucky." The President seeing that he had been shot, asked him at what battle he had been wounded. When Taylor replied, "At Fort Donelson," Mr. Lincoln complimented the work of the Federals there, not supposing for a moment that the soldier whom he held by the hand was a Confederate, coolly planning one of the most daring schemes of the war. Taylor watched closely for some time the daily movements of Lincoln, and then passed quietly down into Virginia and on to Richmond to hold a conference with Jefferson Davis.

In a letter to the writer, dated March 14, 1898, Colonel William Preston Johnston, President Davis's aid-de-camp, says: "I think the date of Taylor's interview was in the early summer of 1862. Indeed, I know it was. It was not a formal affair. Mrs. Davis was not in the city, and I was living with Mr. Davis. I met Taylor and told Mr. Davis he was in town, and he directed me to ask him to breakfast. While we were waiting for breakfast Taylor explained his wish and plan to me before Mr. Davis came down, and toward the close of breakfast I told the President that Taylor had a scheme he wished to lay before him." Colonel Johnston then refers to the following account of the interview: "'Well, Walker, said Mr. Davis affably, 'what is it?' 'Mr. Davis, I want to bring Lincoln a prisoner to you in this city.' 'Oh, pshaw!' said Davis, 'how can such a thing as that be done?' 'Just as easily,' said Taylor, 'as walking out of this town. I came across the Potomac at no great distance from Washington, and while I was there I watched Lincoln's habits closely and know his outgoing and incoming. I tell you, sir, that I can bring him across that river just as easily as I can walk over your doorstep.' 'How could you do it?' said Mr. Davis. 'Lincoln,' replied Taylor, 'does not leave the White House until evening, or near twilight, and then with only a driver he takes a lonely ride two or three miles in the country to a place called the Soldiers' Home, which is his summer residence. My point is to collect several of these Kentuckians whom I see about here doing nothing and who are brave enough for such a thing as that, and capture Lincoln, run him down the Potomac and cross him over just where I crossed, and the next day will have him here.' Davis shook his head and said: 'I can not give my authority, Walker. In the first place, I suppose Lincoln is a man of courage. He has been in Indian wars, and is a Western man. He would undoubtedly resist being captured. In that case you would kill him. I could not stand the imputation of having consented to let Mr. Lincoln be assassinated. Our cause could not stand it. Besides, what value would he be to us as a prisoner? Lincoln is not the Government or the Federal power. He is merely the political instrument there. If he were brought to Richmond what could I do with him? He would have to be treated like the magistrate of the North, and we have neither the time nor the provision. No, sir, I will not give my authority to abduct Lincoln!'"

Major Taylor was a brave soldier and a gentleman and the thought of assassinating Lincoln never entered his mind. The iron-nerved Kentuckian simply desired to capture the chief executive of the United States and to retain him as a prisoner of war. But the tall chieftain of those who wore the gray consented not, for he knew that his great opponent might be killed in the attempt. Was this refusal to sanction the proposed abduction mere sentiment? No, but it was manhood and wisdom. Thus it is seen that Davis not only did not desire the assassination of Lincoln, but refused to countenance even a possibility of it.

When Mr. Lincoln was assassinated, three years later, the whole country was in a state of great excitement. President Andrew Johnson, in his proclamation of May 2, 1865, charged Davis with instigating the assassination, and offered $100,000 reward for his arrest. Davis was captured. The Federal Government at his trial made a thorough investigation into what Johnson had charged. The result of the trial shows that Jefferson Davis was in no wise connected with Lincoln's assassination. Davis prevented a possible killing of Lincoln in 1862, and the world believes to-day that the sad affair of 1865 was wholly without the previous knowledge of the Confederate chieftain. Were Caesar and Lincoln at this time to commune upon subjects martial and civic, they could speak of Jefferson Davis as a Pompey, but never as a Brutus.

COLONEL CHARLES NAPIER.

Colonel Charles Napier was lieutenant colonel in the Sixth Kentucky Cavalry, commanded by Colonel Grigsby; was seriously wounded at Snow Hill; the most of his regiment was captured on the Indiana and Ohio raid. He was ordered to report to me on my last expedition into Kentucky and was organizing a regiment when I was wounded, and had about four hundred men who were afterwards consolidated with other Kentucky commands. His regimental organization was as follows: John Shanks, lieutenant colonel; Coleman, Major; Nelms, of Atlanta, Georgia, adjutant; Neil Helm, captain Company A; Henry Gist, captain Company B; John Head, captain Company C; Alf. Richeson, captain Company D; R. Row, captain Company E; William Quinn, captain Company F.

LIEUTENANT-COLONEL ROBERT SOERY.

Lieutenant-Colonel Robert Soery was born in England, and was but a small child when brought by his parents to Robinson county, Tennessee. He enlisted in the Confederate army at the beginning of the war; was elected lieutenant-colonel of Sypert's regiment; was killed during the latter part of 1864.

Company Officers of the Rangers.

SAMUEL BURK TAYLOR.

Captain Samuel Burk Taylor was born in Jefferson county, Kentucky, in January, 1841, and died in October, 1867. He was a brother of Major J. Walker Taylor and son of Hancock Taylor, who was elder brother to President Zachary Taylor. He was a striking likeness of President Taylor, and had many of his characteristics in battle; he was cool and courageous and always quick to use any advantage. While apparently a small man, he was an athlete, and expert in the use of fire-arms. He joined Colonel Johnson about the 20th of August, 1862, and in a few days after led his company in a fight against the combined forces of Foster and Shackelford. He and Captain Fowler with about one hundred men held Foster's whole command in check. Here Captain Taylor showed his remarkable precision with the pistol. Taking his stand in the middle of the road, he shot down several horses, and when asked afterwards why he killed the horses instead of the men, said that he always found that a dead horse was the best breastwork in the world against cavalry, as it was almost impossible for a trooper to force his steed to go over him or around him.

Captain Taylor led his company in the battle of Uniontown, Geiger's Lake, Owensboro, and many skirmishes before joining the main army. He was with Morgan on his Christmas raid and led one of the parties on the attack at Lebanon, Kentucky. He was also on the Indiana and Ohio raid and aided in capturing the steamboats that crossed the command at Brandenburg.

With one of his lieutenants he rode into Cincinnati and reported the condition of affairs in that city to General Morgan. He and

274

CAPTAIN SAM. B. TAYLOR,
Co. E, 10th Ky., P. R.

Captain Jake Bennett made a gallant fight against Hobson's whole command at Long Bottom, holding them in check all night; was captured with General Morgan and put in the Ohio penitentiary, and greatly aided Captains Hockersmith and Bennett in rescuing General Morgan.

They were very desirous to know where the sewer pipe came out on the outer side of the wall around the prison.

Along the front wall of the prison a veranda ran, reaching to the top of the building, and along the face of the veranda, from column to column were extended horizontal bars or rods high overhead, at each floor, the structure being several stories high. One of the little party who was plotting to escape engaged the superintendent in conversation, and the talk finally led to the bars, which one of them said were separated by such a distance perpendicularly, that a prisoner might escape by springing upward from one to another until he got upon the roof, from which he could descend at the rear. The superintendent hooted at the idea of any man making such high, vertical, dangerous leaps. "Why we have a little fellow here who can do it," responded the officer. This declaration being challenged, Captain Taylor was brought forward as their champion acrobat. Permission was given for him to break his neck, but to the utter amazement of the superintendent, the little captain leaped upward from story to story with the agility of a kangaroo, and was soon on the top of the building from which he gained the coveted view and saw that the sewer ran under the wall at a place favorable for their emergement. This valuable information inspired the conspirators with increased hope and aided much in their escape.

LUCAS WILLIAM TRAFTON.

Lucas William Trafton, son of William and America Trafton, was born in Evansville, Indiana, April 9, 1837. He attended Wabash College, and pursued his studies with a view to the practice of law. While at home from college he met with an accident while out hunting which resulted in the loss of his left arm.

At the age of seventeen he entered the office of the county clerk of Henderson, Kentucky, as deputy under William D. Allison, which position he filled acceptably for four years. At the age of twenty-one he was admitted to the bar and at a special election in October, 1859, he was elected to succeed Grant Green as county judge. He served as such until August, 1862, at which time the Robinson military government came into control of the State of Kentucky. Knowing that he would be forced out of office, he left on or about August 12th, with Captain Ed. Hall and enlisted with the Tenth Kentucky Cavalry at Camp Coleman. Captain Hall's two companies were merged with eight companies under the command of Colonel Adam R. Johnson. This regiment was of the second brigade of General John H. Morgan's division. He followed its fortunes as captain and assistant quartermaster until the capture of Morgan's command at Buffington Island, and rejoined it after being exchanged as a prisoner.

When captured he was taken with other prisoners to Johnson's Island, and afterward to Columbus, Ohio. In a letter dated in November, 1863, Captain Trafton alludes to General Morgan's escape in these words: "There has been a change in our hotel, as just two weeks ago General Morgan and six others escaped from this place." His letters written home while in prison, showed that he was continually in his usual cheerful spirits. His letters, whether written in prison or in the field, deplore the fact of more young, able-bodied men not enlisting in the cause of the South.

On March 24, 1864, Captain Trafton was taken to Fort Delaware, where after a few months he was exchanged. He returned South and joined his command. Late in the fall of 1864, while going with Captain Paul Marrs from Montgomery, Alabama, to join General Adam R. Johnson's command, he was shot at Milledgeville, Georgia, by a drunken man and was severely wounded. Captan Marrs immediately sent for physicians and had them probe for the bullet. This was unsuccessful and the physicians afterward decided that an operation would be necessary. When about to take him to the hospital, Mrs. Mary Spaulding, one of the many noble-hearted and patriotic women of the South, appeared at the hotel and asked that the wounded Confederate soldier be taken to her home. This was done and the operation was performed by Dr. White, removing the bullet. This operation was done without the administraton of anaesthetics.

Captain Trafton, under the kindly ministrations of Mrs. Spaulding, was nursed back to strength and health. Captan Marrs, true to his comradeship, remained with him until he was out of danger. Captain Trafton was at Milledgeville five months. After his recovery he rejoined his command and was with it till the close of the war.

CAPTAIN JAKE BENNETT,
2d Capt. Co. A, 10th Ky., P. R.

Returning home he resumed the practice of law. On November 23, 1865, he was married to Miss Helen Gibbs.

In 1871 Judge Trafton was elected as a Democrat (with which party he always most zealously affiliated) to the Kentucky Legislature, where he served on several prominent committees. He was for a number of years a law partner of Judge H. F. Turner, and this firm was one of the most largely patronized at that time. In social life Judge Trafton was a fine talker and full of humor.

He died August 6, 1877, and is survived by a widow and one son, Spaulding Trafton, who resides with his family in Henderson, Kentucky. Remembering with gratitude the kindly attentions of Mrs. Mary Spaulding, he named his only son for her.

Colonel Johnson first became acquainted with Captain Trafton at school; he had just recovered from the loss of his arm. But he soon taught his school-mates that he did not want nor would receive any consideration on account of his misfortune. In fact in all games he was one among the first to be chosen, and in civil life he displayed the same independence and courage. Colonel Johnson recognizing his ability, appointed him quartermaster and he proved to be one of the most competent in the service. And from that time he was the constant companion of Colonel Johnson, journeying with him through the woods on his frequent visits from point to point. He was with the command at the capture of Clarksville, and was one of the foremost in Martin's attack on Fort Donelson. He was also in the fight at Uniontown, and was one of the thirteen men who fought Shackelford at Geiger's Lake. He went South with Colonel Johnson when he reported at Bragg's headquarters at Glasgow, Kentucky. Returning then to Camp Coleman, he completed his muster-rolls and carried them to Richmond, where he was commissioned, and appointed disbursing officer.

JACOB BENNETT.

Captain Jacob Bennett was the youngest captain in Johnson's Partisan Rangers. He was a second lieutenant in Shacklet's regiment, the Eighth Kentucky. He resigned the day before the battle of Fort Donelson, shouldered a musket and went into the ranks and fought through that great battle. Was sent to Camp Morton, when captured, as a prisoner, but escaped and joined Johnson in June, 1862; was one of the seven men who fought the Federal cavalry at Madisonville; one of the twenty-seven men who captured Henderson, Kentucky, and Newburg, Indiana. Was elected first lieutenant of Company A, and became captain of that company on the resignation of Captain Ray; was at the capture of Hopkinsville, Clarksville, Uniontown, Owensboro, Sutherland's farm, and charged through the streets of Madisonville, carrying off a lieutenant as prisoner; was at the battle of Milton; flanked the Federals at Green river bridge, was in both battles of Lebanon, Kentucky, was one of the three captains who captured the steamboats on the Indiana and Ohio raid, and was one of the most prominent and conspicuous officers in the conflicts and skirmishes that occurred on the expedition until Morgan was captured, and he, Captain Hockersmith and Sam Taylor were the real leaders in aiding John Morgan in escaping from the penitentiary. After which he went west in Tennessee, on Obion river, raised a company of thirteen men, and made a raid through Kentucky to the Ohio river, burning the wharf boat at Owensboro that was loaded with Federal supplies and guarded by negroes. He captured General Shackelford at Madisonville and prepared to shave his head in retaliation for being put in the Ohio penitentiary (Shackelford being in command when he was captured on the Ohio raid). It is said that Shackelford was to be married that night and many of Bennett's friends prevailed upon him to release the general without executing his threat.

He returned to Obion river without the loss of a man, married and settled there, and after the war was elected sheriff and now has a position with the new penitentiary at Nashville.

Captain Bennett's company was a part of General Adam R. Johnson's famous Partisan Rangers. There was, perhaps, no man in that regiment who was bolder or more fearless than was Captain Bennett.

Major William J. Davis, adjutant general of the first brigade of Morgan's division, when the command was stationed near Liberty, Tennessee, early in 1863, was often on scouting parties behind the enemy's lines with detachments of the Tenth Kentucky and other regiments of the brigade. He says of Captain Bennett: "Jake, afoot, seemed a great, overgrown, awkward country youth, but on horseback, his seat was firm, and he had the air of the true cavalryman; in action he was all alive, quick of motion, prompt, a fine shot, and in a hand-to-hand fight always got the best of his adversary—in a melee on the road, when opposing advance guards

CAPT. SAM. G. WALL,
2d Capt. Co. C, 10th Ky., P. R.

were mixed pell-mell, he had no equal.   He did a noble thing on the turnpike road between Lebanon and Murfreesboro, Tennessee, one day: We had borne down on a long wagon train, escorted front and rear by Wilder's brigade of Federal cavalry, but protected by infantry marching on each side of the wagons, who resisted stoutly.   Before we succeeded in cutting out and driving off a few dozen wagons and teams, the fighting was at close quarters and pretty hot.   The Yankee " web-feet," after delivering their fire almost in our faces, used their bayonets to some effect as we rode into them.   It was all over in a few minutes, but Jake got in some fine work.   A sergeant of his company by his side was engaged with a Yankee who was in the act of running him through with the bayonet, while another had a bead drawn on Jake himself; Jake, who saw every thing going on about him and kept invariably a clear head, first shot the Federal who had his sergeant at disadvantage, then killed the one who threatened him—so quick it seemed like sleight of hand."

SAM GARRET WALL.

Captain Sam Garret Wall was born in Cynthiana, Harrison county, Kentucky, on the 22d of January, 1832.   He lived at this place until his widowed mother married again and moved to Morganfield, Union county, Kentucky.   When relieved from farm work he attended the public school at this place until 1849, when he became inspired with the gold fever and went across the plains to California.

In 1851 he returned to his home with plenty of experience but little else, and took charge of the farm, as his step-father had died during his absence.   He was married in January, 1852, to Miss Virginia Winston, and in April, 1853, a daughter was born to them.   At the birth of the child the mother died.

In April, 1862, he married a Miss America N. Metcalfe, and a year afterward a son, Sam G. Wall, Jr who is now living in Durango, Colorado, was born to them.   The Civil War opening just about this time, he raised a company in his home town and enlisted in the Tenth Kentucky Cavalry, commanded by Colonel Adam R. Johnson.

Captain Sam Wall was one of the best officers in the Confederate service.   He was a very temperate man and cool, calm and courageous, always at his post.   His men loved him and obeyed him without a murmur.   He was killed while leading his company in one of the most desperate charges of the war.   His loss was a serious blow to the whole command.   The action taken in the battle of Milton by the Tenth Kentucky has been described in Part I. of this narrative; it was in this engagement that the gallant Captain Wall was killed.

JOHN HAMILTON WALL.

Lieutenant John Hamilton Wall was born in Cynthiana, Harrison county, Kentucky, September 15, 1836, his father George Washington Wall died in 1838, and in 1841 his mother married a second time and with her husband, Colonel Thomas J. Clark, moved down to Morganfield, Kentucky, where Colonel Clark practiced law until 1845.   Securing a farm about ten miles out of Morganfield he moved his family there and put young John in the country school. He attended this school until 1851 when he was sent to Cynthiana to the Harrison Academy where he remained for two years, returning home in July, 1853.   He settled down to farm work until 1861, when he was enrolled in Captain W. M. Sheppard's newly organized company, Company I, Third Kentucky Infantry, as a private and went into camp at Camp Boone on the Fourth of July of that year.   He figured in all the movements of this company until after the Rochester trip.   He returned to Bowling Green with the regiment and was left there sick and for three weeks was unable to join his company.   As soon as he was able to travel he joined his command on Green river and operated with them until after the battle of Shiloh, where, in a hand--to-hand fight he was shot through the body.   Refusing assistance, he worked his way back to the camp out of which they had driven the Federals.   He was placed in the field hospital and remained there some time.   On the seventh of April, in company with several others, he started to Corinth, Mississippi, about eighteen miles off, and arrived at that place on the morning of the tenth of that month, 1862.   He was sent to the Irving Block Hospital at Memphis, Tennessee, and after several weeks stay ran away, getting to his command in time to be in two skirmishes as well as the battle at Corinth.   He was discharged at Holly Springs for physical disability and transportation was furnished himself and comrade as far as Franklin, Tennessee.   From that point they started home on foot and near Hopkinsville fell in with General John Morgan.   Being personally acquainted with the general he was re-enlisted, and at his request was sent to report to Colonel A. R. Johnson, who was then in his department near the Ohio river. He found Colonel R. M. Martin in command of Johnson's regiment at Providence and delivered instructions to him. He assisted both his brother and Colonel Martin in drilling their men until he was compelled to be sent home on a sick furlough. He carried with him orders for Captain E. H. Warthum, but found on his arrival that the captain had already gone South. While still an invalid he was captured by Captain Williams, who tried to compel him to pilot himelf and squad to several places they intended going, and although threatened with instant death if he refused, he was firm and told them they could hold him as prisoner but he would not guide them anywhere. With some others of Johnson's command he was confined in the Caseyville prison, from there sent under guard to Henderson, thence to Johnson's Island. After several desperate attempts to escape, they were exchanged and succeeded in joining their command at Turkey Neck Bend in time to participate in the Indiana and Ohio raid. L. D. Hockersmith was appointed captain and John Wall first lieutenant of Captain Sam Wall's old company. Lieutenant Wall was then placed in command of the wagon-trains and ordered to cross the mountains to Sweet Water Valley. Reaching that place, he reported to General J. C. Breckinridge and was ordered to use his men after the bushwhackers. He was engaged in this until sent to Chickamauga, where, the senior officers being absent, he led his company through that battle. He was in all the engagements with his command until Stoneman's raid, when he was wounded in the left arm, amputation being necessary. Seven weeks later he went with a scout following Sherman's raid until near the coast, where he again fell in with his command and remained with them until the surrender and was a part of the Jeff. Davis Guard. He reached home on the twenty-second of June, 1865, and with his brother began farming. A few months after his return he ran for county clerk, was elected and has served in that capacity for twenty years in Union county, Kentucky. He is still a vigorous and aggressive business man, and takes great interest in all public matters.

PAUL J. MARRS.

Captain P. J. Marrs enlisted under Colonel E. G. Hall in the summer of 1862, who was recruiting a regiment for Johnson's brigade. Was appointed quartermaster of Colonel Hall's regiment soon after the attack on Fort Donelson, where our men killed so many of the Second Kansas regiment. Colonel Hall was sent into Union and Henderson counties for the purpose of filling up his regiment. Being in want of arms, Colonel Hall, with a detail of fifty men made a raid into Indiana on the little town of West Franklin, and captured a lot of guns and horses from the home guards.

Some time in November I was sent with Captain William Quinn's company to arrange camp for the regiment at Shiloh Church, Hopkins county, Kentucky. While we were out obtaining supplies we were attacked by Major Platter and part of the command was captured including Captain Quinn, Lieutenant De-Champ, Jim Quinn, Fred Powell, Chas. Wood, Jonas Noakes, B. M. Clay and myself. We were taken to Henderson, transferred to Mt. Vernon, thence to Evansville and kept in prison for a long time on account of our raid upon West Franklin. Through the persistent efforts of General A. R. Johnson we were transferred to prison at Indianapolis, thence to Johnson's Island, and finally exchanged at Fortress Monroe. On our exchange we were ordered to report to General A. R. Johnson, at Decatur, Georgia, who was then reorganizing the remainder of Morgan's command after the raid into Indiana and Ohio. After General Johnson got together three or four hundred of Morgan's men, he received orders to report to West Virginia and join General Morgan, after his escape from prison.

On my arrival at Wytheville, Virginia, General Johnson placed me in charge of men making saddles, harness, boots and shoes. Remained in charge until relieved by Lieutenant Joe Gathright.

After the fight of General Morgan with General Averill at Crockett's Gap, I was ordered to report to General A. R. Johnson, at Decatur, Georgia, who was then equipping and organizing to go to Kentucky to recruit men in the rear of Sherman's army. The officers under General A. R. Johnson consisted of Colonel Napier, Colonel J. Q. Chenoweth, Colonel Sid. Cunningham, Captain Thomas Johnson, Lieutenant Overton, Lieutenant Thornton, and myself quartermaster, other men selected to be officers of the different companies as they were recruited. Fifty-two men in all left Atlanta on July 3d, traveling the whole distance to Union county, Kentucky, without being molested or attacked by any

Yankee commands, reached camp near Morganfield July 21st.
General Johnson with his colonels, Napier, Chenoweth,
Cunningham and L. A. Sypert, recruited and organized some two
thousand seven hundred men within a short period of thirty days.
During this short stop in Kentucky we created considerable excitement. Captured two or three steamboats on Caseyville bar with
large quantities of commissaries, stores, cattle, horses and large
quantity of money from quartermaster's department. Some two
or three hundred head of cattle were turned loose in Union and
other counties in western Kentucky. During the time that we
were recruiting the Federals sent some fifteen of twenty thousand
men after us, consisting of General Hobson's command of ten
thousand and General A. P. Hovey of Mt. Vernon with five
thousand men. It became evident that we should get out of
Kentucky; Captain Johnson and myself were ordered to locate camp
at Bruce's Mill, for the whole command, couriers being sent to all
commands to meet at that point. Captain Johnson or myself
issued rations for men and horses to the number of one thousand
seven hundred on Saturday and we started that night on our
way South. We struck a trail of a heavy force of Yankees that
night and found them in camp at Grubbs' Crossroads. The
general decided to surround the camp that night and attack them at
daylight. Colonel Cunningham was sent around on the right,
Colonel Napier was sent around on the rear of the camp and
Colonel Sypert's regiment occupied the left. At daylight General Johnson with Colonel Chenoweth's regiment charged them
in front and captured the whole camp with all their horses and
men, with the exception of one company. During the fight it
was so foggy it was almost impossible to distinguish our men from
the Yankees. I think Colonel Napier's men mistook Chenoweth's
men for the Yankees and fired on them. This was when Colonel Johnson was wounded. Colonel Chenoweth's horse was shot
from under him and my horse was wounded in several places.

On account of our command being short of ammunition, we
were compelled to fall back, taking with us some two hundred
prisoners, horses, wagons, etc. Colonel Johnson was led off the
field by Lieutenant Thornton.

Colonel Napier, being the senior colonel, declined to take command of our men and turned over the command to Colonel
Chenoweth. We immediately started on our way South and were

compelled to leave General Johnson at a farm house during the day. Colonel Chenoweth prepared and crossed a large portion of the men over Cumberland river at Canton, Kentucky. Before we had all gotten over we were attacked by Hobson's command and those that did not cross were scattered considerably, but they crossed the river in a few days and reported at camp near Paris, Tennessee. General Forrest being in Tennessee at that time, our command was attached to his and we were all present at the destruction of Johnsonville, Tennessee. After this fight Colonel Chenoweth sent me with a detail of men into Kentucky to pilot Major Owsley's command across the Cumberland and Tennessee rivers, which was done very successfully. Our command was afterwards turned over to General Lyon, who had made a raid in Kentucky of considerable importance.

We were kept in Western Tennessee and Northern Mississippi during the remainder of the war. After the surrender of Lee many of us found our way home, and surrendered to the Federals.

I will add to this something that very few soldiers of the Confederate army can say. The horse that I rode into the Confederate army, I rode home. This needs some explanation. When I was captured by Colonel Platter, the horse was sold in Henderson by the Government and Governor Arch Dixon bought the horse and used him while I was in prison. When I came into Kentucky with General A. R. Johnson, Governor Dixon sent me word that the horse was in fine shape and if I wanted him he would send him to some convenient place that I might get him. I sent for the horse and rode him all through the remainder of the war to Tennessee, Mississippi and part of Georgia, and when I returned home I brought the horse and returned him to Governor Dixon, who used him as a buggy horse for many years afterwards.

BARTLETT LOUIS GOOCH.

Bartlett Louis Gooch, who resides in Nebo county, was a hero during the war between the States. He was born August 24, 1846, and enlisted in the Southern army July 4, 1862, being then only sixteen years old.

Young Gooch joined Captain Adam R. Johnson's company of the Breckinridge Guards, Kentucky Cavalry, and was in all the fighting of the Tenth Kentucky until he was captured at Cheshire, in Ohio, July 20, 1863. After his capture he was taken to Camp Douglas

MRS. FRANK AMPLIAS OWEN.

where he was held prisoner for some time. He surrendered to the inevitable at Washington, Georgia, the last of April, 1865.

Mr. Gooch was with Morgan on his raid through Kentucky, Indiana and Ohio. He served as a private and was in a number of engagements, but managed to escape unharmed. After the war he returned to his home in Kentucky and has for many years been a successful farmer in Nebo county, where he is respected by all who know him.

Major Amplias Owen writes, "I send you Bart. L. Gooch's record. He is a collateral descendant of Governor Gooch of Virginia. The Tenth Kentucky could boast of many brave men but none braver than Bart. Gooch of the Old Guard."

FRANK AMPLIAS OWEN.

Frank Amplias Owen enlisted as a private in Company A, Eighth Kentucky Infantry, at the age of sixteen. He was wounded and captured at the battle of Fort Donelson and imprisoned at Camp Morton, from where he and Thomas Carlisle escaped during a heavy rain and thunder storm. Walking through the country to Evansville, Indiana, he embarked on the steamer Storm, bound for Green river, arriving at his home eight days after leaving Indianapolis. Soon thereafter Colonel Adam R. Johnson and Lieutenant Colonel Bob Martin went into that section to raise a regiment of cavalry. He enlisted with them and was elected second lieutenant of Company A of that regiment.

He commanded the remnant of that old regiment as the rear guard of General John H. Morgan's command from Cheshire to the surrender, near Zanesville, Ohio. He was imprisoned at Camp Chase for three weeks, removed to Johnson's Island, Ohio, and was paroled for exchange but the exchange was stopped and he was there until the war closed. He was released on parole June 22, 1865, and arrived home on the 26th.

MRS. FRANK AMPLIAS OWEN.

To Major Frank A. Owen's courtesy and energy is due most of the material for sketches of the company officers of the Partisan Rangers and the muster-rolls of the several companies. It should be said, however, that in this work he has had the assistance of his accomplished wife, to whom these compilations, on account of her strong Confederate sympathies and connections, have been "a labor of love." Major and Mrs. Owen may be regarded as typical Americans; each is descended from a long line of honorable ancestry, whose services to their country were illustrated in the Colonial and Revolutionary wars; each had many relatives in the Confederate army, distinguished for courage and conduct. Mrs. Owen is the granddaughter of Captain Payne Dixon (brother of Governor Archibald Dixon), a soldier in the "War of 1812," and of the Kentucky contingent at the battle of New Orleans. She is the daughter of Captain Richard M. Allin, who, with his brothers, Major Phil. T. Allin and Lieutenant Jack Allin, served with credit in the Confederate army. This esteemed couple now reside in Evansville, Indiana, and with their five children, Allin, Abram, Ruth, Keturah and Dorothy, constitute a happy family, famous for its hospitality.

WILLIAM CURRENS DIMMITT.

There was perhaps no member of the Partisan Rangers better or more favorable known to the people of this section of the country than was Captain Dimmitt.

He was known in various ways, as a teacher, a citizen, as a preacher, as a warrior, and was esteemed for his high moral character.

He was born in Germantown, Mason county, Kentucky, April 4, 1825. He attended school at Bethany, Virginia, and was a student under Alexander Campbell. In 1846 Mr. Dimmitt joined the ministry and up to the time of his death, less than two years ago, he was a minister of the Christian church. Kentucky has produced few men who have done more preaching during their lives than did this man. He was a man who never seemed to tire in the Master's cause. Hundreds and perhaps thousands were brought into the church under his ministry.

Mr. Dimmitt, being a Southern man with Southern sympathies, went into the Southern army near the beginning of the war. In 1862 he organized Company K of the Tenth Kentucky Partisan Rangers. He held the place of captain for some time and then became chaplain. As a soldier he was brave and fearless and held the respect and confidence of his men. After the war Captain Dimmitt again took up the work of the ministry and for many years was pastor of the church at Grape Vine. He also taught school and as an instructor had great success.

He married Miss A. F. Winstead, and to them were born several children, most of whom are still living. More than twenty-five years ago he removed to Texas where he was actively engaged in the ministry until death came to him on the twenty-first day of December, 1901.

JAMES WALLER.

James Waller was born in Granville county, North Carolina, January, 1837. Emigrated with his parents to Hopkins county, Kentucky, in 1850. He was a brother of Dr. J. S. Waller, of Hanson. His parentage on both sides was descended from Revolutionary stock. A maternal uncle held a captaincy in the Continental army in the struggle for American independence while a cousin of his mother, John Forsythe, was the secretary of State in President Jackson's cabinet. There were other relatives who took a prominent part in securing the independence of this country.

Young Waller received only such attention as was afforded by the common schools at that time. He took advantage of this and by perseverance managed to secure a very good education for boys of his age and opportunity. The young man had just reached the years of freedom from parental restraints and was looking around to determine on a course which he should pursue in the way of a profession, when the war between the States broke out, and as he was an intensely Southern man in his opinions, he was arrested as a Southern sympathizer and sent to prison on Johnson's Island in the fall of 1863, where he remained three or four months.

From Johnson's Island he was sent by way of Washington, D. C., when he was exchanged. He, with a number of other comrades made their way back to Kentucky and enlisted in the Confederate army. In April, 1864, he was engaged with Captain (afterwards Colonel) Hollis in recruiting what was known as Hollis's company. He was engaged with Colonel Hollis in a minor fight at Slaughtersville in July, 1864, when Hollis was killed. Not a great while after this battle Waller was elected First Lieutenant of Company A, Captain January's company.

Company A went into Chenoweth's Kentucky regiment at the formation of General Adam R. Johnson's brigade at Providence

(Bruce's Mill) in August, 1864. About the twentieth of this month, General Johnson began making his way South. At Grubbs Crossroads, seven miles east of Princeton, he encountered a small body of Federals. This was for Johnson an unfortunate affair, as it was here that he lost his eyes and was forever made a blind man.

It was at the battle of Grubbs Crossroads that George Riddle and John Brown, of Hopkins county, two brave soldiers, lost their lives. The writer of this article was a witness to the shooting of General Johnson. He was sitting on his horse about ten paces from the general at the time the wound was received. Johnson was seen to throw his hands to his face and requested to be taken from the field; after being placed in the ambulance about one mile from the battle ground, I did not see him again until about two o'clock in the afternoon. It was then that I heard him give orders that his brigade be taken South and report to General Bedford Forrest for duty. General Johnson had received a wound that shot out both his eyes. He was suffering intensely and it was at his request that he was left at a farm house which was done, a few miles north of Cadiz. The brigade reached Canton, on the Cumberland, about ten o'clock at night, and ignoring the order to cross the river, at once went into camp for the night. About four o'clock the next morning we were surprised by a regiment of Federal soldiers under command of Colonel Hawkins. Lieutenant Waller, in the absence of the captain, attempted to form his company for battle. While engaged in his duty he was shot from his horse and expired in a few minutes. The body of Lieutenant Waller was given decent burial by the good people of Canton. After four months it was taken from where it had been buried, carried by kind hands to Olive Branch Cemetery in Hopkins county where it was deposited. Lieutenant Waller was a brave soldier and now he sleeps peacefully beneath the sod of his beloved county.

MILAM M. SISK.

Milam M. Sisk was born in Hopkins county, July 4th, 1820, and was reared on a farm where he lived till the breaking out of the war in the sixties. He was related to the Sisks of the county and was known as a brave man.

In 1862 he enlisted in Company I, Tenth Kentucky Partisan Rangers and was elected as orderly sergeant of his company.

He was in a number of battles and in all these showed that he was well worthy the name of soldier. He was in fights at Madisonville, Hopkinsville, Clarksville, Uniontown, Owensboro, Panther Creek, Elizabethtown, Ashbyburg, Muldraugh's Hill, all in Kentucky, and was at Liberty and Snow Hill in Tennessee and was on Morgan's raid into Indiana and Ohio where he was captured at Cheshire.

Mr. Sisk was sent to Camp Douglas, where he died the twenty-third day of July, 1864. He left a family of seven children, several of whom are still living.

W. D. BROWN.

I joined Company I, Tenth Kentucky Regiment in the fall of 1862, and that night we went to Hopkinsville, captured some Federal forces early the next morning. In a day or two at Clarksville, Tennessee, we captured Colonel Mason's regiment of Federals without firing a gun. A few weeks later while in company with Captain Christy, and Ide and Charles Robertson, we were attacked in the rear by some Federal troops. In our retreat my horse fell with me, and thinking he was shot, I undertook to make my escape on foot but was captured. This took place where Dawson City now stands; there was no city there then. Was carried to Madisonville, kept a prisoner in court house for a day or two, thence to Henderson, transported to Evansville on a boat. While at Henderson, W. C. McGary and F. W. Nisbet called on me and offered to go my security if I would take the oath and return home. This was of course very kind, but I declined, so that night I spent in jail at Evansville. That was the extent of my jail service. The next day we went to Johnson's Island where we spent the winter. As good luck would have it they did not relieve me of my cash which was about fifty dollars. It came in mighty handy to supplement our supplies, as I was about the only one in the mess that was supplied with cash. I bought flour, butter, lard and whatever else we needed for our comfort. I had the good fortune to get into block No. 2, in a room with George Bronough, Sam Greenfield, Dr. Jack Nisbet, Jim Davis, Dr. M. B. Winstead and Bill Stiles. The last two named were held as spies. A dirty scoundrel got Dr. Winstead to take a letter to deliver to Mat or Chit. Lyon purporting to be about a patent loom, when in fact it was a diagram of the Federal camp at Henderson. The other gentlemen were civilians, except Jim Davis. Stiles and myself would carry in our rations of fuel for the day and night; Davis prepared our meals while the others would entertain company, play seven-up and euchre. Thus time passed until spring, when an exchange was arranged and the civilians were sent home; the soldiers were sent to Jamestown, Virginia. Dr. Winstead slipped out of Johnson's Island on his nephew's name, Frank Winstead. The mistake was discovered and a terrible effort was made to recapture Winstead. We were halted in front of Fortress Monroe and a thorough search was made of our boat, but no one would point out Winstead to the searchers, so he went through. I reached my regiment again at Turkey Neck Bend on the Cumberland river, started on the Indiana and Ohio raid, lost my horse, and was left in company with Captain Christy, Dr. Winstead and Cy. Crabtree. We visited Hopkins county. I made the trip on a blind mule; I set it adrift near my old home and secured a horse from my brother Fletcher's home. After a time a lot of us started out through the Kentucky Purchase; near Princeton we captured a Federal regimental officer and some recruits,while having a high time with their best girls. We paroled them and on we went. We finally reached General Forrest's command, cast my lot with the Eighth Kentucky Regiment, Captain F. B. Harris's company, was captured near Franklin, Tennessee, made my escape, joined the regiment and surrendered at Columbus, Georgia.

THOMAS M. BROOKS.

Mr. Thomas M. Brooks was born in Princeton, Ky., April 21, 1842. At the age of one year moved to Madisonville. With the exception of the time he was in the war, Mr. Brooks has been a citizen of this town. When the war between the States broke out Mr. Brooks, then a young man, enlisted in Company K, Partisan Rangers, Tenth Kentucky Regiment.

He was engaged in many battles and skirmishes during the war, and at all times showed himself to be a brave man. He was in the battles of Baker Creek, Elizabethtown, Muldraugh's Hill—all in Kentucky—and was in the battle of Lookout Mountain, Tennessee. He was with Longstreet at Knoxville; was at Tunnel Hill and Atlanta, and was with General Williams when General Stoneman was captured at Stone Mountain.

Mr. Brooks was finally captured, and at the end of the war paroled at Washington, Georgia, with a comrade whose name was Polk

LIEUTENANT POLK LAFFOON,

Co. I, 10th Ky., Cav.

Prince. Both Prince and Brooks were very much worn and debili-
tated. Prince was not able to travel and Brooks gave a widow by
the name of Arnold a mule to board him and Prince for two months.
Although Mr. Brooks wanted to return home to his family in Kentucky, yet he would not desert his friend till both were able to travel.
Mr. Prince returned home, is now a farmer in splendid condition,
has a happy family and lives near Guthrie.

Mr. Brooks is now a citizen of Madisonville. The kindness he
showed his comrade during the war is an evidence of the kindly
disposition of the man. There is no one who is more ready to help
a friend in need than is Mr. Brooks.

POLK LAFFOON.

Polk Laffoon was born in Hopkins county, Kentucky, on the 24th
day of October, 1844, and remained on the farm till he was fourteen
years old, receiving what education the common school afforded.
He was then placed in school at Madisonville, Ky., under Professor
Maurice Kirby, where he received the most of his education. He
was with Colonel Al Fowler in the battle of Burnt Mill, Webster
county, Ky., on the 13th of July, 1861. He was practically a
soldier from that date, but was not formally enlisted into the Confederate army until the 12th of October, 1861. He was second
lieutenant of Company I, Eighth Kentucky Infantry, commanded
by Captain James Powell, the regiment being commanded by
General H. B. Lyon. His regiment brought on the battle in concert
with the First and Second Mississippi and Seventh Texas Regiments
on the bloody Saturday, and was the largest loser on that day. He,
with his regiment, was captured on that day, was sent to prison,
first to Camp Chase, then to Johnson's Island and was exchanged
at Vicksburg on the 16th day of September, 1862, and went into
camp at Canton, Mississippi, where, owing to the dilapidation of
the companies of the regiment they were consolidated, and by
Lieutenant Laffoon's request he was omitted from the first officers.
He immediately came to Kentucky on recruiting service, and found
that General A. R. Johnson had left the State. He joined General
Johnson's regiment at Camp Winroe, Tennessee, where he was
elected Second Lieutenant of Company I, Tenth Kentucky
Cavalry, commanded by Captain John H. Christy. This was about
the 15th of October, 1862. From that date until the close of the

Indiana and Ohio raid he was with General John H. Morgan on all his raids and in all the battles of any note.

He was captured on this raid and confined in the Pennsylvania penitentiary for nine months, and at Fort Delaware and Point Lookout until the close of the war, when he was released from prison and arrived at his home on the 24th of June, 1865. He taught school in Christian county for two years, and in Trigg and Logan counties, during which time he studied law at night. He entered the practice of law in the fall of '67 and has been a continual practitioner since. He was elected county attorney of Hopkins county in 1872 without opposition. In 1884 he was elected by the Democrats of the Second Congressional District of Kentucky a member of the Forty-ninth Congress and was re-elected to the Fiftieth Congress in 1886.

ALFRED RICHESON.

Captain Alfred Richeson was born in Louisville, Kentucky, July 18, 1830, and was the second son of Alfred Richeson and Elizabeth Williamson Richeson of Amherst county, Virginia. He was educated at the University of Virginia and at West Point. He was six feet six inches in height, with steel gray eyes, light brown hair, and weighed about 275 pounds.

Captain Richeson was a man of wonderful personal magnetism, a thorough linguist, a finished scholar, and having traveled over most of the civilized world, he was possessed of a fund of anecdotes and reminiscences which, accompanied by his intelligent face and most perfect physique, qualified him to be a leader among men.

He was a faithful, devoted friend and a fearless and dreaded foe; and during the troublous times of old Kentucky during the sixties he, with the rest of Colonel Adam Johnson's men, made an imperishable record.

He enlisted in the Confederate service in Union county,, Kentucky, during the winter of '62 or '63 and was made captain of Company E, Colonel Adam R. Johnson's Tenth Regiment, Partisan Rangers, C. S. A.

He was in several engagements, the most important of which were the fight near Clarksville, Tennessee, near Owensboro, Kentucky, at Uniontown, Kentucky, and at Geiger's Lake, Union county, Kentucky, and with several of his men was captured in '63 and sent

CAPT. ALFRED RICHESON.
Co. E, 10th Ky. Cav.

to the prison on Johnson's Island near Sandusky, Ohio, where he was finally exchanged and returned to Richmond for orders.

He was foully murdered by some of the carpetbaggers who cursed West Tennessee with their nefarious plots during '69 and '70. His death occurred in October, 1870.

JOHN D. FIELDS.

After Morgan's Ohio raid in July, 1863, I escaped and joined the command of General John S. Williams, which was camped at Panther Springs, nineteen miles northwest of Saltville, Virginia, and seven miles from Tazewell Court House (or Jeffersonville). This was about July 23d or 24th. I was ordered by General Williams on the 26th to take a volunteer scout and go in the direction of Bland Court House, West Virginia, and ascertain the whereabouts of the enemy. The detachment left camp about two or three a. m., and after proceeding eight or ten miles (in a heavy fog), we heard horses tramping on the Blue Lick and Wytheville Road about one mile to our left; the volunteers refused to proceed further, and I ordered them back to camp. Then proceeding alone to the junction of the roads and being in a blue uniform, I was enabled to maneuver unmolested until the main column of the Federal troops passed by. Falling in the rear of said column, I followed it for a mile, when an officer dropped out of the line and stopped at a house on the roadside for refreshments, which he never got, as I then rode up and captured him, making him mount his mule and accompany me by a circuitous route to General Williams's headquarters. The officer proved to be Captain John Cutler, of Company C, Thirty-fourth Ohio Mounted Infantry, and officer of the day. In 1895 I located the captain at Arkadelphia, Arkansas, where he had lived since 1872. We had quite an amusing correspondence. He wrote me that the capture of him and the " other donkey " caused him nineteen months of prison life. I returned him the officer's sash he wore that day, which he was very thankful to receive. I remained with General Williams until January 18, 1864. Then proceeded to Decatur, Georgia, where General A. R. Johnson was re-organizing the remnant of General Morgan's command. In March we were ordered to Wytheville, Virginia. On our arrival the day was bright and pleasant, and the birds were chirping in the trees as we marched into the fair grounds, and everything indicated that spring had opened. We were thinly clad and had only one thin blanket, and no tent or protection from the weather; and when we awakened next morning we were all covered with snow. We left Wytheville early in May for Saltville, Virginia. Almost immediately after our arrival at Saltville we were ordered aboard of the cars for Dublin, Virginia, to re-enforce General Jenkins. The engine that pulled our train jumped the track a few miles from Saltville, causing considerable delay; hence, when we did reach Dublin, General Jenkins's troops were in full retreat; but when our little band of about four hundred appeared on the field the Federals were driven back for a considerable distance, when they succeeded in making a stand, and re-enforcements being brought up, we were forced back, but in good order, until we crossed New river. They followed us no farther. Afterward we returned to Saltville and Abingdon, where preparations were being made for Morgan's last raid into Kentucky, which began the last day of May, 1864. The first night after leaving Abingdon we camped in Moccasin Gap on Moccasin creek. The second night we camped on Clinch river, and the third night at Pound Gap, on the Cumberland mountains. During the night the woods in which we were camped caught fire, causing considerable excitement. During the confusion a man on a white horse dashed into the camp and out; he was believed to have been a Federal scout, but was not killed or captured on account of the confusion existing. Nothing of interest occurred until on the 5th, when a bushwhacker fired on our men. He was shot and his body left in the fence corner on the roadside. We went into camp nearby. It was at this place that private Ben G. Slaughter (known in the command as "Squirrel") attempted to rob a bee-hive of the old log-make style, during the absence of the owner. In attempting to extract the honey from the hive, his hands became fastened in the cross-pieces and he was fearfully stung. The bees were so wrought up that we had to tear the fence down and pass the column around next morning. "Squirrel" said he had found the remedy for bee-sting, which remedy was honey, and he made a copious application, both externally and internally. We reached the hills above Mt. Sterling, Kentucky, June 8th at sundown, and went into camp in a beautiful small woodland pasture. The command was in fine spirits, but, alas, many of them were to be left on that field to answer no more to roll-call. The Yankees reported that there were found one hundred and forty-seven killed and wounded on the field. The picket was

JOHN] D. FIELDS, M. D.

in charge of Lieutenant Colonel Brent with orders to place them about one and a half miles back on the Ticktown road; but from some cause he placed them only a few hundred yards from our camp. At daylight the next morning, June 9th, the Federals drove in the pickets, and followed them so close that they were right on the camp before we had any warning. A heavy fog was all that saved us from capture. The Federals did not know where we were camped as we were in the pasture a short distance from the road. The first of the Federals passed by on the road, and when the second part of the regiment came up Lieutenant Colonel Martin had succeeded in forming a line of battle over in a wheat-field and behind a fence about one hundred and fifty yards from the road the Yankees were in, and fired a volley into them. They cried out: "Don't fire; you are firing into your own men." Colonel Martin commanded us to give it to them. At this time they ran a piece of artillery up and fired it over in the direction of Mt. Sterling, it seemed to me. The right flank of our line was near the road, so we just dashed over the fence and captured the gun, but they got away with the caisson. So we rammed the cannon full of rock and clay and abandoned it. About this time I was badly wounded by being shot through the right shoulder, which bled very profusely, and in the course of an hour I became so weak and blind I could not go any farther, so lay down in the wheat-field and rooted my shoulder into the soft ground to see if it would not stop the flow of blood. The last thing I can remember was lying on my right side and seeing the heads of wheat dancing about as the bullets hit them. I knew nothing more for some time after the battle was ended. When I came to I was lying on my back and my clothing was wet, for it had rained. I crawled to the fence a short distance from where I had lain down (Lieutenant Joseph Sellers had found me lying on my right side, turned me over on my back and reported me dead), and pulled myself up by the fence. As soon as I got up straight I heard a rattling of a saber in the scabbard of some one on horseback, and knowing that our men did not use them, I let go the fence and lay down just as a drunken Irish soldier came up. He said: "Hello, Johnnie, don't you want to be an angel?" I told him "Yes;" and he said: "I will assist you," pulling his pistol at the same time. Just then a lieutenant rode up and asked the soldier what he was doing. He said here was a Johnnie that wanted to be an angel, and he wanted to assist him. The officer upbraided him, and came up to the fence, asking me if I was much hurt, and after receiving my reply, got off his horse and climbed over the fence, and gave me some apple brandy which revived me very much. Then he ordered two stretcher-bearers to take me to a house near by. A man by the name of Thomas lived there. I was kept here about two weeks under guard with others, when I made my escape and went to Mr. James Hamilton's on or near Slate creek, about seven miles from Mt. Sterling. I was not at Mr. Hamilton's more than two days before a woman betrayed me, and the next morning at daylight a company of Federals were around the house. The captain called Mr. Hamilton to the door and asked him if he had a wounded rebel at his house. Mr. Hamilton replied that he had a wounded boy in the house. After some parley the captain and his lieutenant came in where I was. The captain asked me where I was from. I told him I was from Knox county, Tennessee. He remarked that most of the people in that county were Union people. I said yes, my father was a Union man. He said: "What are you doing in the rebel army?" and I told him I had been conscripted, and that I wanted to take the oath. He then asked me if I could ride horseback. I told him I was so weak I could hardly sit up. He then asked Mr. Hamilton if he had a hack or buggy; but he did not have either. So he said he would leave me there and send an ambulance out for me next morning. When the ambulance came I was twenty-one miles from there, up in the mountains at a Mr. Howard's. After recuperating for a few days, I commenced gathering men together to go South. In one of my trips I went up on the Red Fork of Kentucky river and came near being captured again. We, five of us, had just gone into a house to get breakfast; the men had sat down, and just as I pulled the chair out to take a seat an old hound barked, and I looked out and saw about forty Yanks coming double-quick down on the house. I ordered the men to run out of the front door, as the Yanks were on us. They lost no time in doing so. We kept the house between us and them until we got into the brush, but just as we entered into the woods they fired a volley into us, but, fortunately, did no damage. They got my hat that I had left outside of the house, and hastily departed. After going about a mile they ran across one of my recruits by the name of Thomas Symes and killed him, and in the excitement they lost my hat, which Mrs. Smith, the lady of the house where poor Symes was killed, brought up to me. The

Yankees told Mrs. Smith that they had killed all of us. We gathered together twenty-seven men hastily, including Captain Kidd's " bushwhackers," and followed the Yankees, and made them pay dearly for poor Symes. We killed twenty-seven out of forty men. This was about the middle of August, 1864. In a few days we collected forty-five men and went out, joining General J. H. Morgan at Abingdon, Virginia, August 29th, 1864, only a few days before he moved into Tennessee. He appointed me first lieutenant of Company B, Fourteenth Kentucky, Colonel Dick Morgan's regiment. I was at Greenville when he was killed. My wound became troublesome and I was ordered back to my old home at Abingdon, Virginia, to recruit my company. I was near Pound Gap, Cumberland mountains, when General Lee surrendered.

I was born April 19, 1845, and at the breaking out of the war in March, 1861, joined Captain Tiller's Partisan Rangers. They were disbanded in September, when I joined Captain Thomas Allen's company, Morgan's squadron, near Bowling Green, about the latter part of October, 1861, and was with this company until Quirk's Scouts, of the same command, was organized, and belonged to it until we became Company B of the Fourteenth Kentucky Cavalry.

[Note by the Editor.—Dr. Fields settled in Texas soon after the war closed, studied medicince, and obtained his diploma at New Orleans; purchased land near Manor, Texas, where he now lives, and has been very successful in the practice of medicine; has a splendid farm and several large ranches, and, like all good soldiers, has made a good citizen and is prosperous.]

BEN. F. PERKINS.

I was sworn into the service of the Confederate States by General Johnson on the street in Madisonville, Hopkins county, Kentucky, in August, 1862, and served till the end of the war; was wounded at Cynthiana, Kentucky, at the last battle General Morgan had there. When our brigade was surrounded by an overwhelming force, I escaped by swimming the river, although suffering from a severe wound in the calf of my leg, and made my way to the White Sulphur Springs in Union county, Kentucky, and soon attached myself to the Thirteenth Kentucky Cavalry then in process of formation and commanded by Colonel Sypert.

In a few days I was selected with Major Taylor and White Canton (an escaped prisoner from Johnson's Island) to meet General

Johnson and Colonel J. Q. Chenoweth at —————— old mill, and pilot that command to Sypert's camp at White Sulphur Springs. Soon we all moved several miles above Providence, and while in camp there General Payne, from Paducah, landed a large force of Federals at Uniontown, and I was detailed to go to Morganfield that night, and to send a man back to report to Johnson. I sent Mr. Thomas Omer. I followed Payne down the road to the Dodge Hill in Union county, and just before he reached this point I took a near cut through the woods with my little squad and ambushed his force. There were but six of us, but we stampeded Payne's entire brigade, and thereby saved a good many horses and other property that they were taking off. At Caseyville they reported that they had been attacked by "Stovepipe" Johnson and two thousand guerrillas.

I shall only add that I began as a private and ended, as my parole shows, as first lieutenant.

THE DEATH OF COLONEL WILLIAM HOLLIS.

BY FRANK A. OWEN.

I write the following sketch, hoping that it may be of some interest, at least to my old comrades-in-arms:

Colonel William Hollis was raising a regiment for Colonel Adam R. Johnson's command early in the summer of 1863. Upon the 25th day of June, with all the armed and unarmed men that he had at his command, he chased Payne's company to Uniontown, but his force was not sufficient to take him by assault in his fortified position, so he surrounded the place and kept him and his men close prisoners for three days, capturing some of his outposts every night. Generally he would get all the horses on the picket, the men often escaping on foot under cover of the darkness, to their camps. Learning one day that there was a strong relief coming to Payne's assistance, Hollis retired to Slaughtersville, in Webster county, on the 27th of June, where he had notified his men to rendezvous on the 28th, preparatory to going South to meet Johnson. Colonel Hollis, with about four hundred and fifty of his men, four hundred of whom were unarmed, had arrived in Slaughtersville and had picketed every road in very soldierly fashion. In the early afternoon two of his officers, unfortunately, had a private difficulty, one shooting and badly wounding the other.

Hollis's picket, thinking that it was the enemy firing, rallied upon the camp, and upon discovering their mistake, were returning to their posts near Captain Thomas Drake's farm when they met Payne's battalion of Thirty-fifth Kentucky Infantry, and an Illinois company of cavalry, which had already reached the limits of the town. The Confederate pickets fired upon them from a point near the farm, then retired hastily to their camp west of the creek, an old railroad dump, the road not having been completed at that time. The Federals made a charge and dismounted in the old creek-bed. A hot skirmish ensued and a large number of the unarmed Confederates retreated from the field. At this critical moment Colonel Hollis was shot in the head and killed instantly. As soon as this became generally known among his small force of raw, undisciplined recruits, they fled in despair at losing their leader, and left several wounded and killed upon the battleground. William Duvall, one of Hollis's best men, was found several days later in a briar patch, a Yankee bullet having struck him to kill. Rev. William Wright, a minister in the Old Baptist church, thoroughly reliable and still in active service as a minister of the gospel, made this statement to me: " I was a member of Company D, Captain Payne's company of mounted infantry, and my company was in advance at the battle of Slaughtersville. We met a squad of Confederates and they fired on us from the top of a rise near Dr. Drake's old residence. Captain Payne ordered us to charge and in less than a half minute the dust had obscured both friend and foe. A number of women ran out in the street in front of us and told us not to go on, for the Confederates were too many for us. At the time we thought that they were our friends, but now we doubt it. We did not heed their warning, but charged on to the bed of the old creek, and there dismounted. We immediately began firing upon the rebels who were beyond the main creek that was about half full of water, and about one hundred and fifty yards distant. We had a protected position, as the railroad not then finished was immediately in our front. I took a position about thirty or forty yards to the right oblique, and in advance of our command, and behind a large tree. The captain, in his broken English, said: " Youse there had petter vatch out a lettle or yous'll get yer head off shot." The Confederates soon gave way, leaving their dead and wounded upon the field, as well as some horses tied to trees, most of whom were wounded. I then made a bee-line for the center of the camp and waded the creek, which was thigh deep. I know that I was the first man to reach Colonel Hollis, who was dead, lying on his back. His coat was thrown open exposing his pistols, one an ivory-handled, silver-mounted, twenty-two caliber, the other a forty-two Colt. I relieved him of both of them and thrust them into my pockets. He was dressed in full Confederate uniform, which was new, and a pair of long-legged cavalry boots. Noticing a beautiful horse tied to a tree, rearing and charging to get loose, I left the dead colonel, and ran to the horse before any of our men reached camp, they having gone round by the large bridge, some two hundred yards out of the way. I understood that there was a detail of men to carry Colonel Hollis to William Stidman's blacksmith shop. I saw the dead officer later in the day lying in the shop without coat, hat or boots. I know that all his clothes were on him when I first saw him in the field. I saw a Confederate lying full length on the ground and leaning on his arm. I went to him and asked him what was the matter. He told me that he had been wounded just before the fight by a brother officer because he wanted to pull loose from Hollis's command and go South instantly. I think he said that his name was Captain Moore. Later on I saw Payne's son, Charlie, wearing the dead Confederate's hat which had a large, drooping ostrich plume on it."

Colonel Hollis was a gallant soldier and an elegant gentleman, and his untimely death was greatly lamented by all who knew him.

AL FOWLER.

BY POLK LAFFOON.

Captain Al Fowler, the subject of this sketch, was born in Hopkins county, Kentucky, on the 17th of July, 1835. He enlisted in the Confederate army in the fall of 1861, but had done valuable scouting service before the date of his enlistment.

He commanded the Confederate embryo soldiers in the assault in the battle of the Burnt Mill in Webster county on September 15, 1861, the first battle of the Civil War fought in Kentucky. This battle fully illustrates the character of the man for courage, indomitable energy and unyielding determination. In this battle he captured twenty-five well-equipped and organized soldiers who were fleeing from Hopkinsville, Kentucky, where General S. B. Buckner invaded the State. Colonel Jas. F. Buckner and Captain Wm.

CAPTAIN AL. FOWLER,

1st Capt. Co. I, 10th Ky., P. R.   Killed at Summer's Store, 1862.

Buckner were in command of the retreating forces and were made prisoners. Colonel J. F. Buckner's command was making its escape through Captain Fowler's neighborhood and he determined on its capture.

He had not a soldier nor a military equipment at his command, but from the surrounding towns and country he hastily summoned his friends by night from their quiet homes and pursued the fleeing foe and overtook them fourteen miles from Madisonville, where they were encamped in a frame church. When morning dawned the retreating forces found themselves entirely surrounded and every avenue of escape closed up. After a sharp skirmish, which lasted an hour, Captain Fowler's men sheltering themselves behind trees, the crest of the hill and the bed of the creek, the enemy surrendered with all their guns and ammunition. Buck Madison was the only wounded on Fowler's side.

From this time until his death, he, by his vigilance, bravery and activity, was a terror to the Federal forces in southwestern Kentucky. He enlisted and armed a battalion of fearless men imbued with the spirit and ready at all times to follow their leader in any deeds of daring. To his enemies he appeared never to sleep, and night and day he might be expected to assail them at any moment. Every scheme that the ingenuity of the Federal officers could devise to capture him and his command proved ineffectual. At one time the "Dutch Cavalry" left Madisonville, where they were stationed and gave it out that they were going to Henderson, but suddenly and rapidly returned, hoping to surprise him. He was in town and they knew it, but after a diligent search they failed to find him, he having sought and found safety under the floor of Lem Simon's woodshop, where he remained until darkness enabled him to escape. The most amusing circumstance connected with this incident was the fact that Captain A. Fowler, unknown personally to the Dutch Cavalry and wearing no uniform, helped the officers to place their pickets before he sought his place of hiding, and when he made his exit from the town he knew the exact route to take to evade the enemy.

Chagrined and mad at their failure to capture him and his command, his enemies were unchivalrous enough to burn down his home, appropriate and destroy his crops, devastate his farm and turn his wife and little children out of home and sustenance. How differently did Captain Fowler act toward his Union neighbors. He was importuned to retaliate on them, but with firmness he declined and threatened to punish any of his command who interfered with private property in any way unless the necessity of his soldiers demanded it and such necessity was first to be submitted to him.

He was impetuous and under excitement was sometimes impulsive. In the heat of battle he often emphasized his exhortation to his soldiers by a little profanity. On one occasion in the midst of the conflict when the battle was raging hottest, he exclaimed: "D——n them, boys, give them h—l." At that instant he observed Major Scobee, who was then and is now an eminent divine in the Methodist church, standing near him. Captain Fowler turned to him and apologized for swearing in his presence. Major Scobee replied: "Colonel, if it does you any good let them have it."

Captain Fowler was with General Forrest at the battles of Sacramento and Fort Donelson as a private soldier, at which places he endeared himself to General Forrest by his indomitable courage. After he received his commission as captain and while he was recruiting his command he was one of General Adam Johnson's chief friends and advisers and was present with him in many of his desperate enterprises.

It is not within the scope of this brief notice of his life and career to enter into the details of the many battles and skirmishes in which he was engaged. He took a brave part under General Johnson in the battles of Clarksville and Hopkinsville, where the Confederates were so eminently successful and where he distinguished himself by gallantry.

It is sad to note the untimely close of a life like that of Colonel Fowler's, but that career which had been so brilliant, so dazzling and so grand was fated to come to a sudden end. On the 23d of November, 1862, near Summer's Store, in Muhlenberg county, Kentucky, in the night, he attacked with his command a superior force of the enemy and in this engagement lost his life. When the battle was raging furiously he ordered his men to lie down, and when day dawned he was found dead from a buckshot wound in the head. From the location and the character of the injury it is generally believed that he was killed accidentally at the hands of one of his own men.

Charles Ashby, a truthful Union soldier of Hopkins county, Kentucky, says he was in this fight, and with a comrade or two found Captain Al Fowler the next mornng and there was a pistol ball

CAPT. W. B. ALBRIGHT.

through his head cutting the band of his hat in two on both sides of his head; in addition to this there had passed through his chest two carbine balls, and it's a mistake about his own men having killed him accidentally.

From whatever view point history may record Captain Fowler, it must set the seal of its approval upon his life and career, whether as farmer, citizen, soldier, husband or father. In that life he represented the highest type of civilization and manhood, and when his body was covered in the ground there was only buried all of the heroism that could die.

W. B. ALBRIGHT.

(From the Confederate Veteran.)

W. B. Albright was born near Clarksville, Tennessee, February 28, 1841. In the summer of 1861 he joined Company A, First Tennessee Heavy Artillery, stationed at Fort Henry, was soon appointed first sergeant in charge of gun No. 1, thirty-two pounder. He was in the bombardment from start to finish. He fired the last shot. It was after the fort surrendered and unawares. Before the gunboat landed he escaped. A few days later he went to Fort Donelson, and was in the water batteries there during the battle. He escaped by the river road. He afterwards joined Colonel Adam Johnson's Tenth Kentucky Cavalry, and was put in charge of a piece of artillery, secured in the recapture of Clarksville.

The most noted shot perhaps of that great war was in August, 1862, when Captain Albright hid a cannon by a straight stretch of road near the Cumberland Iron Works, sent all of his men away, waited by the gun until the head of the Federals, the Fifth Iowa Cavalry, was near, then he fired directly down the line. The chaos following that shot can hardly be conceived.

Of this shot Captain Albright has written:

"As they approached, going north before crossing the bridge, the scene was magnificent. It is vivid with me still. When they crossed the bridge, entering the fine stretch of road looking directly into the mouth of my gun, they did not falter, but spurred their horses to greater speed. They came as an avalanche to sweep everything before it. The few hundred feet were soon covered. At a glance I saw that I would get but one shot, and ordered my squad to flee for safety. Having no friction matches, I had to use the torch from a small fire near by kindled for that purpose. There I stood waving my firebrand to keep it alive, and at the same time keeping an eye on my gun and the enemy. It seemed an age for them to cover that short distance leading up from the bridge. I was eager to have it over. I confess that I felt something more than eagerness when they came abreast in columns of eights, their sabers flashing in the light of the sun, which was then just rising. I could not but feel a hesitancy in firing on such men. In these few seconds the head of the column had almost reached me. I gave my firebrand a whirl in the air to make sure of its being a 'go,' and lowered it to the powder. They were so close that the smoke and dust enveloped the entire front of their column; in fact, the whole moving mass was enveloped in a heavy charcoal dust that filled the air until it became as 'dark as Egypt.' I had no time for anything. A jam and crash of men and horses were all around me; the road seemed to be piled full of them. Kind providence and a big beech-tree were my salvation this time sure. Men and horses were all about me, so close I could feel them move about. The charging column was only checked, and imagine my surprise, when the smoke cleared away, not to find the road filled with the dead. Upon looking about for my cannon it was many feet away, having been thrown from its trunnions. The carriage was lying upside down. All this was done by the momentum of their heavy horses and their speed when the gun was fired. At the close of the fight Colonel Martin congratulated me on the part I had so well executed. It was all done with a little 'Fourth-of-July' gun, but promoted me to the rank of captain."

He was in many successful engagements in Northern Kentucky. In November, 1862, he went South and joined Morgan's command; was with him on his famous Christmas raid into Northern Kentucky and was captured. He escaped from his guard, but was soon recaptured by Woolford's Cavalry. He was marched to Lebanon Junction and from there sent to Louisville on an engine. After a few days in prison changed his name, his uniform, and succeeded in being taken as a private for exchange at Vicksburg. Near Cairo the boat was headed for St. Louis, where it ran into a dense fog and was forced to land when he and James Christian escaped and took up the tramp for Dixie, one of great fatigue and hardships. He rejoined his command in time to go with General Morgan on his Ohio campaign, and was captured at Adams' Mills, July 19th. He was imprisoned at Cincinnati, on Johnson's Island,

DR. BENJAMIN REDFORD,
Surgeon 10th Ky. Partisan Rangers.

Allegheny City, Point Lookout, and Fort Delaware. In March, 1865, he was sent South on a special exchange, and at Greensboro surrendered with Joseph E. Johnston's army. He was twelve times a prisoner of war and got his freedom only once by consent of his captors or custodians.

Captain Albright settled after the war at Columbus, Ohio, and was instrumental in organizing the Confederate Camp in that city. He was traveling when, falling sick at Gallatin, Tennessee, he died, and was buried in the Confederate lot in the cemetery there. He left a wife to mourn his loss.

JOHN B. DORTCH.

Captain John B. Dortch was born May 11, 1830. He was a successful farmer at the beginning of the war, when he enlisted as a private in Cyrus Sugg's company which was raised in the vicinity of Guthrie, Kentucky, and was soon after elected lieutenant of the company which was placed in the Fiftieth regiment, of which Sugg was elected lieutenant colonel and Dortch was elected captain.

He escaped with a part of his company from Fort Donelson, and reported to General Albert Sidney Johnston at Murfreesboro. Afterwards he raised two companies of cavalry and reported to me at Camp Coleman, Todd county, Kentucky. Under my orders he burned the railroad bridge between Russellville and Bowling Green, and had a sharp skirmish with General Harrison at Russellville. He commanded one of the battalions of Morgan's men at the battle of Chickamauga, and afterwards, under Bragg's order, reported to General Wheeler, and was never connected with my command any more.

PHILIP JONES.

Philip Jones was born in Henderson county, 1837; enlisted in the Tenth Kentucky Partisan Rangers in August, 1862; was commissioned adjutant and served in that capacity until his resignation.

OSCAR L. BARBOUR.

Oscar L. Barbour was born at Princeton, Kentucky, in 1846. Enlisted in Tenth Kentucky Partisan Rangers in 1862. In February, 1863 he was appointed adjutant of the regiment; although but seventeen years old he was a very brave, active and efficient officer and was always known as Adjutant Barbour. He died at the home of General A. R. Johnson in Texas, in 1882.

JAMES M'CLAIN.

Captain James McClain was born in Henderson county in 1837; moved to Memphis in 1855 and was among the first to enlist in the Confederate army, and served with Forrest's old regiment until 1862, when he was promoted and transferred to the Tenth Kentucky Partisan Rangers, and was appointed commissary in place of Horace Garth, resigned. He was one of the most efficient officers in that line in the service; was promoted to brigade commissary in February, 1863, and held that office until his death, which occurred during the Ohio raid at Buffington Island, where he was drowned.

NEIL HELM.

Captain Neil Helm was born in Missouri, 1836, moved to Texas in 1857 and was employed in surveying with me, and proved to be one of the most faithful and fearless men that were in my employ. At the beginning of the war he returned to Missouri, joined General Sterling Price and remained with him until General Bragg's expedition into Kentucky, when he was captured and was sent to prison at Louisville; escaping he joined me at Walnut Hill in Webster county, remained with me until we joined Morgan, when he got an appointment as captain with permission to raise a company of scouts, and was sent to Texas on recruiting service. Among his recruits was William Hamby, afterwards adjutant general of Tennessee, Thomas Bryson, Charles Taylor, Fletcher Stephens, and a number of others. This company of scouts was my advance guard on the Indiana and Ohio raid, and Captain Helm's skill and care saved us from a number of ambuscades on that eventful expedition. He escaped with me at Buffington Island, and was of material assistance in reorganizing Morgan's command at Morristown, Tennessee, and at the second reorganization at Decatur, Georgia. He was in the fight with Martin at Dublin depot and was with me on my last expedition in Kentucky and commanded company A in the regiment organized by Colonel Napier. After I was wounded he lost all interest in the Confederate army and refused to do any more service, and remained in the vicinity of

CAPTAIN ANDREW RAY,
1st Capt. Co. A, 10th Ky., P. R.

where I was confined from the wound I had received in the fight at Grubbs Crossroads and came with Major Walker Taylor several times to take me South. But being unable to be moved and also being under parole, I declined to go with them, and when I was sent to prison he went to Virginia where my wife was boarding. When I came from prison in February, 1865, he took immediate and special care of me and as we were traveling South he was killed at Chester, South Carolina, as before described.

BRIGADE STAFF.

My brigade staff was, Walter Overton, adjutant; Paul J. Marrs, quartermaster; Thomas J. Johnson, commissary; ——— Long, aid; George Hunt, ordnance officer; Meade Woodson, aid-de-camp.

The brigade organization was to have been the Tenth Kentucky: Colonel R. M. Martin, commissioned June 1, 1864; Lieutenant Colonel G. Wash Owen; Major, Jacob Bennett; Adjutant, Frank A. Owen; Surgeon, Dr. Ben. Redford; Quartermaster, R. R. Kelley; Commissary, Sherwood Hicks.

Second Regiment: Colonel, J. Q. Chenoweth, Commissioned August, 1864; Lieutenant Colonel, S. P. Cunningham, August, 1864; Major, Jones; Adjutant, Waller Bullock; Surgeon, Netherton.

Third Regiment: Colonel, Lee Sypert, commissioned 1864; Robert Soery, lieutenant colonel; J. Walker Taylor, major.

Fourth Regiment: Charles Napier, colonel, commissioned August, 1864; Lieutenant Colonel, Shanks; Mark Coleman, major.

Fifth Regiment: Colonel, William Hollis.

MISS LIDE CARICO, Daviess County, Ky.

"The Daughter" of the 10th Ky., P. R.

Ashly, Walter.
Bacon, Gillie.
Brown, Theodore.
Brown, Lee.
Barr, ———.
Barnard, Pink H.
Beal, Andrew.
Beel, John.
Barber, Oscar L.
Bowers, Samuel.
Burnett, James.
Burnett, Pious.
Brooks, Robert
Browder, Josiah.
Buchanan, R. H.
Bryant, Simeon.
Bradon, John.
Burwell, James.
Burnett, Elijah.
Burress, Murry.
Burress, John.
Bryant, Jas. H.
Burras, Dan.
Brown, Henry C.
Carlisle, R. R.
Carlisle, R. W.
Cobb, Wm.
Chappell, Thomas.
Chandler, James W.
Coleman, Wm.
Corbett, James.
Corbett, John.
Coffman, Theodore.
Crockett, John W.
Clure, Lafayette.
Clove, F. L.
Carico, Miss Eliza,
"Daughter of the Regi-
ment."

Coffman, Jas. R.
Culver, Thomas.
Donley, John.
Dothett, J. G.
Dixon, George.
Darnell, B. W.
Darnell, R. W.
Duvall, Archibald D.
Dwyer, ———.
Edwards, P.
Eubanks, S. J.
Eubanks, A. S.
Favers, Travis.
Fraser, Wm.
Friend, Jacob.
Fenwick, Wm.
Fenrich, Wm. H.
Farley, John.
Farley, Henderson.
Farley, Joseph.
Floyd, Robert.
Gooch, Bartlet L.
Glover, Joseph.
Glove, Wm.
Glover, Thomas J.
Gooch, Thomas
Gudgil, Dan.
Gates, ———.
Harte, Ben E.
Hicks, B.
Hawkins, R.
Humphrey, George.
Humphrey, Thomas.
Humphrey, Isaac.
Hicklin, Thomas.
Hicklin, Lem.
Humphrey, R. H.
Hicklin, John L.
Hollis, Wm.

Huffman, ———.
Harden, James.
Humphrey, Sam. C.
Hussey, Chas.
Hobgood, Simeon.
Jones, Willis H.
Jackson, Thomas.
Johnson, B.
Johns, Bud.
Jenkins, Wm.
Jones, Thomas.
Jones, Robert
Jenkins, Dr. Warren L.
Lockett, Wm.
Marion, John.
Mulligan, John.
Mullins, John W.
Mason, Wm.
Moore, Wm. P.,
   "Judge."
Moore, Wm.
Morehead, Enoch.
Madison, Wm.
Myers, Marion.
McCowan, C. L.
McGowan, Chas. W.
Meffiord, Andrew J.
Myers, James.
Nance, J. H.
Owen, ———.
Owen, B.
Ogden, Wm.
Osburn, J. D.
Osburn, Harden,
Prather, H. C.
Priest, E. Pam.
Pennington, M. J.
Pritchett, G. W.
Pruitt, James Robert.

Priest, E. R.
Purdue, Chin.
Pendrus, Wm.
Paterson, John.
Porter, Dr. George W.
Quin, Ben F.
Ray, John Wes.
Rheam, F. R.
Rust, Lemuel T.
Robinson, Ben.
Robinson, George.
Robertson, Burtram B.
Ramsey, Andrew P.
Riley, John.
Sayres, Louis.
Sayres, J.
Stodghill, Dan.
Stodghill, J. Harry.
Sizemore, James.
Stubblefield, D.
Thomas, J. W.
Slayton, Vm.
Slayton, A. J.
Son, C. J.

Son, Samuel.
Siers, Louis.
Sellers, L.
Smith, John.
Sigers, Wm.
Spinny, George W.
Sutton, L. B.
Spencer, George.
Scott, C. M.
Sutton, W. M.
Sursey, F. B.
Sutton, Wm. H. H.
Sayers, W. C.
Straud, John.
Tippett, C. C.
Thomas, Pack Pascal.
Smith, C. A.
Triplett, J. H.
Tippett, J. Hinton.
Thomas, Wm.
Tippett, Pres.
Townsend, A. W.
Timmons, Felix.
Thomas, George.

Thomas, James R.
Thompson, P.
Thompson, James.
Tapp, Jes Anderson.
Townsend, James L.
Tapp, James.
Thomison, Zack.
Utley, Zac.
Veazey, N.
Veazey, Edward.
Wilkerson, John.
Ward, John J.
Weldon, T.
Wilson, E.
Wilson, A.
Woodward, J. M.
Warren, J. A.
Woodward, F. H.
Wood, Frank.
Yarbrough, Ingraham.
Yarbrough, John.
Yarbrough, C.

Lieutenant Robert Sugg, of Henderson county, Kentucky, says: "Captain Ed. Hall's company was commanded by Captain Montgomery Swope, after Captain Hall resigned; First Lieutenant, Robert A. Sugg; Second Lieutenant, Frank DeSchamp; Third Lieutenant, John W. Lockett. This was after Captain Hall resigned."

The company was consolidated with Company A, "Mont" Swope becoming first lieutenant and Robert A. Sugg, third lieutenant, both of whom resigned soon after the fall of Clarksville, Tenn.

COMPANY B.   REORGANIZATION.

In the reorganization Company G was consolidated with Company B. Company G was Captain L. D. Fisher's company, and he was killed in 1862; hence, the consolidation of the companies.

THOMAS GOOCH,

One of the first eight enlisted, Co. A, 10th Ky., P. R.

First Captain, L. D. Fisher.
Captain, Wm. M. Marr.
First Lieutenant, Hugh Dunlap.
Second Lieutenant, B. B. Kirby.
Third Lieutenant, S. S. Hicks.
First Sergeant, S. Wilkins.
Second Sergeant, S. Burns.
Third Sergeant, G. Allen.
Fourth Sergeant, Henry Perdue.
First Corporal, Joseph Stalls.
Second Corporal, John Turpin.
Third Corporal, G. W. Smith.
Fourth Corporal, Thos. Knight.

PRIVATES.

Allen, J. H.
Allen, E.
Anderson, **G. W.**
Applegate, F.
Armstrong, W. T.
Burnett, J. H.
Bethel, C. W.
Biggs, W. T.
Biggs, A. T.
Biggs, P. B.
Brasher, L.
Bard, J. S.
Brandon, G.
Buchanan, Wm.
Beck, Wm.
Covington, Geo.
Crews, Rufus.
Copeley, James.
Chicon, Chas.
Cherry, Geo.
Cox, W.
Cobb, T. J.
Clarke, W.

Clarke, W. E.
Cheaney, W.
Denton, S. P.
Davis, J. H.
Dunbar, W.
Elder, Chas.
Ezell, A. D.
Edwards, H.
Emerson, John.
Freele, J.
Fields, Willis.
Frazer, W. H.
George, J. M. A.
Griffin, D. A.
Giles, R.
Griffin, J. C.
Gudgell, D. E.
Griffin, J. A.
Gallagher, P.
Green, Wm.
Hargis, L. D.
Hargis, H. L.
Howell, J.

Hughes, A.
Howell, T.
Hargin, R. A.
Higginson, E. R.
Johnson, F. B.
Jones, P.
Jones, W. T.
Jennings, R. B.
Jennings, O. T.
Justice, N. J.
Linthicum, E.
Long, W. B.
Lester, J.
Luckett, J. H.
Lancaster, N. N.
Lewis, J.
Martin, J. D.
Mattingly, M.
Morton, T.
Mitford, C. F.
Masterson, T.
Masterson, G. W.
Malloy, G.

Morris, M. L.
Madden, W.
Nichols, D.
Osburn, V.
Orange, T.
Parker, T. H.
Parker, T.
Parks, F. M.
Parks, N. J.
Pirtle, E. S.
Pirtle, J. C.
Pirtle, J.
Pugh, W.
Pemberry, R.

Pirtle, J. B.
Reed, J.
Reed, H. D.
Roberts, G. F.
Rhodes, Wiley.
Rose, John.
Smithson, John.
Spatchel, John.
Ambrose, B.
Shirley, John.
Sandefur, T. H.
Sheets, J. D.
Sheets, O.
Sandefur, T.

Sandefur, A. H.
Taylor, D. H.
Taylor, L. D.
Vititoe, G. T.
Willingham, A. J.
Willingham, Jackson.
Willingham, H. D.
Woodburn, W. W.
Wilson, S. L.
Williams, Wm.
Williams, H.
White, Brantley.

REORGANIZATION.

Company B, Tenth Kentucky, Partisan Rangers.
Captain, Wm. M. Marr.
First Lieutenant, Hugh Dunlap.
Second Lieutenant, B. B. Kirby.
Third Lieutenant, S. S. Hicks.
First Sergeant, S. Wilkins.
Second Sergeant, S. Burns.
Third Sergeant, G. Allen.
Fourth Sergeant, Henry Perdue.
First Corporal, Joseph Stalls.
Second Corporal, John Turpin.
Third Corporal, G. W. Smith.
Fourth Corporal, Thos. Knight.

PRIVATES.

Allen, J. H.
Allen, E.
Anderson, G. W.
Applegate, F.
Armstrong, W. T.
Burnett, J. H.
Bethel, C. W.
Biggs, W. T.

Biggs, A. T.
Biggs, P. B.
Brashear, L.
Bard, J. S.
Brandon, G.
Buchanan, Wm.
Beck, Wm.
Covington, Geo.

Crews, Rufus.
Copeley, James.
Chicon, Chas.
Cherry, Geo.
Cox, W.
Cobb, T. J.
Clarke, W.
Clark, W. E.

CAPTAIN L. D. FISHER,
1st Capt. Co. B, 10th Ky., P. R.

Cheaney, W.
Denton, B. P.
Davis, J. H.
Dunbar, W.
Elder, Chas.
Ezelle, A. D.
Edwards, H.
Freale, J.
Emmerson, John.
George, J. M. A.
Griffin, D. A.
Giles, R.
Griffin, J. C.
Gudgell, D. E.
Griffin, J. A.
Gallager, P.
Green, Wm.
Hargis, L. D.
Hargis, H. L.
Howell, J.
Hughes, A.
Howell, T.
Hargin, R. A.
Higginson, E. R.
Johnson, F. B.
Jones, P.
Parks, N. J.
Pirtle, E. S.

Jennings, R. B.
Jennings, O. T.
Justice, N. J.
Linthicum, E.
Long, W. B.
Lester, J.
Luckett, J. H.
Lancaster, N. N.
Lewis, J.
Martin, J. D.
Mattingly, M.
Morton, T.
Mitford, C. F.
Masterson, G. W.
Masterson, T.
Malloy, G.
Morris, M. L.
Madden, W.
Nickols, D.
Osburn, V.
Orange, T
Parker, T. H.
Parker, T.
Pirtle, J. C.
Pirtle, J.
Pemburry, R.
Pirtle, J. B.
Pugh, W.

Reed, J.
Reed, H. D.
Roberts, G. F.
Rhodes, Wyley.
Rose, John.
Spatchel, John.
Shirley, John.
Sandefur, T. H.
Sheets, J. D.
Sheets, O.
Sandefur, T.
Sandefur, A. H.
Taylor, D. H.
Taylor, L. D.
Viditoe, G. T.
Willingham, A. J.
Willingham, Jackson.
Willingham, H. D.
Woodburn, W. W.
Wilson, S. L.
Williams, Wm.
Williams, H.
White, Brantley.
Jones, W. T.
Frasier, W. H.
Fields, Willis.
Smithson, John.
Parks, F. M.

Company B, Tenth Kentucky, Partisan Rangers.

Captain, L. D. Fisher.
First Lieutenant, J. M. A. George.
Second Lieutenant, D. A. Griffin.
Third Lieutenant, S. S. Hicks.
Orderly Sergeant, Jas. O. Keach.

PRIVATES.

Armstrong, W. T.
Allen, J.

Applegate, F.
Anderson, G. W.

Allen, E.
Bethel, C. W.

Beck, Wm.

Biggs, W. T.

Brashear, L.

Baird, J. S.

Biggs, A. T.

Cobb, T. J.

Clark, Jerome.

Clark, William.

Curry, Ed.

Clarke, W. E.

Cheaney, W.

Davis, J. H.

Duvall, A. D.

Elder, Chas.

Freels, J.

Freney, John.

Farley, H.

Farley, Jno.

Farley, Jo.

Giles, R.

Griffin, J. C.

Gudgell, D. E.

Griffin, J. A.

Griffin, Dan.

Griffin, Dave.

Hagan, R. A.

Hollis, Wm.

Higginson, E. R.

Hix, Sherwood.

Jennings, R. B.

Jennings, O. T.

Justice, Jas.

Justin, N. J.

Keach, O. J.

Keach, Jas., Orderly S.

Long, W. B.

Linthicum, E.

Lester, J.

Luckett, J. H.

Lancaster, N.

Logan, Wm.

Mefford, Andy.

Mattingly, M.

Morton, T.

Mitford, C. F.

Masterson, G. W.

Masterson, T.

Osburn, V.

Orang T.

Pickett, J.

Parker, N. S.

Pirtle, E. S.

Pirtle, J. C.

Pirtle, J. B.

Pemburry, R.

Pirtle, J.

Pew, W.

Reed, J. A.

Reed, H. D.

Roberts, G. F. (K.).

Stoll, Jo.

Stoll, Jno.

Sherley, Jno.

Smith, Jno.

Stewart, Jo.

Sparks, Frank.

Sparks, Nick.

Spatchel, J.

Sandefur, T. H.

Sheets, J. D.

Sheets, O.

Sandefur, T.

Sandefur, A. H.

Turpin, Dick.

Taylor, D. H.

Taylor, L. G.

Vittitoe, J. H.

Willingham, A. J.

Willingham, H. D.

Willingham, R. C.

Woodburn, W. W.

Wilson, S. L.

Watkins, J. W.

Willingham, Jackson.

Williams, Wm. Dr.

Williams, Parson Bill.

Williams, Alvis.

Scoffield, Green.

Company G, Tenth Kentucky, Partisan Rangers.

Captain, Wm. Marr.

First Lieutenant, Wm. Kirby.

PRIVATES.

Cherry, G.

Chicon, C.

Cokely, J.

Cruse, R.

Dunbar, W.

Eathery, Wm.

Edwards, N. .

Greer, W.

Gentry, G. W.

WM. H. MOORE,
Co. A, 10th Ky., P. R.

Howell, J. E.
Hughes, Alex.
Johnson, F. B.
Jones, Finis.
Hargus, D.
Kennedy, Mat.
Jones, Bill.
Morris, L.
Moore, Jas.

Miloy, Geo.
Night, T.
Parker, J. H.
Parker, T.
Rhodes, W.
Rollins, Ed.
Smith, Ben.
Sherry, J.
Smith, Doc.

Stubbs, Joe.
Underwood, H.
Williams, W. S.
Williams, Rich.
Williams, Will.
Williams, Henezy.
Wilkins, C.
Welch, D. C.

In reorganization was consolidated with and made Company B, which was L. D. Fisher's company, Fisher having been killed in 1862.

COMPANY C, TENTH KENTUCKY.

First Captain, John E. Prow.
Second Captain, Sam Wall.
Third Captain, L. Dow Hockersmith.
First Lieutenants: John W. Head, John Brooks, Dr. B. M. Long, L. Dow Hockersmith.
Second Lieutenants: Van B. Prow, Thomas J. McGraw.
Third Lieutenants: W. A. Kuykendall, T. B. Pearson, Thomas Guthrie, Henry S. Jones.
First Orderly Sergeant, J. H. Jones.
Second Orderly Sergeant, B. R. Wear.
Third Orderly Sergeant, Thomas Guthrie.
Second Sergeants: A. Gibson, J. B. Head, E. Wallace, R. Young.
Third Sergeants: Cave Johnston, J. E. Hunter.
Fourth Sergeants: Samuel Withers, Calvin J. Tapp.
First Corporals: J. McKinley, E. Wallace.
Second Corporal, W. A. Bird.
Third Corporal, Theo. B. Clare.
Fourth Corporal, W. Truder.

PRIVATES.

Agnew, R. T.
Agnew, J. M.
Arnold, Sam W.
Anderson, J. N.

Azel, C. F.
Aud, Henry C.
Agnue, Abner.
Agnew, P. M.

Agnew, R. F.
Aldridge, John.
Beacon, Chas. A.
Bird, W. T.

Bird, J.
Brantley, Bluford.
Burton, J.
Bell, James.
Bishop, Geo.
Burton, J. Henry.
Brantley, David B.
Birchfield, U. G.
Bean, J. F.
Bean, C. A.
Brantley, John.
Broadfoot, Ben. C.
Bentley, John.
Cannon, W.
Cannon, E. S.
Clayton, L. W.
Clayton, G. W.
Click, P. M.
Conroy, John.
Conway, J. W.
Cole, W. C.
Clark, J. H.
Clark, B. H.
Caspar, J. C.
Conger, Thomas.
Cromwell, Nathan.
Cook, James .
Cook, John.
Cook, Joe.
Coon, Joe.
Chandler, D.
Conn, David.
Con, C. F.
Con, H. C.
Chandler, Thomas W.
Clark, J. M.
Conger, J. N.
Creder, D. V.
Cain, David.
Chandler, Tom.

Con, I.
Clavis, Robert.
Caspar, T. C.
Covey, T. H. B.
Cromwell, Nace.
Cook, James Y.
Cannon, G. W.
Clore, Theodore, B.
Dillbeck, W. W.
Dye, J. W.
Dilleck, Chas.
Dills, John.
Dills, Jesse.
Dunn, D. M.
Dye, John R.
Davis, Robert.
Dillbeck, Wm.
Dye, R. T.
Dons, D. B.
Dye, Wm.
Dills, Phil.
Eddings, R. E.
Endsley, J. M.
Evans, James.
Edwards, George.
Edmondson, H. R.
Elliott, L. P.
Eddings, B. F.
Elliott, Lewis.
Edmonds, H. C.
Edmonds, H. A.
Farmer, Ben C.
Grayson, B. F.
Grayson, S. W.
Gains, Bernard.
Guess, J. S.
Grayson, J. J.
Grayson, G. W.
Gibson, Allen.
Givens, James.

Guess, D. F.
Hartley, B. S.
Holman, T. J.
Haley, Ben.
Head, James B.
Holman, Sam.
Hale, Thomas G.
Hunter, Jasper.
Howard, Chas.
Harrell, C. F.
Henry, Alec.
Hughes, James.
Harold, J .C.
Henry, Thomas.
Hillman, T.
Hackley, J.
Hackett, J.
Head, Wm.
Haley, B. S.
Hunter, J. M.
Huckleby, Jim.
Hunter, Pres.
Hughes, Joseph.
Henry, Joe D.
Hutchinson, Henry.
Hazel, C. F.
Holliman, Dr. Daniel.
Imboden, Geo.
Jones, J. M.
Johnston, J. R.
Jones, M.
James, W. B.
Johnston, J. M.
Kuykendall, Frank M.
Kemp, J. L.
King, Thomas.
Lucas, Geo.
Land, Thos.
Lowry, S. H. B.
Messick, Samuel.

CAPTAIN JOHN PROW,
1st Capt. Co. C, 10th Ky., P. R.

Mobley, J. M.

Mobley, T. M.

Milton, R. S.

Mobley, D. R.

McKinley, W. H.

McKinley, J. J.

McKinley, A. R.

McGraw, I. C.

Miller, Wm.

Madden, Patrick.

Marshall, Wm.

Moore, James.

Metcalf, Coates F.

Monan, Wm.

Morse, Jas.

Murphy, F. M.

McGraw, John.

Manly, John.

Morse, Joe.

Mabby, Bryan.

Myrick, Samuel.

McKinley, Jonathan.

Melton, Robt. S.

Nelson, Wm.

Nesbitt, A. G.

Nichols, R.

Neal, M. Dock.

Nonticutt, W. W.

Nelson, M.

Osborn, H. N.

Osborn, Randolph.

Osbern, R. M.

Osbern, J. H.

O'Nan, Leo.

Prow, John E., Jr.

Phillipps, R. E.

Prow, Wm.

Pitts, T. L.

Parish, Wm.

Pearson, T. B.

Potts, T. B.

Query, Wm.

Query, Morton.

Query, Thos.

Quarles, Thos.

Rich, Obadiah.

Robertson, Benoni.

Rowe, David.

Robertson, P. D.

Ryan, John.

Rice, N. N.

Ritter, Obadiah.

Rhyle, W. H.

Smith, Polk.

Smith, Holden.

Stallians, Geo.

Smith, J. Crit.

Simpson, John.

Smith, B. F.

Snodgrass, Dave.

Stephens, Michael.

Snow, J. M.

Smith, ———.

Simpson, I. M.

Smith, I. P.

Smith, Nat.

Stalions, John.

Tapp, J. Calvin.

Tetherington, R. M.

Talley, A. W.

Thurman, Q. S.

Thurman, W. R.

Thurman, J. S.

Talbott, Geo.

Trader, A .W.

Utley, R. Y.

Vaughn, B. N.

Vaughn, J. W.

Vaughn, B. F.

Vaughn, J. D.

Vaughn, Isaac W.

Vaughn, Henry.

Wallace, Jas.

Waskum, Jas.

Wise, C. C.

Wells, W. E.

Wheatcroft, Jas.

Wheeler, Edward.

Walker, Lewis.

Walker, G. W.

Walker, A. J.

Wall, Lewis.

Withers, H.

Withers, S. W.

Williams, Wm.

Wallace, C.

Weir, B. R.

Withers, Wm. M.

Warren, N. B.

Yager, J. P.

Young, R.

COMPANY D.   REORGANIZATION.

Captain, T. M. Hammack.

First Lieutenant, W. J. Alloway.

Second Lieutenant, W. J. Gardiner.

Third Lieutenant, Omer.

First Sergeant, Geo. H. Goodwin.
Second Sergeant, Felix Jewell.
Third Sergeant, J. P. Flannigan.
Fourth Sergeant, J. D. Henry.
First Corporal, Ben L. Moore.
Second Corporal, Reuben Reasor.
Third Sergeant, T. F. Hal.
Fourth Sergeant, W. F. Christian.

PRIVATES.

Anderson, James.
Albutt, James.
Bask, John.
Collins, Jerry.
Cannon, W. A.
Cullen, Richard.
Christian, Sam
Dodge, J. R
Day, O. B.
Dyer, James.
Francis, Henry.
Fowler, P. L.
Fitzhenry, M.
Graves, W. P.
Graves, G. M.
Griffin, George.
Hardy, John.
Hampton, J. W.
Hamilton, W. F.
Hancock, D. C.
Hager, W.
Holt, C. G.

Hanner, C. H.
Jeffries, Thomas.
James, M. B.
Lackland, Robt.
Lackland, H. H.
Mitchell, Silas.
Montgomery, M.
Mitchell, W. M.
Mitchell, Geo.
McClelland, James.
McGill, J. C.
McKinley, T. M.
Neal, John.
Omer, T. D., Jr.
Perkins, J. W.
Perkins, B. F.
Peters, D. M.
Peters, G. W.
Peters, J. H.
Potts, C.
Poe, John.
Rudd, J. W.

Rice, James.
Robinson, W. S.
Robinson, J. M.
Reynolds, Levi.
Sanders, L. J.
Scarce, Daniel.
Smith, Adam.
Stone, W. J.
Swingle, H. F.
Slaton, Tom.
Stone Jasper.
Taylor, J. W.
Taylor, Richard.
Threlkeld, W. H.
Thompson, W. P.
Thompson, John.
Utley, M.
Wade, Daniel.
Walker, J. K.
Whitecotton, G. H.
Young, J. O.

REORGANIZATION.

Company D, Tenth Kentucky, Partisan Rangers.

Captain, T. M. Hammack.
First Lieutenant, W. J. Alloway.
Second Lieutenant, Wm. J. Gardiner.
Third Lieutenant, Thos. Omer.

CAPTAIN JOHN H. HAMBY AND WIFE,
Co. H, 10th Ky., P. R.

First Sergeant, Geo. H. Goodwin.
Second Sergeant, Felix Jewell.
Third Sergeant, J. P. Flannigan
Fourth Sergeant, J. D. Henry.
First Corporal, Ben L. Moore.
Second Corporal, Reuben Reasor.
Third Corporal, T. F. Hall.
Fourth Corporal, W. F. Christian.

PRIVATES.

Anderson, Jas.
Albutt, Jno.
Bask, Jno.
Collins, Jerry.
Cannon, W. A.
Cullen, Richard.
Christian, Sam.
Dodge, J. R.
Day, O. B
Dyer, Jas.
Francis, Henry.
Fowler, P. L.
Fitzhenry, M.
Graves, W. P.
Graves, G. M.
Griffin, Geo.
Hardy, Jno.
Hampton, J. W.
Hamilton, W. F.
Hancock, D. C.
Hager, W.
Holt, C. G.

Hamner, C. H.
Jeffries, Thomas.
James, M. B.
Lackland, Robt.
Lackland, H. H.
Mitchell, Silas.
Montgomery, M.
Mitchell, W. M.
Mitchell, Geo.
McClelland, Jas.
McGill, J. C.
McKinley, T. M.
Neal, Jno.
Omer, T. D., Jr.
Perkins, J. W.
Perkins, B. F.
Peters, D. M.
Peters, G. W.
Peters, J. H.
Potts, C.
Poe, Jno.
Rudd, J. W.

Rice, James.
Robinson, W. S.
Robinson, J. M.
Reynolds, Levi.
Sanders, L. J.
Scarce, Daniel.
Smith, Adam.
Stone, J. W.
Swingle, H. F.
Slaton, Tom.
Smock, Jno.
Stone, Jasper.
Taylor, J. W.
Taylor, Richard.
Threlkeld, U. H.
Thompson, W. P.
Thompson, Jno.
Utley, M.
Wade, Daniel.
Walker, J. K.
Whitecotton, Geo. H.
Young, J. O.

Company D, Tenth Kentucky, Partisan Rangers.

Captain, T. M. Hammack.
First Lieutenant, Will J. Alloway
Second Lieutenant, John Thompson.
First Sergeant, Daniel Scarce.

PRIVATES.

Anderson, Jas.	Holt, C. G.	Potts, C.
Albutt, Jno.	Hamner, C. H.	Rudd, Geo. W.
Collins, Jerry	Jewell, Felix.	Reasor, Reuben.
Cannon, W. A.	Jeffries, Thos.	Robertson, W. S.
Cullen, Richard.	Lackland, Robt.	Robinson, J. M.
Dodge, J. R.	Lackland, H. H.	Reynolds, Levi.
Day, O. B.	Mitchell, Silas.	Smith, Adam.
Dyer, James.	Moore, L. B.	Stone, J. W.
Fowler, P. L.	Montgomery, W. M.	Swingle, H. F.
Flannigan, J. P.	Mitchell, Geo.	Swingle, Jno. S.
Francis, Henry.	Mitchell, Wm. M.	Slaton, Thos.
Fitzhenry, M.	McClelland, Jas.	Sanders, L. J.
Goodwin, Geo. H.	McGill, J. C.	Taylor, J. W.
Graves, W. P.	Neal, Jno.	Taylor, Richard.
Hampden, J. W.	Omer, T. D., Sr.	Threlkeld, U. H.
Graves, G. M.	Omer, T. D., Jr.	Thompson, W. A.
Hamilton, W. S.	Perkins, J. W.	Walker, J. R.
Henry, J. B.	Peters, D. M.	Whitecotton, Geo.
Hancock, D. C.	Peters, I. H.	Mitchell, Wm.
Hall, T. F.	Peters, L. U., Jr.	Threlkeld, Henry.
Hager, Wm.	Perkins, B. F.	Threlkeld, Wm.
Hardy, Jno.	Peters, W. L.	

COMPANY E. REORGANIZATION.

Captain, Sam B. Taylor.
First Lieutenant, T. S. White.
Second Lieutenant, J. W. McLean.
Third Lieutenant, H. S. Jones.
First Sergeant, R. W. Taylor.
Second Lieutenant, J. A. Jones.
Third Sergeant, W. Fisher.
Fourth Sergeant, B. F. Fields.
First Corporal, W. M. Eaves.
Second Corporal, T. M. Howard.
Third Corporal, W. Hixton.
Fourth Corporal, B. W. Taylor.

BARTLETT GOOCH,
Co. A, 10th Ky., P. R.

PRIVATES.

Ambrose, B.
Ambrose, L. F.
Ashby, J. A.
Austin, W.
Allgood, W.
Arnold, W. H.
Bell, G.
Bradley, J.
Boswell, W.
Bradley, W.
Butts, R.
Blythe, W. H.
Bell, C. F.
Baker, G. C. P.
Blanford, J.
Carico, J.
Cudney, H. H.
Carlisle, Cyrus.
Cox, W. T.
Carlisle, J. P.
Chandler, J. H.
Camp, S. A.
Dobyns, D. G.
Ellis, L.
Emerson, C. A.
Freels, F.

Grady, W.
Gough, J. S.
Higgs, D.
Hewitt, J. W.
Head, R.
Hobbs, J.
Howard, H.
Houston, B.
Harrison, W. T.
Hayden, M. S.
Harrison, J.
Head, H. R.
Harrison, J. W.
Johnson, M. A.
Johnson, W. A.
Johnson, Frank.
Jenkins, J.
Kinneer, J. A.
Kinneer, E. H.
Kendall, T.
Lancaster, B. F.
Long, T.
Millen, J. H.
McClellan, A.
Mitchell J.
McIntyre, Joe.

Morris, J. C.
Munford, John.
Pritchett, J.
Robinson, T.
Rummage, J. B.
Roberts, J. A.
Riddle, T.
Quigley, R.
Richardson, A.
Regan, C.
Rhodes, J. L.
Rhodes, Charles.
Sutton, J. S.
Stewart, G.
Stewart, J. P.
Smith, W. P.
Sandefur, A. D.
Sands, James.
Stofield, Fred.
Snider, G. G.
Todd, T. J.
Tierce, Wm.
Vincent, J. H.
Wright, F. M.
Watson, J. H.

REORGANIZATION.

Company E, Tenth Kentucky, Partisan Rangers.

Captain, Sam. B. Taylor.
First Lieutenant, T. S. White.
Second Lieutenant, J. W. McLean.
Third Lieutenant, H. S. Jones.
First Sergeant, R. W. Taylor.
Second Sergeant, J. A. Jones.
Third Sergeant, W. Fisher.
Fourth Sergeant, B. F. Fields.

First Corporal, W. M. Eaves.
Second Corporal, T. M. Howard.
Third Corporal, W. Hixton.
Fourth Corporal, B. W. Taylor.

PRIVATES.

Ambrose, B.	Freels, F.	Mitchell, J.
Ambrose, L. P	Grady, W.	McIntyre, Jos.
Ashby, J. A.	Gough, J. S.	Morris, J. C.
Austin, W.	Higgs, D.	Munford, Jno.
Allgood, W.	Hewitt, J. W.	Pritchett, J.
Arnold, W. H.	Hobbs, J. P.	Robinson, T.
Bell, G.	Head, R	Rummage, J. B.
Bradley, J.	Howard, H.	Roberts, J. A.
Bell, J.	Huston, B.	Riddle, T.
Boswell, W.	Harrison, W. T.	Regan, C.
Bradley, W.	Hayden, M. S.	Rhodes, J. L.
Butts, R.	Harrison, J.	Rhodes, Chas.
Blythe, W. H.	Head, H. R.	Sutton, J. S.
Bell, C. F.	Harrison, J. W.	Stewart, G.
Baker, G. C. P.	Johnson, M. A.	Stewart, J. P.
Blanford, J.	Johnson, W. A.	Smith, W. P.
Carico, J.	Johnson, E. C.	Sandefur, A. D.
Cudney, H. H.	Johnson, Frank.	Sands, Jas.
Carlisle, C.	Jenkins, J.	Stofield, Fred.
Cox, W. T.	Kinneer, J. A.	Snider, G. G.
Carlisle, J. P.	Kinneer, E. H.	Todd, T. J.
Chandler, J. H.	Kendle, T.	Tearce, Wm.
Camp, S. A.	Lancaster, B. F.	Vincell, J. H.
Dobbins, D. G.	Long, T.	Wright, F. M.
Ellis, L.	Mullin, J. H.	Watson, J. H.
Emmerson, C. A.	McClellen, A.	

Company E, Tenth Kentucky, Partisan Rangers.

Captain, S. B Taylor.
First Lieutenant, T. S. White.
Second Lieutenant, J. Handley.
Third Lieutenant, J. W. McLean.
First Sergeant, R. W. Taylor.

CAPTAIN JOHN H. CHRISTY,
2d Capt. Co. I, 10th Ky., P. R.

Second Sergeant, S. Jones.
Third Sergeant, J. Hewitt.
Fourth Sergeant, T. A. Jones.
Fifth Sergeant, B. T. Field.
First Corporal, W. Eaves.
Second Corporal, T. Robertson.
Third Corporal, B. Taylor.
Fourth Corporal, T. Howard.

PRIVATES.

Ambrose, L. F.
Ashby, John.
Armstead, Wm.
Austin, W.
Baker, George.
Backbarron, Sam.
Backbarron, E.
Bell, G. E.
Bradley, J.
Bell, J.
Boswell, D. S.
Bradley, W.
Butts, R.
Blythe, W. M.
Bell, C. F.
Cottrell, J. P.
Chandler, J. H.
Camp, S. A.
Carrico, J.
Christe, C.
Dollins, B. G.
Ellis, L.
Fisher, W.
Fields, Ben.
Fields, John.
Frields, F.
Grady, W.
Head, B.

Head, W.
Head, Richard.
Higgs, Ed.
Higgs, D.
Hibbs, Del.
Head, Dick.
Howard, T. Y.
Haws, Dick.
Harrison, Al.
Howard, H.
Houston, B.
Hobbs, T.
Harrison, W. T.
Haden, M. S.
Jones, Thos.
Johnson, M. A.
Johnson, W. A.
Johnson, E. C.
Johnson, F.
Jones, Thos.
Jones, J. H.
Kinneer, J. A.
Kinneer, E. H.
Kurtz, H. R.
Kemble, T.
Lancaster, B. F.
Luckett, T. D.
Lucket, Jo.

Mullins, J. H.
Morton, David.
McLean, N. C.
McClon, A.
Peggins, C.
Pritchett, J.
Quitrell, J.
Rummage, J. B.
Riddle, T.
Roberts, J. A.
Sales, Jas. A.
Slover, Fred.
Sutton, J.
Stewart, G.
Stewart, J. P.
Smith, W. F.
Sandefur, A. D.
Smith, Al.
Sands, J.
Thirston, W.
Todd, T. J.
Teare, W. A.
Vincell, H.
Vidito, J.
Wright, F.
Webber.
Yeizer, Broz.

COMPANY F. REORGANIZATION.

Captain, John S. Chapman.
First Lieutenant, Henry Cromwell.
Second Lieutenant, J. M. Hewitt.
Third Lieutenant, Louis Schimmet.
First Sergeant, Ben Buckman.
Second Sergeant, A. M. Perine.
Third Sergeant, James Lynn.
Fourth Sergeant, Henry Gilchrist.

PRIVATES.

Alvey, William.
Austin, William.
Bowen, J. W.
Blackwell, Robert.
Beauchamp, W.
Braddock, J. L.
Berry, G. W.
Ball, L. D.
Baker, James.
Buckman, W. C.
Burch, Robert.
Beauchamp, N. P.
Catlett, Robert.
Catlett, George.
Chapman, Ben.
Conway, John.
Culver, John.
Clark, Yeatman.
Coleman, Thomas.
Coleman, Z.
Connell, Frank.
Coleman, Jack.
Coleman, Smith.
Drury, A. J.
Delaney, Chas.
Davenport, James.
Fendrick, Thos.

Girten, Thos.
Girten, Valentine.
Gray, Nevill.
Gobin, J. D.
Gough, H. C.
Graham, E.
Gore, John.
Greenwell, Sam.
Hughes, Graham.
Howell, Walker.
Harris, Fendle.
Haskins, Robert.
Hutchends, Henry.
Herndon, John.
Herndon, Thos.
Hughes, Robert.
Hughes, Willis.
Hedges, James.
Johnson, James.
Lynn, Robert.
Ladd, James.
Ladd, Ben.
Ladd, Z.
Lynn.
Lynn, James.
Lynn, H. J.
Mattingly, L.

Moore, W.
Moore, R.
Mitchell, B.
McCullough, J. B.
Nailor, E.
Quigley, R.
Richardson, A.
Riddle, J.
Ray, Wm.
Riley, M.
Roach, John.
Rayborn, C.
Shanks, J. J.
Stewart, John.
Smith, Chas.
Staffor, J.
Spaulding, E. M.
Staples, Geo.
Storey, M. B.
Trumbo, O.
Trumbo, Ben.
Vandiver, L.
Wood, Chas.
Wathen, Wm.
Wallace, Robt.
Yates, Wm.

CAPTAIN JNO. S. CHAPMAN,
Co. F, 10th Ky., P. R.

REORGANIZATION.

Company F, Tenth Kentucky, Partisan Rangers.
Captain, Jno S. Chapman.
First Lieutenant, Henry Cromwell.
Second Lieutenant, J. M. Hewitt.
Third Lieutenant, Louis Schimmet.
First Sergeant, Ben Buckman.
Second Sergeant, A. M. Perine.
Third Sergeant, Jas. Lynn.
Fourth Sergeant, Henry Gilchrist.

PRIVATES.

Alvey, William.
Austin, Wm.
Bowen, J. W.
Blackwell, Robt.
Beauchamp W.
Braddock, J. L.
Berry, G. W.
Ball, L. D.
Baker, Jas.
Buckman, W. C.
Burch, Robt.
Beauchamp, N. P.
Catlett, Robt.
Catlett, George.
Chapman, Ben.
Conway, Jno.
Culver, Jno.
Clark, Yateman.
Coleman, Thos.
Coleman, Z.
Connell, Frank.
Coleman, Jack.
Coleman, Smith.
Drury, J. A.
Delaney, Chas.
Davenport, Jas.

Fendrick, Thos.
Girten, Thos.
Girten, Valentine.
Gray, Neville.
Gobin, J. D.
Gough, H. C.
Graham, E.
Gore, Jno.
Greenwell, Saml.
Hughes, Graham.
Howell, Walker.
Harris, Fendle.
Haskins, Robt.
Hutchins, Henry.
Herndon, Jno.
Herndon, Thos.
Hughes, Robt.
Hughes, Willis.
Hedges, Jas.
Lynn, Robt.
Ladd, Jas.
Ladd, Ben.
Ladd, Z.
Lynn, H. J.
Mattingly, L.
Moore, W.

Moore, R.
Mitchell, B.
McCollough, J. B.
Nailor, E.
Quigley, R.
Richardson, A.
Riddle, J.
Ray, Wm.
Riley, M.
Roach, Jno.
Raibourne, C.
Shanks, J. J.
Stewart, Jno.
Smith, Chas.
Stafford, J.
Spalding, Ed. M.
Staples, Geo.
Story, M. B.
Trumbo, O.
Trumbo, Ben F.
Vaudever, L.
Wood, Chas.
Wathen, Wm.
Wallace, Robt.
Yates, Wm.
Johnson, Jas.

Company F, Tenth Kentucky, Partisan Rangers.

Captain, Alfred Richardson.
First Lieutenant, J. H. Beauchamp.
First Sergeant, N. P. Beauchamp.

PRIVATES.

Austin, Wm.
Bowen, J. W.
Blackwell, Robt.
Beauchamp, Wm.
Braddock, J. L.
Berry, Geo. W.
Ball, S. D.
Clark, Yateman.
Coleman, Thos. C.
Coleman, Zebidee.
Conrad, Frank.
Coleman, Jack.
Coleman, Smith.

Coleman, Presley, B.
Drury, J. A.
Delaney, Chas.
Greenwell, Samuel.
Harris, Fendle.
Haskins, Robt.
Hughes, Green.
Lynn, Robt.
Howell, Walker.
Mason, Reuben.
Mitchell, Bryant.
McCulloch, J. B.
Mattingly, Leonard.

Moore, Wm.
Naylor, Edward.
Quigley, Robt.
Richardson, Henry.
Riddle, Jas.
Ray, Wm.
Strong, M. B.
Wood, Chas.
Vandiver, Lafayette.
Trumbo, Oliver.
Trumbo, Ben F.

COMPANY G.   REORGANIZATION.

Captain, J. N. Taylor.
First Lieutenant, F. G. Eakin.
Bob Sugg was the first second lieutenant of this company; Mallure succeeded him.
Second Lieutenant, G. F. C. Mallure, (in first organization was bugler).
Third Lieutenant, O. L. Barbour.
First Sergeant, Jack Allin, succeeded O. L. Barbour as second lieutenant when Barbour was made adjutant.

PRIVATES.

Arnold, G.
Bell, Chas.
Blanford, J. T.
Berry, J. H.
Blanford, I.
Barbour, Phil.

Buckman, J.
Black, R.
Clay, B. M.
Culver, T. R.
Chase, W. N.
Cook, Z.

Dixon, J. S.
Drury, F. F.
Drury, J. H.
Dance, R. T.
Dance, J. E.
Everett, E. R.

CAPTAIN J. N. TAYLOR.

Eblin, J.
French, Leo.
Floyd, R. T.
Fowler, Peter.
Fowler, J.
Fowler, Joseph.
Fowler, R.
French, W.
Floyd, W.
Hardwick, Tom.
Hancock, Laz.
Hargrave, J. M.

Hart, T. E.
Horseman, Wm.
Grady, Bill.
Mattingly, Charles.
Mattingly, "Miles."
Mills, L.
Mills, M.
Nally, N.
Lock, H.
Penticost, Benjamin.
Pritchett, John.
Powell, B.

Sights, J. B.
Sights, A. B.
Sights, L. B .
Sanderfur, A.
Sanderfur, P.
Thomas, G. W.
West, H.
Williams, W. C.
Wilson, W. J.
Willing, Henry.
Willing (Another).
Wilburn, J.

REORGANIZATION.

Company I, Tenth Kentucky, Partisan Rangers.
First Captain, Al. Fowler.
Captain, John H. Christy.
First Lieutenant, F. Ferris Brown.
Second Lieutenant, J. K. P. Laffoon.
Third Lieutenant, S. Hick Woolfolk.
First Sergeant, Ben Newton.
Second Sergeant, M. M. Sisk.
Third Sergeant, C. M. Hall.
Fourth Sergeant, H. Laffoon.
First Corporal, D. A. Bondurant.
Second Corporal, T. C. Hunt.
Third Corporal, Jesse Tapp.
Fourth Corporal, O. B. McCulley.

PRIVATES

Ashby, Jno. A.
Alvis, Henry.
Brown, C. M.
Barron, N. D.
Barton, Wm. H.
Barron, N. D.
Browning, John.
Barron, Wm. E.
Bowlen, H. R.

Buras, W. B.
Blandford, T. C.
Baldwin, I. A.
Clark, F. M. P.
Cunningham, Jno.
Chinn, F.
Chinn, Jas.
Clark, Thos.
Cox, Wm.

Cox, Jo.
Cargile, John H.
Cargile, Jas.
Davis, H. T.
Davis, W. T.
Davis, D. D.
Davis, M. H.
Davis, Wm. P.
Dollins, D. G.

Figley, Geo.
Fowler, L.
Fortune, E.
Griffin, J. Y.
Hill, Harrison.
Heron, A. M
Howell, A. J.
Howell, Wm.
Howell, Jas. (Died.)
Hardwick, William.
Hardwick, Ambros.
Hibbs, I. T.
Hicklin, K.
Hollbrook, W. O.
Hunt, Thomas.
Johnson, J. W.
Kennett, W. F.
Loving, Jas. D. W.
Loving, John.
Lyle, W. R.
McQuigg, Byron.
McCulley, Orlean.
More, Morris.
Mitchell, S. D.
Morton, Jno. H.

Mitchell, W. I.
Nelson, W. A.
Nance, J. G.
Nailer, E. W.
Montgomery, Geo.
McLean, J. Frank.
McClain, I. T.
Marshall, T. S.
Neal, I. C.
Newell, Jas.
Oates, W. A.
Oates, George M.
Oates, Jas. M.
Oldham, D. H.
Porter, Jack.
Price, Chas.
Price, M.
Robertson, Jo.
Walker, John B.
Wood, H. O.
Radford, R. R.
Ray, H. W.
Robertson, C. J.
Roark, Jno.
Ray, Jack.

Southard, K.
Sisk, Barney.
Slayton, S. B.
Slayton, W. D.
Stone, Amos.
Sisk, Milan.
Skales, Thomas.
Slayton, Jo. P.
Timmons, Polk.
Taylor, Thos.
Walker, A. C. R.
Wingold, Thos.
Whitefield, I. W.
Wicks, I. E.
Walker, I. E.
Woolfolk, Jno. B.
Spirey, Wm.
Wicks, Jos.
Laffoon, S. B.
Webb, Jas.
Todd, O. C.
Winstead, Dr. M. B.
Walker, John B.
Wood, Hillie.

REORGANIZATION.

Captain, H. C. Merriweather.
First Lieutenant, D. Chipley.
Second Lieutenant, J. A. Monday.
Third Lieutenant N. B. Dupuy..
First Sergeant, L. T. Banks.
Second Sergeant, W. P. Neal.
Third Lieutenant, James Falls.
Fourth Lieutenant, George Green.
First Corporal, S. S. Loyal.
Second Corporal, J. S. Morgan.
Third Corporal, Wm. Pence.
Fourth Corporal, J. A. Quick.

1. CAPT. T. H. HAMBY.   2. CAPT. H. CLAY MERIWETHER.

3. LIEUT. I. K. ALLEN.

And other officers of the Partisan Rangers in camp.

PRIVATES.

Absden, J.	Johnson, J. C.	Powell, Fred.
Bell, Wm.	Kelley, E.	Quinn, James.
Boswell, G. W.	Kincaid, Jesse.	Quinn, Bud.
Boardman, Samuel.	Lawson, J. W.	Ross, F.
Clore, L.	Lawson, Pat.	Robbins, J. L.
Christian, J. T.	Lockett, James.	Rollins, Thos. L.
Carlisle, B. L.	Lockett, J. W.	Summers, S.
Cavendar, Thomas.	Laycock, Fred.	Sebree, J.
Corbett, Wm.	Mitchell, J. H.	Shields, Wm. B.
Combs, E. S.	McMahan, J. W.	Simmerman, T.
Davidson, B.	Morgan, T. B.	Sledge, A. D.
Estez, J. G.	McQuiddy, O.	Sherrod, Wm.
Estez, Richard.	Morrow, Stephen.	Trafton, L. W.
Fisher, H.	Malburn, G. T. C.	Trimble, Thos.
Fowler, G. H.	Newman, N. H.	Tryte, H. G.
Hayden, Joseph.	Newman, N. M.	Wilhelm, F.
Hayden, J. H.	Newman, R. L.	Williams, F.
Henderson, J.	Newman, T. M.	Wood, Chas. T.
Hall, F. A.	Nokes, J.	Wood, Charles.
Hanna, W. M.	Nance, Jno. W.	Woodward, Wm.
Hewell, Samuel.	Osburn, Chas.	Willey, Henry T.
Henry, Thos. B.	O'Bannan, C. S.	Winstead, W. T.
Henel, Sam.	Parker, J. C.	Winstead, T. Jeff.
Johnson, G. W.	Parker, R. L.	Walker, Henry.

REORGANIZATION.

Company H, Tenth Kentucky, Partisan Rangers.

Captain, J. N. Taylor.
First Lieutenant, F. G. Eakin.
Second Lieutenant, G. F. C. Mallure.
Third Lieutenant, O L. Barbour.
First Sergeant, Jack Allin.

PRIVATES.

Arnold, G.	Berry, J. H.	Buckman, J.
Bell, Chas.	Blanford, I.	Black, R.
Blanford, J. T.	Barbour, Phil.	Clay, B. M.

Culver, T. R.
Chase, W. N.
Cook, Z.
Dixon, J. S.
Drury, F. F.
Drury, J. H.
Dance, R. T.
Dance, J. E.
Everett, E. R.
Eblin, J.
French, Leo.
French, Henry.
Floyd, R. T.
Fowler, Peter.
Fowler, J.

Fowler, Jos.
Fowler, R.
French, W.
Grady, Wm.
Floyd, W.
Hardwich, Tom.
Hargrave, J. M.
Harte, T. E.
Horseman, Wm.
Mattingly, Chas.
Mills, L.
Mills, M.
Nally, N.
Lock, H.
Penticost, B.

Pritchett, Jno.
Powell, B.
Sights, J. B.
Sights, A. B.
Sights, L. B.
Sandefur, A.
Sandefur, P.
Thomas, G. W.
West, H.
Williams, W. C.
Wilson, W. J.
Willing, Henry.
Wilburn, J.

Company H, Tenth Kentucky, Partisan Rangers.

Captain, J. N. Taylor.
First Lieutenant, F. G. Eakins.
First Sergeant and Lieutenant, Jack Allin.

PRIVATES.

Arnold, Giles.
Bell, Chas.
Blansford, J. T.
Berry, J. H.
Blansford, Ignatius.
Buckman, Thos.
Barbour, Phil.
Biggs, Peter.
Black, Richard.
Clay, B. M.
Culver, Thos. R.
Culver, Wm. H.
Culver, Randal.
Chase, W. A.
Cook, Zack.
Dixon, Jos. S.
Drury, F. F.

Drury, J. H.
Dance, R. T.
Dance, J. E.
Everitt, E. R.
Eblin, Jno.
French, Leo.
French, Henry.
Fowler, Peter.
Floyd, Robt.
Fowler, Jas.
Fowler, Jos.
Fowler, Robt.
French, Willis
Floyd, Wm.
Hargood, J. M.
Hart, Thos. E.
Horseman, Will.

Lock, Henry.
Mattingly, Church.
Mills, Tim.
Mills, Martin.
Pentecost, Ben.
Sights, J. D.
Sights, L. B.
Sights, A. B.
Sandefur, Philip.
Sandefur, Arch.
Thomas, P. W.
Vest, H.
Williams, W. C.
Wilson, W. J.
Wilburn, Jno.
Willing, A.
Wally, Henry.

COMPANY K. REORGANIZATION.

First Captain, Rev. W. C. Dimmitt.
Second Captain, John H. Hamby.
First Lieutenant, A. R. Prince.
Second Lieutenant, Ben White.
Third Lieutenant, Crit. McKnight.
First Sergeant, P. Giles.
Second Sergeant, W. T. Jackson.
Third Sergeant, R. L. Baker.
Fourth Sergeant, M. V. Darnell.
First Corporal, D. H. Howton.
Second Corporal, I. H. Boyd.
Third Corporal, M. B. Howell.
Fourth Corporal, Wright Crockett.

PRIVATES.

Allen, James.
Allen, John.
Allen, Mat.
Armstrong, John.
Ausenbaugh, Charles.
Ausenbaugh, Bailey.
Brooks, T. M.
Beckner, A. N.
Claxton, Wm.
Clayton, W. L.
Dillingham, W. R.
Dockery, James.
Eagen, Nicholas.
Eison, Charles.
Ellis, John.
Grissom, M. C.
Herron, J. H.

Herron, Elisha.
Higgins, Nick.
Hunter, W. J.
Hunter, H. C.
Handley, J. W.
Hill, Lewis.
Holbell, J. H.
Hayes, G. W.
Jackson, J.
Lamb, Winfield.
Lewis, T. S.
McKnight, D. H.
Mounts, William.
Mercer, T. L.
Martin, Robert.
McKnight, W. T
Nichols, Wm.

Pasteur, Frank.
Robertson, J. H.
Self, W. M.
Self, J. B.
Stallions, I. M.
Scott, G. R.
Scott, H. L.
Stovall, D. M.
Trusty, W. M.
Tapley, John.
Yates, W. M.
Utley, A.
Veal, Thos.
Van Dorn, ———.
Williams, S. W.
White, David.
White, William.

REORGANIZATION.

Company K, Tenth Kentucky, Partisan Rangers.

First Captain, Rev. W. C. Dimmitt.
Captain, Jno. H. Hamby.

First Lieutenant, A. R. Prince.
Second Lieutenant, Ben White.
Third Lieutenant, I. C. McKnight.
First Sergeant, P. Giles.
Second Sergeant, W. T. Jackson.
Third Sergeant, R. L. Baker.
Fourth Sergeant, M. V. Darnell.
First Corporal, D. H. Houton.
Second Corporal, I. H. Boyd.
Third Corporal, M. B. Howell.
Fourth Corporal, Wright Crockett.

PRIVATES.

Allin, Jas.
Armstrong, Jno.
Ausenbaugh, Chas.
Ausenbaugh, Bailey.
Brooks, T. M.
Beckner, A. N.
Claxton, Wm.
Clayton, W. L.
Dillingham, W. R.
Dockery, Jas.
Eagin, Nicholas.
Eison, Chas.
Ellis, Jno.
Grissom, M. C.
Heron, J. H.
Heron, Elisha.
Higgins, Nick.

Hunter, W. J.
Hunter, H. C.
Hill, Lewis.
Holbell, J. H.
Hayes, G. W.
Jackson, J.
Lamb, Winfield.
Lewis, T. S.
McKnight, D. H.
Mounts, W.
Merser, T. L.
Martin, Robt.
McKnight, W. T.
Nichols, Wm.
Pastur, F. A.
Robertson, J. H.
Self, W. M.

Self, J. B.
Stalian, I. M.
Scott, G. R.
Scott, H. L.
Stovall, D. M.
Trusty, W. M.
Tapley, Jno.
Yates, Wm. M.
Utley, A.
Veal, Thos.
Van Dorn, ——
Williams, S. W.
William, ——
White, David.
Allen, Jno.
Handley, J. W.

Company H, Tenth Kentucky, Partisan Rangers.

Captain, J. S. Chapman.
First Lieutenant, H. Cromwell.
First Sergeant, A. M. Perrine.

PRIVATES.

Alvey, T.
Buckman, N. C.

Birch, R.
Catlet, R.

Chapman, B.
Davenport, J.

Grayham, E.	Hardeiter, T.	Stafford, J.
Girten, T.	Ladd, J.	Smith, C.
Girten, V.	Ladd, B.	Stewart, J.
Gabin, J.	Ladd, Z.	Shanks, J. J.
Gough, C.	Lynn, H. J.	Fenderick, T.
Hopkins, B.	Lynn, J.	Wathen, J.
Holcomb, E.	Riley, M.	Waller.
Hughes, J. G.	Rouch, J.	Yates, W.
Hughes, J.	Reburn, C.	Gray, N.
Hodges, J.	Schimmel, N.	

FIELD AND STAFF OFFICERS OF THIRTEENTH KENTUCKY CAVALRY.

Colonel, L. A. Sypert, Christian county, Kentucky. Died since war.

Lieutenant-Colonel, Robert Soery. Killed at Bear Creek, Tennessee.

Second Lieutenant-Colonel, L. D. Hockersmith, Madisonville, Hopkins county, Kentucky.

First Major, Walker Taylor.

First Adjutant, Joseph Walker, Madisonville, Hopkins county, Kentucky.

Second Adjutant, Geo. Whitecotton, Sullivan, Union county, Kentucky.

Surgeon, Dr. Hugh Crowell, Crittenden county, Kentucky. Killed after war by Captain Frank Hawkins, U. S. A.

Quartermaster, Ely Nunn, Repton, Crittenden county, Kentucky.

Commissary, Frank M. Kuykendall, Union county, Kentucky. Promoted from first sergeant major.

Second Sergeant Major, Amplias Timmons, Hopkins county, Kentucky.

COMPANY LIST OF CAPTAINS.

Company A, Wm. C. Kuykendall, Webster county, Kentucky.

Company B, Henry Wilson, Clarksville, Tennessee.

Company D, Geo. Sellers, Union county, Kentucky; First Lieutenant, Ben F. Perkins; Second Lieutenant, Lon McKinley; Third Lieutenant, Wm. Funk, all of Union county.

Company C, Presley Carr, Union county, Kentucky.

Company E, Nath. Calhoun, Kentucky.
Company F, ——— Webster, Kentucky.
Company G, B. F. Wallace, Kentucky.
Company H, Neil Helm, Kentucky.
Company I, Captain Al. McGoodwyn, Caldwell county, Kentucky.
Company K, Captain Nelson, Kentucky.
Official Scout, Jack Tomblin, Hopkins county, Kentucky.

This Thirteenth Kentucky Regiment was consolidated with the Twelfth and Eighth Kentucky Regiments February, 1865, commanded by (that grand old soldier of two wars) Colonel A. R. Shacklett, of Island, Kentucky, who, though totally blind, enjoys a talk with old comrades. This June 10, 1904, make somebody happy by going to see him. You will be better by the visit.—Frank A. Owen.

COMPANY A, THIRTEENTH KENTUCKY CAVALRY.
C. S. A.

Commanded by Captain Wm. C. Kuykendall

First Lieutenant, Cokendolpher. Afterward promoted to captain.
Second Lieutenant, Jno. H. Crudup. Afterward promoted to first lieutenant.
Third Lieutenant, Thos. M. Brown. Afterward promoted to second lieutenant.
Second Lieutenant, Jas. Gist. Afterward promoted to third lieutenant.
Orderly Sergeant, Geo. E. Price, Clay, Kentucky.

PRIVATES.

Adcock, Can., Hopkins county, Kentucky.
Aldridge, Jno. H., Webster county, Kentucky.
Anderson, Bud, Hopkins county, Kentucky.
Allen, John, Georgia.
Brooks, John, Webster county, Kentucky.
Buck, Theo., Webster county, Kentucky.
Burnett, Pat., Hopkins county, Kentucky.
Bennett, Richard, Union county, Kentucky.
Black, Huston, Webster county, Kentucky.
Brown, John, Webster county, Kentucky.

Bails, P., Webster county, Kentucky.

Bean, John, Webster county, Kentucky.

Cunningham, John, Webster county, Kentucky.

Cardwell, G. H., Christian county, Kentucky.

Catlett, Al., Union county, Kentucky.

Clark, Marsh, Webster county, Kentucky.

Cardwell, Geo. S., Webster county, Kentucky. Desperately wounded at Grubbs' Crossroads.

Cap, Red, Texas.

Coleman, Jas., Union county, Kentucky.

Dunning, Ben., Union county, Kentucky.

Doris, Saml., Webster county, Kentucky.

David, Jas. A., Webster county, Kentucky.

Dye, Enoch, Webster county, Kentucky.

Daves, Thos., Webster county, Kentucky.

Dills, Ben., Webster county, Kentucky.

Dills, Jas., Webster county, Kentucky.

Dial, E., Webster county, Kentucky.

Day, Jas. D., Manitou, Kentucky.

Day, Ben, Manitou, Kentucky.

Davos, Lige, Hopkins county, Kentucky.

Davis, Sam, Hopkins county, Kentucky.

Edings, Nathaniel, Webster county, Kentucky.

Farwell, W. H., Webster county, Kentucky.

Fletcher, Jas., Webster county, Kentucky.

Fowler, Jas., Webster county, Kentucky.

Fowler, Thos., Webster county, Kentucky.

Givens, W. H., Webster county, Kentucky.

McGill, Riley, Webster county, Kentucky.

McGill, W. R., Union county, Kentucky.

McGill, Jas. Harvey, Union county, Kentucky.

Gilmore, Frank, Union county, Kentucky.

Herin, ———, Webster county, Kentucky.

Hall, Hill N., Webster county, Kentucky.

Hunter, Ben, Webster county, Kentucky.

Hill, Jas., Webster county, Kentucky.

Hardin, Jno., Webster county, Kentucky.

Herron, Buck, Webster county, Kentucky.

Herron, Esq., Webster county, Kentucky.

Hall, Wm. V., Webster county, Kentucky.

Hyman, Hazel, Webster county, Kentucky.
Holeman, Thomas, Webster county, Kentucky.
Hoff, Wm., Webster county, Kentucky.
Howton, Ben, Hopkins county, Kentucky.
Hammock, Steve, Union county, Kentucky.
Hazel, H., Union county, Kentucky.
James, Miles B., Webster county, Kentucky.
Johnson, Noah, Jr., Webster county, Kentucky.
Johnson, Noah, Sr., Webster county, Kentucky.
King, Jas., Henderson county, Kentucky.
Kuykendall, Jas., Webster county, Kentucky.
Kuykendall, Frank M., Webster county, Kentucky.
Kezee, Huston, Webster county, Kentucky.
Lewallen, Pedney, Webster county, Kentucky.
Lynn, Isaac, Webster county, Kentucky.
McLendon, Geo., Webster county, Kentucky.
McLeon, G., Webster county, Kentucky.
Mitchell, Henry, Webster county, Kentucky.
Matthews, Geo., Webster county, Kentucky.
Mangum, Thos., Webster county, Kentucky.
Monroe, J. G., Webster county, Kentucky.
Matthie, Andrew Ben, Webster county, Kentucky.
Montgomery, Wm., Webster county, Kentucky.
Martin, David, Webster county, Kentucky.
Music, Sam, Webster county, Kentucky.
Monrowe, Wood, Webster county, Kentucky.
Monroe, J. G., Webster county, Kentucky.
Mangum, Cam., Hopkins county, Kentucky.
Nunn, Jno., Crittenden county, Kentucky.
Nunn, Ely, Crittenden county, Kentucky
Nisbett, Cris. C., Webster county, Kentucky.
Philipps, Wm., Crittenden county, Kentucky.
Phillipps, Ed., Crittenden county, Kentucky.
Phillipps, Thos., Crittenden county, Kentucky.
Potts, Tillman, Webster county, Kentucky.
Potts, Robt., Webster county, Kentucky.
Patterson, Jno., Tennessee.
Price, G. E., Webster county, Kentucky.
Price, Elihue, Webster county, Kentucky.

GEORGE BERRY.

Powell, ———, Daviess county, Kentucky. Executed by General Burbridge's order.

Powell, Wm., Sebree, Kentucky.

Royster, Wm., Henderson county, Kentucky.

Roland, ———, Webster county, Kentucky.

Saler, Jas., Webster county, Kentucky.

Skinner, Ashburg, Webster county, Kentucky.

Smith, Roley, F., Hopkins county, Kentucky.

Stites, Jack, Hopkins county, Kentucky.

Shaw, Jno. (Uncle Jack).

Thornton, Geo., Webster county, Kentucky.

Thurman, Barney, Webster county, Kentucky.

Urby, Dudley, Webster county, Kentucky.

Vaughn, J. S., Webster county, Kentucky. Quartermaster of regiment.

Vaughn, Johnson, Webster county.

Vaughn, Jo. C., Webster county, Kentucky.

Vaughn, Allen, Webster county, Kentucky.

Vaughn, Jeff., Webster county, Kentucky.

Wagoner, B., Webster county, Kentucky.

Wallace, Abram, Webster county, Kentucky.

Wallace, Collen, Webster county, Kentucky.

Whitecotton, Geo., Webster county, Kentucky.

Wallace, Ben. F., Webster county, Kentucky.

Wallace, Abe C., Webster county, Kentucky.

Wallace, Jas. T., Webster county, Kentucky.

Wallace, W. R., Webster county, Kentucky.

Woodard, Ben E., Webster county, Kentucky.

Wynn, Wm. C., Webster county, Kentucky.

Wicks, Jas. W., Webster county, Kentucky.

Wiley, Geo., Hopkins county, Kentucky.

Wilson, Wm., Crittenden county, Kentucky.

Williams, H. B., Crittenden county, Kentucky.

FIELD AND STAFF OFFICERS OF SIXTEENTH KENTUCKY CAVALRY.

Colonel, J. Q. A. Chenoweth, Harrodsburg, Kentucky.

Lieutenant-Colonel, Sidney Cunningham.

Major, ——— Jones, Bowling Green, Warren county, Kentucky.

Surgeon, Norborn Berry, Henderson county, Kentucky.

Quartermaster, David A. Brooks.

Commissary, John Lynn, Lyon county, Kentucky.

Adjutant, Dr. ———. Acted at beginning.

Captain Harris, of Mississippi, had few men in this command.

Captain John Head, from Colonel Wm. Hollis' regiment, 42 men.

Captain Jos. H. Payne, Missouri, number of men, 42.

Captain Wm. Quinn, number of men, 83.

Captain Nelson, number of men, 36.

Captain Lindsey Duke Buckner, number of men, 73.

First Lieutenant, J. P. Pearce, Marion, Kentucky.

Second Lieutenant, Dave Varnell, Lyon county, Kentucky.

Third Lieutenant, Wm. White, Lyon county, Kentucky.

Orderly Sergeant, Sam C. Barnett, Caldwell county, Kentucky.

Captain ——— Rushing, Kentucky.

Captain George B. Payne, number of men, 56.

Major Housley's Battalion, number of men, 320.

Names of his captains misplaced.

Captain J. J. January, number of men, 65.

Captain John Brooks, number of men, 32.

Captain or Major Dorch, number of men about 300; was connected with the command first, and afterward became the Fourth Tennessee Battalion of Cavalry.

Total number of men, 1,059.

Respectfully submitted,

FRANK A. OWEN.

COMPANY D, SIXTEENTH KENTUCKY CAVALRY.

This company belonged to Colonel Chenoweth's Regiment, Sixteenth Kentucky Cavairy.

Captain John J. January's company was regularly organized at Brice's Mills, in Webster county, August 17th or 18th, 1864.

Letter of Company was D. Chenoweth's Regiment.

First Lieutenant, James Waller, of Hopkins county. Killed at Canton, Kentucky, August 23, 1864.

Second Lieutenant, Chilton Reed, of Warren county. Went through the war; whereabouts not known, if living; was promoted to first lieutenant; some say, later to captain.

Wm. Quinn, of Henderson, Kentucky, became captain in September.

DR. GEORGE PORTER,
1st Surgeon 10th Ky. Partisan Rangers.

Bub Quinn, of Henderson, Kentucky, became first lieutenant in his company.

George Riddle, of Union county. Killed at Grubbs' Crossroads.

Sam Riddle, of Union county. Killed at Grubbs' Crossroads.

Marshal Clark, of Union county. Living.

Clint Balough, of Union county. Living.

Robert Pots, of Union county. Died in Camp Chase.

James Pots, of Union county. Died in Camp Chase.

——— Herron, of Webster county. Died in Camp Chase.

——— Herron, of Webster county. Died in Camp Chase.

Thos. Skinner, of Webster county. Died in Camp Chase.

Asbury Skinner, of Webster county. Living.

Jas. Michill, of Webster county. Living.

Wm. Wise, of Webster county.

Sam C. Humphrey, of Webster county.

Bud Sizemore, of Webster county. Living

A. Lee Brown, of Webster county. Living. St. Louis.

John Brown, of Hopkins county. Killed at Grubbs' Crossroads.

Dr. J. S. Waller, of Hanson, Hopkins county. Living.

Jonah Tippitt, of Hanson, Hopkins county. Living.

James Hibbs, of Hanson, Hopkins county. Living.

Ben F. Heart, Manatoe, Hopkins county. Died after war.

Henry Mitchell, of Manatoe, Hopkins county. Wounded in fight with negro regiment; died after war.

Hyram Yeates, of Manatoe, Hopkins county. Killed in fight with negro regiment between Eddyville and Johnsonville same day that Colonel Soery was killed.

James Sales, of Pleasant Grove, Hopkins county. Living.

Robert Hall, Madisonville, Kentucky. Living.

David Cryder, of Union or Crittenden county; don't know.

Cameron Mangum, of Hopkins county. Died in Texas.

Thomas Mangum, of Hopkins county. Living in Texas.

John Burton, of Hopkins county. Died at Camp Chase, 1865.

Jesse Burton, of Hopkins county. Killed near Burksville, Kentucky, December, 1864.

Wm. Wilkerson, of Hopkins county. Living in Texas.

John Tomllnson, of Hopkins county. Living at Ashbysburg, Kentucky.

Finas Timmons, of Hopkins county. Died in 1873.

John Crabtree, of Madisonville. Living.

(Supplied by Jack Tomlinson.)

—— Larah Dossett, Sacramento, Kentucky. Living in Texas.

Zachariah Thomeson, of Webster county. Living near Nuckels, Kentucky.

Garland (Frosty), of Springfield, Webster county. Living near Sebree, Kentucky.

George W. Wiley, of Hopkins county. Living near Hanson, Kentucky.

Polk Walker, of Hopkins county. If living, near Hanson, Kentucky.

Andrew Staton, of Hopkins county. Murdered by order of General Burbridge at same time with John Brooks.

Sim Hobgood, of Hopkins county. Living near Slaughtersville, Kentucky.

Pleas. Cobb, of Webster county. Living in Owensboro, Kentucky.

Frank Kuykendall, of Union county. Living in Missouri; acting lieutenant.

Thomas Jewell, of Webster county. Living near Delaware, Kentucky.

Sam C. Humphrey, of Webster county. Living at Guntersville, Mississippi.

James Gist, of Webster county. Living at Providence, Kentucky.

Theo. Brown, of Hopkins county. Living in Texas.

Henry Brown, of Hopkins county. Living in Texas.

Jo. Ashby, of Hopkins county, Ky. Died in 1898.

David Johnson, of Hopkins county. Living in Texas.

Wm. J. Clayton, of Hanson, Kentucky. Living.

Richard D. Clayton, of Hanson, Kentucky. Living.

Calvin Yarbrough, of Hanson, Kentucky. Prisoner at Hopkinsville, Kentucky, December, 1864, and murdered by order of General Steve Burbridge at Louisville, January, 1865.

Geo. S. Cardwill, Hopkins county. Living at Louisville, Kentucky. Desperately wounded at Grubbs' Crossroads.

Marion McCormick, of Hopkins county. Died in Mississippi, 1875.

Wm. Yarbrough,, of Hopkins county. Living at Nebo, KeKntucky.

Frank Myers, of Hopkins county. Living near Sebree, Kentucky.

Marion Myers, Company A, Tenth Kentucky. Killed during war; place not known.

THOMAS M. BROOKS (and Grandson, Robert Thompson)

Co. H, 10th Ky., P. R.

Eaf Roby, of Webster county, orderly sergeant. Living in Mississippi.

Robert Buts, a brave Irishman, of Union county. Don't know.

Buford Carlisle, of Hopkins county. Died about 1893.

John Carlisle, Jr., of Hopkins county. Died in Missouri in 1880.

John Brooks, of Hopkins county. Murdered by General Steve Burbridge's order at Louisville, 1864.

Amplias Timmons, of Hopkins county. Living in Texas.

Wm. Ashley, of Hopkins county. Died in 1895.

W. B. Anderson and others whose names we can not get now.

FIELD AND STAFF OFFICERS OF ELEVENTH KENTUCKY CAVALRY.

Colonel, William Hollis, Webster county, Kentucky.

Lieutenant-Colonel, Holmes ———.

Major, James Waller, Hopkins county, Kentucky.

Adjutant, J. Thomas Greer, Hopkinsville, Kentucky.

Quartermaster, Fred Kline, Henderson county, Kentucky .

Commissary, A. " Coney " Owen, Hopkins county, Kentucky.

Captain, Thomas Henry, Union county, Kentucky, 71 men.

Captain, T. Basham, Bonham, Texas, 32 men.

Captain, Ad Anderson, Texas, 40 men.

Captain, J. J. January, Kentucky, 85 men.

Captain, ——— Lindsey, Kentucky, 27 men.

Captain, ——— Nelson, Benton, Kentucky, 33 men.

Captain, H. J. Buck, Tennessee, 16 men.

Captain, Alex. Uttley, 22 men.

Captain, Henry Wedding, Corydon, Kentucky, 18 men.

Captain, Ollie Steel, Henderson county, Kentucky, 30 men.

Captain, Jas. Wallace, 36 men.

Sergeant Major, E. D. Arnett, Henderson county, Kentucky.

Total number of men, 410.

This regiment was organized thoroughly, but fifty-two men of the four hundred and ten were armed, and two hundred and five had horses. On 22d of June, 1863, they were attacked by five companies of the Thirty--fifth Kentucky U. S. Cavalry. Colonel Hollis and Lieutenant Wm. Duvall were killed, eight wounded, six captured and the battalion put to flight, who subsequently joined other commands. This was the end of the Eleventh Kentucky Cavalry as an organization. Respectfully,

FRANK A. OWEN.

CAPT. NEIL HELM'S SCOUTS.

Captain, Neil Helm.
First Lieutenant, Wm. Hamby.
Second Lieutenant, Chas. Taylor.
Third Lieutenant, ——— Rogers.
Orderly Sergeant, Tom Bryson.
Second Sergeant, Fletcher Stephens.
Third Sergeant, Henry Sampson.
Fourth Sergeant, Phillip Smith.
First Corporal, Geo. Uttley.
Second Corporal, Marion Dunn.
Third Corporal, John Ashley.
Fourth Corporal, Fred Frazier.

PRIVATES.

James Donally.
David Phillips.
S. J. Scurry.
Theodore Davidson.
Wm. Sugg.
Jno. Divine.
Peter Smith.
Henry Hardwick.
Salem Frazier.
Cyrus Garth.
Daniel Simms.
Henry Simms.
J. J. McCormick.
Ed. J. Johnson.
Thos. Phillips.
S. G. Threadgill.
P. B. Snodgrass.
E. G. Brown.
O. B. Dodd.
Z. T. Bush.

Fred. C. Foster.
D. T. Wood.
Thos. Shannon.
Jno. Saxton.
Henry S. Sexton.
David Bean.
Jno. O'Conner.
Ben C. Thorpe.
Henry Dixon.
Bailey Traweek.
Robt. Ridgley.
F. Ainsworth.
Geo. Furgeson.
Frank V. Stephenson.
Phillip Fowler.
Geo. Johnson.
Chas. Abney.
A. C. Bullett.
B. L. Caraway.
J. L. Curtain.

Vincent Dalton.
Conrad Clayton.
Sandy Slocum.
L. D. Farmer.
R. Y. Robins.
Linzey Leslie.
Thos. Dyer.
D. G. Vincent.
Volney Paine.
Z. P. Denison.
Alex. Benton.
Tom. C. Posey.
A. B. Van Zandt.
I. C. Pinson.
G. D. Galloway.
C. O. Foster.
David Kinkead.
Henry A. Chadwick.

CAPT. WILLIAM BRANK McLEAN,
Commander Steamer "Curlew."

Incidents and Adventures.

CAPTAIN WILLIAM BRANK McLEAN.

Commander of Steamer " Curlew."

Captain Wm. B. McLean was born at Harrodsburg, Kentucky, June 25, 1820. He handled the steamer " Newsboy " during the war, plying between Henderson and Evansville. Previous to the war he owned and managed the steamer " Bowling Green," running between Evansville and Bowling Green. During the war he was arrested on suspicion of aiding the Southern cause, was kept under military guard at Indianapolis for about six weeks, but failing to make out a case against him, he was released without a trial. Captain Lew Wallace, who had him in charge, treated him with every courtesy he could ask, and was instrumental in obtaining his release.

He died December 1, 1880, at the age of sixty years, and is buried in " Oak Hill " Cemetery at Evansville, Ind. He was a warm friend of the South, and ran many risks to furnish us supplies. He brought me the proposition from the Sons of Liberty previously mentioned.

AN OUTLINE HISTORY OF THE PARTISAN RANGERS.

By Frank Amplias Owen.

This abridged history is useful as a succinct summary of the incidents hereinbefore related in Part I, particularly as it gives dates which are lacking in the fuller account.

On the first of June, 1862, F. A. Owen became my first recruit. Older men who had raised a nucleus of companies had refused to follow me as their leader on account of "youth and inexperience," men who afterward led to my standard companies of gallant and enthusiastic young soldiers, all of whom, both officers and men, thenceforward manifested the utmost confidence in their commander and always stood by me faithfully and manfully in every emergency to the bitter end.

Owen was then only seventeen, but had been in a Federal prison and had escaped. He was a quiet, amiable boy, and his round, pleasant face made him appear more youthful than he was. A brave, patient, earnest, model soldier, true as steel to those whom he professed friendship for and loyal always to his country's cause. He is still living, his home now being in Evansville, Indiana; and though white-haired, he still holds in his business the same standard of downright honesty that was so marked in the gallant young soldier.

OWEN'S STORY.

Johnson, Martin and Owen alone attacked and utterly demoralized the Federal provost guard company stationed in the National Hotel at Henderson, Kentucky, on June 7, 1862. Subsequently they were engaged in recruiting the Breckinridge Guards until the thirteenth of the same month, when Captain Johnson, with six men at-

MAJOR FRANK AMPLIAS OWEN.

tacked a Union force of three hundred and fifty men. The enemy were camped at Woodson's or Browning's Spring in the outskirts of Madisonville, and had with them two pieces of artillery. Johnson's little handful of determined young Confederates drove this large force pellmell from their camp.

On the fourteenth of June they received twenty new recruits and at once started in pursuit of the fleeing Federals and followed them to Henderson. The citizens of that town, hearing of their approach, sent out a delegation of the prominent men of the city headed by the Mayor, Colonel Ed Hall, accompanied by the county Judge, Trafton, ex-Congressman John Young Brown, afterwards Governor of the State, J. H. Barrett, and others to meet Johnson and request him to state what his action toward the Union men of the town would be. The young Confederate told them that he was not making war upon private citizens, and rode into the town and raised the Confederate flag over the court house, though the captain of the gunboat lying off the town seriously objected.

The next day this same squad of daring young soldiers, led by the gallant Johnson, captured Newburg, Indiana, paroled one hundred and eighty prisoners, and carried off five hundred stands of arms, though not a gun was fired.

Johnson and Martin now received recruits until the 4th of July, when a big barbecue was arranged for them by the citizens of Slaughtersville who wished to show their appreciation of this first daring invasion of Northern soil by such a small force of brave " wearers of the gray." While this band of loyal Southerners were enjoying the good things that the ladies of the town had prepared for them, news was brought to them that a large force from Newburg and Evansville, Indiana, who had captured and shot John Patterson, was fast approaching. The forty-seven new recruits gathered by Johnson and Martin were quickly organized and preparations made to meet the advance. That night this little band of Confederates attacked the Federal pickets on the several roads and so demoralized them that they retreated in confusion to their homes.

Owen and Johnson went to see poor Patterson, who had been removed from Samuel's farm to a cabin in the woods some distance from the battleground, and where he was safe from the Federal soldiers. They found him suffering intensely, but brave enough to stand the move to old man Jesse Brown's, seven or eight miles in the interior, safe from any chance of capture and where he received every attention possible from the kind family and the neighbors who called, Dr. Jenkins's people and others too numerous to mention. This splendid nursing finally restored Patterson to health, and soon he wedded a young woman who did not mind his being blind, and the two settled down and made their living and raised a family, being good and thrifty citizens. Patterson only died within the last few years, and left his widow and several grown children to mourn his loss.

From this time on Johnson and Martin recruited rapidly, for nothing "succeeds like success" in military affairs as well as in the quieter walks of life, for soldiers, like other men, worship a rising rather than a setting sun. Soon their forces increased to three hundred and fifty men, and they advanced upon the city of Hopkinsville and captured a small force of Federals and home guards without firing a gun. Emboldened by this success, they next attacked the larger and more strongly-fortified and fully-manned city of Clarksville, Tennessee, where they took Colonel Mason's Seventh Ohio Regiment, no resistance being made to their reckless charge right up to the enemy's breastworks. This occurred in the month of August, and the next thing the little band of Confederates decided to recapture Fort Donelson, but on ascertaining that this place was too strongly fortified for their small force, they made a gallant charge upon the troops concealed behind these historic breastworks, then retired in good order toward Clarksville. On reaching Rolling Mills, on the Cumberland river, now known as Bear Springs, Furnier, Tennessee, they had a lively fight with a band of Federal cavalry from Fort Henry, and came off victorious, with colors flying. This engagement was also in August, 1862.

Ever active and enterprising, and like the proverbial Irishman at a country fair in the "ould country" always looking for a fight, they moved northward and charged and blazed away at a regiment of infantry from Hoosierdom at Uniontown, Kentucky. Here these successful Confederates captured the entire force with all their camp equipage. After paroling their captives, Johnson and Martin moved their captured stores to Geiger's Lake, left a small company to guard them, then disbanded and went home after the manner of partisan rangers or ancient Scottish clans. It was understood that they were to rendezvous at a certain date at the

Holman farm in Webster county, in the hills between Dixon and Boxville.

After disbanding, it was learned that Colonel J. M. Shackelford, commanding a Yankee regiment, had received information that there was a small Confederate camp at Geiger's Lake, where Johnson had stored all his captured goods, including the cannon taken from Mason at Clarksville, Tennessee, and that he intended marching there. Lieutenant Bob Martin, with about fifty men, hastily formed an ambush where it was supposed the enemy would have to pass going from the north. Colonel Johnson was sick, but with twelve other invalids, guarded their camp. While the ambushing party were quietly waiting for Colonel Shackelford to walk into their nicely-laid trap, where all their men were well placed and their cannon masked, they were surprised at hearing firing in the camp on the lake in the rear. Martin was sitting on his horse, the others having dismounted, and upon hearing the shots at once galloped back to the camp and found that Colonel Johnson had gone around the end of the lake when he discovered the advance of the Federals from the south instead of the north, and through a by-path that the Confederates had not been aware of. Johnson, ever a close--quarter fighter, allowed Shackelford's force to come up to the lake without interference. Thinking that the Confederates had deserted their camp, the Yankees gave shouts of exultation, for they believed they were to meet with no opposition and were quite jubilant in their delusion. Just at this juncture, when they were in disorder, pillaging the tents they had so easily captured, our little invalid corps, under their strategic leader, suddenly fired into them from the other side of the lake, then quickly fell back some distance out of view, and while Shackelford was forming his men for an attack upon the men who had so unceremoniously spoiled their fun, Martin dashed up from the rear. Two Federal squads at once turned their fire upon his daring figure, one ball taking effect in Martin's horse. Nothing disconcerted, Martin galloped back, and in a short time brought the ambushing company with their cannon into action on the bank of the lake. The weeds being high in this bottom, Shackelford could not see them until he charged up to within about fifty yards, and did not even know that the artillery was in the neighborhood, as was afterwards learned by the Confederates who now opened fire. Upon the discharging of that cannon, loaded with cut bars of lead, the Yankees fell back in confusion. The gallant Shackelford was wounded in the foot and neither he nor his officers could rally his fleeing men.

Johnson and Martin had such a small force, and had heard from the citizens such exaggerated stories of the Federal numbers that they did not follow up this victory. They afterwards believed that had they pursued them closely they could have captured the entire demoralized command before they could have gotten on the steamboat at Caseyville for safety. This memorable fight occurred upon the third or fourth of September, 1862.

Colonel Johnson now went South, leaving Martin in command. Martin met the other companies at the Holman farm on the sixteenth of September, and marched to the neighborhood of Slaughtersville, Kentucky; thence to Ashbysburg on the Green river, which he crossed on the eighteenth, and moved in the direction of Owensboro. They camped part of the night on Panther creek at Glen's bridge. Colonel Martin, Major Scoby and Captain Owen got lunch at Mrs. Oglesby's. As all of them were devoted Southerners, both she and her daughters treated them with the greatest kindness. The young ladies were then unmarried, but later became the wives of physicians who became very prominent in their profession. One of them was then a gallant Confederate soldier in the First Kentucky Cavalry. He was the late Dr. Soyars, of Slaughtersville, Kentucky, who died about nine years ago. The other was a noble citizen of the same town.

Colonel Martin now advanced upon the beautiful city of Owensboro at daylight, September 19, 1862, and found there Colonel Netter with about four hundred men and one piece of artillery. They were camped in the fair grounds below the town. The Confederates captured a few soldiers who were found in the town, and so far as the city itself was concerned, they had it all their own way. Martin sent in a demand for the surrender of the camp to Colonel Netter, but was refused. Martin had previously sent the companies of Captain S. B. Taylor, J. S. Chapman, and Clay Merriwether below the camp, and thus had the enemy completely surrounded. Netter came out with a company to reconnoiter the force below his camp and see, it has been recently learned, if he could find any way to save his horses if he was compelled to surrender. This Federal commander was killed in a skirmish with this force, but the Confederates did not know it until the next day. Martin decided that it was not best to attack the Federals in the position they held as they had already captured in the town what they most needed—ammunition. They quietly marched out and camped on the Southerland farm ten miles out on the Halford Road, with the intention of attacking a regiment that was being formed by Colonel Shanks, to be called the Twelfth Kentucky Cavalry. It was heard next morning that the Indiana Legion had come across the river to Owensboro and would give the Confederates battle if they would wait for them. The next morning the Twelfth Kentucky charged the Confederate forces in great style, but upon being repulsed they retreated and appeared no more upon the scene.

Martin requested Owen to accompany him upon a reconnoisance of the Indiana forces. Riding through the woods parallel to the road, they came within sight of their infantry and artillery a quarter of a mile beyond Panther creek upon the Owensboro Road. Both of these Confederate officers could not resist taking a pop at the nearest of the enemy, then galloped back to their camp, and much to their surprise their fire not being returned. Martin at once marched his regiment down to a level meadow, relinquishing the strong position they were occupying on the hill and ridge near the Southerland residence. He formed his men about eighty yards from a heavy stake and rider fence running parallel to the big road and within a few feet of same, and there awaited an attack. There was a ditch between the fence and the road which Martin had failed to discover until too late to remedy the mistake, as the Yankees had crawled up that ditch and put the muzzle of their guns through the fence just above the bottom of the ground rails. Thus entirely shielded, they poured a murderous fire into the Confederate forces, killing a number of splendid men, among them James Keach, orderly sergeant of Captain Fisher's Company B; George Berry, of Company F; Richard Dunville, orderly sergeant of Company A, as well as many others, numbering thirty-six in all, killed and wounded. The Federals being much greater in numbers and shielded by their strong breastworks, the Confederates were compelled to withdraw after standing their ground bravely for some time. They were not followed more than a half a mile, then recrossing the river at Ashby's ferry, they camped for the remainder of the night on the opposite bank. The next morning they were confronted by two Federal battalions with two brass six-pounder cannon. The wearers of the gray took refuge in an earthen fort made by Colonel Shackelford in 1861, and as it was upon a high hill overlooking the river and town, they repelled the charge of the enemy, then slipped out at the rear of the fort and marched down the river and flanked the Union forces. Company A of the Confederate force had a small skirmish with one of the scouting parties, and the Federals, fearing that a trap had been laid for them, crossed the river and went into camp on the other side. Later they recrossed the river at Clarksville and returned to Henderson.

The next morning the Confederates sent their cannon to a place of safety, concealing it in a thicket near Mr. W. H. Jackson's, this gentleman being familiarly known as Uncle Hal. A few days later the Confederates learned that one of Uncle Hal's negroes had seen their hidden treasure, and fearing that he would tell the Yankees of its whereabouts William Wilkerson, James Waller, Thomas Washington and others covered it with a wagon sheet and hauled it through the fields to the very head of the east fork of Deer creek, where it remained about a year, when the Yankees captured Wilkerson and scared him into telling where it was. The Federals then unearthed it and carried it to Owensboro, where it was used for a morning and evening gun as long as the Thirty-fifth Regiment remained there. Upon the anniversary of the death of Colonel Netter this gun was said to have been fired a hundred times on the bank of the river until it exploded and badly crippled the gunner, Kelley Shelton, of Pratt, Kentucky, who is yet living, minus his right arm.

In a few days these Confederates were disbanded again with instructions to prepare heavy clothing and make ready for a winter campaign. In October three hundred and fifty of them were marched South to Camp Winnow, Tennessee, where they met Colonel Johnson, who had been to Richmond, Virginia. They soon joined John H. Morgan's command and went into Kentucky with him on what is generally called the " Christmas raid."

A running record has now been made of all the engagements of Colonel Johson's regiment up to the time they joined the main army.

After the capture of Clarksville, Johnson sent Captain Fowler and his regiment back to Madisonville, where Dimmitt's company (afterwards Captain John Hamby's) was recruiting. Receiving a dispatch that a Federal force would leave Henderson for Madisonville, Colonel Johnson sent warning to Fowler and Dimmit, who united their forces and warmed the blue coats well. This little band met the enemy at William Wilson's farm, a mile north of the court house of Madisonville. There were after this skirmishes between the men who remained in Kentucky and the Yankees. Upon one occasion George Thomas, of Company A, who had first served out twelve months' enlistment in the First Kentucky Cavalry of the Confederate army, and Joseph Browder, who had been on a scout, were leaving Slaughtersville when they overtook Miss Annie Ogden and Miss Ellen Jenkins, who were riding slowly along on horseback. Thomas rode with the first and Browder with the second young lady, and they had not gone very far when they met Major Platter of the Federal amy, and another soldier in citizen's garb. These two rode with the little party until near the Platter place, when Major Platter drew his concealed weapon and suddenly fired across Miss Ogden's lap at Thomas. The ball missed its mark, and the other, fired at Bowden, also flew wide. Major Platter wildly fled, closely pursued by the brave Bowden who shot him in the top of the head, which wound finally caused his death. Thomas is a successful farmer, yet living near Morgantown, Butler county, Kentucky.

Another skirmish occurred just after the nocturnal fight at Henderson on the seventh of June, 1862. Johnson had gone to Union county and Martin and Owen heard that there had been a large lot of government supplies put off the boat at Ashbyburg, Kentucky, and a lieutenant and twenty men left to guard it. As there were no other Yankees on Kentucky soil nearer than Louisville that they knew of, Martin decided that it would gladden Johnson's heart for him and Owen to slip down there and capture the twenty-one soldiers and the goods in their custody. They advanced but a short distance when they met the Ninth Pennsylvania Cavalry, who had gone to chase them and captured Owen's gray Indian pony which was so slow that he had to abandon him and trust to his heels through the woods, while Martin, being better mounted, escaped after firing both barrels of his trusty shotgun at them. Owen fired but one barrel at the start, and it was lucky for him that this was so, as it saved his life shortly afterwards, when an orderly sergeant ran up to him with a huge saber, not knowing of his reserved shot, and crying: " O, blast your little soul, I got you now! " Owen discharged his other load at him, but he jerked his horse up so that but one shot struck him in the left arm. This he told Owen when they met later, when Owen was a prisoner and he a commissioned officer who called the roll on Johnson's Island for a time in 1864. Once these two men of opposite armies were telling yarns, when this Federal officer boasted of his splitting a Confederate's head open near a brick church in the neighborhood of Slaughtersville. Owen then related his side of the story so circumstantially that the other was compelled to admit his falsehood and to bear much guying for wagging his boastful tongue.

There was another little fight June 22, 1863, in which Colonel William Hollis, who was raising a regiment, the Eleventh Kentucky, for General Johnson's command, was killed as well as some six or eight wounded.

THE FLAG OF THE PARTISAN RANGERS.

Letter From the Lady Who Presented It.

Mrs. J. J. Massie (formerly Miss Tennie Moore), of Fort Worth, Texas, has been so kind as recently to write the following letter:

In visiting my old home last summer after an absence of sixteen years, I learned the sad fact that out of the number that stood with me on the upper veranda upon that memorable morning when I presented that beautiful Confederate flag to your command, I alone am left. All the rest have passed over the river and are resting in the shade of the trees. I was so young at the time, and so many years, freighted with the sorrow, cares and responsibilities of life, have intervened, I find some difficulty in recalling with accuracy all the incidents of that day and the enthusiastic welcome we gave you as our deliverer from the Yankees. A much loved uncle of mine, who watched with pride and pleasure my warm and zealous espousal of the cause of our beloved Confederacy and remembered how untiringly he had seen me day after day go to the sewing-room, where we were busy making the uniforms of our brave soldiers, who, at the first call went forth to battle for their dear country; and how, at our private expense, my mother, sister, and myself, with some assistance from him, made over one hundred soldier caps and gave them to our brave boys in gray, having for a model a cap of a cousin who was being educated at a military institution, and who hurried home as soon as Tennessee seceded, to fight her battles, this uncle wishing to reward my fidelity and devotion, bought rich and handsome material for a large and magnificent Confederate banner and gave it to me on the condition that I would present it to the Forty-ninth Tennessee infantry, in which he had enlisted and which was then under General Buckner, at Fort Donelson. We made the flag, a boat was chartered, a brass band was engaged, and a day appointed for its presentation. The battle ensued, Fort Donelson fell, and in his hurried retreat South, he sent me a message to present it to the first Confederate regiment that captured Clarksville. Never will I forget the happy day when Colonel Johnson, stationing his troops on the outskirts of the town at the college which was then the headquarters of the Federals, came in alone at a very early hour in the morning, proceeded to the headquarters of Colonel Mason, and demanded the unconditional surrender of Clarksville.

Colonel Mason, astonished and bewildered at the daring bravery of this noble Confederate officer, sprang from his bed, hastily drew on a few articles of clothing, thrust his feet into a pair of slippers, and entered his room at headquarters, followed by Johnson, to whom the guard on the outside seemingly paid no attention. Mason asked Johnson how much artillery and how many troops he had in his command. " Enough to use you up, and I am going to give you only a few moments in which to decide," Colonel Johnson replied.

A fiery-headed captain, with a volley of oaths, was the only one who protested against capitulation. He was for a fight, when Colonel Johnson bade him be quiet—said that his soldiers were only waiting for a signal to make the attack. Mason sent out a squad to investigate, and Colonel Martin so adroitly maneuvered his troops as to cause them to be counted twice. The Confederates had only one piece of artillery which had been taken from the Federals a short time before. Mason made an unconditional surrender.

Not long subsequently he was relieved of his command for not resisting the small force of Confederates sent against him.

When the glad news reached my home, I hastily sent a messenger to Colonel Johnson, telling him of my great desire to present to him an expensive and beautiful flag as a tribute to his daring bravery and an expression of our gratitude to the gallant soldiers of his command. Accordingly, at eleven o'clock his whole force marched up in regular file and took position in front of our home. There in that upper porch, was Mrs. Tompkins at my right, who was one of the grandest old mothers of the Confederacy, and whose zeal and energy and deeds of heroism and self-sacrifice will be cherished as long as a member of the Fourteenth Tennessee survives, while on my left stood my devoted old colored nurse—my black mammy of blessed memory—and to whose faithful charge I had entrusted the care of the flag.   In commencing my address, when I said, " I bring this flag from its long hiding-place, a faithful negro's cabin," she proudly laid her hand on her heart, and making a profound bow to the command, said, " That's me! "

This proud, laconic speech elicited a round of applause from the boys.   And when I lowered the flag into the keeping of Colonel Johnson, three rousing cheers went up for Miss Tennie Moore, and made the welkin ring, while the air was full of caps tossed upward with the hearty prayer, " God bless her, we are wearing her caps now."

That day was one of the happiest of my girlhood.

Before closing this sketch I wish to pay a little tribute to dear Mrs. Tompkins, a woman of wonderful decision of character and executive ability, and to whose loyal devotion and patriotic zeal the Fourteenth Tennessee was greatly indebted for their splendid equipment for their long march to the front.   It was just as fine as tender hands and loving hearts could make it.   Mrs. Tompkins opened a sewing-room over a large store, and we eagerly rushed with our thimbles and needles to her assistance in fashioning the garments in which our brothers, fathers, sweethearts, and friends were to march to glory, and alas, in so many sad instances— the grave.

She cut out hundreds of garments with her own hands and personally directed the putting together and sewing the pieces. Sometimes we were praised and encouraged, and then scolded for our want of common sense.   But upon one notable occasion the climax of her indignation was reached when a young lady who so patiently tried to make a pair of pantaloons for her boy-lover, and brought them for her inspection, and she discovered, to her dismay, that she had put the pockets in the seat of the breeches instead of the places she had so carefully marked for her guidance.

Many a poor fellow died blessing Mrs. Tompkins for her kindly ministrations to the sick and dying, who had been brought up to Clarksville from the Fort Donelson battlefield.

I feel in this day when the loving devotion of the colored race to the master and mistress of the household is passing forever into oblivion a desire to speak of my own black mammy already alluded to. Into her keeping we gave all our ready money and jewelry, fearing they might fall into the hands of the Yankees. As soon as the Federals took possession of our city, a treacherous negro boy belonging to a neighbor, informed them that we had a large Confederate flag concealed in our home, and our house was repeatedly searched and twice set on fire with the sworn declaration that they were going to burn up the rebels, and we were subjected to many other indignities as unwarranted as galling.

I remember for four months we children didn't step out on the porch. The houses on each side of the street as far as we could see were occupied by Federal troops, inmates having fled South for protection within the Confederate lines. General Grant's head-quarters for a short time were in the handsome house of a banker a few doors above us.

This faithful slave had taken the flag and after carefully wrapping it in cloth and papers, she had placed it at the very bottom of her chest, throwing on top of it a bundle of carpet rags. A tidy negro, she always kept her cabin neat and homelike. One day a searching party entered her door, demanded her keys, and proceeded to toss the contents of her drawers and wardrobe upon the floor. When they unlocked her chest she exclaimed, " The Lord knows I thought you all were the nigger's friend, sent here to give us our rights and our freedom, and that we could look to you for protection. You ain't our friends at all. Just look how you have gone and mussed up my nice, clean cabin. I'd like to know what a poor nigger like me has got that you can want. For goodness sake, don't tangle up my carpet rags." The lieu-tenant in charge of the searching party said, " Come along, boys, and let the old nigger's rags alone."

But right underneath these rags lay the large flag, five by seven feet, our one hundred dollar treasured ensign for which they had been so diligently searching.

One dark, rainy, dismal night, while the city was full of Yankees, my cousin, a captain in the Confederate army, hearing of the illness of his mother who was a member of our family, made his way across the river and through familiar by-ways and stealthily tapped at our rear door. My mother stealthily opened the door and discovering who it was, let him in quickly. A Federal soldier was pacing his beat in front of the house. Our cousin was cold and hungry, weary and footsore. I went in the darkness and roused mammy and she cheerfully came and soon had prepared him a warm tempting supper and food to last him several days. Before day dawned our kinsman had crossed the river and was on his way back to the Confederate camp. Even after the war she never left us, notwithstanding the fact that her husband, a smart, likely negro, wanted her to go back with him to his old home in Richmond, Virginia. She declared that she would never leave us as long as she lived, my mother, and her children.

It was my pleasure and privilege to watch over her during a long illness, for she died of dropsy and could not lie down. My brother furnished her with the cosiest of chairs and the downiest of pillows, and I carried her meals to her, and would allow no one else to administer her medicines. When she was dying she gave me her little girl, my name sake. Our grief at her death was sincere and deep, and when I reach the other shore I know she will be there to welcome me, for the promise is, " Be thou faithful unto death and I will give thee a crown of life." Though her skin was black her soul was white.

Very truly yours,

MRS. J. J. MASSIE,
Fort Worth, Texas.

MORGAN AND HIS MEN.

BY GENERAL BASIL W. DUKE.

In October, 1861, Morgan organized a "squadron" as it was termed, of three companies of Kentucky cavalry, the nucleus of that formidable and renowned division which he subsequently commanded. This squadron was constantly and actively engaged in picketing and scouting in the front of General Albert Sidney Johnston's army while it lay at Bowling Green, and was scarcely ever out of sight or hearing of the Federal host, which, under General Buell, confronted that army. It witnessed the Confederate rear guard leave Nashville when General Johnston evacuated the city, and fired on Buell's advance when the Federal army entered. It remained in the immediate vicinity of Nashville for several weeks after the Confederate army had crossed the Tennessee river in daily and nightly combat with the Federal outposts, and quitted that region only to take part in the battle of Shiloh.

The history of Morgan's squadron closed with its active and audacious campaign of six weeks in Middle Tennessee, where it was ordered immediately after the battle. During this period Morgan won his first considerable success and also sustained his first disaster. He attacked the enemy, of twice his own strength, at Pulaski, completely defeating him and taking over three hundred prisoners. But a few days after he was himself attacked by General Dumont's cavalry brigade at Lebanon, and his command, about three hundred strong, after a desperate fight, was almost cut to pieces.

In June, 1861, Morgan began the organization of his regiment, the Second Kentucky Cavalry, at Chattanooga. It was composed of the remnant of the "squadron," some three hundred men of

the First Kentucky Infantry, C. S. A., who, having served out
their term of enlistment of one year in Virginia, elected to re-
enlist in cavalry service; one company of Mississippians which had
served a similar term in infantry, and recent recruits from Kentucky; in all about four hundred strong.

With this partially completed regiment, a battalion of Georgia
partisan cavalry and two companies which had just arrived from
Texas to join him under Captain (afterward General) R. M.
Gano, Morgan started from Knoxville on the Fourth of July,
1862, on what is known as his "first" Kentucky raid. His
command numbered about nine hundred men. The raid
was efficiently conducted and full of adventure, and the results are
best told in his own brief report of it:

"I left Knoxville on the fourth day of this month with about
nine hundred men and returned to Livingston on the twenty-
eighth inst. with nearly one thousand two hundred, having been
absent just twenty-four days, durng which time I have traveled over
one thousand miles, captured seventeen towns, destroyed all the
government supplies and arms in them, dispersed about one
thousand five hundred home guards and paroled nearly one thousand two hundred regular troops. I lost in killed, wounded and
missing of the number I carried into Kentucky about ninety."

With the recruits obtained in Kentucky and those which soon
after came out to join him, Morgan in a very short time, raised
his regiment to the maximum. During the remainder of the
summer of 1862, he was employed on the north bank of the
Cumberland, as was Forrest on the south, in harassing Buell's
army, which was stationed at and around Nashville, and perhaps
no cavalry leaders ever did more effective service than did these
two in that brief period.

Morgan accompanied Kirby Smith in Bragg's invasion of Kentucky, was actively engaged during the Confederate occupation of
the State, and aided in covering the retreat of the army.

Rapidly growing into a brigade, and then into a division, Morgan's
command continued on a large scale the peculiar service it had performed so efficiently with less strength. The two most notable
exploits if its commander until he undertook the famous raid
through Ohio and Indiana, were the battle of Hartsville and the
" December raid " into Kentucky.

At Hartsville, after a long and rapid march, crossing the Cum-

berland river in bitter cold weather, he attacked two thousand
five hundred Federal infantry in a strong position, his own force
numbering only twelve hundred and fifty; killed and wounded
two hundred and sixty-two of the enemy and carried off eighteen
hundred and thirty-four prisoners, although he was himself assailed
in turn by several thousand additional troops.

He made the "December" raid with nearly three thousand
seven hundred men, captured a great number of prisoners and
destroyed completely nearly fifty miles of the Louisville and Nashville railroad, the main line of communication by which the Federal
army in Tennessee received its supplies and reinforcements.

But the most remarkable expedition ever undertaken by him
was the "Indiana and Ohio raid." It was not merely sensa-
tional, but it was well conceived and most ably conducted. Had
he returned with his command from that raid to the Confederate
lines, he would have been beyond question foremost in reputation
of the cavalry leaders of the Civil War.

At the time it was undertaken General Bragg was menaced by
vastly superior forces. His retreat from Middle Tennessee and
across the Tennessee river had become a necessity. But to safely
accomplish it, and to fight with any hope of success after crossing
the Tennessee, it was also necessary that the attention of the hostile forces should in some manner be diverted from his movement
and that a part of the Federal troops which might otherwise
participate in the battle to be fought south of the river, should
be attracted to some other quarter.

General Bragg could do this only by a judicious use of his
cavalry. He therefore directed Morgan to make a raid into
Kentucky with two or three thousand men, and if possible, hold
there all of the cavalry and a large part of the infantry which were
about to move against him. Morgan advised that he could not
with so small a force adequately do such work. He suggested
that he could, if permitted to cross the Ohio river and enter Ohio
and Indiana, create such consternation in those two States that
the Federal Government in response to the popular demand for
protection would be compelled to withdraw troops from the army
of the Cumberland and thus weaken the demonstration about to
be made against Bragg.

Morgan finally proceeded on that plan. He rapidly traversed
Kentucky, crossed the Ohio river thirty miles below Louisville,

and invaded the North with about two thousand veteran cavalry. The picturesque features of that great raid are familiar to all who have read much about the Civil War. The long, swift marches by night as well as by day, with scarcely a halt; the dismay of the communities through which the grim column passed, bringing in its turn "something of the agony and terror of invasion;" the swarming hordes of militia striving to hinder the progress of the gray-coated riders, and finally the onslaught of the trained and veteran troops, whom it was the purpose of the raid to summon. The nerve displayed in passing the big river and penetrating to such a distance into hostile territory has also been generally recognized. But few people realize how skillfully the expedition was managed, and the stategic shrewdness employed to avoid or overcome the numerous perils to be encountered; nor to what extent the main object, the luring away the troops which might have impeded Bragg's retreat or overwhelmed him at Chickamauga, was accomplished. The safe extrication of the command was prevented only by a matter which no intelligence could have foreseen or provided against. Morgan reached Buffington Island, the point on the upper Ohio contemplated in his original plan as the one where he could recross the river, and found the stream, usually fordable at that season, deep and impassable except by boats. The "June rise" almost invariably followed by very low water, came that year in July, and he reached the river when the flood was at its height. The greater part of his command was captured, but the chief object, indeed, the sole object of the raid, was perfectly accomplished.

The division was never gotten together again, and although General Morgan, after his escape from prison, did excellent work, displaying in full measure the enterprise and quick intelligence which so characterized him, his early good fortune seemed to have deserted him. After his death the men who had followed him so faithfully still fought on bravely and stubbornly, but no other leader could arouse in them the same spirit.

There can be no doubt as to Morgan's extraordinary capacity. As a commander of partisan cavalry he exhibited not only exceptional audacity but a resourceful genius which could meet every contingency. Notwithstanding the great disaster of the Ohio raid, that he was some months a prisoner, and that he was killed a year before the close of the war, he accomplished results almost unequaled. " The creator and organizer of his own little army, with a force which at no time reached four thousand, he killed and wounded nearly as many of the enemy and captured more than fifteen thousand."

He was more remarkable, however, in the influence he exerted over his followers than in aught else.   It was almost limitless. No other Confederate officer was so completely identified with his command, and no other body of men regarded themselves as so completely belonging to their commander.   They accepted the appellation of " Morgan's men " in its literal sense.

CAPTAIN L. D. HOCKERSMITH,
3d Capt. Co. C, 10th Ky., P. R.

MORGAN'S ESCAPE FROM IMPRISONMENT.

By Captain L. D. Hockersmith.

Colonels R. Morgan's and W. W. Ward's regiments were captured July 19th, 1863, at Buffington's Island, Ohio.   Colonels B. W. Duke's and D. H. Smith's commands were captured July 20; Lieutenant Colonel Coleman and command were captured July 20, at Cheshire, Ohio, General Morgan and the remainder of his command captured July 26, and taken at once to the Ohio State prison, as I was informed, while we, the first that were captured, were carried to Cincinnati, confined in the city lockup about forty-eight hours; taken from there to Johnson's Island, where we remained four days, and then were removed to the State penitentiary at Columbus, Ohio.   The following is the plan of the cells in the prison and the disposition of the prisoners:

EXPLANATION.

1.—Entrance to hall in front of cells.
2.—Outside wall of main building.
3.—Hall in front of cells.
4.—South side of cells in first range and east wing of prison.
5.—Stove flue.
6.—Ventilation in flue.
7.—Sentinels.
8.—Stove.
Partition wall between convicts and prisoners of war.

CELL PLAN OF PRISON.

4	4	4	2

9	Magee	35	3	
		34		
		33		
		32	4	2
		31		
		30		
	Bennett	29		
	Hockersmith	28		
		27		
9		26	3	2
		25		
		24		
		23		
		22		
	Col. R. Morgan	21		
	Hines	20		
		19		2
	Sheldon	18		
9		17		
		16		
	S. Taylor	15		
		14	4	
		13		
		12		
		11		
		10	8	6	5
		9		
		8		
9		7	4	
		6	3	
		5		
		4		
		3		
		2		
9		1	7 1 7	2

These cells were three feet six inches wide, about seven feet long and about seven feet high, with a heavy iron grate door to each, with spring locks and were in tiers or ranges. The diagram shows range No. 1, while range No. 2 was immediately above. On the left were the cells in which the convicts were confined. The floors were arched with three arches of brick, while the top was made of sand cement called concrete, making the floor about two and one-half feet thick. In addition to this there was in each cell a broad plank in front of the bed fifteen inches wide and five feet long. This plank was to keep the feet off the damp concrete floor. The bedstead was a small skeleton, hung to the partition wall by small iron hinges, so that it could be turned back against the wall to allow the prisoner room for a small promenade; there was also a small three-legged stool to each cell, and a strip of plank one inch thick, three inches wide and three feet long which was used as a prop to the bed. This completed the furniture.

The following was the disposition of the prisoners in the cells, with the number and range.

PRISONERS OF FIRST RANGE.

Name of Prisoner.	No. of Cell.
Col. W. W. Ward,	1.
Capt. P.. H. Thorpe,	2.
Capt. J. L. Jones,	3.
Capt. Thos. W. Bullit,	4.
Capt. A. Thomas,	5.
Lt. Col. J. T. Tucker,	7.
Capt. E. T. Rochester,	8.
Capt. Thos. H. Shanks,	9.
Capt. R. E. Roberts,	10.
Capt. L. W. Trafton,	14.
Capt. Sam B. Taylor,	15.
Capt. R. D. Logan,	16.
Lieut. Tom Moreland,	17.
Capt. R. Sheldon,	18.
Capt. E. W. McLean,	19.
Capt. Thos.Henry Hines,	20.
Col. R. C. Morgan,	21.
T. E. Earton, Lt. Master,	22.
Capt. G. C. Mullins,	23.
Capt. J. L. N. Dickens,	24.
Capt. M. S. Edwards,	25.
Capt. M. Griffin,	26.
Capt. L. D. Holloway,	27.
Capt L. D. Hockersmith,	28.
Capt. J. C. Bennett,	29.
Maj. J. B. McCreary,	30.
Col. D. Howard Smith,	31.
Capt. James N. Taylor,	32.
Capt. B. S. Barton,	32.
Capt. H. C. Ellis,	33.
Capt. J. B. Hunter,	34.
Capt. J. S. Magee,	35.

SECOND RANGE.

Name of Prisoner.	No. of Cell.
Col. R. S. Cluke,	1.
Capt. T. M. Coombs,	2.
Capt. J. H. Hamby,	3.

Capt. C. C. Morgan,	4.	C'p. W. R. Cunningham,	21.
Capt. E. F. Cheatham,	5.	Capt. Isaac Baker,	22.
Maj. H. A. Higby,	6.	Capt. G. M. Coleman,	24.
Capt. Hall Gibson,	7.	Capt. C. L. Bennett,	25.
Major W. G. Owen,,	8.	Major R. S. Bullock,	26.
Capt. D. R. Williams,	9.	Gen. Basil W. Duke,	27.
Capt. E. D. Warder,	10.	Capt. A. S. Brunner,	28.
Capt. S. Morgan,	11.	Capt. J. S. Chapman,	29.
Lieut. J. H. Croxton	12.	Capt. Jas. W. Mitchell,	29.
Capt. Buford A. Lacy,	13.	Capt. M. D. Logan,	30.
Capt. T. R. Boyd,	14.	Capt. C. H. Morgan,	31.
Wash. C. Shame,		Maj. W. G. Bullitt,	32.
Aid-de-Camp,	16.	Lieut. Jos. B. Cole,	33.
Capt. E. S. Dawson,	17.	Maj. W. P. Elliott,	34.
Capt. J. S. Ambrose,	18.	Gen. John H. Morgan,	35.
Lt. Col. C. Coleman,	20.		

OHIO PENITENTIARY.

Major Theoph. Steele in hospital.

Captain C. C. Campbell sick in hospital.

Captain John H. Woolf sick in hospital.

The main outside wall which inclosed this hall as well as the cells, was some taller than the cell building. The cells are five tiers or ranges high. The floor of this hall was stone and laid in solid earth with no ventilation under it. This outside wall had no connection with the cell walls whatever, with the exception of the ground floor. I have been thus particular in giving the names of parties, with their cells and locations, as I shall frequently in after communications have need to refer to many of them. We wish the reader to study well the various positions laid down in this article, with the names of the parties connected therewith. In my next I shall commence with the plans suggested and adopted for our escape.

LAYING PLANS.

In the last chapter, in describing the cell floors, I omitted to explain a fill of eight or ten inches, made of spalls of rock, from the size of a grain of sand up to six inches or more in size. These spalls are pieces or chips which fly from rock or brick in dressing them when getting them ready for use. The object of this filling was to give a level base for the six inches of concrete which formed the floor of the cells.

The entire building was covered with a metal roof, through which there are several skylights. About the middle of the outer main wall there was a down pipe or tin spout to convey the water from the roof to the ground,, and which was fastened to the wall with iron cleats. Mr ——— Scott, who was one of the wardens of the penitentiary, one day gave us the history of two convicts who had managed to make their escape by going through one of the skylights on the roof, and then by climbing down this pipe or spout to the ground. The relation of this wonderful escape I honestly believe led to ours.

Up to this time I had scarcely entertained an idea or thought that there was any chance for us to get out of the prison, except by being turned out through the door by which we had come in. But Scott's story set me to thinking that I could at least manage some means to regain my liberty. The architect, in laying out his designs for the erection of this prison in the Buckeye State, intended no doubt to build a house from which no man should ever be able to escape.

But he failed, as all others had done before. It is said that man can not build what man can not pull down or destroy. Yet when one passes through one of these immense iron-grated doors as a prisoner, and the turnkey, with his lever, throws one of those one by three inch bolts into its socket, he leaves all hope behind.

JAKE BENNETT.

When Captain Jake Bennett was taken to his cell the guard gave him a shove as he ushered him in and said: " Go in there, you damned Reb, and let's see if you can get out of there." The Captain cast his eyes to the ceiling and exclaimed: "No, my God! I might as well try to get out of hell."

Jake Bennett was captain of Company A, Tenth Kentucky Cavalry, and from some cause had been sent to Camp Chase, where the privates of Morgan's command were confined. While there he attempted to make his escape, but failed and was sent to Columbus for safe keeping. When I heard Captain Bennett make his remark about the infernal regions I at that time thought that he was correct. It was after this that I conceived the idea of regaining my liberty.

STUDYING ABOUT ESCAPE.

On the 27th of October, 1863, I began looking around to see how and where there might be a possibility of getting away from under the surveillance of those Yankees who were watching us so closely. While walking through the hall-way I was impressed with the idea that I could crawl through the stove flue and thus get out on top of the prison. I soon caught an opportunity to examine the ventilator in the flue, which was located near the floor. I believed that there could be but one thing in the way to prevent a success, and that was the guards who were stationed so near the outlet. It seemed at first that it would be a difficult matter to get the ventilator from the place assigned to it by the architect. However, I ventured near enough that day to see that it could be removed without disturbing the wall. I did nothing more then, as it was getting late in the evening and not being long until our supper would be ready.

SHAM READING.

That night while in bed I thought the matter over again and again, and the next morning at nine o'clock, the 28th, I was at my post with Testament in hand, seated on the stone floor leaning against the wall, near enough to the ventilator to touch it with my right hand, and more eager, if possible, than the day before to accomplish my purposes. You may rest assured that my mind was more upon the undertaking than it was upon the Testament I was reading. Four o'clock in the afternoon came and found me no nearer out than when I first began. Again I was locked in my cell for the night to dream of liberty. At six o'clock the next morning we were all turned out of our cells to prepare for breakfast, and, as the usual custom, marched in single file to the well or hydrant, where there was a large trough filled with water, where we performed our morning ablutions and then ate our morning meal.

THAT VENTILATOR.

At ten o'clock my opportunities were better than ever before. The guards seemed to be more careless than usual. I succeeded in getting the ventilator loose, and fully intended some time during the day to take my departure from the hall, through the stove flue to the top of house, and about dusk to go down the pipe and forever shake the dust of Columbus from my feet. While I was rejoicing in my own mind at the thought of my early deliverance, Captain Sam Taylor, who had been watching my maneuvers, suspected me, approached me and in an undertone, to my surprise, said: "What in the hell have you been sitting at that hole all day for?" meaning the ventilator in the flue. I replied: "None of your business," all in good humor, of course; for we were the very best of friends.

CAPTAIN SAM TAYLOR.

We immediately walked to the rear of the hall. The captain took me by the arm and walked with me as far as cell No. 35. We then turned around and returned to cell No. 28, which we entered and sat down upon my bed. Captain Taylor had all the time been trying to find out what I had been planning. At first I gave him no satisfaction. He then appealed to me to tell him the truth, and asked me if I had not been planning an escape through that stove flue. I answered him that I was not only planning, but that I intended to make my exit through that same place, and requested him to keep silent upon the subject.

VENTILATOR PLANS ABANDONED.

He insisted that I could not succeed, and gave several reasons for his belief. I did not agree with him, and gave him to understand that I could not afford to abandon my plans unless something better was offered. He then suggested that as I was a mechanic and brick mason that I could perhaps cut through these walls. That idea had never before presented itself to my mind; I had almost forgotten that I ever knew how to handle the trowel or to lay brick, but the idea was a good one and I liked it. Several suggestions were made and abandoned, as to how we should proceed. We then separated. By this time I had about abandoned the plan of going out through the flue.

LAYING PLANS.

On October 30th, at eight o'clock a. m., Captain Taylor and myself got together in his cell, No. 15, and renewed the conversation of the evening before. We laid many plans and made many suggestions, none of which seemed to be feasible. I then proposed that we go through at the floor and cut under the foundations. My knowledge and experience taught me that there must be a ventilation under the cell floors, otherwise it would be so damp that men could not live in them.

SOUNDS THE FLOOR.

While thus reasoning, Taylor picked up the strip of plank used to prop up the bed and with the end knocked on the floor of the cell. It sounded hollow, and he then stepped out of the cell door and with the same plank knocked on the floor of the hall, which produced a dull, dead sound. We were then satisfied that my suggestion was correct—that the ventilation was beneath the cells.

PLAN AGREED UPON.

Then my plan to cut through the floor was at once agreed upon. We at that time knew nothing of the thickness of the floor, and there was no way of gaining the desired information but to go to work and cut through and find out. The difficulty now was to secure tools with which to begin work, as we had nothing but pocket knives and some other small tools, such as files and saws, which we were permitted to have to make rings and such like with.

I proposed to do the work—the cutting of the cement—while Captain Taylor was to conceal the mortar or whatever rubbish might be taken out as the work progressed. His proposition was to take the rubbish out in his pockets, throw it in the stoves, in the spit-boxes, scatter it around in the saw-dust on the dining room floor or put it in any or all places where it would not be discovered. Captain Taylor and myself by this time pretty well understood the task before us, and were selfish enough to undertake the job by ourselves, as up to this time we had taken no one into our confidence.

We had, as we supposed, all our arrangements made, ready to begin work the next day. It was understood that our work would have to be done by daylight, because we were locked up in our cells during the night, and there could be no communication one with another between the hours of six p. m. and six a. m.

On the morning of the 31st of October at eight o'clock Captain Taylor and myself were in my cell, No. 28, further discussing the subject which had been uppermost in our minds for some time;

when the question arose as to whose cell we should begin the work in; not that we were particular as to the cell, but how should we get together after the work should be completed. We were separated at night, and we knew that the escape must be made in the dark. If we cut through the floor in his cell I should be left; if in mine, then he would be left.

CAPTAIN HINES COMES IN.

While we were thus planning and talking Captain Thomas H. Hines walked up to the door of my cell and addressed himself to us by saying: "Are you fellows plotting against the whites?" or words to that effect. Captain Taylor replied: "You are mighty damned right." It was not long until Captain Hines was let into the secret, Captain Taylor communicating the same to him. Captain Hines endorsed the plan with delight. We also informed him of the difficulty we had just been considering. He proposed that the work should be commenced in his cell, agreeing to take upon himself the responsibility of detection. Then the question came up again in reference to getting to the cell when the work was done, when Captain Hines proposed to have the doors open at the proper time by sawing the bolts or eating them off with aquafortis. We accepted his proposition which was the condition.

ACCEPTED HINES' PROPOSITIONS.

Captain Taylor and myself having heard Captain Hines' propositions, and accepting them, we told him that we had been considering a plan for getting General Morgan out with us. The difficulty that presented itself was to get him from his cell after the completion of the work, his cell being No. 35, second range, just above that of Captain McGee, No. 35, first range. Yet it was determined that we would take him with us if possible. We at length agreed to lay the matter before him and see what he thought of our plans.

CALL ON GENERAL MORGAN.

We three went to General Morgan, Captain Hines acting as spokesman, while Captain Taylor and myself listened and occasionally threw in a word. He heard us through, questioned us closely and was much surprised at the audacity of the undertaking.

! do not believe at the time that he had any great confidence in the success of the enterprise. We informed him that he was to have nothing to do with the work, but must keep himself in the background so as to keep down suspicion. We left the cell and it was proposed by Hines and Taylor to take Captains McGee and Sheldon into our confidence, while I selected Captain Jake Bennett. There being no objections to the three persons named, they were invited into Captain Hines' cell and informed of our plans, and all readily agreed to them. Captain Sheldon made some good suggestions as to how we should begin work, and how we should get the tools to begin with. I regard him as being one of the most determined men of the six.

PLANS FOR ESCAPE.

Captain McGee was a mechanic, a carpenter by profession, and the right man in the right place; Captain Bennett expressed himself as being ready to do anything that we might impose upon him. I being a brick-layer, Captain Taylor proposed that I should superintend the work. Captain Hines was to act as guard or sentinel, while Captain Taylor should conceal the rubbish, which he had formerly agreed to do. Each man having been assigned to his work, we yet had some other things to look after. We were not well supplied with tools. We had but two pocket knives among us. Sheldon's proposition to get knives from the table of course was adopted, with the understanding that we were to take but one at a time, for fear they should be missed.

CONFIDENCE GAME.

The next thing was to manage to get the confidence of the guards so as to keep down any suspicion they might have of our intentions. It was the custom of the wardens to sweep and inspect the cells, or cause it to be done by the convicts, at least once every day. The hall was looked after twice each day. They were particular in keeping a clean prison. We were not allowed to spit tobacco juice on the floor, neither were we allowed to throw apple or peach parings or seed, strips of paper or litter of any kind on the floor. So in order to prevent their sweeping our cells, Captain Hines proposed that we get brooms and do our own sweeping. We were allowed to furnish our cells with any kind of furniture or ornaments we chose to buy; and some of them were handsomely furnished, which helped to keep down or hide any suspicion that might arise from our proposed sweeping.

We were also forbidden to make any unnecessary noise, such as singing, whistling, or reading aloud. Captain Bennett determined to overcome this difficulty by getting a few of the boys together, joining our hands in a circle around the wardens or any guards that might be near, and singing such songs as "The Old Cow Crossed the Road," or "Grasshopper Sitting on a 'Tater Vine," etc. This seemed to take all right and met with no objections from the guards. We were also to make as much noise as possible while making breast-pins, rings, etc. With our plans matured for the future, and in our imagination again breathing the air of liberty, we betook ourselves to different points of the prison, and in due course of time ate our supper and were locked up in our cells for the night, where we further planned for the future.

WORK BEGINS.

November 2d. We thought it better to keep separated this morning and not allow more than two together at any one time. We now had two of the table knives, secured, I think, by Bennett and McGee. We put the two edges together and by striking them with a poker managed to make saws of them, which were to be used in cutting the cement mortar. They were of soft iron, driven into a block of pine or poplar wood handle. Captain Hines swept his own cell that morning and so did one or two others, as we thought it best to do. At half past eleven o'clock we went to dinner, when I managed to procure another knife, making the third one now in our possession, besides the pocket knives, which we thought to be sufficient with which to commence work.

Captain Sheldon and myself went to Captain Hines' cell No. 20, and on that evening we made a beginning. My recollection is that we worked all that evening, but at night could scarcely tell what had been done. The cement or concrete proved to be harder than ordinary rock. Our knives were of soft metal and made but little impression on the floor, consequently Captain Taylor had not much more than his vest pocket full of rubbish to dispose of. Yet we felt that we had made an excellent beginning. Captain Hines was at his post all the while, keeping a sharp lookout lest some intruder should step in unawares.

November 3d.　Bennett and McGee went on duty, while Taylor, Sheldon and myself staid out in the hall, doing our best to entertain the guards and officers so as to keep them from cell No. 20. Strange to say, the guards knew every prisoner so perfectly that they would miss any of us if we were absent from the crowd more than an hour at a time. Therefore, at first we had to be released from work frequently, so that we could make our appearance in the hall where we could be seen by them. But not so towards the close, because we all seemed to be well contented and had given the wardens so little trouble, mixed with a good deal of "taffy," that they believed us to be resigned to our fate. All things considered, our day's work was very satisfactory.

November 4th.　The size of the hole which we cut in the cement I suppose was fourteen inches square, though I never measured it. We got through the cement that day. Everything passed off quietly with no changes made in our arrangements, except that Taylor proposed to carry the straw out of Hines' bed-tick, burn it in the stove, and fill the tick with the brick, mortar, stone, etc. We also concluded that one was enough to work at a time, as more would be in the way and impede the progress, and that also one would not be as likely to arouse suspicion as would more.

November 5th.　We began work as usual. It was but a short time until we had reached the arch, but we still had no idea how far it was to the air chamber. We made no new discoveries until late in the afternoon, at which time I was at work, when my knife slipped through the joint of mortar between two arched brick. I knew then that it would be no difficult job to reach the air chamber. Now came the exciting time with me. I wanted the pleasure of getting under that floor first. I cut and sawed the mortar from between three of these brick as rapidly as possible, lifted them out and then took one of the loose ones and knocked several others through to the ground, by striking them on the end. I then had a hole large enough for a small man to go through. I ventured down into this hole. I think it was the darkest place I ever saw before; it was about four or four and a half feet to the ground. I could see nothing. I called to Captain Taylor, who was the only one who knew that I had gotten through, to bring me a candle. I lighted it and soon found out the full extent of the air chamber. At the west end it was about eighteen inches from the arch to the floor, while at the east end it was not less than twelve feet.

There seemed to have been a room cut out of these for some purpose, but no door or entrance to it except a large air grate in the end wall. I could see no entrance to this chamber except the hole we had cut, and this air grate, the latter being stopped up with plank outside, which cut off all light. I had now seen all that there was to be seen underneath the floor, and thought it best to report the same to General Morgan and the boys. It is useless to try to describe my feelings while beneath the floor, as I thought of the near approach of our deliverance. I leave this to the imagination of the reader. I came out again into the light and started to General Morgan's cell. He was engaged in talking to some of his men in the hall, but left them and followed me and invited me to take a seat and said: "Captain, what is the news?" I told him that I had been out reconnoitering. When he asked me what I meant by that I replied: "I have been all under this building." He slapped me on the shoulder and said: "Captain, do you really mean it?" After describing things the best I could I proposed that he walk down to cell No. 20, lift up the black carpet sack, which we kept over the hole, and see for himself. He did so and was satisfied with the result. The brick and mortar was taken from the bed and thrown into the air chamber where there was plenty of room for it.

November 6th. We were not able to understand why the plank was against the air grate, and the ventilation and light cut off from the chamber. I was determined to find out, because I thought that would be the next place for us to commence work, as at that point we would have only to cut through one wall or take out the air grate. I proposed when we went out to the wash trough (to wash our faces) that we should learn the cause of this obstruction. It was not long until we were marched to the wash trough, and while some were washing, two or three of us sauntered about the yard in the direction of the end wall, above mentioned, and to our disgust found hundreds of bushels of coal piled against this wall and air grate. I saw at once that if we removed the grate that the coal would come down on us in an avalanche. It was, therefore, necessary to find some other place to begin work.

We began cutting through the cell wall. The first rock which we attempted to get out was an odd-shaped one, with the larger end back in the wall, with a sharp point next to us; it gave us much trouble; it required three days' work to get it from its place.

November 10th. Captain Taylor had not been well since the sixth; Sheldon, Bennett, Magee and myself had been doing the work. These walls being so thick, we were compelled to cut in the face a space of six or seven feet wide so that we might have an opening on the opposite side large enough for a man to go through. During the 11th nothing of importance transpired, but on the 12th the whole thing came near being a failure. Before commencing the work we agreed upon a system of signals by which we were to be governed. The bed prop was again to be brought into use: one tap with this on the floor was to notify those at work to come out and let others take their places. Two taps was a signal for dinner and was usually given a half an hour before time for eating. Three taps was the signal of danger and we were to come out as quickly as possible when this was given. By some oversight on this day, those whose duty it was to give me the signal for dinner failed to do so. The others were called in line and marched into the dining hall, leaving me in the air chamber. General Morgan made some excuse for not going to dinner, and as soon as they all passed out of the gate he gave me the alarm signal. I came out as quickly as possible. They had missed me at roll call at dinner and Scott came on a hunt for me. I had just time to get out and brush my clothes when I heard him ask the general, who was standing between the gate and the cell, "Where is Captain Hockersmith?" The general replied, "I left him lying upon my bed a few moments ago complaining of not being well. I had missed him and I came to look him up. Let's go up into my cell and see if he is there." As soon as they got far enough beyond, that I could get there without detection, I went into it and covered myself up in bed. I saw that I would have to feign sickness which I did the best I could. When Scott found that I was not in Gen. Morgan's cell, he immediately came to mine and found me in bed and inquired as to my disease. He seemed satisfied, and as he left I asked him to bring me a little sick diet. In a short time he sent me some nice toasted bread, stewed chicken and a cup of tea. I remained in my cell until 4 p. m., when the doctor came in and left me some medicine, which, as soon as he left, I threw in the stove. No work was done that afternoon.

Nov. 13th found me still on the sick list, though improving rapidly. Some of the boys were at work under the floor. The doctor came in again and left some more medicine, which went into the stove to keep company with yesterday's stuff. It cured me and soon I went down to work again and found Bennett, Sheldon and Magee had done well. This day we completed the journey through the first wall.

On the 14th of November we began digging the ditch from the cell wall to the outer wall of the main building, which was a distance of twenty feet. The first eighteen inches of this was loose dirt, made so by filling the trenches of the foundation walls. We supposed that the digging of the ditch would be an easy job, judging from the first foot and a half. But we soon discovered our mistake, for after getting through the stratum of loose dirt we came to a hard, tough clay, which did not yield very readily to our knives. I procured an additional knife, made by a convict out of an old razor blade; it proved to be the best tool for digging that we had been able to secure. I sharpened the end of it on a brick, and thus formed a kind of chisel of it. Captain Taylor managed to get a shovel from a convict who was wheeling in coal, but we could only use the shovel in the loose dirt after we had digged it out with our knives. The ground was too hard and the ditch or hole too small to use it as a spade.

After we had gone some four or five feet into the ditch Captain Taylor brought us a box eight by ten inches square and eight inches deep. It had been sent filled with provisions to some of the boys. In the box we bored a hole with our pocket knives, tied a rope to it, made of a piece of bed ticking, and with the stick used to prop our beds we would push the box back into the ditch, where it would be filled by the man who was at work. When full it would be hauled out and emptied into the air chamber.

On the 17th of November Captain Bennett was reported as not being able to work, on account of having blistered his hands; that left Sheldon, Magee and myself to complete the work, though Bennett sat at the mouth of the hole and drew out the dirt and emptied it. We were just seven days in cutting this ditch which was in size eighteen inches wide three feet high and twelve feet long. One day while engaged in this work I came near being caught. I had traded one of the convicts out of a prison cap which was

made of the same material as their clothing.   I wore it while
at work to keep the dirt out of my hair.   One day while at work
our candles gave out and I went up to get a fresh supply and
in the hurry forgot that I had on the prison cap; but fortunately
the man from whom I had gotten it was sweeping the hall immediately in front of the cell I was going out of.   He noticed the
cap and told me to take it off, which I did and threw it back into
the cell without attracting any further notice.   Had this been
discovered by the officers I would have been sent to the dungeon
for my indiscretion.   I secured my candles and went back to
work.   I think we used something near nine pounds of candles
while engaged in this underground work.   We had the privilege
of buying them provided we paid for them ourselves.

By the 21st of November we had completed nearly all the underground work except cutting through one wall.   There had been
no effort made to get the cell doors open as yet.   Taylor and
myself went to remind Captain Hines of his promise.   We found
him in General Morgan's cell and reminded him of his promise.
He replied that it was impossible for him to get the doors open.
The General then asked what was to be done.   I proposed that
we cut a hole through the floors of each one of our cells proposing
that we work up from underneath.   I had made the same proposition to Taylor and Bennett before.   They at once approved of
the plan, and seemed to be relieved.

We worked four days getting through the outer wall and cutting four feet up the wall toward the top of the ground, leaving
about two feet to cut after other work was completed.   We then
went to work cutting through our cell doors.   On the 25th I had
another conversation with General Morgan.   He inquired as to
how we were progressing.   I told him that in two days more the
work would be completed.   He expressed surprise at the progress we had made.   He then proposed to me that if we made
our escape and that if I would go with him to Richmond that he
would give me $10,000 in gold. I thanked him, of course, but told
him that it was freedom and not money that I was after.   He
replied: " That makes no difference; you must have the money."
Captains Bennett and Taylor were present at the time and one
of them—Bennett, I think, —made the statement: " We never
would have gotten through these arches and walls had it not been
for Captain Hockersmith, or some other bricklayer."   The General

sanctioned what was said.   He also proposed to give $50 or $100 to any one in the first range of cells who would exchange cells with him the night we were to make the escape.   The arrangement was effected with his brother, Colonel Dick Morgan, and on the night of the escape they exchanged cells.

Sheldon, Magee and myself worked faithfully on the 26th and 27th, and just about completed the work of cutting through the other six floors, Sheldon and Magee cutting three of them—their own and Colonel Dick Morgan's—while I cut three—Captains Taylor, Bennett and my own.   We did not cut quite through the six inches of concrete, but just nearly enough so that by a stroke of the foot from the top it would be broken through.   The first hole made was under the bed in cell No. 20, the one through which we entered the air chamber, while the others were under the fifteen-inch plank which lay in front of the beds.   In estimating the place to work up through from the bottom, it was only necessary to get the width of the cells and the thickness of the partition walls.   Again we brought into use the bed prop, using it as a measuring pole.

On the following page is a diagram of the cell in which we worked, showing the cement and arches we cut through; also the ditch and two stone walls we cut through.   The diagram represents cell No. 20, although it was cell No. 1 with end wall taken out, showing the end of it, and also ends of the air chamber. Also back of bed with wall taken away, giving view of floor under the floor·

Profile of Prison Cell.

No. 0.—Hall floor.

No. 00.—Hall way.

No. 1.—Door way to cell.

No. 2.—Bedstead.

No. 3.—Concrete floor.

No. 4.—Arches.

No. 5.—Hole cut through to air chamber.

No. 6.—Filling between arch and concrete.

No. 7.—Wall between convicts and prisoners.

No. 8.—Wall of prison cells.

No. 9.—Between outer and inner walls.

No. 10.—Outer wall.

No. 11.—Hole digged upward as escape.

No. 12.—Opening made from air chamber.

No. 13.—Tunnel from wall to wall.

No. 14.—Cut through outer wall.

No. 15.—Air chamber.

No. 16.—Rock removed from No. 11.

No. 17.—Where we came out from under the prison.

Several parties had helped us in various ways. Captain C. H. Morgan made our rope by tearing up a bed tick and platting it into a rope sufficiently large and strong to hold the weight of any ordinary man. Everything was now ready for us to make the attempt. Liberty was just before us; in a short time we should bid farewell to prison and prison rules. It had been determined that we should leave on the night of the 27th, just after the guard made his midnight round; but just before we were locked up in our cells all agreed that the night was too light to make the attempt.

We had formed our plans to elude the watch. It was the custom of the night guard to examine the cells three times during the night—once at ten o'clock, then at twelve, again at three. The guard carried with him what I call a coffee-pot lamp—that is a lamp with a spout to it—and as he approached the cell door if he saw no one therein by the dim light he would stick the spout through the bars and throw the light upon the bed. We knew that we should have to resort to some means to deceive him. It was agreed that we would always if possible have our heads covered up when he came and in the event he stuck the spout in, to throw off the cover as if frightened. By this means he came to believe that we slept with our heads covered. So the night we escaped we stuffed our drawers and undershirts with straw taken from the beds, and after he had made his midnight round we covered the stuffed clothes up in bed and slid down into the air chamber.

It was agreed that on the night of the 28th we should make the start. The understanding was that Taylor should go down into the air chamber first and knock on the thin cement as a signal for us to go down. I followed him to complete the hole to the top of the ground which work perhaps, required some twenty or thirty minutes. I went up into the yard and found all quiet. It was then raining slowly, though it had been raining hard just before. The guards and their dogs had all gone under shelter. I went back and reported. Our rope was ready, with a good grab-hook made of a bent poker. We all now marched out into the yard. After getting there we found an inner wall about twelve feet from the main wall. That wall was only twenty feet high, while the outer one was twenty-five feet high. This lower wall had in the end a slat gate which was not less than twelve feet high. The gate had a brace or two nailed on it. Taylor climbed up on the braces to the top of the gate, tied a rock to the end of the rope, threw it over the wall, let it swing down until he could reach through the gate, caught the end and tied it. The rope was made with loops, which made the climbing an easy matter. After we had gotten to the top of the lower wall we then had only five feet more to climb to get on top of the twenty-five-foot wall. We jumped on that, went round to the sentinel box or stand fronting the railroad, fastened our rope to an iron rod near the guardhouse, and after changing our clothing, we went down the rope to the ground. General Morgan left his carpet-sack; Taylor and myself went back into the yard and got it. We were now outside the prison walls forever and were bidding adieu to Columbus. We then separated for a while. Bennett and myself agreed to travel together, General Morgan and Hines were paired, Taylor and Sheldon together and Magee by himself. Bennett and myself went to the depot and procured tickets to Cincinnati. General Morgan had given me seven dollars, and I already had about the same amount. After procuring our tickets we took seats in the coach. It was but a few minutes when Morgan and Hines came in. We pretended to be asleep until the train moved off. They ran near enough to the prison walls for us to see our rope swinging

in the breeze.   General Morgan took his seat by the side of a
Federal colonel. I know not what passed between them, except
a bottle of brandy, of which they both partook.   Not long after
that Morgan remarked that he saw two of his old Kentucky friends
sitting just ahead of them, and that he wished to speak to them. He
came where we were, shook hands with us, and after talking a
moment went back to his seat by the colonel.   We said nothng
more to him until we reached Cincinnati.   Bennett and myself
were standing on the platform when he came out where we were,
and told us that he and Hines were going to jump off, and insisted
that we do the same.   I told him that we had purchased om-
nibus tickets for Covington, and that we would cross the river
that way. He thought that if we went to the depot we should
be captured.   He bade us good-bye and jumped off.

Bennett and I remained in Covington until eleven o'clock a. m.,
let ourselves be known to a fifteen-year-old clerk who gave us our
breakfast and got us out of the city.   We went to Owen county
and after gathering corn for two or three weeks we left there
and came to Hopkins county.   I left Captain Bennett sick near
Ashbyburg, on Green river, and came to Madisonville.   I remained
at home two nights and one day, when I again took up my line
of march, made my way to the Confederate army, was again
captured, made my escape, to be the third time a captive of war,
and the third time made my escape.

Forty years have passed since these stirring times, and a majority
of those who went into that struggle now lie beneath the sod of
the valley. The brave General Morgan did not live to see the
close of the struggle or witness the failure of the " Lost Cause."
A nobler, truer, or braver man than he never led men to battle.

The memory of this gallant soldier and his daring deeds are em-
balmed in the hearts of those who stood by him amid the trials
and duties of war.

For my comrades who shared with me the toils and privations of
a prison life, I have nothing but the kindest feeling, and pray that
when the last trump shall sound that each and every one of them
may have on the armor of salvation and all be happy throughout
eternity.

AN INDORSEMENT.

Nashville, Tennessee, January 20, 1899. I wish to state I have carefully read and examined Captain L. D. Hockersmith's account of General Morgan and his companions' escape from the Ohio State Penitentiary and find it to be a correct and impartial

J. C. BENNETT, CAPTAIN TENTH KY. CAV., C. S. A.

P. S. I also authorize Captain Hockersmith to attach my name to said account whenever he desires to republish it.

A PARTISAN RANGER MARRIES AN OHIO GIRL.

BY CAPTAIN JOHN G. ROACH.

Joe Williams, of Company K, Colonel Adam R. Johnson's Tenth Kentucky Cavalry Regiment, was severely wounded during Morgan's raid through Indiana and Ohio. Captain John G. Roach, of Louisville, relates this story: "A mutual friend and myself, feeling sure that our comrade must soon bleed to death, carried him by main strength into a dwelling-house near by. As his clothes were dripping with blood, the ladies of the house · protested most vehemently against our entering the door, declaring that their carpets and floors would be ruined, but in we pushed regardless of what the women said, and laid him on the floor. I then assured the discomfited and agitated ladies that our comrade's devoted mother was a woman of means and would amply repay them for any and all the care and attention they would give her beloved son. We then left hurriedly, as firing was going on all around us and we feared capture.

"Some years after the war, never having heard a word of my wounded comrade since he was left in the house of the strangers, I was in some town in Southern Kentucky when I chanced, greatly to my astonishment, to meet my old comrade, Joe Williams, whom I had long thought dead. But there he was in fact, sound and well. Joe naturally insisted upon my accompanying him to his home in the country some miles from town, saying that he gratefully recalled how I and our mutual friend had saved his life at the imminent risk of our own. I accepted his pressing invitation, and we were so busy talking about our former military experiences that I forgot to ask him if he were a married man; and was much surprised when, upon reaching the house I was introduced to one of the ladies with whom I had left Williams, in Ohio, as Mrs. Williams.

"She was one of the protesting daughters of the protesting mother, but had nursed him kindly, and his gratitude was great, and his affection for her became so strong that he went back after the war and married her."

WM. WILLIAMS, M. D.,
Co. B, 10th Ky., P. R.

A PRIVATE'S RECOLLECTION OF MORGAN AND HIS MEN.

BY DR. W. WILLIAMS, OF CHURCH HILL, KENTUCKY.

I.   ACTIVE SERVICE.

I am prompted by a notice of the death of Colonel R. M. Martin, (Bob Martin as he was familiarly called), to present a few reminiscences that may bring to memory some of the cherished recollections of the "boys in gray" whose ranks are becoming decimated by time.

It was my good fortune to belong to the Tenth Kentucky Cavalry, the regiment of which this daring spirit was made colonel by the promotion of the no less gallant officer, Colonel Adam R. Johnson, to the brigadier generalship of the Second Brigade of Morgan's division of cavalry.   Under the leadership of these gallant officers as partisans, Johnson's regiment became famous throughout Kentucky.   On reporting to General Morgan for duty near Murfreesboro, they at once ranked with the best troops, and from then on they participated in all the daring undertakings of that dashing cavalier.

After remaining in camp for a month we started on the raid into Kentucky, known as the " Christmas raid," made memorable by the hardships endured, the rigors of winter, the swollen streams to be forded or swum, incessant pursuit of the enemy, and the night marching and frequent engagements, all of which told upon the physical man; but it went to make veterans of boys wholly unaccustomed to the hardships of army life.   The fruits of this raid were immense.   The capture of towns with their army supplies, the destruction of railroads and government property, the capture and paroling of hundreds of prisoners of war, the equipment of our men with the best of arms, the addition of recruits to our ranks, thereby relieving General Bragg as he quietly fell back upon Tullahoma. It was while crossing one of these rivers (Rolling Fork) that General Duke received a wound from the explosion of a shell, a fragment of which ripped its way through the side of his head. As we supposed him killed, gloom hung over the command like a pall; no officer possessed the confidence and esteem of his men to a greater degree.

As we passed out of Kentucky into Tennessee we took position at the forks of the pike near Liberty. It was here I think, that Colonel Johnson received his appointment of brigadier general. It was while here that the battles of Milton, Woodbury and Snow Hill were fought. It was while here that Colonel Martin so delighted in his characteristic scouts, one of which I call to mind and would be glad to relate. General Rosecrans had issued an order that all Confederates caught within the Federal lines wearing Federal uniforms should be treated as spies. The order was intended for Morgan's men more especially, as they frequently wore the captured overcoats. In fact if I remember correctly, General Morgan wore one of the overcoats himself, and it was not an unusual thing to see a private dressed completely in a Federal uniform, boots and spurs included. Colonel Martin ordered a detail of one hundred and twenty-five men to represent Federal cavalrymen as nearly as possible. Of this detail the writer was one. After preparing two days' rations we started on our march, a perfect counterpart of a Yankee scouting party. That night we bivouacked in a dense grove of cedar, within hearing of the Federal army, the noise of which reminded one of some great monster as it lashed itself into repose. As we rested ourselves on our arms, ready to move at a moment's notice, I thoughtlessly removed a spur from my foot which was unpleasantly tight, thinking I would get it before leaving, but unfortunately I failed to think of it. It had been borrowed of my captain who prized it highly, as it was one of a pair presented him by some friend. We had gone about three miles before I missed the spur. Riding up to my captain I told him of my loss. He seemed to be much worried, and asked me to gallop back and get it. In the face of Rosecrans's order and my probable capture, I hesitated, but recalling the fact that I was mounted on one of General Harding's Belle

Meade race horses, I felt that I could outrun the entire Yankee army, if it became necessary. Without delay I galloped back just as the sun was creeping above the tree tops. I was never more impressed with the beauties of the morning. On turning an angle in front of a small church, and almost in sight of the coveted spur, I ran face to face with two Yankee cavalrymen. Instantly my Sharp's carbine went to my shoulder, with the command to halt, which they did without a moment's hesitation. I asked them what company they belonged to. They said the Twenty-first Cavalry. I ordered them to take the road bearing to my right and watched them as they disappeared in the cedars. I lost no time in recovering the spur and making all haste in getting away from so unwholesome a locality.

Early that morning Colonel Martin halted us near the pike, Franklin or Alexandria, I forget which. The rumbling of wagons and the tramp of horses on the road denoted a foraging expedition. Leaving us to await his command, he quietly rode in the direction of the passing train of wagons, looking the ideal Yankee colonel. The wagons began to come to us. In a little while our ruse was found out and the alarm given. The Yankees began to stampede and I have never witnessed such a stampede.

Wagons were turned over, mules killed and we were not able to make off with our captures on account of the obstruction and the dense growth of cedars. Eight wagons, thirty-two mules and sixteen prisoners, Colonel Martin had captured, you might say, entirely alone. We lost no time in getting them out of the way. Placing a guard over them they were started back in a different direction to the one they came.

Going in the direction of what is known as Union Hill, Colonel Martin learned that a regiment of Federal cavalry was ahead. He though to capture or disperse them. By rapid marching we were soon near the crest of the hill, and just here we were ordered to charge, not cavalry, but an entire regiment of infantry, who sent a withering volley into our little party. Here I lost my Belle Meade thoroughbred, shot in two places. That brave soldier and comrade, John T. Sherley, came back under fire and carried me out behind him. As we were far into the Yankee lines and they were becoming thoroughly aroused, we lost no time in getting back to camp, there to await orders pending other movements.

In a short while we were ordered to move in the direction of Cumberland river to a more favorable camping ground (Salt Lick Bend), leaving many of the rank and file behind in killed and wounded. I think it was at McMinnville about this time that Colonel Martin received the wound through the lung which troubled him ever after and which finally caused his death. Major Owen assumed command of the regiment, putting the men in the best possible position. Leaving the convalescents in camp, we began crossing the river into Kentucky. Brushing away a small force of cavalry that opposed us, we reached Green river on the morning of the Fourth of July, and had a most spirited engagement with some Michigan troops, who fought from a splendidly constructed fortress. We lost here in killed and wounded fifty or sixty of our brave boys. Among the killed was Colonel Chenault. Passing on to Lebanon, Kentucky, we were soon hotly engaged with and stubbornly resisted by Colonel Hanson, a brother of General Roger Hanson, of Confederate fame. It was here that Lieutenant Tom Morgan was killed, the younger brother of General Morgan, a mere boy, but noted for his daring bravery and his devotion to the cause.

After the capture and paroling of Colonel Hanson and his men, we at once began the march. Reaching Brandenburg, we captured two steamboats, one a United States packet, a magnificent side-wheeler, the Alice Dean. Holding in check a gunboat by the well-directed fire of our artillery until the last man had been ferried over, as we ascended the hill on the Indiana shore, the heavens were lighted by the blaze of this magnificent steamer as it was rapidly reduced to ashes. Never doubting our leaders, Generals Morgan, Duke and Johnson, we pressed forward to Corydon, to be met by several thousand militia and home guards, who had thrown up breastworks in front of their little city. They, however, were no match for the dauntless Morgan, for soon we were in possession of the town. I shall never forget the abundance of eatables that the good dames had prepared for their patriotic lords, who evidently anticipated a siege of several days' duration.

On, on we swept like the wind, overrunning by sheer audacity all resistance. At Salem, bridges, railroads, and government supplies were destroyed, amounting to thousands of dollars. Citizens fled in consternation, regarding us as a band of ruffians who would spare nothing. From every hillside the crack of rifles was heard as they fired into our jaded ranks. But on, on we swept like some mighty cyclone, from Salem to Vernon, on to Harrison, even into the suburbs of Cincinnati, where the pickets were driven into the city. . Traversing three great States, our men were utterly exhausted. Reaching the Ohio, the Federals began to swarm around us like bees, like suggestions of a diseased brain with its horrible hallucination of blue-devils dancing in their joyous glee amid sulphuric flames. The heroic General Johnson plunged into the Ohio with a few followers, in utter disregard of grape and cannister as it belched forth from the port-holes of a gunboat in livid flames. After a lapse of nearly two score years the horrible scene is as vivid as yesterday, horses and men struggling amid stream, many to sink to rise no more, and we powerless to help them.

As the capture and imprisonment of General Morgan with most of his officers and the indignities heaped upon them are matters of history I will not enter into its details; but, in the next paper, will describe the treatment of some of us privates at Camp Douglas.

II. PRISON LIFE.

As Morgan failed to cross the Ohio after the capture of nearly his entire command, he made for the interior, hoping to get into Pennsylvania territory and cross into Virginia. He had only the remnant of his command that had succeeded in getting away at Buffington, not more than three hundred, if so many. Pressing on all day and night as fast as jaded horses and worn out men could, we reached a little town, Irvington, Ohio, where we surprised and captured the garrison. After paroling the Federals, General Morgan said to us: "All who have horses unable to travel will ride to the front." Fifty-four of his decimated command rode forward, this writer among the number. He briefly addressed us, saying that he would press no fresh horses but that he would turn us over to Colonel Sontag, who would treat us as prisoners of war. With this he waved us an adieu and passed on with that lordly bearing like some knight of old, never to be seen again in life by us.

Colonel Sontag proved to be a gentleman and a soldier; he allowed us the ·choice of turning over our horses to the citizens or the United States Government. I gave mine to his major; I have forgotten his name, but I shall ever think of him kindly. · We were marched to Portsmouth, Ohio, where we were kept over night, then we were placed on a packet and sent to Cincinnati, and then to Camp Morton, Indiana, where our prison life began in reality. After being searched and stripped of everything of value, even a pocket knife being denied us, we were counted and allotted to the barracks (I think originally intended for horses) without floors.   Vermin could be seen crawling upon the ground, but having traversed three States, we were so utterly exhausted that we defied graybacks and dropped upon the ground or in bunks and gave ourselves up to that great restorer of over-taxed nature, sleep. We slept long and profoundly, I do not know how long.   We were summoned to roll call by the sound of the bugle.

It was here at our first roll call that Morgan's men appeared most ridiculous.   Some wore stove-pipe hats and linen dusters, with pants stuffed in cavalry boots, some in shirt sleeves and no shoes; others in a combination of Confederate gray and citizens' clothes, and some in linen suits.   I had on an article of apparel, low-necked and short sleeved (which I had hastily secured from a burning building, thinking I was getting a much needed shirt), all my clothes miserably dirty from an accumulation of dust and perspiration, the dust giving a ground-in appearance, making it difficult to distinguish their real color.   In addition to their ridiculous appearance there was an irritability pervading the entire command, doubtless due to an overtaxed nervous system, brought about by the hardships endured.   I have counted several fights during a day; they were usually of a harmless nature, fisticuffs, as there was nothing to do harm with, all having been deprived of all weapons. However, there was one man killed during our stay of a month at Camp Morton; a Texan killed a fellow prisoner.   What the Federal authorities did about it I never learned; they removed him from prison.

After a stay of one month at Camp Morton, we were transferred to Camp Douglas, near Chicago.   We were kept here eighteen months, guarded by the First Michigan sharpshooters and Indians, who were finally sent to the front in time to participate in the charge after the mine explosion in front of Petersburg, leaving but few to tell the tale. " Old Red," whom all of Morgan's men recall with a shudder, was a sergeant in this regiment, and noted for his harsh treatment of the prisoners.   Captain Sponable, I remember quite well, was the proud owner of a magnificent Newfoundland dog, which followed him into prison and strayed into the barracks of the Second Kentucky, Duke's old regiment.   No sooner had it entered than the boys had a blanket thrown over it, and in a short while had a feast savory beyond description. Rats were eaten with avidity when they could be caught about the sinks. In fact there was a sense of everlasting hunger that could not be appeased by prison allowance, which was barely sufficient to keep soul and body together. Those who were so fortunate as to have friends outside were permitted an occasional meal that the many were denied; and in this connection, I recall the kindness of Mrs. Waller, of Chicago, also Mrs. Philip Laerman as well as Mr. Copeland and Rev. E. B. Tuttle, who, I think is now bishop of Missouri. If it should be the same he will doubtless recall the boy who was placed in White Oak, with his friend Clore, for having rolled off a barrel of pork from the Federal commissary department.

In the spring following our first winter, smallpox in all its fury broke out among the prisoners, carrying many to their final resting-place out on the cold cheerless prairie, to be swept by the bleak winds and chilling frost of an inhospitable clime. But even there beside that great expanse of water, loving hands from the beloved Southland have erected a shaft of marble perpetuating the memory of those who so willingly gave up their lives for a cause they loved. The most touching incident of devotion I ever saw was a negro boy some sixteen or eighteen years of age, a body servant of one of Morgan's men, and the only negro in prison; he persistently refusing his liberty, preferring to remain with his master. He finally died and was carried to the deadhouse, where he was partly devoured by rats.

Seven-up, poker and dice were the prevailing forms of amusement; every form of literature, more especially newspapers, were denied us. Many utterly lost hope of ever being exchanged, and would take any risk to make their escape, which, in spite of the vigilance of guards, they often succeeded in accomplishing, either by scaling the walls or by tunneling. This was finally made impossible by raising the barracks several feet above the ground and doubling the guards and establishing a deadline, which was made as plain as day by large lamps lighting up the entire streets from one end to the other.

The Federals had various methods of punishing the prisoners for violations of prison rules. One often practiced was riding them on "Morgan's Mule," which was a two-inch scantling set up edgewise, and about eight feet from the ground, which they were forced to mount and sit astride. After remaining there awhile one felt as though the spinal column was being pushed out at the top of the head. (I speak from experience). Another mode, of punishment was to tie one up by the thumbs with the feet barely reaching the ground. Incarceration in the dungeon with or without shackles, depending upon the offense, was another punishment. Firing into the barracks, if lights were seen after taps, was sometimes resorted to. Our sergeant major, Frank Porter, now county clerk at Princeton, had his arm shot off at the shoulder in this way.

The winter of 1863-4 was one of the coldest on record. The suffering of the prisoners was great in the extreme. I have seen great, stout-hearted men who had faced death in many forms weep from the intense cold.

There were several thousand prisoners confined at Camp Douglas, many of them Hood's men, who were captured at Franklin on his ill-fated march into Middle Tennessee.

In the spring of 1865, Morgan's men were electrified by the news of their speedy exchange. The visions of the green fields of Kentucky and the mountain fastness of Tennessee, with its rippling waters and genial clime, were soon to be realized, after nineteen months of hardships and denials, which are made sacred by memory. In a few briefs years the last Confederate will have passed into the portals of the Great Beyond and, like their colors at Appomattox, will be nothing more than a memory.

ESCAPE FROM CAMP MORTON.

BY FRANK AMPLIAS OWEN.

The prisoners belonging to my regiment, Eighth Kentucky, C. S. A., were quartered in the fair ground stables, all open in front. The back wall of these stables was made of one and one-fourth inch board about twelve feet long set upon ends, this making the outer wall of the prison in February and March, 1862. What it was later, I do not know. Through this wall a door was cut by the United States carpenters, using one of the horse stalls for a passage or door way into a lot containing about one-fourth of an acre of land that was fenced in an oblong square with rough boards fourteen to sixteen feet long, set on ends, and the two ends of this fence were joined to the main wall of the fair grounds or prison. Thus a long ditch was dug in this space and used as an out-house by the prisoners.

On a day of April, 1862, late in the afternoon, a little storm blew down the eastern section of this out-house wall, leaving only about three planks standing at right angles and joined to the outside wall running east and west, parallel with the out-house ditch, making a snug corner.

Through this breach I determined to try to make my escape. having just the day before secured a suit of citizen's clothes from one of the United States guards on duty about the prison, for which we paid him (three of us, Owen Glass, of Henderson county, Thomas Carlisle, of Webster county, and myself) seventy-five dollars in greenbacks and fifteen dollars for betraying his trust, and from the quality of the clothes I am satisfied he made equally as much, if not double the amount that we had paid him for his perfidy. At any rate we were satisfied, for they were only about two sizes too large for us, and we wanted to wear them over our uniforms on account of the cold weather of that climate in March. Carlisle and I bunked together. Owen Glass had a bunk in Dr. Broy's prison office. This Dr. Madison J. Broy was the prison surgeon and lived in Evansville, Indiana, until 1899, when he died at the ripe old age of ninety years, honored and loved by every one. Owen Glass and I were distantly related and were warm personal friends; and as I had a minie ball in my leg that I had brought from Fort Donelson, and it was causing me more trouble than pleasure, as soon as I got to prison I called on Dr. Broy and formed his acquaintance and he really seemed to enjoy the job. I did not make as much fun about its removal, the boys said, as Clive Brown did about having a tooth extracted by this selfsame surgeon a few minutes before. The truth of the matter was, I was afraid to go to the hospital down in Indianapolis, and I somehow or other always dreaded a hospital. From some cause the Yanks put an extra line of men on guard this special night, running through the prison length, and thus separating us from Dr. Broy's office-building, hence Owen Glass was left behind. However, he escaped a few weeks later and was killed by the Yanks somewhere in Union county, between Henderson and Morganfield, Kentucky. I never saw him after I left Camp Morton. A braver boy never wore the Confederate uniform than Owen Glass; he would have made his mark if he had lived. Quite a number who bunked near us learned that Carlisle and I were surely going to make the attempt that night, and some fifty or more determined to run out after us while the guard's gun was empty after firing after us. Their leader, whose name I do not remember, promised me that we should have the right of way first, and no man was allowed to enter the out-house lot after "Taps" until his party had heard the Yankee guns; then their plan was to rush out and take their chances, every man hoping to make good his escape in some way or other. It is amusing now to look back and see how some of that party were gotten up for their charge and long trip through the enemy's country. I shall mention one (but not his name): A member of my company (A) whose getup was only a little exaggerated over many in that party. First, he had fully six days' rations, was in heavy marching order with bedding strapped on, and to this, frying pan, coffee or camp kettle, an old clock that struck the hours, like a jackass's first notes before each strike, with a camp-stool with an old oilcloth table cover over all to keep the outfit dry. What a pity these boys were doomed to disappointment, for the guards' guns were not fired at us, but Carlisle and I got out all the same, and this is the manner in which we did it: Just as the guard or sentry cried, "Half past twelve o'clock and all is well," I went to the out-house lot and approached the long ditch rapidly as though I was on business bent, and as soon as the sentries met and separated at the corner of the house from which we expected to make our break for liberty, I took my stand in the corner; a moment later Carlisle came and took his stand just behind me, and when the two sentries met just outside and within two feet of us and separated and were thirty or forty feet apart and were walking in opposite directions, we slipped out from our hiding place and passed between them with as little noise as possible, and walking rapidly. When we were some forty yards outside of the sentries' beat, and about half way to a low farm-fence of rails, it lightened and we could see the long line of guards, and took to our heels and ran as fast as we could. Forgetting the fence, we both struck it and fell over it on the other side, just as another flash of lightning lit up the heavens. Right here we laid very close to mother earth until we could get a breath and steady our nerves. After another flash of lightning, we arose from our muddy bed and made double-quick time till we got to a ravine out of sight of our enemy. Then we struck a match and got our bearings with a compass. Our plan was to skirt around the city on the east side, which we did, reaching the White river below the city just at daylight. We then followed down the east bank of the river for quite a long distance, half wading and swimming sloughs and branches, until we discovered a skiff on the opposite bank of the river. I stripped and swam the river with much difficulty, as the water was very cold and the current swift; making a safe landing however, nearly a half mile below my objective point. When I finally reached the skiff it was chained and locked to the roots of a small red elm-tree. I secured a fence rail, broke it and with the thin, flat, sharp end of one piece I dug the earth from the root for a distance of at least twenty feet, to a point at which the root was small, yet I failed to break it until I had gnawed the bark from the top of the root with my teeth, and then with a fence-rail I succeeded in breaking it and pulling it far enough back under the bank of the river to get the chain off. About this time a lady came out on a veranda or porch of a farm-house on the rise just above me, some one hundred and fifty yards, or more, distant from the river. She held out her hand and let the water from the dripping eaves of the house run on it for an hour it seemed to me in my excited state of mind, before she finally disappeared in the house. I got into the skiff and allowed the current to take me down the river out of sight; with my half flat rail I paddled the canoe to the east side and took in my comrade, donned my clothes and again put our craft in the middle of the current, feeling most glorious, thinking we had a clear river into the Ohio and all our main difficulties were gone. About three o'clock in the afternoon we stopped at a cabin on the bank and bought a loaf of corn-bread and a piece of boiled hog-shoulder. We then resumed our journey down the river, happy as any two boys you ever saw. We knew that we were no "small punkins," and just while we were exulting over our wonderful success, and thinking that the boys we left behind were all fools for letting a thing as small as the Fair-Grounds Prison keep them from home and friends we rounded a point and came in full view of Waverly, Indiana, and, oh, horrors, a mill-dam and a fall sufficient to make it dangerous for our craft! As we neared the town we saw several blue-coats and as all eyes seemed to be on us we boldly steered our craft to the nearest point to the crowd, tied up and walked into the middle of them in front of the store and addressing the man that looked most like a merchant we asked him how far from town Mr. Smith lived. He said, "Which? Squire Smith?" We said "Yes," and he looked south and said it was nearly four miles. After getting directions, we did not tarry long enough to be questioned. We learned afterward that Squire Smith was a recruiting officer at that time. Our desire to see "Esquire Smith," or having any previous knowledge of any such person, was all a hoax; believing that there were Smiths in every neighborhood, we only wanted a pretext to get out of town and away from those bluecoats without arousing any suspicion in their minds as to what we really were. For this reason we played Yankees and asked questions so fast that it gave them no opportunity to quiz us, and as Esquire Smith lived south of the town it suited our purpose to leave in that direction. When we were less than a mile from Waverly we were overtaken by a young Mr. Armstrong, who asked us a great many questions as to our homes, occupations, destination, and even politics. I was a Douglas Democrat. He said he had no use for Stephen A. Douglas or any of his followers. Then I told him my friend here was a Lincolnite and a black enough one to suit him no doubt, and that it was as much as I could do to stand him, although we were raised together. Armstrong said that was worse and more than he could stand, that he was a Breckinridge Democrat and did not care who knew it. So we were getting into a pretty warm argument when we came to the forks of the road neither of which ran south, the direction we wanted to travel; so we asked him which road went to Esquire Smith's and he told us the left hand and that we could not get to Smith's until in the night. We asked him then where would be a house on the road that we could likely get to stay for the night. He said his father lived about one mile further on, and that he sometimes took in travelers, but if we were what we said we were politically, he did not think he would let us stay. However, we might try him, but to him he did not think we talked at all like Northern people. This we did not argue with him, but bade him good-bye after he had given us the direction to his father's farm. We were not long in reaching the senior Henry Armstrong's. The old gentleman was standing under the shed of the farm work-shop which we came to before we got to his residence, a white frame cottage. We stopped and asked him if he could or would take care of us till morning. He said "That depends on who you are. My son told me a long story about you a few minutes ago and said he was in Waverly and that you came down White, etc. Now, young men, I have made up my mind from what my son told me about you and what I hear and see that you are Southern soldiers escaping from Camp Morton. If I am right in my conjectures, that's my home and you will be at home there as long as you think it is safe to remain. If you are what you told my son you were, you can go on. I have to feed the stock, it's getting late and I only waited here to see you, so goodbye," and he turned and went on, my comrade insisting that it was only a trap to catch us, but by the time we got opposite the house I persuaded him to take the chances with me and we walked right into the house. And such a fire as was roaring on that family hearth, I would like to see once more and the big fat biscuits and coffee, steak and brown gravy. We were still wet and our heels and toes blistered. As soon as the old gentleman and his son came in, he asked the wife and mother to give us dry clothes, which they did from tip to toe. I thought we would never get done rolling up those breeches' legs; they were about thirty-six or thirty-eight inch legs and we wore thirty

and thirty-one, but they were warm and dry and after a good
supper the senior Henry Armstrong said he wanted to hear us
talk some, but ah, how sleepy we were; we could hardly hold our
eyes open half an hour after supper. Besides the family at home,
composed of five or six, there was a Jew whom I did not fancy
much on account of his talking so much and asking so many questions; and the old gentleman noticed it and said to us, "I am a
native of Virginia, my wife is also and so is my oldest son; this
Jew is a peddler and has been making this his home for several
years; in fact ever since he came to this country and you need not
be afraid of him; tell us who you are and where you are from and
what State troops you belong to, and then you may go to bed, and
to-morrow is Sunday and you must put it all in telling us about
the South, your escape, etc."

We complied with his demands and then went to bed, the first
feather-bed we had touched since we had joined the army.   Such
a night's sleep! We did not (it's strange to say) even dream of
home or Yanks.   Next morning for breakfast we had more real
coffee, biscuit and some of the best sausage with gravy I had tasted
up to that time in my life.   It quit raining about noon, Sunday,
but the creeks were overflowed so we could not cross them if
we had been so disposed.   We remained with the family and the
Jew until after noon, Monday, spent a very pleasant time, bought
a lot of receipts from the Jew, a few of them I remember now.
Receipts for rats and mice extermination, one for each for making
red and blue ink, one bottle Perry Davis' painkiller, one bottle
cherry-bark bitters and twelve small one-fourth ounce phials.   In
these we put our painkiller and cherry-bark bitters, labeling each
with Latin technicals.   And as I had so often heard my father, Dr.
Abram B. Owen, of Hopkins county, Kentucky, prescribe for
people and tell them more about how they felt than they could
tell themselves, I knew pretty well the lick it was done with, and
I was going to make my knowledge in this line do us a good
turn in hours of extremity, as we had but little money left after
getting our outfit of clothes, and this Jew was the exception to
the rule; and as he did not offer to knock off anything, we did
not ask it, for we were glad to get his advice.   He told us that
we could not travel far through that State without some occupation or trade. If it was horse or cow hunting we must have a
rope, and he gave us this parting shot, that with all our safe-

guards we would get caught any way and taken back to Camp Morton or hung most likely. Mr. Armstrong sent us on horses twenty miles or thereabouts, Monday afternoon, the —— of April, 1862, and wished us much success after the war with the independence of the South gained. We left Mrs. Armstrong and the small children in tears; "God bless them" has been my prayer often since and is to-night, this November 25, 1900. After this ride we footed every step of the way to Evansville, Indiana, passing through Johnson, Morgan, Monroe, Green, Martin, Daviess, Pike, Warrick, Vanderburg counties. We rested every night where there were Union soldiers at home on furlough, some wounded, some sick, some had just joined, some had their uniforms and were getting ready to go to the front. I practiced medicine on some of them, had many funny experiences, and paid every night's lodging with our wares through the State of Indiana.

We crossed one stream on the old Erie canal aqueduct at Pittsburg, Indiana, and walked the tow path to Evansville, Indiana. When we reached the wharf at Evansville we found the steamer Storm, Captain Drinkwater, nearly ready to leave for Green river and all way-points, loaded from hurricane to boiler deck with Union soldiers, destination, Calhoun, Kentucky, where there was quite an army in camp of instruction. We were threatened with trouble at the wharf as there was a strong guard of soldiers with an officer to examine and see that no one left the city on the boat that did not have a pass from Major Robinson, the provost marshal of the city. I learned this much quick, and we made no attempt to get through the line but stood near and were apparently disinterested spectators until we heard the mate say to the captain that he would have to coal as there would be no certainty of getting any at Spottsville, as they heard there were rebels in the town that day. The mate with a lot of deck-hands (all white) started up the river to some coal barges. We fell in with them while a part of the soldiers followed and surrounded the barge that we were on by this time, and the first coal box filled Carlisle and I 'toted' on to the boat, emptied it, threw the box down behind the boiler where we saw some empties, and both walked up into the cabin which seemed to be occupied by Union officers, most of whom were playing cards. We went immediately to the office paid our fare to Ashbyburg, Kentucky, and went to our stateroom and to bed without supper. We slept well the early

part of the night, but the latter half we did not close our eyes.
We were in such a fever to get off that boat that the minutes
seemed hours, and hours seemed months. · Just as daylight came
the clerk knocked on our stateroom and called, "Ashbyburg," and
by the time the plank was on the bank, two young "Johnnies"
were on the top of the plank just over the top of the river bank.
We met Providence Mounts, the steamboat agent, who was a
Union man and knew us both, and you bet this was a trying
moment, for he recognized us and was so surprised that he could
not articulate a word for a moment; but offered each of us a hand,
which we grasped quick and drew his arms in each of ours, one
of us on each side, and we walked him, or rather dragged him
behind the nearest house on the bank, the boat puffing off well
in the meanwhile, when Mounts suddenly recovered his senses
somewhat, and said he must go to the boat to pay some freight
bill; this we told him he could attend to on her down trip. By this
time he saw the point and said he would not report us for anything
in the world. We told him we knew he would not, for the
reason that we were not going to give him a chance, explaining
after the boat and Yanks were all out of sight, that we had walked
too far and risked our lives and health too much on that little trip
to take even a little chance of being recaptured when we were then
within fourteen miles of mother and home, which we reached
without farther adventure that afternoon. There were many
little incidents that occurred along this trip from Camp Morton,
Indiana, to Hopkins county, Kentucky, where my parents lived on
a farm twelve miles distant from Madisonville, Kentucky, my
native town. My father had retired from the practice of his profession several years prior to this.

One incident that seems more ludicrous than any other, I will
relate. At a point in Johnson county, Indiana, I think it was,
we stopped for the night at a farm house. The old man said if
we could put up with his fare he would keep the two of us for
one dollar and fifty cents. When he took us right into his
family room the first thing we saw was a Yank with his arm in
a sling, so we soon learned there was no danger from him in the
present if there were no well ones around.

Turning to the other side I saw a middle-aged woman in bed,
but she did not look sick a bit to me; but to keep from being
questioned I commenced asking questions as to her troubles from

the old man who seemed to want to do all the talking. I learned that his wife had been all the doctors' care in that section for about a year or near about it, and he related what he had paid each, the aggregate running up into the hundreds. I thought I saw a chance to make our night's lodging, so I commenced work by asking all the symptoms from the beginning and what each doctor had said and done, and all along I made suggestions as to how she felt and the effect each doctor's medicine had produced, giving each, save one, a "cut." The old family doctor was quite old and had offi- ciated at the birth of each of their children and had just died a short time before. I bragged on his methods and told them that if they had stuck to him all the way through he would have cured her finally, that the dark drops that he gave her and the liniment he prescribed, with one more addition, would have cured her in a month. I made up my mind that her trouble was more of the mind than anything else, and I told the old man that I could save his wife and have her well in less than a month, I knew, and that I had a medicine with me that I knew would cure her if she would try it according to directions. The old man said they had agreed between them that they would not spend any more money on the doctors. I then told him that if he would try my medicine that night I would guarantee that his wife could stand on her feet in the morning, a thing she had not done for months past, and if I did not cure her sound and well in a month I would quit the practice and say I was no doctor. He then asked if this was not some trick to get his money, and said if I would want no money for the medicine—that there would be some catch in it, some way. At this point I told him I would take the cure on the insurance plan, furnish all the medicine free that was necessary, and that his wife would say she was well and I would not ask for one cent until even her neighbors said she was well and able to attend to all her duties as she used to do. At this point the old lady said," Old man, I believe the young doctor can cure me." We then and there agreed upon a price upon the aforesaid conditions. After supper I got my medicines, one bottle I gave to the husband of the patient and told him to put the contents in a quart of hot water and to keep it on the warm embers and to rub his wife with a woolen rag saturated with the medicine every hour, commencing on the muscles of the back and hips and to continue this on down to the ankles and especially the bottom of the feet, and stipulated that each rubbing should not be less than twenty minutes at a time. After careful directions to him I turned to the old lady and called her attention to how small a quantity of medicine it took to do good if it was only the right kind, telling her that I did not care especially for her husband's one hundred dollars, but I wanted to convince him that man did not have to be seventy-five or one hundred years old before he could have some sense, and that I knew she would be able to stand alone by breakfast though she would be a little dizzy-headed. After this we retired to our bed which was in an adjoining room and slept until near morning. We heard the old lady cry out, "Old man, you are rubbing the skin off, you are." "Well, you know the doctor said I must rub it in well and you must have the quart of medicine rubbed in by morning and it is nearly all gone now." To make a long story short, to my great delight the old lady stood up that morning and blessed God that she was well, but she was all but skinned. The old man said he was not satisfied with her being well, but that he had more faith in me now than he thought he would ever have in any doctor—that I was nothing but a young upstart of a quack when I started talking about curing the old woman in a month. I told him that it would take three more bottles of the medicine to cure her sound and well and I would send it to him by mail as soon as I got to Evansville; that I had but one left with me. He said he must have that, and I told him I could not let him have it, and he wanted to know why. Then I told him that I thought I might have an opportunity of getting a similar case on my way home, and another one hundred dollars; that he would not have to give her another application for seven days and by that time he would have the three bottles due him. He asked me how I sold it by the bottle, and I told him five dollars, so he offered me five for this last bottle; I declined it, telling him I was honest and had contracted to supply him with all the medicine free of cost, and I would do it, but for the reason given could not let him have this. He then asked me to let him see the medicine, that he had so little confidence in it the night before that he did not even read the name on the bottle till this morning and only knew it was dark in color. So I handed him over my last one-fourth ounce phial of cherry-bark bitters for his inspection. He asked me if it was poison to taste it and would it hurt him to taste it. I told him that in some rare cases I gave it internally. He looked at it, smelt it, and tasted it, and compared it with the label of the bottle he had used, then shoved a five dollar bill into my hand and said I need only send him two bottles instead of three. I remonstrated with him but with no effect; he said he had the medicine and I had the money, and that was the end of it. Then I pulled the same bill only rolled in a different shape and asked him to take out our bill for the night and he would not have a single cent. He knew the woman would get down again if he charged me anything, and thus we left him with a promise to return at the end of the month for my one hundred dollars, and the stingy old badger said, "Ninety-five you mean, you've already got five dollars," I told him, however, that was all right. Soon after reaching my Kentucky home, Colonel Adam R. Johnson and Lieutenant Colonel Robert M. Martin came to my father's house with a commission from the C. S. A., to raise a regiment of cavalry, and I joined them, and we raised the Tenth Kentucky Cavalry, C. S. A., which I served with till the close of the war.

The Breckinridge Guards, the first company made up by General Johnson in Kentucky, in 1862, was the foundation of the Tenth Kentucky Partisan Rangers. Adam R. Johnson, captain; Robert M. Martin, first lieutenant; Frank Amplias Owen, second lieutenant; Felix Eakin, third lieutenant.

The men that went to Newburg, Indiana, were in this first company; most of them became members later of Captain L. D. Fisher's Company B. However, several other companies were blessed with a part of them, nearly all of them becoming officers of some kind in the other companies.

When the regiment was partially made up it was officered by Adam R. Johnson, colonel; Robert M. Martin, lieutenant colonel, and F. Amplias Owen, major, without commission, and I was so recognized; but when the regiment was fully organized, Rev. Scobey, a man of age and great mental as well as physical power, defeated me for major, and I was made adjutant, and later captured and taken to Camp Chase, and stayed three months or less, during which time I messed with Lieutenant Shane, of Nashville, Captain McLean, of Nashville, and Lieutenant Clarence Prentice, of Louisville, Kentucky, whose father, George D. Prentice, of the Louisville Journal, supplied our table with all the good things the market afforded. I was exchanged at City Point, Virginia.

During my absence Lieutenant Phil. Jones was appointed adjutant; after he was captured, I again filled his place for a time and during my furlough in which I visited my old regiment at Grovesport, Mississippi, Lieutenant Oscar L. Barbour was appointed adjutant and served in this capacity till the Ohio raid. Further than this I am not informed, as I was captured on July 26, 1863, with General John H. Morgan in Ohio.

General Morgan put me in command of the remnant of the Tenth Kentucky Cavalry as soon as we were safe out of sight of the forces of Generals Hobson and Shackelford at Cheshire, Ohio, and I commanded that squad of men with great pride, and General Morgan said, with ability, in evidence of which he said he would add another bar to my collar on account of the manner in which we took care of the rear, especially at the Woodman Taylor farm. The last night of the raid the Yanks captured two of my best soldiers, Merce and Crow Johnson, who were on picket. The Yanks coming into the road through a narrow lane near the picket base, after firing one volley into my men lying flat on the ground, ran out the main road, taking in the two Johnson brothers. The third brother, William Allen Johnson, and William Gradey (now a large farmer on Diamond Island, in Henderson county) stood by me and fought with bravery worth recording here.

Some of the boys ran away but returned in a very short time, but the Yanks had also gone. While there was no blood shed, so far as I knew, it looked right scary, for the blaze of fire from the Yankee's guns seemed to reach us as we were all sound asleep, and as you may well suppose, I did not blame the boys much. However, the three that remained kept their courage up by shooting in the direction of the enemy, but we felt awful lonesome for about three to five minutes till the other boys got their bearing properly adjusted. Not one of them ever flickered for a moment after that. Most of them have now answered the long roll, and are resting peacefully, I trust, on the other shore.

On the afternoon of this same twenty-sixth of July, General Morgan captured a militia colonel or captain, or a captain who was in the regular service, who was at home on a furlough, and who had command of the militia in our front and on our flanks. My information at the time was that General Morgan flattered this militia colonel and surrendered to him on the condition that he would stop his men from firing on us from the hill on our left and not delay us any longer. When we came into contact with this larger force of militia-men, we were out of ammunition, the main body having given what they had to the rear squad, as they called for it, from time to time, along the way after leaving Cheshire, Ohio.   General Morgan's great anxiety was to get to this ford before Shackelford's force, which was then traveling a parallel road. We had seen the long line of dust on our right and would have beaten them had it not been for the delay the militia caused us.   I know this, that after the above described capture of the colonel and a short parley, the colonel went forward with some of our men and a flag of truce up at both ends of our column of not over two hundred and fifty to three hundred men.   We were then running for dear life with empty guns as well as empty stomachs, but alas, the mountain made a bend to the right and ran us right into the arms of Shackelford's parallel force.   They wheeled their column into line not a hundred yards ahead of us where their road intersected ours.   I heard that Shackelford and Hobson and their men made much sport of the gallant militia colonel, and I am sorry that he did not contend for his rights before the War Department, for Shackelford's force would never have captured us on Ohio soil had it not been for this force of militia under command of this captain or colonel.

He wrote to me several years since but I have for the moment forgotten his name, though I have his letters yet with my war papers.

PRISON LIFE AT CAMP DOUGLAS.

BY T. B. CLORE, TENTH KENTUCKY CAVALRY.

While many have written of the inhuman treatment of the Confederate prisoners at Camp Douglas, Chicago, they have not related by a large majority all the terrible cruelties they were subjected to. I shall here relate some incidents that occurred in 1864, and which I have never seen in print.

Upon a winter night, while lying in my bunk, I heard a noise in the barracks just back of the one in which I was sleeping. The head of my rude bed being close to the side of a window, I looked out and saw our men coming out with a rush and one of the patrol guards cursing and rushing them. In a case of this kind it was usual for all the men to try and get out first as the last one would get thumped on the head with a club such as the guards carried, it being part of their outfit, including two revolvers. After all had gotten out of the barracks, they were ordered to form a line and remain there until the guard returned. He was gone but a few minutes when he returned with two more guards. Our men, many of them boys, were again ordered to form a line. The weather was bitter cold and the ground covered with snow and ice, but these gallant Confederate soldiers were compelled at the muzzle of a revolver, to partly undress and sit in a half-naked condition upon this frozen ground with its sheet- of ice and snow. One of the guards stood at the head of the line while the others stood in the rear of the column and discovered that some of the miserable fellows had pulled their coat tails down for partial protection to their nudity from the awful contact with the cold earth. Every one that was detected was mercilessly kicked in the back with the

408

SERGEANT T. B. CLORE,
Co. C, 10th Ky., P. R.

heavy shoes of the brutal guards. After having them sit thus from ten to fifteen minutes, which must have seemed an hour to these luckless heroes, one of the brutes said, " Now, God damn you, I guess you have had enough, haven't you?" One of the boys allowed his pride to get the better of him and talked back, though he said nothing that the Yankee should have gotten angry at, but the fiend in human shape made him keep his painful, agonizing seat, and after giving all the rest a round of cursing, he allowed them to go back to their barracks but kept the unfortunate one there for a half hour longer. There were so many thousand men in that prison, and such diabolical deeds were perpetrated that I could not follow up all the cases, but one should not have been surprised to hear that all treated as these I have mentioned died with pneumonia or pleurisy.

The next day I learned the cause of this devilish punishment of these hundred and fifty Confederate soldiers. One of them had thoughtlessly spit upon the floor and for this petty act all of them were made to suffer. Some of those guards would have rivaled the Comanche Indians in their brutality. I have known them to be passing along at the dead hour of the night and just for downright meanness fire into the barracks where we were asleep. As a protection many of us nailed a board across the head of our bunks and filled in between that and the outside boards with earth and stones. Mort Quincy was one of the cooks for part of the time and slept in the kitchen. He had a fifty gallon kettle that he cooked in, and one night one of the guards shot in at him, the ball striking the iron kettle and glancing off went clear around the room, but luckily did not hit him.

At one time, a few men, nine in number, concluded to try and make their escape from this hell on earth, and for genuine bravery and true grit their attempt has perhaps never been excelled. The crowd was composed of Henry Gilchrist, Charlie Eden, Hamp Jones, ———— Chase, and others whose names I have forgotten. The day before the night on which they were to make their strike for liberty, one of them came to me and asked me if I would not join them. After I had listened to all their plans I promised to go with them, but later in the day I decided that the odds were too great against us and withdrew from the doubtful enterprise. They had selected a wide plank in the prison fence that they would cut through. This fence was twelve or fifteen feet high with a gangway all around about three of four feet from the top, and day and night guards walked this and kept a sharp lookout over the yard.   On the inside there were posts with lamps with reflectors on them and a bright light was thrown from one lamp to another.   These posts were about six feet high.   The time set for the charge was about nine p. m.   Charlie Eden and Frank Jones were to lead in the desperate attempt.   They were to advance together and throw a blanket over the lamp nearest to the wide plank, while Jones was to cut the plank with a dull old ax he had found.   Their only arms were this old ax and pocketsful of brick bats.   All of them collected in a barrack nearest to the point of attack, and at the appointed time made a rush for the fence. Eden threw the blanket over the lamp so as to partially obscure them from the sight of the guards, and Jones went to work with his ax, while the other stopped a few feet from the fence and began stoning the sentinel.   One was knocked off his elevated station but the others fired upon the assaulting party.   The rest of the ptarol guards rushed from their house and fired upon these poor fellows while they ran between them and their barracks. Unfortunately, it was found that the plank they were trying to cut through was nailed to a big post instead of the parallel girders and did not readily yield to Jones' blows.   Seeing that they would be killed before their sturdy axman could make an opening for them to pass through, they turned upon the guards who were firing from behind and fighting desperately, succeeded in putting all of them to flight toward the prison gates, not once stopping to use their clubs or pistols.   Of course this raised a general alarm, and it was amusing to see these cruel bullies in their mad race pursued by this handful of half-starved, ragged Confederates with their weapons of stone.   One company came close by my window and peeping out I could see and hear them.   The captain was giving orders in a very low, quivering voice, "Close up, boys, close up; steady, steady, now close up."

Seeing that effort was hopeless, the strikers for freedom ran to their barracks and hastily undressed and jumped into their bunks. Warner Scroggins, now living in Louisville, Kentucky, and S. B. Withers, of Sturgis, same State, had occasion to be out of their barrack at this time on a more peaceful mission, and were near their door, returning, when the firing began.   Not understanding what all this rumpus meant, they ran in and got into their bunks with all their clothes on. Their teeth chattered with the apprehension of their being suspected and punished by the heartless guards. Their cunning availed them not, for discovered under such suspicious circumstances, no explanation would be listened to by the guards and they were marched off to a dungeon and confined in "durance vile" for thirty days and fed so scantily that they almost died of hunger. This dungeon was eight feet square and built directly over a sewer that drained all the filth of the prison. A hole had been cut into the floor to serve as a flue but which let in such an awful stench that it was almost impossible for human beings to exist in such a place. These two innocent Southern gentlemen were kept in this confinement for a month, and though the guards told them they would give them liberty if they would divulge the names of the others concerned in the plot, they refused to do so to the last. Finally they were released, coming out with the faces of corpses but the souls of living heroes.

PRISON LIFE AT CAMP DOUGLAS.

BY J. M. LYNN, BOXVILLE, KENTUCKY.

In the winter of 1864-65, B. L. Mitchell, Henry Gilchrist, George Staples and Jack Porter were defeated in their efforts at digging a tunnel to escape from that hell on earth, Camp Douglas. Half starved, half frozen, cruelly beaten, and mercilessly forced to ride "Morgan's Mule," as painfully straddling a sharp-edged piece of timber, with feet dangling in the air sometimes heavily weighted, the unhappy prisoners were constantly contriving some means to get out at the great risk of being shot in the attempt, or terribly punished afterwards, if the effort failed.

The Federals found the tunnel, but could not find the men who had the intolerable impudence to thus try to regain their precious liberty. The Kentuckians were the suspected parties, so the Tenth Kentucky and a part of the Second Kentucky Cavalry were ordered up near headquarters, one hundred and fifty in all, and forced to huddle up in a mass. The commander of the prison came out of his office, and instructed a corporal to demand that some one step over the line and tell the names of the men who had dug the tunnel. The corporal did so, and after waiting a minute and no one moving forward, he returned to the commander, reported, received fresh orders, and came back to within ten feet of where

Sergeant Beck and myself were standing and whispered to one of the armed guards near us.   Instantly the guard cocked his musket, and fired into the helpless mass of prisoners.   The bullet struck William Coles, killing him, and the buckshot wounded Henry Hutchins in the groin, passing through and tearing his hip frightfully. His suffering was terrible and pitiful, and he did not die till morning.   Both had lived in Union county, Kentucky.

Soon after the shots had been fired, the chaplain brutally re-marked to the commander, who had come forward with several of his staff, " General, that was a fine shot." We could not hear the reply, but all of them seemed satisfied at the results of this mur-derous order.

We were then commanded to take our foully assassinated brother to the dead house, and the wounded one to the hospital, when it would have been more merciful for them to have put him out of his terrible agony at once.

I would solemnly swear before any court, to the truthfulness of this account.   Many occurrences of killing and wounding and beating prisoners took place there under the excuse that they had broken some rule, sometimes a very trivial one.   The prison guards had the full power of killing or maltreating the prisoners in any way they fancied without any word from the officers, and tyrannically they exercised their unwarrantable authority.

THE BATTLE OF BLUE'S POND.

BY BEN. F. PERKINS.

The battle of Blue's Pond was fought a few days after the Bell's Mines Fight, between Colonel Sypert, commanding the Confederates, and Colonel Burgess, the Yankees. The latter was in camp at Morganfield when Sypert returned from Bell's Mines with forty-eight prisoners, whom he intended to parole in that city, but finding that the town had been occupied in his absence, he was compelled to go to Blue's Pond, a few miles west of Morganfield, where he established camp, paroled his prisoners, and sent them under guard north of the Ohio. The next night he sent Captain Gaar to annoy the Federals, declaring that as long as they stayed in Morganfield they should neither eat nor sleep, as he intended to have his guns popping by night as well as day. After spending two nights without sleep, the doughty Yankee colonel said he was going to Blue's Pond after Sypert's head. They moved out in that direction, and had hardly reached the outskirts of the town before Sypert was informed of their plans. The gallant Confederate at once began preparations to give them a warm reception by moving his men across the pond which is about a mile long and very muddy, and only to be crossed in two places. Colonel Sypert formed his men on the north side of the pond in the woods, his men concealed behind trees and logs, and anxiously awaited the advance of the enemy. In a short time, we could hear the sound of moving cavalry and the orders given, and in a few moments a long blue line swept into the camp we had deserted a short time before. After a while they were convinced that we had vamosed and rode into the treacherous mud to water their horses, their line reaching a distance of seven or eight hundred yards. At

413

this suitable juncture our signal gun was fired and its explosion seemed to simultaneously ignite our three hundred double-barreled shotguns. I never saw such a laughable mix-up of horses and men during the whole war as this bemuddled Yankee command as their horses reared and veered and snorted and cavorted in a wild, crazy effort to free themselves from the sticky mire. Here and there along the line some horses and riders would tumble together into the mud, while others would plunge, scattering the slush and slime all over the men. The soldiers kicked, cursed, yelled and spurred in vain attempt to get away from the terrible rebels whom they had boasted about greasing and swallowing alive. But the scene is absolutely indescribable, defying both words and imagination to reproduce it, and it is not likely that any other such odd or ludicrous farce was ever played upon the stage in the theater of war, in all the history of this sublunary orb as the glorious and uproarious battle of Blue's Pond. But "Blue's Pond" is entirely too prosaic a title for the scene of this contest and it is respectfully and most urgently suggested that the county that has the honor to possess such an historic treasure, petition the Legislature of Kentucky to change its plebeian cognomen to the statelier, more dignified appellation of "Indigo Lake," or any other more elegant or majestic if not descriptive and characteristic denomination for this now classic locality.

But to return to our more immediate subject. The field was soon full of men and horses running in the wildest disorder through the woods toward Morganfield. Colonel Sypert, seeing that the Yankee force was at least one thousand strong, and not knowing how utterly demoralized they had become, "every man for himself and the Devil for the hindermost," instead of rallying and forming again for battle as he naturally expected such a superior force to do, retired now to Curlew Hill instead of vigorously pursuing the disorganized mob, and established his camp, there near the famous Anvil Rock.

The writer of the sketch, with a command of twenty men, visited the scene of the stampede a few days after the affair, and saw bodies of some twenty fine horses, seven new made graves near the Saul Blue home, and found four or five wounded Yankees at the old Blue farm. He also ascertained that some twenty-six Federals less severely wounded were taken away from Morganfield when evacuated by the Yankees the next day.

THE DADE HILL YANKEE STAMPEDE.

BY BEN. F. PERKINS.

I think it unnecessary to relate all the preliminary movements of my single assistant and self, and shall begin with the skirmish itself after a few introductory remarks necessary for the proper understanding of the subject. General Payne, or " Butcher Payne," a sobriquet he had won by his many cold-blooded murders of Confederate prisoners, a hard-hearted villain whom even George D. Prentice denounced in the Louisville Journal for his numerous bloody crimes and fiendish outrages, had just made a raid through Union county, which will never be forgotten by General Johnson's men nor the citizens in general. General Johnson had ordered the writer, with a single companion selected by himself, to go to Morganfield and find out how many men Payne had and in what direction they were going.

I chose T. D. Omer and started for Morganfield and arrived there the next morning at daylight. The town was occupied by about three thousand Federals of all colors and hues, some being only sixty-day men. After gaining all the information that was possible, I sent Omer back with a dispatch for General Johnson who was near Providence, Webster county. When Omer left, Payne was just moving out in the direction of Caseyville. I followed on a parallel country roadway, a little to the left of that which he had taken. Near where the village of Gum Grove now stands, I met Lieutenant S. M. McKinley with six men of my own company and proposed to him that we ambush Payne's army at Dade Hill, about two miles from the place at which the said Gum Grove is now situated but which, at that time had no existence. He said he would adopt the suggestion if I would take command.

I did so and we moved as rapidly as possible down the road until we reached a place opposite to Dade Hill, then we turned through the Calin's farm and proceeded to the top of Dade Hill with the intention of crossing the Caseyville road and taking position on the north side.   When we got in sight of the road, we found that the Federals had already reached the top of the hill and halted, and were pillaging Mr. Luther Calin's house.   We two charged up to within forty or fifty yards and opened fire.   `Absorbed in their robbery, they were completely surprised and retreated in great disorder into the woods without firing a gun or even sending a scouting party back to investigate our numbers. As a result of our fire, one Yankee was severely wounded and three slightly, while the entire party was stampeded for several miles, scattering in their wake the supplies they had stolen from the farmers.   Bacon, flour, meal, etc., were afterwards picked up by the wagon-load by the people living along the route they had traveled, and quite a number of cattle that were lost in the stampede, were subsequently recovered by their owners.

THE OLD GRAY LEGGINS.

An incident related to Ben. F. Perkins by Mr. John Kibby

Mr. John Kibby, living between the present site of Gum Grove and Dade Hill, relates a funny little story of the war. The doughty General Payne had ordered Kibby's residence searched for "concealed rebel soldiers," and, after they had examined all the rest of the premises in vain quest of "gray coats," Kibby suggested that they look in the garret so that they would feel fully satisfied that they had left no stone unturned. A ladder led up to a hole in the ceiling of a small room through which the garret had to be reached. One of the Yankees was ordered by an officer to ascend this ladder and search every corner. He ran up and stuck his head in the hole, and almost fell to the floor, and he scrambled down, his face white with fright. "There are some guerrillas hiding up there," he whispered excitedly, and flatly refused to go up again. The officer cursed him for his womanish cowardice and ordered several to go up together, believing that numbers would inspire confidence, but these declined to move a step upon such a perilous venture. The commander's face flushed with wrath at thus being disobeyed, and, cursing loudly, swung himself up the ladder and put his head in the hole. Evidently a very fearsome sight greeted him, for he turned loose of the ladder and fell back to the floor, his teeth chattering and his knees popping together. His leg caught under him and broke the bone, but he did not seem to mind this and shouted: "They are up there, sure, and I intend to burn down this house and them in it." To save his property Mr. Kibby ascended to investigate, and soon the frightened Yankees were greeted with a shout of laughter as he appeared and threw in their midst a pair

417

of his father's old gray leggins that had been hanging upon a rafter and in the half light resembled a pair of human legs. There was the cheapest looking set of fellows that gathered around and inspected these harmless thngs, all humiliated at the thought of their being scared by such a small thing as a pair of leggins, but half excusing themselves upon the plea that they were gray. Burglars are often scared away by imagined footsteps of the landlord of the place they are trying to rob, and a kindred feeling terrified these house robbers who, conscious that they were doing wrong, were made cowards and easily intimidated by going into dark places which their inflamed imaginations peopled with a lot of wild, murderous guerrillas. Thus it is with all of us when tempted to wrong-doing. That wonderful reader of human nature, who always hits the nail upon the head, has truthfully declared,—

"Thus conscience doth make cowards of us all;
And thus the native hue of resolution
Is sicklied over with the pale cast of thought;
And enterprises of great pith and moment,
With this regard, their currents turn awry,
And loose the name of action."

If these Yankees are gracious enough to accept this apology for their timidity, they are perfectly welcome, as the Southern people are wonderfully magnanimous and forgiving anyway.

LIEUTENANT JOSEPH W. BELL.

A DARING ESCAPE.

BY JOHN A. STEELE.

About the first of June, 1864, General Morgan started from the vicinity of Abingdon, Virginia, on his last raid through Kentucky. His command consisted of about 1,500 cavalry and 750 dismounted men who had joined him there without horses. I shall not attempt to relate the details and hardships of that march through the mountains, as it has doubtless left a lasting impression upon you, as it did upon me. Let it suffice to say that after enduring great hardships and fatigue, the cavalry marched into Mt. Sterling on the morning of the 8th of June, and after a spirited engagement captured the garrison, and also a large quantity of quartermaster and commissary stores. After sending back a number of captured wagons to haul up the exhausted foot men, General Morgan moved toward Winchester and Lexington. The brave horseless men who had kept so close to the heels of the cavalry all the way through the mountains of Virginia and Kentucky reached Mt. Sterling about dark on the same day, and encamped just outside of the limits of the town. Weary, footsore, exhausted, they at once yielded to the already neglected demands of nature, and fell into a profound slumber from which alas, many of them never awakened.

Through the criminal carelessness of the officer commanding the rear guard, who had but recently been assigned for duty with our command, before daylight on the morning of the 9th, we were surrounded by a vastly superior force under General Burbridge, which fired at close range into our camp before a single man was awake. Completely surprised, but nothing daunted, these heroic men sprang from their blankets, seized their rifles and standing singly or in squads and groups, fought with the energy of despair. At length under the leadership of the gallant Colonel Martin, of the Tenth Kentucky, they formed in compact mass and forced their way through the Federal lines, making good their retreat, the enemy being slow to follow. Our loss was about 300 men in killed, wounded and captured. Among the latter were Captain Jos. W. Bell and myself. We were all taken to Lexington, and after being held there for two days were placed in box cars on the Louisville road and started for our prison home. The tops of the cars were lined with Federal soldiers; besides these, there were four to each car to guard the doors on the inside. They sat on each side of the doors with their bayonets crossed. Captain Bell and myself were in the same car, After leaving Frankfort on our journey, Bell said to me, "John, I am going to take a nap, please wake me up before we reach Lagrange, as I intend to leave you there." He placed a stick of cordwood under his head as a pillow, and was soon lost to the war and its wild alarms. I did not regard his request seriously, but when the whistle sounded for Lagrange I complied with his request and said playfully, "If you are determined to desert this excursion, I wish you Godspeed." When the train stopped at the platform there was quite an assemblage to see the "Rebels," among them a little boy who had ridden up and hitched his horse just in front of our car. The captain in command left our car and walked up and down with a sort of bantam-cock stride, and a look that seemed to say, "Behold the conquering hero, I'm a bigger man than old Grant;" although I do not think he ever saw us until after our capture. Finally, after exhibiting us to his satisfaction, the train started on its way, and he ran to get aboard. Captain Bell was standing with his left hand resting on the jamb of the open door; as the freight car was in motion and the step rather a high one, Bell, very courteously extended his right hand to assist him; being a powerful man he easily drew him in, and just as he got him on a balance, with a sudden jerk he threw him against the soldier who was upon the right of the door and sent both sprawling to the floor, at the same time with a left-handed slap he laid the opposite soldier out as flat as a pancake. Then out he sprang like a catamount, and in a moment was on the back of the horse of the aforesaid little boy, and by dint of kicking and beating with his slouched hat he forced the slow animal into a run. Every moment I expected to see him riddled by those upon the top of the car, but their astonishment at the daring act was so great that not a shot was fired. The last I saw of him he was passing behind the courthouse square at full speed, with his auburn locks floating in the summer breeze.

It took the doughty captain in command some time to realize what had happened, and when he did, he ordered the soldiers to shoot the first one who made a demonstration to escape, but that pleasure was denied them as none of us demonstrated.

I have now written you an account in my feeble way of one of the most daring episodes that occurred within my knowledge during the Civil War, and although forty years have passed, it is still fresh in my mind. The subject of it, my old friend and comrade, big-hearted, generous, brave Joe Bell, has passed that dark river to which we are all rapidly approaching. As one by one we cross over I trust we will meet in a reunion more joyous than any this world can afford.

WAR REMINISCENCES.

BY J. S. WALLER, M. D.

The writer of this article was born in Granville county, North Carolina, in February, 1846, and at the age of four years came with his parents to Hopkins county where they settled in a new home near the town of Hanson. In July, 1864, I enlisted in the Confederate army, joining Company A, Twelfth Kentucky. I was with General Johnson at the time he was shot and lost his eyesight at Grubbs' Crossroads, and was within a few paces of that brave man when that terrible calamity befell him. The remembrance of the event will go with me to the grave. At the fight at Canton, I hid in a ravine near the river, after our men were scattered, waited for a favorable opportunity, made my escape and returned to Hopkins county.

When I reached home, I procured a horse and with Captain Hockersmith and others we made our way to Paris, Tennessee, and reported to his command. This was in September, 1864. The brigade was placed under the command of General H. B. Lyon. The brigade consisted of Sypert's regiment, Chenoweth's, later Cunningham's regiment, and Owsley's battalion, in all about fifteen hundred men. While here we were drilled and a detail of soldiers was sent to Corinth, Mississippi, for arms and ammunition.

Our first engagement of importance after we were in Tennessee was when we went to Johnsonville to support General Forrest in an engagement with quite a large force of the enemy. Fortunately for the enemy and perhaps for us also, the river was between the contending forces. General Forrest, however, succeeded in accomplishing his purpose, which was the destruction of a large quantity of Federal stores estimated to be worth a million and a half dollars.   A reminder of this artillery duel can yet be seen at Johnsonville when the river is low, in the hulls of seven steamboats and three gunboats, besides some barges which lie rotting in the sand and water.

After this engagement we returned to Paris, remaining there until about the twentieth of November, at which time General Lyon made his way into Kentucky.   Leaving Paris with about fourteen hundred men, two pieces of artillery, and some ammunition, we crossed the Tennessee river five or six miles south of Johnsonville, and struck out for the Cumberland river which we crossed twelve miles east of Dover.   At Cumberland river we destroyed quite a number of boats that were loaded with stores for the enemy at Nashville.

After leaving the Cumberland river, General Lyon divided his forces, half going by the way of the Princeton and the other to Hopkinsville.   We reached Hopkinsville with about five hundred men and were very soon engaged in a fight between the city and the asylum, where we were attacked by a force of about fifteen hundred men.   The battle lasted about two hours, when our command withdrew from the field losing about forty men, most of whom were made prisoners.   We also lost one piece of artillery.   From Hopkinsville, we marched in a circuitous route and came to Madisonville, at which place we were joined by that part of the command which had come by the way of Princeton.

At Madisonville, the court house suffered the same fate that had befallen these temples of justice at Princeton and Hopkinsville, that is, it was burned down.   From Madisonville, the command took up its march for Hartford, the county seat of Ohio county.   We crossed Green river at Ashbyburg, and after crossing were encountered by a force of Federals, but we kept on our way to Hartford. At the latter place we encountered a small force of the enemy, about fifty in all, but they surrendered without giving us a fight. From here we went to Elizabethtown, where we destroyed a stockade and near the town we derailed a train containing about three hundred Federal soldiers.   After a slight resistance, they were made prisoners of war.   We then went from there to Hodgenville, then to Campbellsville.   At or near the latter place, General Burbridge came up on our rear and this had the effect to accelerate our motion and get us started in a Southern direction.

We passed through Columbia and Burksville, crossed the Cumberland river and made our way back into Tennessee. With the exception of some slight annoyance in the way of bushwhackers we had but little trouble and passed out of Tennessee into Alabama north of Huntsville. We again crossed the Tennessee river a few miles west of or below Guntersville. After crossing the river we went to the village of Red Hill where we encamped for a few days, proposing to take a needed rest, having been on the go continuously from the 20th day of November until this date, which was the 13th of January.

The men and horses were greatly worn from their long and arduous travel. Very few if any of the men had stopped within doors during the whole march. The winter had been a severe one and the men had suffered greatly. We had lost by killed, wounded and desertion the main part of our command. We numbered now not more than four hundred men. Sypert's and Cunningham's regiments were depleted until there were scarcely enough to form a respectable company of soldiers fit for duty. Major Owsley's battalion was reduced to three men, one major, a captain and a private.

On the morning of the 15th of January, we were surprised by an attack by the Fifteenth Pennsylvania Cavalry. This was attributed to a mistake in picketing. The enemy were upon us before we were aware of their nearness to us. The attack was made about four o'clock in the morning. General Lyon and his staff at headquarters were surrounded before they knew the enemy were in the country.

Sergeant Lyon of the Federal army went to General Lyon's headquarters, knocked on the door, announced who he was and demanded a surrender. This brought on a parley and General Lyon asked the privilege of putting on his pantaloons. The request was granted, when General Lyon drew his pistol and shot the sergeant dead in his tracks. The live general marched out over the dead body of the sergeant; the staff and others followed and all except about forty who were made prisoners, escaped and made their way farther South, where they reported to General Forrest.

The writer happened to be one of the forty unlucky fellows who was made a prisoner. I was sent North by way of Nashville,

Indianapolis, and thence on to Columbus, Ohio, arriving at Camp Chase near Columbus on the twenty-fifth day of January, 1864.

There were eighty-two of us Johnny Rebs in the prison at Columbus. Of course there were many hundreds all told, but of our crowd when we started, to the forty were added at other points forty-two more, which made the number stated. We remained in prison about four months, and it is useless to say that to us they were four long weary months. Of the eighty-two in our crowd, only twelve men survived and came away alive from that prison. The other seventy sleep in the North in a burying-ground that is near the prison.

There are several reasons which may be assigned for this fearful mortality: exposure during the cold winter, lack of proper food and clothing, and the rigors of the winter that we had to endure while away up North.

On May the 12th, 1864, the war being over, we all took the oath of allegiance and pledged ourselves to support the government of the United States the remainder of our lives. Those of us who still live, are loyal to that oath, and to--day the government has no more loyal friends than those who fought for the cause of the South in the sixties. Four days after leaving Camp Chase in Ohio, I was at my home in old Hopkins county, where I have ever since lived and among the people of which county I expect to spend the remainder of my days, be they few or be they many. Within my breast rankles no hatred or ill-will to those who may have fought on the other side. We are now a united people, living under the best government over which the sun ever shone.

THE REMINISCENCES OF BRIGADIER GENERAL SAMUEL WOODSON PRICE, WHILE IN COMMAND AT LEXINGTON, KENTUCKY.

I was appointed to the command of the Twenty-first Kentucky Volunteer Infantry, the 25th of February, 1864, to fill a vacancy caused by the death of E. L. Dudley, of Lexington, Kentucky, and assumed command on the 10th of the following month. After I was wounded in a battle at Kennesaw Mountain June 20, 1864, having a sick leave of absence, I returned to my home at Lexington, and after being restored to health, I assumed command by the order of General Stephen Burbridge as commandant of the post at Lexington, which position I held till mustered out on the 27th of July, 1865.

During my administration the troops under Burbridge captured a man by the name of George Owens, of Louisville, Kentucky, in Henry county, Kentucky, but a mere youth. He was brought to Lexington and put in the military prison then in my charge. This was near the close of the war. I went with Mrs. Owens, his mother, to see Burbridge and intercede for her son, George. He refused to give her any satisfaction. Then I advised her to apply in person immediately to Mr. Lincoln. He, being a merciful man, wired an order to suspend the sentence of death till further orders.

One day I found in my mail a letter from Owen informing me that Lieutenant Vance, provost marshal of Burbridge's staff, had selected him and four other Confederate prisoners to be sent that afternoon by rail to be shot in retaliation for a Union man who had been recently killed in that county. I, immediately, as the orders should have been sent to me by Burbridge to the prison, asked my provost marshal if such an order had been received. Receiving a negative answer, I at once repaired to General Hobson's headquarters in a room above mine, and at once made known to him the object of my visit, which was to ascertain if such an order had passed through his office. Upon inquiring of his provost marshal I found such an order had passed through his office. Having no time to lose, as it was then two o'clock, and the train had left with the prisoners, I, without delay, at once proceeded to General Burbridge's quarters. Finding the general out of the city, I inquired of Vance by whose authority he had sent Owen off with his fellow prisoners to be executed the following day. He replied by order of Burbridge. I then asked him if President Lincoln's telegraphic order had not been to suspend the execution of Owen, the response being he knew of no such order from the President. I had him then go with me to the adjutant general's office and make inquiries of him about said order, and on inquiry he said the order which was on file in office had not been revoked, and furnished a copy to Vance. As the question of veracity was in dispute between the two men, I was indifferent about their dispute, but wanted a telegraph order to recall Owen, and put the dispatch in my hands to be telegraphed to Colonel Bulkley, who was charged with the execution of the men. The provost marshal replied that that could not be done without it included the other four Confederates. My reply was, "So much the better," as there was no military necessity for murdering these men. They gave me the dispatch and I remained at the telegraph office till I received an acknowledgment of its receipt, and the next day they were all returned to the prison under my charge. And after that there were no more men sent away from my prison to be executed by Burbridge.

SAMUEL WOODSON PRICE.

THE SONS OF LIBERTY.

BY T. M. FREEMAN.

In company with Captain Fowler and two lieutenants. (I believe of Colonel Clay's battalion, Giltner's brigade) I went into Kentucky in July, 1864. We had orders to collect all the scattered members of our commands we could find, and enlist as many recruits as possible, each going to the community where his command was raised. This was thought necessary from the number of Giltner's brigade which were scattered from the main command in our reverse at Cynthiana in June 1864, and who evaded capture and got to their homes. My orders directed that if I thought it advisable and could do so, to pass over into Southern Indiana for recruiting purposes. Lieutenant Archie Smith who had brought out a body of recruits had among them a half dozen or so from South Indiana. It was this portion of my orders that I considered justified me in going on to Chicago and reporting to Captain Tom Hines and becoming identified with the movement of which he had charge, so far as the Confederate Government was concerned.

After parting with my comrades in Bath county I stopped at Mrs. Lindsay's, mother of Captain James Lindsay of our brigade. Mrs. Lindsay introduced me to a minister (whose name I forget), assuring me he had information that she felt I should have, and adding that I could confer with this gentleman with perfect freedom as she knew him to be trustworthy, and I could depend on all he told me.

This gentleman gave me first information of the scheme of the "Sons of Liberty" to establish a "Northwestern Confederacy,"

428

CAPT. T. M. FREEMAN.

the first overt movement toward which would be the release of the Confederate prisoners by the Sons of Liberty with the aid of a band of Confederates then in Chicago and other points under the orders of Captain Hines. He stated that Hines had reporting to him some one hundred and twenty-five men, but that he needed all the additional Confederate soldiers he could get. He stated that there was to be a general conference of the officers of the Sons of Liberty in Chicago on the 22d of July, 1864 (then about a week off) at which all the details of the movement to be made some time in August were to be determined. He said Hines, as the representative of the Confederacy, would be at the conference. He also stated that he was informed that Hines was authorized by the Confederate Government to take command and control of the movements of all prisoners released. He urged upon me the necessity of Hines having with him as many old soldiers as possible and that I should go at once and report to him. He told me that he was engaged in getting as many of our boys as he could to go to Hines. He said, " If we succeed you will not need to do any recruiting in Kentucky; your boys will flock to the released army of Confederates in Illinois and Indiana at once; to help this movement to success was the quickest way to get all the scattered boys in Owen, Trimble and Carroll into the ranks again." As my orders stated that I could, if I thought it advisable, cross over the Ohio, I concluded to go. I went as soon as I could get to the railroad. I boarded the train at Kaiser's Station not far from Paris, Kentucky, and reported to Captain Hines at Chicago. This is how I became connected with this movement.

I found the information given me by the friend of Mrs. Lindsay correct. The conference was held at the time stated. I was not present but learned generally what took place and got acquainted with a number of the leading officers of the Sons of Liberty. I was initiated into this order (the only secret order I ever belonged to, except the Ku-Klux) by Judge Morris, at whose house I was concealed with Captain Hines. Before leaving Chicago, Colonel W. A. Boles (of Buena Vista fame) who was a major general in the Sons of Liberty organization, learning that I was in the adjutant general department of our command, stated to Captain Hines that he needed such an officer to assist him in organizing his men in Southwestern Indiana, and asked Hines to order me to go to Indiana with him.   This Hines did, and I went to French Lick Springs (Colonel Boles' residence), and was with him constantly till after the fifteenth of August, the time set at the Chicago conference for the attack on the prisons.

On leaving Chicago I carried a message from H. H. Dodd, who was the commander-in-chief of the Sons of Liberty for Indiana, to a Mr. Elliott, a leading spirit among the Sons of Liberty.   1 found Mr. Elliott to be a former Kentuckian from near Lawrenceburg; he knew a number of my relatives in that region.

After he became convinced that I was a Confederate, he was quite communicative.   He took me into the cellar or basement of his store—a large warehouse—and there he showed me what I would say was several wagon-loads of hand grenades or shells, which he told me were filled with Greek fire to be used in the attack on Camp Morton.   He also showed me the Greek fire in several different sized bottles; poured some on the stone floor of the cellar which, after a few seconds burst into flame.   He also took me in his buggy and we drove to the country and used several vials of the Greek fire, dashing it into some piles of driftwood in a creek bottom, which set the piles of drift afire.   He also drove me all around Camp Morton, which I reconnoitered closely, noting location of the roads and approaches to the prison, the entrances, location of the camp of the guard, and the battery of artillery bearing on the prison.   Later when I finally started back toward Kentucky to return to the army, Mr. Elliott furnished me with several bottles of the Greek fire to take back, and also gave me the formula for making the same.   (If Colonel Stoddard Johnston is still living he will tell you of the report I made through him as acting adjutant general to General Breckinridge at Wytheville, on arrival in Virginia.   I know he remembers about it, for we talked it over when he was at Fort Worth, some fifteen or sixteen years ago.)

As I stated before I was with Colonel Boles till after the fifteenth of August.   I found him a man of most sterling qualities.   He was also a magnificent specimen of manhood, over six feet high, broad-shouldered, straight as an arrow, very soldierly in bearing, with eyes and features which bespoke the greatest firmness and courage.   He was a man of fine attainments and wide information, and in all a most striking character.   He was as true to the South as you or I, and would certainly have been in our ranks had he not believed that he could be of more service where he was. His wife, a New Orleans lady, was just as devoted to the South as was Colonel Boles. He was no mere adventurer or even an ordinary citizen, but a man of large wealth and as far as I could judge, the leading citizen of that whole section of country, and a man of the greatest influence throughout Southwestern Indiana.

While I was there, daily, men (Sons of Liberty) were coming to the Springs, and reporting full organized companies ready for service at his call. I assure you I was astonished at the preparations he was making, and that so perfectly and quickly. He was the owner and proprietor of a health resort (the French Lick Springs).

It was the height of the reason, the place was full of visitors, and in the midst of all this company, this grand old man was perfecting his arrangements, had collected at various points quantities of arms and ammunition, and had two pieces of artillery concealed. All this I had from his own lips, and I fully believe. One day there appeared a stranger who excited my suspicions. You see I was traveling those days, as the saying is, with a halter around my neck; I "kinder" sized him up for a detective, but the old colonel relieved my anxiety when I spoke to him about it. Said he, " That man, Freeman, is a messenger of mine. He is direct from Richmond here, and I may add, direct from President Davis. I maintain a direct communication with Mr. Davis, independent of the Sons of Liberty, independent of Captain Hines and everybody else. Mr. Davis has assured me that he hopes to enter Kentucky with a strong force under one of his best generals in September, or maybe later, and in case our move on the prisons is successful, and the Sons of Liberty rally, as expected, to the twenty-five or thirty thousand released Confederates, the immediate invasion of Kentucky and the capture of Louisville and Cincinnati by Southern troops is, I believe absolutely certain. I have the utmost confidence in Mr. Davis's assurance." " But," he added, " even though the prisoners are not released and the Sons of Liberty fail to meet our expectations, if a Southern army appear in Kentucky this fall, I shall cross the Ohio river with the men I can control, I am safe in saying several thouand, and cast my lot with my Southern friends."

This messenger left in a day or two as quickly as he came. Matters went on very favorably till the morning of the 11th of August, when Colonel Boles ordered me to take the train to

Indianapolis and report to H. H. Dodd, the commander-in-chief of the order for Indiana; that he (Boles) was ready to move, at a moment's notice, on New Albany (the point which it had been arranged he should attack), with five thousand men and two pieces of artillery.   Arriving in Indianapolis about nightfall, I went after supper to Dodd's residence; his house was a few feet back from the sidewalk; I passed his parlor windows which were open; as I approached the front gate Dodd and two or three other men were in the parlor. He saw and recognized me and met me at the gate.   Without a word he took me by the hand and led me back to the sidewalk.   There I delivered Colonel Boles' message as above.   Dodd replied, "Well, it is too late; within the last twenty-four hours we have been betrayed by a member of our order from New Albany; the government knows all our plans. They are rushing in reinforcements to the prison guards as rapidly as possible.   Everything is known.   We are all spotted.   The United States marshal (who is a brother-in-law of mine) is in my parlor now, and I expect to be arrested before he leaves the house." (And he was.)   "You must get out of the city as quickly as possible and go back to Boles and tell him the whole plan must be indefinitely postponed."   Next morning I returned to Colonel Boles.   When I delivered Dodd's message to Boles he was the maddest man I ever saw.   He swore a little, under provocation,   and with an oath he swore that Dodd was the damnedest idiot on the "footstool."   "The moment he found we were betrayed, instead of postponing the matter he should have ordered the attack at once. We were better prepared than they were.   He has thrown away the best chance we will ever have."   I think Boles took the right view.   And I believe now as he believed then, that we would have been successful.   I know we would had all the Sons of Liberty had the grit and backbone of Colonel Boles. But, as he remarked, there were too many political soldiers in the Sons of Liberty, and it is about as hard to make a real soldier out of a politician as a "silk purse out of a sow's ear."

As a matter of course, things were at a standstill after this unfortunate set-back.   There was "nothing doing" at the Springs, and I told the old colonel I could not see that I could be of any service to him in the present condition of affairs, and I would like to rejoin Captain Hines in Chicago.   To this he consented, and I went to Chicago.   I found that Hines agreed exactly with

Boles as to the course Dodd should have taken. And he said, "Freeman, Boles is the only soldier among the whole lot."

I remained with Captain Hines at Judge Morris's some time, till finally he requested me to accompany him to Toronto, Canada, where he went to confer with the Confederate commissioners, Thompson, Clay and Holcombe. The second day after we got there, Captain Hines notified me I was to bear a message to Colonel Boles. This message I always supposed was the result of this conference between the commissioners and Hines, but I never knew the purport of it.

I went at once to Colonel Boles and then back to Chicago where I found Hines. And here I remained till the meeting of the Democratic convention which nominated McClellan for President. This was the date set for the second attempt on the prisons.

I always supposed that the setting of this date was one of the results of Hines's conference with our commissioners at Toronto. But the enemy evidently got wind of it, and by the time the convention was under way, the guards at Camp Douglas were increased from fifteen hundred to ten thousand men, with artillery in proportion. This display had its effect upon the leaders of the Sons of Liberty, and the movement was again deferred. They then hinged their hopes upon a division they predicted in the resistance of the draft ordered for some time in September, I think. But the expected resistance did not occur, except possibly in New York and a few other places, and then everything was for the time being "in the air." Shortly after the Democratic convention, Captain Hines considered it advisable to leave Chicago.

He went to Southern Illinois. By agreement I went to French Lick Springs. I soon found that Colonel Boles was beginning to despair of anything being done by the Sons of Liberty, and it was daily becoming evident that Mr. Davis could not spare any force to invade Kentucky though the information was that Kentucky would join us in force.

I at last said to the colonel that I wanted to return to the army, and that I wanted to hunt up Captain Hines and get him to order me to return. He interposed no objection. I really think he had before this despaired of anything being accomplished. I found Captain Hines at Vandalia, Illinois. When I expressed my opinion of the outlook and wish to return to Virginia, he said, "Freeman, like yourself, I have no faith in anything being done.

There are too many politicians in this order; you can consider yourself under orders to return to your command, and I would go too if I could; but my orders keep me here, and I have got to see the thing out to the bitter end. And I really never expect to come out of the thing alive."

I returned to Owen county, Kentucky, taking with me three young men, two of them citizens of Chicago. I soon gathered in the hills of old Owen about one hundred and fifty men, somewhere about a third of whom were members of my old regiment, Fourth Kentucky Cavalry. With these boys I started from Owen, 20th of October, 1864. We captured a train on the Kentucky Central as we crossed it, a short distance west of Cynthiana; had quite a spirited little affair with the Yanks near Olympia or Mud Lick Springs. The enemy outnumbered us somewhat, and came especially to take "us out of the wet." But those Fourth Kentucky Boys, with their side partners, the new recruits, astonished the Yanks (and me too), for they " wiped the earth up with them." After about a fifteen minutes' scrap, there wasn't a Yank to be seen, except a bunch of prisoners who could not run fast enough to get away. This little affair was, I believe, the last combat in Kentucky. I lost some horses, but no men, and captured more horses than I lost. Reported at General Breckinridge's headquarters without the loss of a man; and this ended my connection with the Sons of · Liberty and their scheme to establish a Northwestern Confederacy, with the released Confederates as a nucleus.

I understand that there are some who pronounce all statements as to the existence of the extent of this conspiracy as romance. Well, I don't much blame any one who knew little or nothing about the matter for so declaring. But I saw and heard enough from others as worthy of belief as the above mentioned doubters, to believe fully that had there been even half a dozen as military men as Colonel Boles among the leaders of the Sons of Liberty, the whole theater of war would have been transferred to Ohio, Indiana and Illinois in the fall of 1864, and the final issue would have been a Southern, a Northwestern, and an Eastern Confederacy.

In writing these statements I have mentioned the names of only a few persons, avoiding the use of any who might be offended at my taking such a liberty. Those I have mentioned I know were always proud of all they did toward helping their Southern friends, and will not be offended. I found also in writing the statement that it was most convenient to do so in the first person. I have not the slightest disposition to parade before the public any part I took in this matter, for it was slight, and really accidental.

Another thing before closing. I understand it has been claimed that another and not Hines, was the leader, as you might say, of the Confederates engaged in this matter. It is difficult to restrain my indignation.

When I met the minister at Mrs. Lindsay's, one of his strong arguments for my going to Chicago was that the Confederates were to be led by that brilliant, dashing officer, Captain Hines. Arriving in Chicago, I found it as he stated. Hines' relations with the Sons of Liberty and with the commissioners at Toronto, as I witnessed them, as well as the statements of Colonel Boles and others that he was the leader, would have satisfied me on that point. But Captain Hines's own statement to me would alone have been sufficient. He told me that his orders were direct from President Davis; that he was sent Northwest to co-operate in every way possible with the leaders of the Sons of Liberty, and that he was specially commissioned to take command of any and all Confederate prisoners that might be released. And if I had no other evidence than this statement of Captain Hines, I would believe it in the face of a score of pretenders, who, after his death have arisen and claimed that they, not Hines, were the leaders of the Confederates.

The denouement of this affair is well known. A final effort on the prisons was to have occurred the night of the presidential election in November, 1864. The night before, the Federals effected the capture of every Confederate soldier, except Hines then in Chicago.

Our old friend Colonel Henry St. Leger Grenfel, who was acting with us and had placed himself under Hines's orders, was one of the captured. Hines succeeded in reaching our army. Colonel Boles, after one or two unsuccessful attempts by the Federals, was finally surprised and captured by a cavalry force.

He, with two other Indianians, Humphries and Develin, were tried and sentenced to be shot. H. H. Dodd escaped after arrest to Canada.

Judge Morris and his noble wife, Charles Walsh, of Chicago,

and our comrade, St. Leger Grenfel, were all tried for conspiracy; and Captain Castleman (who was captured somewhere in Indiana).

You know St. Leger's hard fate. Judge Morris and wife, after months of confinement in McLean Barracks, were released. Charley Walsh served six months in Camp Chase pen, with Boles, Humphries and Develin, who had been surprised. I am always averse to appearing in print on any subject, but at General Johnson' urgent request, I write the above statement. I am ready to be qualified to every fact stated in the above, and were it not for the death of many, indeed a large majority of those familiar with the above facts and who were participants in them, I could establish everything as abundantly as could be required, and by people as creditable as any in the whole country. I have endeavored to be as brief as possible, but even after this extended statement, many matters have been omitted corroborative of the facts stated. If this hastily written statement is of interest, I do not regret the time taken writing it, but it has been hurriedly done.

There were four of us boys in the Confederate service. The oldest, Colonel D. C. Freeman raised a battalion of infantry while Bragg was in Kentucky, and served for some time with General Humphrey Marshall in West Virginia, but was finally transferred to General Joe Johnston's army. Before the close of the war he was compelled from broken health to resign and go to Southern Alabama.

The next oldest, Captain G. R. Freeman, commanded Company D, Twenty-third Texas Cavalry throughout the war. The next, Captain C. T. Freeman was orderly sergeant of Company A, Terry Rangers (Eighth Texas) till the battle of Shiloh where he received a wound which disabled him for over a year. Dr. Yandell, the surgeon general, discharged him, saying he would never be fit for service again, but he managed to get back to Texas, and about eighteen months after was made commissary of the Frontier Regiment, but finally he re-entered the cavalry and closed his service under Colonel "Rip Ford" in our final victory on the Rio Grande.

The youngest, the writer, joined the Second Kentucky Infantry, Company B, Colonel Roger Hanson's regiment. But after the capture of Donelson I escaped from the Yankees, and when the regiment was exchanged, was adjutant of Fourth Kentucky Cavalry (Giltner's regiment). About December, 1864, I was commanding Company A, of Major Bart. W. Jenkins' squadron of scouts, which position I held till the close. Went with General Duke to Charlotte, North Carolina, after Lee's surrender and was with him till, by order of the Secretary of War, General John C. Breckinridge, he disbanded his command at Woodstock, Georgia.

[Note.—I have a personal acquaintance with three of these Freeman brothers. One of them I knew for years in the city of Austin as a business man. He ranked high in the estimation of all who knew him. The second, who lives in the Bluegrass region of Kentucky, lost an arm in the Confederate service. The third, our correspondent, I have associated with on such a familiar footing as to know that he needs no endorsement as a gentleman and a scholar.—A. R. J.]

AFTER THE GREAT RAID.

NARRATIVE OF JOSIAH B. GATHRIGHT.

I.

On the sixth day of July, 1863, Morgan's command was well started on that extraordinary ride, the Indiana and Ohio raid. I was then first lieutenant of Captain J. Taylor Berry's company, Colonel Roy S. Cluke's regiment, Johnson's Brigade, Morgan's Division of Cavalry.

During the night of the above date, our regiment had reached Mt. Washington in Bullitt county. Here our company and Company D, Second Kentucky Cavalry (Duke's former regiment), First Lieutenant George B. Eastin commanding, were detached under command of Major William J. Davis of the staff, with instructions to make a detour around east of Louisville, cut communications between that city and Central Kentucky, make the greatest possible demonstration for our numbers to create the impression that the whole command was moving in that direction, and then to cross the Ohio where we could, and rejoin the command in Indiana.

It was night, but when any important move was on, the command never halted for night, and the battalion moved on rapidly through Jefferson, Builitt, Shelby, Oldham and Henry counties, everywhere leaving the impression that we were the advance guards of the command. This was to mask the movement of the main command to Brandenburg, which point had been selected for crossing the river, and it effectually deceived the enemy, as events hereafter related will show.

We visited Simpsonville, Shelbyville, Eminence, Smithfield,

438

LIEUT. JOS. B. GATHRIGHT.

Jericho and Sligo, and approached Westport on the Ohio with the view of crossing there, but we found that the enemy had anticipated us and had taken away or destroyed all craft of every sort. As the enemy's gunboats were encountered by us, as hereafter related, and the crossing of the main command at Brandenburg was not interfered with by them, we had evidently created the desired impression that the command itself was moving around above Louisville, and the destruction and removal of all craft along the river above Louisville showed apparently that the enemy was aware of Morgan's intention to cross the Ohio.

In the march the detachment came within a short distance of my home, and of course I seized the opportunity to ride by and see my parents. I arrived there about noon, and greatly to my pleasure, I found quite a number of the neighbors there assembled for dinner. Among them were several prominent Unionists, and I was gratified at this evidence that notwithstanding the great strain these old neighbors were still maintaining friendly social relations. These seemed as glad to see me as the Southern sympathizers, and all were completely surprised, for we had moved so steadily and rapidly that none of them knew we were in this part of the State.

Failing to find means for crossing at Westport, we moved towards Louisville, sending scouts to search for small craft along the river. Two small wood boats (flat-boats for carrying wood) were collected at the Barbour place opposite Twelve Mile Island, and we made a night march to that point. A few incidents of the night march are worth relating to show the condition of the men at this period of that most extraordinary ride. The last part of the march that night was over a "corduroy road"—a road made of poles cut to same length and laid close together upon the soft earth. Its uneven surface made the march over it very trying upon weary men and horses, and the noise of the hoofs clattering over the poles, could be heard in the stillness of night for more than a mile. I was in command of the rear guard on this march, and, though a confirmed insomniast, I went to sleep while riding at the head of the guard and my horse left the column and wandered off nearly a half mile . before I was aroused by being nearly unhorsed by the limb of a tree. I could not have known which way to ride but for the noise of the tramping hoofs on the corduroy road. Riding back I found that I had crossed a pretty

deep valley in my slumbers and when I reached my command and
took my place at the head of the guard, I found that no one had
noticed my involuntary absence, which   meant   that   though
they had kept the road, they also were practically asleep.
Had I not told it, no one would have known that under military
law I had become entitled to a court martial and a death sentence.
Other similar incidents occurred,—a member of my company falling from his saddle upon the road and not awaking until aroused
by his comrades and placed in the saddle again. The command
reached the river about daylight, and at once began to cross, one
boat being used to ply between the Kentucky shore and the Island,
and the other between the Island and the Indiana shore. By about 8
o'clock all had crossed to the Island except myself and the videttes,
(eight in number)—which I had posted to guard all approaches during the crossing. Calling these in, we rode down to the river to cross;
but just as we reached the bank, my attention was drawn to three
suspicious-looking steamers that had just turned a bend, and were
in full view only a short distance down the river. Watching them
intently for a few moments to determine their character, all doubt
was dispelled by puffs of white smoke from their decks towards the
Indiana shore, followed by the roar of artillery, and I knew that we
were cut off from our command.   A shout from the Island revealed
the fact that some of our men were still on the Island.   I learned
that about thirty-five had crossed to Indiana under Major Davis,
with Lieutenants Eastin and Hopkins. Quickly manning the boat, we
succeeded in making two turns to the island and back, but on the last
turn the boat narrowly escaped shots from the gunboats, which were
rapidly moving up, and further attempt at rescue would have been
folly. The rescue of the men being the chief object, the boat was on
each trip loaded with them to its full capacity, and this meant the
abandonment of horses, arms and accoutrements of every kind.
From some cause unknown to me, no commissioned officer was
among those rescued, and I found myself the only commissioned
officer, with eight men mounted and armed, and thirty-four men
without horses, arms or equipments of any kind. It was now about
half past nine of the morning; we were only nine miles by land from
Louisville and our presence, and perhaps our actual condition, known
to the enemy. I at once moved the men back to a high point on
the river hills, and, as the men belonged to different companies, proceeded to form a temporary company organization by appointing

the requisite number of officers. Believing that it would be a fatal mistake to disclose our condition by daylight marching, I decided to proceed by night marches only, and to take the chances of remaining where we were until nightfall. I sent messages to some residents of the vicinity, whom I knew to be friendly to our cause, requesting them to send in cooked food, and late in the afternoon, a nice old gentleman rode into our camp, bringing a bushel basket full of excellent food excellently prepared. We were hungry, and ate ravenously, but there was more than enough for us all. It was now growing dark and we fell into line and started on our march to the Confederacy, the nearest point then being Knoxville, Tennessee. Four of the mounted and armed men marched with me in advance, the thirty-four unarmed "infantry" following,, and the other four mounted men forming the rear guard. Just as we were passing out of our camp, the old gentleman (Mr. Frank Snowden) who had so kindly and bountifully supplied us, came rushing to my side and informed me that one of the men was on his horse—the horse upon which he had brought in the good dinner. I turned back with him and meeting the rider, or riders rather, for there were two on the horse, I ordered them to dismount and give Mr. Snowden his horse. They began to plead earnestly to be permitted to ride the horse for the night at least, promising to procure another horse and turn this one loose to return home. Under the circumstances, I could not possibly permit it, and told them they must give up the horse. The noble old man, however, could not resist their appeals, and he told them to ride on and turn loose his horse. But we soon found the task of procuring horses for the dismounted men more difficult than we had expected. I do not believe that nights were ever darker than these first few nights of our march, and the horses of the good Union men of that section, apparently knowing our preferences, had taken to the woods. We made frequent stops and sent to farms to get horses only to find the barns empty, and it was too dark either to find or catch a horse in the open fields. The men were almost exhausted and when a halt was made and a detail sent to a barn in search of horses, the remaining men would drop down in the fence corners and be so sound asleep by the time the detail returned, that it took some time to get them awake and started again. Chiefly from these causes the men who had taken Mr. Snowden's horse, did not turn him loose as promised, and I did not know of their failure to do so, until it was too late. I have always regarded this as about the meanest thing I ever knew one of Morgan's men to do, but the situation was a very trying one, and when I came to know this soldier, I found him to be a man of good character. On our first night's march we fortunately avoided an ambuscade that a company of home guards had prepared for us. They had taken position behind a church-yard fence skirting the road by which we were expected to come from the river. They were armed with shot guns loaded with slugs. Had we followed the usual route that night, this narrative would probably never have been written, for there is no weapon so deadly in a close ambuscade as a shot gun loaded with slugs.

On our second night's march we passed right through my father's farm, and near the residence, but I could not stop, for in the weary and demoralized condition of the men, I felt it incumbent upon me to be with them every moment. All the next day we were in camp within half a mile of the home of my sweetheart. I did not, however, leave camp to visit her, for the same reasons given above, and for the further reason that the discharge of the extra duties devolved upon me in our situation had left me but little time to get a little sleep, which the long fast made absolutely necessary if I was to keep going. That evening we broke camp a little earlier,—in fact a while before sundown. We were going right through her father's farm and right by the house. Perhaps I started early with the hope of getting at least a glimpse of her; anyhow we started earlier than we had been starting. We passed along through the farm and by the side of the house, and then through a gate that led to the open in front of the house. A young lady was standing upon the front stile. I said to the column "Move on," and wheeling my horse, I galloped up to the stile; it was her sister. Shaking hands without dismounting, and asking and answering a few hasty and eager questions, in the course of which she told me that her sister had ridden over to a neighbor's, I was just wheeling to ride on, when I saw her coming in full gallop, for she was a good horsewoman. I rode quickly to meet her, and after a hasty exchange of greetings and expression of pleasure at this accidental meeting after so long a time, I turned very reluctantly and galloped away calling back to her,—

"And steadfast keep in mind
The soldier-boy will ne'er forget,
The girl he left behind."

After the war (when I had established myself in successful busi-

ness as a result of knowledge obtained in the discharge of special
duties to which I was assigned in the latter part of the war, and
which will be specially mentioned in this narrative), this young lady
became my wife.

That night we reached a point on Salt river, near Taylors-
ville. By this time we had succeeded in mounting all the men,
but had found it impossible to get arms of any kind. As we were
lying in camp each day, it was desirable to have the most
secluded spots obtainable in each locality,, in order that our presence and our condition should be kept from the enemy. I had
therefore, from the beginning of the march, kept a continuous chain
of names of those to whom I could apply for information and direction, and so complete was this kept up that at no time during the
march was any question asked of any one except of those who had
been commended to me.

The next camp was in the Chaplin Hills, of Nelson county.
Reaching this vicinity before daylight, I halted at the house of Henry
Russell, a fine old farmer whom I knew to be a good Southerner,
and myself went to the door and roused him up. When he came
to the door I told him who we were and that I wanted him to dress
and mount his horse and guide us to the most suitable camping place
in the vicinity, where we could escape observation. The old gentleman was at once suspicious and doubtful as to our pretensions, and
declared he was a quiet, peaceful citizen who was minding his own
affairs and taking no part in war matters. I tried to assure him
that we were really Confederates, but he seemed to think it was a
scheme of the Yankees to inveigle him into the commission of an
overt act, and he continued to object. Seeing what was the real
trouble with him, I said, "Mr. Russell, you can not be held account-
able for what you are compelled to do; I order you to dress at
once and go with these guards to the stable. They will help you get
mounted and see that you report to me here in the road as quickly
as possible." This settled it,—the old gentleman soon appeared
mounted and ready to guide us, and in great good humor. He told
me he thought we were Yankees trying to entrap him, and he was
delighted when he became convinced that we were genuine. He
guided us to a delightful camping place near the Grigsby farm,
and we and our horses were bountifully fed that day. We had also
the pleasure of a visit from several pretty girls, not an uncommon
and always an agreeable event. There were in this body of men,

a few who evidently had never been subjected to proper or in fact any discipline, and others who were ambitious beyond their abilities or their deserts. I learned afterwards that four or five of these had agreed not to go out of the State, but to remain as guerrillas. I had no knowledge of this and heard no complaints from the men, and was therefore taken by surprise when the following incident occurred: We had just broken camp on Chaplin Hills, and had nearly reached the public road, when one of these rode up to my side at the head of the column and in a somewhat insolent tone demanded to know my plans, saying that I had not consulted them about these and that many of the men were dissatisfied, and they must be informed as to what route I proposed to take and where I proposed to go. This act was so unexpected and so extraordinary, that I lost my self-control for a moment, and denouncing him, I drew my pistol to shoot him, but quickly recovering my equilibrium, I ordered him to the rear of the column and decided to at once develop and discard any mutinous members of the company, knowing that they were only a source of weakness, and that without resorting to summary methods, I could not discipline them otherwise than by requiring good soldiers to lose much needed rest to guard the unruly ones. So at once wheeling my horse, I ordered the company to form in a circle, and riding into the circle, made this little speech which I still remember almost word for word because this little painful incident has so often recurred to me: "Soldiers! Four days ago we were cut off at the Ohio river, only nine miles from Louisville—the enemy's headquarters. Thirty-four or five of you were rescued from the Island without horses, arms, or equipments of any kind. We have now marched more than one hundred miles through the enemy's lines; you are all now well-mounted, and we have not lost a man. No man who is a soldier would be dissatisfied, disheartened, or disappointed after what we have accomplished. As the only commissioned officer left on this side of the river, it is my duty to command you, and to lead you back if possible to the Confederate lines. Under present conditions, I can not compel you to go through the lines against your will, and I will not further exhaust good soldiers by having them stand guard over insubordinate ones. When I have finished speaking, I shall wheel my horse and resume the march and shall go through to the Confederate lines or get killed or captured in the attempt. All those who wish to follow me will fall in column behind me, but I want no man to follow me from this point who has not the courage and the sense of duty to follow me to the end." Then wheeling my horse I rode away, and every man promptly fell in line and followed. The attempt to disorganize and scatter the company had completely failed.

In this connection I will state that during this march through the lines, quite a number of men came into our camp who stated that they had been wounded and left during some former Confederate inroad into the State, or had been "cut off" and were waiting for an opportunity to go through the lines. In every instance I offered to take them with me, though they were without arms, but not one of them reported back to go with us, and I think they were all skulkers if not deserters. In each case I learned that they were being harbored by some good Southern sympathizer who thought he was doing the cause good service, but was really exposing himself and his family to more danger than these recreants would have encountered in going through the lines to their commands. Perhaps it was just as well; for a soldier that would remain "cut off" under the conditions then existing was not worth issuing rations to.

We continued our night marches after the same plans without incident worthy of note, until we reached the Cumberland river at Burkesville. We had crossed here on previous expeditions, but not at night. We managed to obtain two skiffs and getting a small beacon light on the other shore, we crossed the men in the skiffs, the horses swimming beside them. A continuance of our great good luck found us in due time across the Clinch river, not far from Knoxville and safe within Confederate lines, and for the first time in more than a fortnight we felt that we could take a rest.

In looking back over these events, it appears to me discreditable to the enemy that we were able to elude them and were permitted to march through their lines from a point on the Ohio river above Louisville to the vicinity of Knoxville, Tenn., and that too with so helpless a force. Every soldier knows that the thirty odd unarmed men were not only of no advantage, but were a serious source of weakness; in case we were attacked, those without means of resistance would at once seek safety in flight, and that would have great tendency to confuse, demoralize, and stampede the armed men, and their horses as well. Indeed I can yet recall that when the gunboats on the Ohio opened fire, and I realized that I was cut off with only my eight videttes, a feeling akin to elation came over me, for I felt that I could go almost anywhere with that squad, experts in fighting or running as the occasion demanded. But after the rescue from the Island, and I found thirty-four unarmed and un-mounted men added to my little squad with no other officer and no organization, I realized that the situation was entirely changed, and that I had a task before me.　Still I believe that at no time did I lack confidence in our ability to get through (although it is diffi-cult in looking back, to see upon what that confidence was founded); but that confidence was not felt by the most of the men, which only made my task greater.

The day after crossing the Clinch river, I left the men in camp and rode to Knoxville and reported to General Buckner. He in-structed me to remain in camp where we were until further orders, and in a few days he notified me that General Adam R. Johnson with a portion of Morgan's command had arrived at Morristown, East Tennessee, and ordered me to report with my company to General Johnson.

II.

Arriving at Morristown, East Tennessee, I reported with my com-pany to General Adam R. Johnson, who, as before stated, had es-caped from Ohio with about 300 men. The camp was on the waters of the Nolichucky, in a productive region, and we had a good sup-ply of food and forage. With the exception of General Johnson and Lieutenant Colonel Bob Martin, there was no officer present of higher rank than that of captain. There was not a complete com-pany organization, the men present representing every regiment and almost every company in Morgan's command. A reorganization was necessary, and two battalions were formed of those who were mounted, commanded by Captains Kirkpatrick and Dortch. One company was formed of all members of the 8th Kentucky, Colonel Cluke's Regiment, and of the 10th Kentucky, Colonel Johnson's Regiment, and I was as ranking officer placed in command of it. Most of the horses of the command were in bad condition, and many of the men were without horses, arms or accoutrements.

An effort was being made in some quarters to dismount the command upon the plea that it would be impossible to mount and properly equip these men, and I regret to say that this scheme was abetted by one regimental officer of the command who, however, was not then with us. It was necessary for General Johnson to go to Richmond to defeat this scheme, and he succeeded in doing so, pledging his word to the war department that he would have 500 mounted and equipped men ready for service within ninety days.

Within sixty days we received orders to join General Bragg in North Georgia, and General Johnson reinforced him with more than five hundred effective cavalry.

The march from Morristown to Bragg's army in Georgia was without incident worthy of note. About the third day after our arrival, we received orders to prepare several days rations, and we knew that meant that there was going to be "something doing." The next day we were on the march toward the enemy and the great battle on the Chickamauga.

We had been placed in Forrest's division, which suited us exactly, and Forrest had the right wing of the advancing army. Our battalion was on the extreme right. We became engaged with Federal cavalry in the afternoon of the 19th of September, the fight beginning in a woods, and drove the enemy from this and up over a hill partly cleared of timber into an open field. When I reached the crest of the hill with my company the enemy's cavalry had reformed and were apparently about to charge. They were just across the narrow open field, and just behind them was a line of trees and undergrowth that plainly outlined the river. As soon as we reached the crest however, we opened fire again at pretty close range, and they immediately moved in column by the left and retreated across the river.

Colonel Bob Martin in command, and General Forrest, both rode behind our lines during the fight, cheering and encouraging the men in gallant style. Reforming our line we also crossed the bridge, without resistance from the enemy, and deploying moved forward through the apparently endless forest. We had orders to keep in touch with the command on our left, but I have an impression that the left of our line did not faithfully carry out this instruction. When we had penetrated the forest for perhaps a mile, without again encountering the enemy, firing was heard in our rear, and apparently right in the direction of the bridge over which we had just crossed. I was ordered by the commanding officer to take an escort and find out what that firing in our rear meant. Taking six of my company I rode, or attempted to ride back to the bridge. It was now about sundown, and rapidly growing dark in the dense forest. When we had reached a point near the bridge, as I supposed, we heard the sharp cry of "Halt," very close to us, and by the dim light could just discover a considerable body of cavalry in front of us and not over fifty feet from us.

Their commanding officer had the advantage of having the sunset behind him and could see us more plainly than we could see them, and they may have been at halt when we approached and could judge our numbers by the noise we made. He seemed, anyhow, to know the smallness of our squad, for he peremptorily ordered us to come in and surrender or be shot to pieces. I declined the invitation telling him that I would do nothing of the kind. Believing, however, that they were Confederate cavalry, I told him I would send one man in to see who they were. One of my escort at once rode to my side and offered to go in. I said in low tones to him, "Ride in and if they are Yankees, remove your hat the instant you discover that fact." He started and I was watching him, as closely and well as the darkness would permit, to see if he doffed his hat, but before he reached the officer my escort suddenly made a lateral dash out through the woods, leaving me alone in the road. I afterwards learned that one of the men had caught sight of the tall conical hat of one of the troopers in front of us, and knowing by this that they were Yankee cavalry, he whispered the fact to his comrades, and they all made a sudden dash out through the woods to avoid the volley which they thought would quickly follow the discovery that we were Confederates.

Intently watching my man I did not know the cause of this stampede and, thinking it only that abundant caution which sometimes prompts even very good soldiers to take an early start for safety, I remained watching his movements until he reached the officer. He had not removed his hat and I might have been deceived, but after a few words in undertone between them, the officer in still more lurid terms than before, ordered me to come in at once or take the consequences. The undertone conversation followed by the peremptory order left no doubt that my man had disobeyed orders in failing to remove his hat, and that he was actually betraying me.

I may say here that this suspicion was subsequently confirmed: about eighteen months after, when the war was over and I was on my way home, I saw this man at a stage-station in Kentucky near his home, and was told he had taken the oath and had been at home a long time.

Putting spurs to my horse I dashed at full speed out through the woods in the direction my men had taken. No volley was fired, and I supposed the enemy was pursuing, but the ground in the dense woods was covered with dry leaves and small brush, and the plunging of my horse through these made so much noise that I could hear nothing else. Riding straight ahead at about right angles to the road I had left, I came suddenly and unexpectedly square up against a tall rail fence with an open cornfield beyond. The fence was only about one hundred and fifty yards from the road, and practically parallel with it and I at once decided to make my horse take the fence rather than follow it in either direction. Riding straight into an angle of the fence, I threw myself on my horse's neck, and using both hands, threw off the top rails and gave him the spur. Rearing as if to leap the fence, my horse, a recent capture, came down on the fence with one foreleg on each side. I knew he was dead-locked, but there was nothing to do but give him the spur again, for there was no time for dallying. I gave it promptly and sharply, but his best effort only sent us rolling over into the field.

Neither was hurt in the fall, however, and I was instantly on my feet rallying my horse. He attempted to rise, but in the fall had thrown a leg through the bridle rein and this threw him back to the ground again. Not stopping to look or listen for the enemy, I sprang forward and quickly, though with some difficulty, releasing his foot from the rein, soon had him on his feet again. In the tumble however, the saddle had slipped back from the withers and turned half way down the side of the horse. Still not taking time to look or listen, I thrust the saddle back upon the horse and attempted to spring into it. My horse was excited, however, and sprang forward at the instant, with the result that the saddle turned and I was thrown back to the ground, dragging the saddle completely around under the body of the horse.

Knowing now that the saddle could not be gotten upon the withers and properly secured without ungirthing it, I stopped for the first time to look and listen for the enemy. Not hearing any sound in the woods, nor seeing any one, I took off my saddle, replaced it securely, and mounting rode leisurely across the field, debating what I should do. On my right a narrowed part of the field extended about three hundred yards, and the woods which I had just left extended all around this to a point on the opposite side, almost in front of me. I rode directly across to this corner of the woods, and when I reached it, thought I heard the tramp of horses up in the woods. Had the enemy circled around the field to cut me off or were these my own men?

I wanted to get my men together, so dismounting, I noiselessly opened the fence, as well to afford an exit in case of need as an entrance, and rode carefully along a path that led up toward the top of a hill. It was now pretty dark, but when I came near the top of the hill I saw outlined against the sky several mounted men, some distance apart, sitting motionless on their horses, and apparently waiting for or watching me. And now again the question was, are these friends or enemies awaiting me, and how shall I find out with a chance of escape if they are enemies? I decided on a plan and riding still closer to them and turning my horse a half-wheel to the left, so that my pistol arm would be toward them and my horse could complete the wheel quickly, I called in quick, sharp tones, "Vincent"—the name of one of my escort. I thought this would disclose me to my own men, but would have no meaning to the enemy. To my great relief Vincent answered, and I was again with my escort. But where were we? We had just ridden right into the enemy, apparently in force, right on the ground as we thought which our line had passed over only a little while before without finding any enemy.

I decided that the best thing to do was to get my little squad back across the Chickamauga for the night and hunt my command by daylight. But the enemy we had just run into were as I thought right near the bridge on which we had crossed, and I had heard that it was difficult to ford the stream on account of its very muddy bed. However, from the top of the hill we were on we could see the outlining trees, showing that the river was not far away, and we rode directly to it. The banks were low and flat on that side, but it could be seen that the other bank was a steep, wooded bluff. Was the stream fordable at this point, and could we get up that bluff with our horses?

I decided to make the test myself, and ordering the squad to remain, I rode into the river and carefully made my way across, finding however that when I had reached the other shore my horse was still waist-deep in water. By climbing over his head and with the aid of a small tree which stood on the very brink, I succeeded in landing, and began to explore the bluff. I found it thickly covered with small undergrowth and vines, but luckily a pig path led right up through the bushes at that point, and clambering up this I reached the terrace above the bluff and found myself in a public road. I could see numerous camp-fires starting up only a few hundred yards distant, but whose? Turning back I took my knife and cut away the small branches and vines overhanging the pig-path to enable our horses to pass up. The cliff from the water's edge to the terrace above was very steep, too steep for horses to climb it unaided, but I made up my mind to try it and ordered two men to cross over. My horse was still standing in the water hitched to the small tree mentioned above and the water was between three and four feet deep at the very edge. Could a horse plunge out of this pool and climb that acclivity? Certainly not, I thought, unless aided; so, when the two men reached the bank I told the foremost one to land as I had done, bringing the bridle-rein over the horse's head, and I assisted him in doing so. Then I told him to aid his horse, when started, by pulling with all his strength on the rein with one hand while seizing limbs and bushes with the other, and thus to clamber up the path as fast as possible.

Planting myself against the small tree at the margin, I ordered the other man to force the horse to a leap. The horse had little inclination to make the plunge and had to be forced to it. When he made the plunge, landing on his knees, with my back braced against the small tree, I threw myself against his hip, bracing him with all my strength while the man above was pulling on the rein with all his force. We thus prevented the horse from sliding or falling back into the water and enabled him to recover his limbs for another plunge, and the horse after a great struggle successfully made the ascent.

The same plan was followed until all the horses but my own had been safely landed. Each horse, however, as he sprang from the water had added something to the wet and slippery condition of the bank and thus had made the ascent more difficult; but each man as landed was added to the "bracers," so that each succeeding horse had one more to assist him. Meantime my own horse had been standing in the water hitched to the tree which I had been so vigorously using as a base of operations. He had been a close observer of all the desperate struggles of his comrades and the sight seemed to have somewhat unnerved him. Besides, I had been so busy and so well satisfied with our success with the other horses, that I had overlooked the fact that there would be no one behind my horse to make him take the leap. When I unhitched him and tried to get him to do this, he would not budge. We had made repeated ineffectual efforts and had almost despaired of getting him to make the plunge without some one going into the deep pool, when suddenly he made the leap out of the water. Being taken somewhat by surprise, we did not afford him our best support. The result was that the horse came to the ground several times, finally making the ascent, but in his violent struggles had left the saddle behind. The question now was where to go. There were numerous campfires on our right only a few hundred yards distant, but I was by no means sure that they were those of Confederates and I decided to wait till daylight to find my command Across the road was a cornfield extending up the hill as far as we could see by night, and beyond it to our left was a high timbered knob plainly outlined against the sky.

We made our way through this field, very rocky and rough, to the top of this knob and camped for the night without unsaddling, however, or building any camp-fire. During the night one of the men who was sleeping close to me aroused me by shaking me, and whispered that there was a lot of soldiers out there, pointing in a certain direction. "Don't you see them right there?" said he, excitedly, but in whispered tones. "No," said I, "I don't see anybody." "Can't you see them standing right yonder?" said he. Still I could not see any men in that direction, and as we were so high above surrounding objects that our horizon in that direction had the sky for a background, I could see plainly that no one was there and succeeded in convincing him that he had been dreaming.

We were up and in the saddle early next morning trying to find out "where we were at." Before mounting, I sent a man to a fence near by, next to the open, with instructions to climb as high as possible and survey our surroundings.

He reported seeing a mixed body of mounted men passing along a road to the south of us, part of them being in Confederate and part in Federal uniform. These were evidently prisoners and their guards, but at the distance it could not be made out which were the prisoners and which the guards.

Riding down from our lofty perch and making inquiry of citizens, we ascertained that we were on Confederate ground and soon found the place where our battalion had camped the night before. They were already up and gone, however, and we hunted up headquarters to find out to what part of the field they had been ordered. It would be a tedious story to tell of the many visits we made to different corps, division and brigade commanders to get the desired information, only to find after long rides that in each case when I received any directions they proved incorrect. Suffice it to say that I spent the entire day in hard riding from one point to another of our lines without finding my command.

This will doubtless seem strange to those who have not had occasion or opportunity to know the great extent of territory covered or operated over by two such armies as those that met at Chickamauga, and my experience will give some little idea of the great difficulty a commanding officer must encounter in keeping in touch with and efficiently handling even the large units of such armies in such extensive battle-fields as this. I had ridden all day in vain and at night I crossed back over the Chickamauga to go into camp with my little squad.

Riding a short distance up the stream, I saw a body of cavalry going into camp off to the right of the road, and as I was passing I heard the name of one of my company called aloud in the camp, and thus at last I stumbled upon my command.

The battle of this day had begun early and at times the fighting was terrific and the rattle and roar of the guns something awful. I was at some time during the day on almost every part of the field, from our center to our right, and had an unusual opportunity of watching the struggle. At one time I rode apparently entirely around the left wing of the enemy, having been told that Forrest could be found in that direction. I did not find him nor did I encounter any Federals, and it seemed to me that the situation afforded a fine opening for a flank attack. Had Bragg known the situation on this flank and had thrown a good division or more on the flank and rear of the enemy's left wing, I believe that day's fight would have ended the struggle on that field.

On this second day of the battle when the roar of the hundreds of cannon was something awful, and the rattle of tens and tens of thousands of small arms swelled through the woods into an uproar almost as deafening as that of the artillery, I was passing by a farm-house just behind where the battle was thickest. The farmer's wife was standing alone in the front yard listening to this tumultuous uproar, the like of which, perhaps, no woman had ever before heard. She called to me and eagerly asked me how the battle was going. When I had replied, she told me she had six sons and that they were all over there in the battle. Though showing a very earnest concern as to how the battle was going, she was perfectly calm and collected, and I have thought exhibited more nerve than any woman I have ever known.

Only those who have heard the awful turmoil and incessant roar of a great battle can form any conception of the awe-inspiring effect of listening close at hand to such a struggle as that of the second day's battle of Chickamauga. Only those accustomed to it can feel otherwise, I imagine, than that very few of those engaged can escape in such a maelstrom of destruction. It is awe-inspiring to be near the crater of a Vesuvius, to hear the incessant hissings, rumblings, and explosions; but the noises of ten thousand craters in eruption would scarcely equal that of Chickamauga. Yet this Georgia mother, within half a mile of the thickest of the battle, listened earnestly but calmly to this awful uproar, as of hell literally turned loose on earth, though every one of her six sons, from her first to her youngest-born, was just over there in it, and she knew that they were in it. War may said to be harder on women than on men, but the God of battles usually most mercifully spares them such ordeals as this. The battle was renewed the third day all along the line, our forces taking the initiative.

The enemy resisted stubbornly and for the most part successfully during the morning, but the assaults upon them were stubbornly and persistently renewed until near night, when their whole line gave way, broken, and the greater part of it demoralized.

The next day our battalion under Colonel Martin went on a scouting expedition towards Chattanooga. We drove in some of the enemy's cavalry and approached the city almost near enough to look down into it.. It was on this day that Forrest sent urgent messages to General Bragg begging him to move on the demoralized enemy. This Bragg failed to do and lost one of the great opportunities of the war.

The writer has since the war talked with many Federal officers and soldiers who were at Chickamauga, and in every instance they have said that the greater part of Rosecrans's army was a demoralized and confused mob and that Chattanooga and surroundings were so congested with these remnants, stragglers, wagons, etc., that it would have been impossible for any order to have been brought out of this chaos had our army promptly moved against them.

General Forrest took occasion to compliment our two battalions for their gallant conduct on this field; and it was no empty or unearned compliment, for Morgan's men promptly and effectually accomplished each time everything they were sent in to do.

In his report of this battle, General Bragg explains his failure to follow up his advantage by stating that his supplies were greatly reduced and his transportation not sufficient to subsist his army at any advanced position. This might have been good reason for not advancing against an unbeaten enemy, but the Federal army had been on the defense for three days of hard fighting, and had been finally driven from the field badly demoralized and disorganized.

General Bragg certainly knew this and must have known the enormous advantage of assailing troops in that condition. Had he vigorously pressed the enemy on this fourth day with even half his army, there is every reason to believe that the Federal army would have been destroyed, and Bragg had more than that number still in condition to do good fighting. The distance was so short that nothing more than extraordinary effort was necessary to supply the advanced force from the same base that was supplying it at Chickamauga. The advancing force might have had to encounter severe privation for several days, but Southern soldiers always willingly submitted to this when something was to be accomplished by it.

The fact is that the war had been almost fought to a finish before many of the old trained martinets of the army learned that they could make a move without taking headquarter-wagons and dress-parade suits with them. The great successes of Forrest, Morgan, Johnson, Duke and others, were largely achieved by discarding all transportation except for ammunition, taking chances of obtaining subsistence and putting horses and men to the utmost of their endurance. Morgan's command not only discarded the usual company-wagon used for carrying tents, cooking utensils, etc., but never used tents from the beginning; and, as time brought experience, actually discarded their cooking utensils when entering upon any important movement.

Neither of these successful leaders would halt a column to eat, sleep or rest when there was any emergency on, or when time was an element of success. A soldier animated by the true spirit and a horse of good blood may break down from long continued lack of food and rest, but on less than half rations of food, and with little rest, they will last through the period of almost any emergency and promptly recuperate when it is past. Had therefore the command of Bragg's army fallen to Forrest on that fourth day, when he was sending urgent messages to Bragg beseeching him to move on, there would have been no lack of any necessary transportation. Many army wagons might have carried loads the like of which they were unaccustomed to, and many farm wagons might have suddenly gotten into the game, but in any event the army would have followed promptly and relentlessly upon the heels of the enemy, giving them no chance to mend the morale or the organization of their beaten and disorganized army.

Had this been done there is good reason to believe that their entire army would have been destroyed or captured; the battles of Lookout Mountain and Missionary Ridge would never have been fought, and Sherman would never have marched to the sea.

Soon after the battle of Chickamauga our battalion under Colonel Martin was ordered into East Tennessee with General Forrest, and I was never again with the army of Tennessee.

But I have heard from many of my old comrades who remained with that army, that the weak defense made by it at Lookout Mountain and Missionary Ridge was the result of loss of confidence in the commanding officer, largely caused by the failure to reap any advantage from the decisive victory at Chickamauga. Old soldiers are the most practical of men. They fight only for results and they will not fight tenaciously if they know in advance that results if achieved will be thrown away.

Who can contemplate the spectacle of that army under Bragg driven from such strongholds as Lookout Mountain and Missionary Ridge without serious loss to the enemy, and then under Johnston standing like a wall in the path of Sherman, repulsing every attack and never driven from any position nor abandoning any position except at the command of its officers, and not realize what a costly curse Bragg had been to the cause of the Confederacy. This is meant only as a criticism not as condemnation. General Bragg was a fine organizer and disciplinarian, but as commander in the field he was an utter failure.

As before stated our battalion went with Forrest into East Tennessee. We were camped for a time at each of the three places,

Cleveland, Athens and Sweetwater, finally reaching the vicinity of Knoxville.

While at Cleveland I was ordered to move with my company up into the mountainous section toward the North Carolina line, and disperse a lot of bushwackers and disloyalists who were organizing and making trouble up there. We effectually scattered them, but they were so alert that we succeeded only in bringing back two prisoners.

The barking of dogs revealed our approach to their rendezvous and enabled most of them to escape.

Longstreet had been sent to re-capture Knoxville. This was another mistake. Had Bragg used his whole army against Chattanooga with reasonable promptness and vigor, its capture would almost certainly have been the result, and then Knoxville would have been ours without the asking. But Bragg divided his forces, laid weak and tardy siege to two cities, giving the enemy time to bring from long distances sufficient force, and was defeated and driven away from both.

It may seem incredible, but it is a fact that our battalion had been detached by Forrest from his command and sent to Longstreet, to circumvent a settled purpose of General Bragg to dismount Morgan's men and put them into infantry commands. Think of these restless and intrepid young Kentuckians, these incomparable riders, who would with enthusiasm remain a week in the saddle without a regular ration or an allotted moment for sleep; who could ride hundred of miles through the enemy's lines, and at every point be the first to announce their coming; think of these men being taken off their own horses and put in an infantry camp to die of ennui or of dry rot.

Yet such was General Bragg's purpose, and it required all the skill and influence of General Breckinridge, General Forrest and General A. R. Johnson to defeat it. General Johnson about this time made more than one visit to headquarters at Richmond to prevent the consummmation of this purpose. When it is remembered that General Morgan''s command furnished their own mounts and particularly all their equipments of every kind, and turned over to the government captured equipments and supplies far in excess of all obtained from the government; that the command at no time numbered more than about two thousand men, and that it required more than one-third of all the forces of the enemy opposing Bragg to keep open their communications and protect their line of supplies, and that, notwithstanding this, Morgan's command repeatedly broke their lines of communication, destroyed their railroads, bridges and telegraph lines; destroyed millions of dollars worth of their supplies, and killed, wounded and captured in many of its expeditions a number of the enemy greater than the total number of men in the command; when all this is borne in mind, this purpose of Bragg to dismount the command is wholly inexplicable. The writer believes that if complete records could be had, they would show that up to that period, Morgan's command had inflicted as much damage upon the enemy as had all the infantry in General Bragg's command. This is no reflection or criticism upon the officers and men of his command. They doubtless accomplished all that their opportunities permitted. But there is no doubt that the Southern soldier was at his best when in the saddle. The rapid movement, the dash, the opportunity for adventure, were all suited to his nature and he was equal to it all.

General Sherman states in his memoirs that he could easily manage our infantry, but not our ubiquitous cavalry—and it may be said that General Sherman seldom had to deal with the best of our cavalry commands; with some of the very best, never at all.

But General Bragg should have never been other than an inspector general. He was as before said a martinet, a good organizer and disciplinarian, but his military capabilities ended there. Had the Kentucky campaign ended his career as commander, as it should have done, the story of the army of Tennessee would have been quite different.

He much overrated the value of discipline when applied to Southern soldiers. These were full of confident self-reliance, ready for any initiative without waiting for command or asking leave; acknowledging no superior and calling no man master. If such men could be thoroughly disciplined, they would be like fine steel with the temper drawn. Severe repression of their individuality might make orderly camps, but it would take away that " esprit de meme " which, in the field is valuable next to " esprit de corps."

When our battalion was near Knoxville, I was again sent with my company to capture or disperse some bushwhackers who lived in a rough and rocky section out towards the mountains. They had just fired into a squad of our men, wounding one of them. We rode rapidly into their section and, deploying as skirmishers, moved over miles of rocks which overspread the whole surface of the ground, and were by age seamed and cross-seamed into crevices lined with a scrubby growth of cedar and forming natural stone rifle-pits perfectly impregnable if defended. We found and thoroughly explored a cave; searched every barn, every hay or fodder stack, and every thicket or forest in that locality. We dislodged some, capturing their abandoned outfit, but the country was so rough and they so familiar with it that we carried back only one prisoner. They might have inflicted serious damage upon us had they made a fight, but we thoroughly scattered them and gave them a scare which they did not soon forget.

When our battalion reported to Longstreet, we were ordered into camp on the river several miles below Knoxville and were assigned to the delectable duty of foraging for food supplies for the army at Knoxville. The boys did not relish this duty, but as we were an unattached battalion (orphans) we might have expected assignment to some such detached service. There was much rain at this time and our camp ground being near the river and on rather low, flat ground, we were exposed to much mud and dampness of feet, resulting to me in a period of bad health which outlasted the war.

In the preceding July, while we were marching through Kentucky on the "Ohio raid," I stopped at my home for a brief half hour, and going to my room, my eyes fell upon a pair of pump-soled boots, such as the young men of that day wore in "society." For the benefit of the present, and some past generations, I will say that these boots had soles hardly as wide as the foot and scarcely thicker than ordinary pasteboard, while the upper leather covering the foot was about as thick as a good quality of writing paper. It was hot riding in that July sun, and I was tempted when I saw those light boots and cast off my heavy ones for them, thinking that I would be able to replace these with heavy ones by fall. I had not done so, and these thin boots soon went to pieces in the mud of our camp, resulting in the serious impairment of my health referred to.

The battle of Lookout Mountain and Missionary Ridge now occurred and General Bragg fell back to Dalton, Georgia. General Sherman came up from Chattanooga with a strong force to relieve Burnside besieged in Knoxville. General Longstreet swung his army around to the northeast of Knoxville and our battalion was ordered to cross the mountains into North Carolina and thence proceed to General Bragg at Dalton, Georgia.

I I I.

Our battalion started on the march to Georgia by the way of North Carolina.   This indirect route was necessary to avoid Sherman's army which was rapidly coming up the valley behind us. We were none too soon, for we passed through Marysville just in time to avoid being cut off by a column of Federal cavalry which formed the right wing of the Federal army and which was pushed forward rapidly, doubtless to prevent the return of any of Long street's force to Georgia.

The crossing of the Great Unaka Mountains was the most picturesque and interesting ride we had during the whole war.   So steep were the western inclines that the roadway was necessarily laid out in zigzag fashion.   Several stretches of this zigzag road were in view all the time and as they were only thirty to forty feet apart and nearly parallel, the several lines of cavalry moving in alternate directions formed a pretty sight, more resembling a fancy drill or dance movement than a march on the road.   It afforded much amusement to the men who were always ready to make the most of every opportunity, and the efforts of those in each line to convince those in the next line that they were going in the wrong direction created much merriment.

This is a beautiful mountain section, sparsely settled, but abounding in large game, it being said to contain more wild animals than any other section of equal size in this country.   The few dwellings seen were nearly all of the most primitive character and were nearly always located in valleys or coves that afforded sufficient space level enough for a building site and a small patch of tillable ground.   Many of these homes seemed so far below the crests of the mountain ridges which apparently encircled them completely, that some of the wits of the command called for Bibles to roll down to the dwellers upon the supposition that the story of the cross had in all probability never reached them.   When we had gotten over into the foothills of the mountains on the North Carolina side I awoke one morning to find myself ill—too ill to proceed with the command.   Keeping with me two good men, Mark Coleman, of Fayette, and Dick Stonestreet of Oldham county, partly for protection, for there were bushwhackers throughout all this mountain section, I went to the residence of John Siler, whom I found to be one of nature's noblemen. He gave us a hearty welcome and expressed a most cordial willingness to take care of me through my illness. His boys were all in the Southern army, and he had already lost two of them. In thought and feeling he associated us with his boys and he could not do enough for us. He constantly talked of his lost boys and always with a tear in his eye, yet he maintained a cheerful demeanor, and behind his grief there seemed a feeling akin to exultation that while his boys were lost to him they died as he would have had them die.

Believing that my illness was brought on by bad boots and wet feet at Knoxville, as soon as able I rode to Franklin, the nearest town to have a pair made. While sitting in the shoe shop, which was a sort of wing to the hotel of the town, a man came in and said to the shoemaker, " General Morgan is in the hotel." " What General Morgan," said I. " General John Morgan, the great cavalryman," he replied. Now I knew, or thought I knew, that our general was a prisoner in the Ohio penitentiary, and I jumped at once to the conclusion that here was an " old soldier " imposing on the credulity of these people for the many good things that would surely be his. I said to the man "Please direct me to him," and I followed him into the hotel and to the parlor to expose the rascally impostor. Imagine my surprise when I stepped into the parlor and found myself in the presence of the real thing —our general. He was surrounded by a bevy of ladies, and was looking as " chipper " and gay as though he had never been in a penitentiary. He was almost as glad to see us as we were to see him free once more, for we were the first of his command, and in fact, the first Confederates to meet him after his arrival within our lines. He and his little party of escaped prisoners had been closely pressed by the enemy on Clinch river, near Knoxville, and Morgan only had escaped. He had made his way alone across East Tennessee and over the mountains to this town of Franklin. Captain Hines told the writer after the close of the war that he permitted himself to be captured on the Clinch river in order to divert the pursuers and aid Morgan's escape. He also told me that from the time their escaping party reached the Kentucky side of the Ohio river General Morgan persisted in letting his identity be known. And here I found him alone in this semi-mountainous section, in which were many disloyal bushwhackers, ready and willing to shoot down a soldier or citizen for his war politics or for anything of value, any one of whom would have risked his life for a shot at this great chieftain, and he was making no attempt to conceal but was openly making known his identity.   As heretofore stated, I had been twice sent into the Tennessee portion of these mountain ranges to capture or scatter armed bands of disloyalists and bushwackers.   And when I was left sick a few miles west of Franklin, the battalion commander directed me to keep two good men with me for protection.   One of these Dick Stonestreet, as good a soldier as we had, was afterward killed by a bushwhacker in this same range in upper East Tennessee.   Yet here was General Morgan, whose life—or death rather—would have been a sweet morsel to one of these partisan murderers, and worth a fortune to him besides, coming alone into this dangerous section and openly making known his identity to every one.   I mention these things in greater detail because they illustrate a strong characteristic of General Morgan.   He did not expose his men recklessly even in action.   I recall but one occasion when he even appeared to do so; that was at Green River Bridge, Kentucky, July Fourth, 1863, but he was careless of his personal safety, and this finally cost him his life.

At this meeting at Franklin General Morgan informed me that he was going immediately to Richmond; that he would there select a point of rendezvous for the reorganization of his command and publish it in the Richmond papers, and he directed me to watch for the announcement and report at the place designated.   In a few days I saw his announcement designating Decatur, Georgia, as the place of rendezvous, and with my comrades, Coleman and Stonestreet, I at once started for Decatur, a small town near Atlanta, and arrived there after three days of riding.   I found General Adam R. Johnson there, and he had already several hundred men in camp with Colonel J. B. Bowles in charge of the camp.   General Johnson had decided upon a reorganization and had begun to assemble the remnants of the command at Decatur before General Morgan arrived at Richmond, so that General Morgan found that his plans were already being carried out.   The object of General Johnson was to complete the work begun at Morristown, which had been interrupted by our orders to march to Georgia for the battle of Chickamauga.   I expected to find our battalion already at Decatur and to resume the command of my company but it had not arrived. The men of these battalions were of course expected at Decatur, to be reorganized with their old comrades, but incredible as it may seem the battalion to which my company was attached, composed of many of Morgan's oldest and best soldiers, members of two or more of his old regiments, were never permitted to report at Decatur nor even to General Morgan again. Not only that, but General Bragg attempted to have officers ordered back to this battalion who had served with it, but who were at the time by proper orders serving in the old command, and under General Morgan himself. My own case will illustrate this and show the attitude of General Bragg towards General Morgan. When I left North Carolina and went to Decatur, Georgia, I was acting in strict obedience to the instructions given me at Franklin by General Morgan. On my arrival at Decatur I was assigned to duty by General Johnson as quartermaster on his staff. When our command was transferred to Virginia I was a member of the staff and went of course, acting at all times under the orders of my proper superior officers. Notwithstanding this, a requisition by General Bragg for my return to the army of Georgia came to our headquarters at Wytheville, Virginia (having been approved by the authorities at Richmond, who were ignorant of the facts), the requisition being based upon the statement that I was "absent without leave." Our general treated the order as it deserved, simply ignoring it. He did not inform me of the existence of such an order and I only learned of it in confidence from his adjutant general.

I have already referred to the efforts of General Bragg to have Morgan's command dismounted, and to the successful fight made by General Adam R. Johnson to prevent it; the above facts show General Bragg's attitude towards the command while at Decatur and even after General Morgan had escaped and was in command again. There is no doubt, however, that Johnson would have been in better favor with Bragg than Morgan was had he not thwarted Bragg's designs upon the command. Johnson was a stricter disciplinarian than Morgan, and Morgan was charged with disregarding and disobeying some of Bragg's orders, just as did Forrest, who, at Chickamauga, where he led us so gallantly, was actually under arrest technically for refusing to report to or to be subordinated to a certain other cavalry officer. The pity is that Forrest was even subordinate to Bragg on that occasion.

The refusal of General Bragg to permit the greater portion of the

command, as reorganized and equipped at Morristown, to go to
Decatur made the reorganization at Decatur more like a rehabilitation than a reorganization.

The three hundred men brought out by General Johnson from
Buffington Island and the company which I had brought out from
Twelve Mile Island formed the nucleus for the reorganization at
Morristown; but the greater part of these were not permitted to
come to Decatur, and the task there was thus more difficult, for the
camp was largely composed of convalescents, escaped prisoners,
dismounted men of all conditions, men without suitable clothing
or equipments, and odds and ends, including not a few chronic
never-do-wells and stragglers.   The effort had once more been
made to put these into infantry commands, but General Johnson
had again gone to Richmond and had a second time succeeded in
getting the authorities to permit him to try to mount and equip
them as cavalry, the authorities declaring their inability to provide
mounts and equipments.   General Johnson went at this task
with the same energy and self-reliance which characterized all his
efforts.   Doubtless no officer in the Confederacy was more competent to meet such an emergency than General Johnson.   The
"regulation" officer has usually exhausted his resources when he
has made requisition upon the proper departments for equipments or
supplies.   But Johnson had been educated in a very differen
school.   His several years of border-life in Texas, surveying
teaming and fighting Indians, had made him very resourceful and
self-reliant.   Coming into Southwestern Kentucky in 1862 with only
two comrades he began a series of bold operations that soon made
a department of his own.   He carried on a successful war against
the greatly superior forces of the enemy, while constantly increasing
his own, until he soon· had over a thousand mounted and equipped
cavalry.   The equipment and maintenance of this force within
the enemy's lines showed him to be very resourceful and had given
him valuable experience.

As before stated, upon my arrival at Decatur General Johnson
appointed me acting brigade quartermaster.   He explained the
situation and outlined his plans for equipping and mounting the men.
I was especially charged with the duty of providing equipments.
He instructed me to find out and detail every mechanic in the
command, and he sent all the chaplains out through the country
to procure materials, any and every thing needful for the men.

Our headquarters were in a large vacant hotel building, affording plenty of room for workmen. Our first detail was of tailors, of whom we had several, and they were put to work on cloth obtained by the chaplains, repairing, etc.; during our brief stay here they did good service.

Paul J. Marrs, of Henderson, and George W. Hunt of Lexington, were my chief assistants, and were very efficient, keeping our horses well supplied notwithstanding the great scarcity of forage in that section at the time. But my most important find was that of several Texas saddle-tree makers, who were skilled in making the Texas or Mexican styles of saddle-trees—so much preferred by our troopers to any other style of saddle-tree; we were in great need of saddles. Being informed that several men were engaged in making and selling saddle-trees only a short distance from Decatur, I immediately went to their place and upon investigation found that they were members of our command. I at once took charge of them and set them to work making saddle-trees for the command.

We had only gotten these undertakings started, however, when General Johnson received orders to proceed with the command to Southwest Virginia, General Morgan having decided to make that his base of future operations. Arriving in Southwest Virginia, our headquarters were first at Abingdon where we promptly renewed our efforts to manufacture articles needed by the command. Before we had gotten fairly started, however, our headquarters were moved to Wytheville, and it was decided to discontinue all except the manufacture of horse-equipments, the need for these being most urgent.

Soon after reaching Wytheville General Morgan took command, relieving General Johnson who had long desired this, in order that he might return to his department in Southwestern Kentucky and resume his warfare within the enemy's lines. At the same time Major Llewellyn of Morgan's staff relieved me as brigade quartermaster. General Morgan complimented us for our success in our manufacturing enterprise, and requested me to give my entire attention to that for a time, saying that these supplies were greatly needed by the command and could be had in no other way. He made it as a request, not as an order, for he naturally thought it was not such an assignment as I would prefer. I told him I appreciated the importance of the work in the condition of the command and would willingly continue in charge, with the un-derstanding that he would relieve me whenever I should request it. Several reasons prompted me to accept willingly this assign-ment. I knew the needs of the command and believed, with the knowledge and experience already acquired, I could get quicker results than would any newly assigned officer and I felt a natural pride in seeing this undertaking accomplish its object. Besides, my health was still bad, and I hoped that by avoiding exposure I might fully recuperate by the time my company, then in Georgia, should be returned to the command. Some time after this when General Morgan was at Saltville, organizing for his last expedition into Kentucky, he ordered me to turn over my charge to Lieutenant Milton Barlow and report to him at Saltville. When I reached Saltville my health was such that the brigade surgeon advised against my going with the Kentucky expedition, and Gen. Morgan ordered me back to Wytheville to resume charge of that work.

For a while previous to this Lieutenant Barlow being unassigned had given me voluntary assistance in the work, especially in de-signing and constructing some much needed machinery, for we had very little, and that of the most primitive sort. He was something of a mechanical genius, having been his father's assistant in design-ing the well known planetarium, which, I believe, was exhibited at the Crystal Palace Exhibition in London.

I had no mechanical training or experience when ordered by General Johnson to undertake this work, but like most boys was naturally fond of mechanics, and my collegiate education covering most of the sciences, partly compensated for lack of practical experience, I entered into it with zeal and confidence. As we were thrown almost entirely upon our own resources, there was ample scope for the exercise of all my ingenuity and that of the men detailed for the work. We had all seen some years of cavalry service, and next to a good horse we valued a good saddle. Every one of these men had his idea of what a saddle should be and each wanted to follow his ideal. I of course had ideas also, and besides was charged with the duty of seeing that all that was done was practical and not too elaborate or expensive. The result was the composite known as the "Morgan saddle," which soon became famous all over the Confederacy and after the war came into extensive use throughout the country.

About six months before Lee's surrender I was again assigned to quartermaster duty in the field and again turned over this work to Lieutenant Barlow.   At that time the command was well supplied with horse-equipments and our wareroom at Wytheville contained a nice surplus available when needed.

MRS. ADAM R. JOHNSON.

BY COLONEL JAMES B. BOWLES.

Josephine Eastland was born upon the 24th day of August, 1845, near Sparta, Tennessee, but moved with her parents to Texas when only two weeks old. She received her education at LaGrange and Austin, Texas, her last teacher being Mrs. Amelia Barr, the celebrated authoress. She was married to Adam R. Johnson at Burnet, Texas, January 1, 1861.

At this period the Indians were infesting Burnet county, and several times she came very near falling into their hands and succeeded in eluding them only by her skillful horsemanship.

When General Johnson came home on furlough in 1862, the danger in Burnet county had been increased by lawless bands of white men, and he concluded to take his wife east of the Mississippi, where he could see her and hear from her more frequently.

On this journey they came in contact with Banks's army near Alexandria, Louisiana, and were compelled to make a flank movement to evade them by crossing Red river some distance above this city. Upon their arrival at the Mississippi, they found it swollen outside its banks, and so were obliged to travel many weary miles through back water. They met many soldiers who assured them that it would be impossible to cross, but this daughter of Texas, inured to continued perils all her life, was the general's compeer in courage and determination and almost in physical power, having always led a healthy, active outdoor life, with constant horseback exercise. So nothing daunted, they finally succeeded in reaching a point upon the Mississippi river, just opposite the city of Natchez. Just as they arrived at this point a gunboat passed up the river so near them that the brass buttons upon the officers' blue coats were plainly visible. Taking it for granted that this couple were peaceable citizens, they did not molest them. After the danger had passed, a little sunken ferryboat concealed from the Yanks, for fear it would be destroyed to prevent communication, was raised by its owner, and they were slowly transported across the turbulent tide of the Great Father of Waters. They now traveled toward Brook Haven, Mississippi. Near this place General Johnson and his wife were in imminent peril of falling into the hands of the Federal General Grierson, who was raiding that part of the country, having started from Memphis and meeting "none to molest or make him afraid," but they put into practice the "Indian dodge" they had learned upon the wild frontier of Texas and escaped his clutches.

Upon their arrival at Jackson, the capital of the State of Mississippi, they found that it had been evacuated recently by Sherman. Many of the streets were flowing with molasses, and the railroad had been destroyed, with a large portion of the city by the vandal's fire. Finally, reaching railroad transportation, they went to the pretty little town of Marietta, Georgia, about sixteen miles from Atlanta, and here Mrs. Johnson was established, at least temporarily. Through all his lengthy tedious dangerous journey of several weeks, Mrs. Johnson never once complained of fatigue, or manifested any signs of fear; her answer to inquiries upon this point always being that her husband was fully competent to take care of her.

Later she went to Virginia, and fell into the hands of Averill, who was making a raid through the mountainous region of the western part of Virginia. With Averill there was a number of negro troops who had been burning and robbing houses. There was no man upon the place where Mrs. Johnson was staying, and she boldly went to the officer in command of them and demanded that a guard be placed around the house for the protection of the ladies. This officer proved to be a gentleman, and not only granted her request, but took his position on the porch till all the men had passed.

After General Johnson's release from imprisonment, he rejoined his wife, at her temporary residence near Fincastle, Virginia, at the hospitable home of Mr. Rufus Pitzer. Notwithstanding the blindness of the general and his crippled condition, still requiring the use of crutches, they decided to go to Macon, Mississippi, where a portion of the command was in camp. When in the vicinity of Montgomery they encountered Wilson's cavalry on a destructive

raid through Georgia. General Adams, of the Confederate forces,
assured General Johnson that it would be impossible for him to pass
Wilson's command, but the latter's motto being still, "Where there
is a will, there's a way," he determined to make the attempt. Procuring a wagon and horse, and accompanied by Captain William
Moore, who now resides in Memphis, Tennessee, and a young
man by the name of Frazier, from Arkansas, they drove around
the army of raiders, eluding them entirely, and after many ups and
downs arrived safe at the city of their destination, only a little the
worse for wear. His escort, Captain Moore, reported to his old
commander, General Forrest, while General Johnson immediately
engaged in active preparations for taking his men, whom he found
at this place, back into Kentucky, to recruit, and fight.

But here the partner of his life, who had so long added to his
happiness and his pleasures and divided with him his sorrows and his
discomforts, now demurred, and probably for the first time during
their marriage relationship seriously opposed his plans, at least
delaying him until he had to unconditionally surrender to fate, if
not to her; for in April General Lee surrendered to the inevitable,
and General Joseph E. Johnston and Dick Taylor soon did likewise.
This of course destroyed all prospect of another expedition into
Kentucky by Johnson and his men; and Mrs. Johnson with her
husband started for their old home in Burnet, Texas, going by way
of Vicksburg and New Orleans. The sequel of Mrs. Johnson's history will be found in that of her husband, whose blindness has not
prevented him from succeeding as a business man almost as well
as a military chieftain, though it has prevented him from watching
his fortune closely and effectually, for not many men in the Lone
Star State have made more money by their own efforts, and lost
more through the efforts of others.

In planning and building near his old home the pretty and
flourishing town of Marble Falls, with its picturesque environment,
he has reared to his own honor and memory, however unconsciously, a handsome monument, which will most probably endure
long after all our tall white cemetery columns have crumbled into
dust. Blessed with health, cheerfulness, competency, and a family
of children and grandchildren worthy of their noble parentage, they
afford a signal type of genuine "American sovereigns," independent,
true, kind, gracious, magnanimous, and beloved, as they gently
rule over many loving hearts of relatives and friends.

GENERAL ADAM R. JOHNSON.

A TRIBUTE FROM GOVENOR LUBBOCK, OF TEXAS.

To the children of General Adam R. Johnson, of Marble Falls, Burnet County, Texas:

You having expressed a desire for me to tell you my acquaintance and friendship for your father, I beg to say, that in 1857 I, being the Democratic candidate for lieutenant governor of the State of Texas, determined to canvass the then frontier counties of the State.

With my wife I arrived in Burnet, and having made a speech there, signified my intention of proceeding at once to Llano. Adam R. Johnson, then quite a young man, insisted that it would be quite dangerous to make the trip, that the Indians were numerous and would attack us, we being alone and unarmed. He said, "If you will go, I will accompany you." And he with two others saw me safe to Llano. We saw fresh Indian signs in abundance, and I have ever believed that the presence of those young men more than likely saved our lives.

This circumstance led to a warm friendship, that has never faltered in all time from that day to the present moment.

General Johnson has been my warm political friend, supporting me for lieutenant governor, and then for governor. As soon as I was inaugurated governor at the commencement of the Civil War, he called on me for information about raising troops in Texas. I could give him no positive information, at that time; he was determined to go at once to the front and to his native State and enlist there. He did so, and was at once a prominent figure. He continued to perform deeds of valor and became known as "Stovepipe Johnson" from the fact that he improvised stove-pipes and wagon wheels to represent cannon and pounced down on the Yankees on the Ohio river, making reprisals, very much to their consternation and the benefit of the Confederate cause.

Unfortunately for our cause as well as for him, he lost his eyesight and became totally blind while in the active discharge of his duty, and was made a prisoner. After suffering every indignity and privation that could be inflicted upon him, he was exchanged (they were willing to exchange a blind Confederate, not dreaming that he could be again a soldier). Upon his reaching Richmond, as soon as notified of his presence, I sought him out, standing ready to do him any service that I could. I called at once to see General J. C. Breckinridge, the then Secretary of War, who immediately called to see him at the Spotswood Hotel, where he was confined from his wound and a severe fall while in prison. The Secretary of War said to him that he saw nothing for him to do but retire in consequence of his blindness; the tears fell down his cheeks. He asserted that he could do good work in the ordnance department, that he could fill cartridges as well as other work, and that he would never retire as long as the war lasted. He then took occasion to say to the Secretary of War that he knew every foot of land in Kentucky, and if furnished with proper authority could enter Kentucky and bring out and put into the Confederate army a large number of good men. He was so earnest and intelligent in his talk that he was granted the authority and I am firmly persuaded that he would have carried out his intentions had not our cause so suddenly collapsed.

President Davis also manifested much feeling in regard to General Johnson's misfortune, and told him if it could be of any consolation to him to know that his efforts in Kentucky had prolonged the war, he could assure him that they had done so.

I was soon after captured and put in prison, where I was kept till near January, 1866.

Your father returned home, and you know how he went to work to repair his shattered fortunes, how he lived on his farm guarding the place, gun in hand, although blind, the Indians not knowing of his misfortune. Finally with great energy and big intellect he forged ahead as a business man, engaging in his former land business and projecting great enterprises for the State.

In 1878, when I was candidate for State Treasurer, he was my fast friend, and has from that time ever been my political and personal friend. How could I do otherwise than admire and respect him for his manhood and brilliant record as a Confederate soldier, and love him as my dear friend?

God bless and keep and prosper him and his dear and true wife and his children and his children's children!

Your sincere friend,

F. R. LUBBOCK.

GENERAL ADAM RANKIN JOHNSON.

A SKETCH BY COLONEL MILLER, OF AUSTIN, TEXAS.

It will be impossible, in a brief sketch, to do justice to the merits of the distinguished civilian and soldier, General A. R. Johnson; for if there is one man more than another whose memory should be perpetuated for an example to the youth of Texas, it is the subject of this biography.

Though a true son of the "Bluegrass State," he longed for the freedom of the broad plains of Texas, and in 1854 he settled down in Burnet, Burnet county, and cast his lot with these true-hearted frontiersmen who were then striving to protect themselves and property from the ravages of the Indians. Burnet was then a border county, and monthly raids were made upon it by the Comanches, and General Johnson had been engaged in several fights with the savages in sight of his now peaceful home, "Airy Mount." As a surveyor and land agent, he has been specially active in inviting and obtaining a sturdy and intelligent population to the county.

As noted and distinguished as he has become in peace, he was more notable and distinguished in war. Paladin of old was not more daring and heroic than this Southern knight on the field of battle. General Johnson's training as a soldier was received in Indian fights in Texas, and the peculiar character of warfare with the savages when he was contractor of the government, carrying the mails on the Overland Route from the stake plains station and El Paso, gave character to the kind of guerrilla warfare he waged so successfully, and from which he gained such celebrity in the Civil War. In his early manhood he distinguished himself for bravery and strategy upon the Texas border, and in defense of his home in Burnet county.

General Johnson had just closed his contracts with the government, and returned with his young bride to his home in Burnet, in 1861, when the Civil War of 1861-5 startled the land from Maine to the Rio Grande. Great excitement prevailed in every village

and hamlet in the State of Texas. Johnson resisted the natural
impulses of his birth and education, and attempted to stay at home,
at least until he could get his business in condition to leave it, but the
fever of battle increased too rapidly.   He found that it would
take too much time to arrange his business affairs satisfactorily,
.and in company with Judge Vontrice, he started for his native State,
Kentucky. He went to Hopkinsville, and there finding General Forrest, he offered his services and was readily accepted, and proved to
be Forrest's right-hand man.   Forrest soon found that Johnson was
highly endowed with courage, prudence, and judgment, and associat-
ing him with another young man of the same stamp, Bob Martin,
he used them as scouts.   It is impossible to follow these two scouts
through all their adventures and wonderful escapes, but when it
is known that they hovered along the line of march with the enemy
and often spent the night within a few feet of the Federal soldiers,
sometimes in the same house, each playing to perfection the many
different characters, and that they were never captured, it will be
readily concluded that Forrest was wise in his choice, and that he
received from them the valuable information that enabled him to
make his name such a terror to the enemy, and that the story of
their adventures would read more like a romance, only that romance
would not venture to tell the facts that did really occur, because
seemingly too marvelous for belief.

Captain Ray, of Slaughtersville, Kentucky, who had a company
of his own held in readiness to enlist in the Confederate army when
a proper leader came along, refused to recruit with Johnson as
their commander on account of his youthful appearance; but after
this daring young soldier, with Martin and Owen, attacked the
provost guard at Henderson, his fame was noised abroad, until
hundreds of the young men in Kentucky, anxious to do battle
in the Southern cause, flocked to Johnson's standard, and he soon
found himself in command of a regiment, with Martin as lieutenant-
colonel; and after the capture of Newburg, Indiana, they were
well organized, the arms and ammunition captured at that place distributed among them, the little band assuming the appearance
of an army.

The capture of a small city like Henderson, Kentucky, and a
village like Newburg, Indiana, may seem but a small and insignificant
matter, while armies of the Union were sweeping South; but it
was mentioned in the London Times and other foreign papers as an

evidence of the resuscitating power of the South in organizing new armies and achieving victories in a country supposed to have been conquered by the Federal forces; and it must be remembered that the Southern Confederacy was seeking recognition at that time, and the importance of securing that recognition can not be over-estimated. No man in the Southern army, no matter how high his rank, displayed more military skill or intrepidity than General Adam R. Johnson. Hundreds of miles in the rear of the regular Confederate armies, in a territory occupied by the enemy, and on a river swept by the Federal gunboats, and in the face of orders subjecting all persons who attempted to recruit for the Confederate army in the State, or who were found with arms in their hands, to a trial by a drum-head court martial and a summary execution, he organized a gallant body of troops, captured Hopkinsville, Kentucky, Clarksville, Tennessee, with arms and supplies, and many other smaller towns, occupying at his pleasure any town south of Green river, as his headquarters, to which he boldly and publicly invited recruits, and by swift movements engaging in battle and defeating Federal detachments of superior force before they were able to concentrate. He was literally the "Swamp Fox" of Kentucky. His forces were daily increasing in numbers and efficiency, and he was daily enlarging the area of his operations, when unfortunately in a battle in Southern Kentucky, he received the serious wound that blinded him for life, and put an end to his usefulness as a Confederate partisan ranger. The ball was fired from a covert, to which he presented a side shot, and striking one eye, passed over the bridge of the nose destroying the other in its course.

The people of that section of the State regarded him with highest admiration and affection, and as the news of the loss of his eyes spread over the country, they were filled with despondency and personal grief for their champion, for he had made it unsafe in that section of the country for the Federals to domineer and hector over Confederate sympathizers, and had enforced upon the enemy the rules of civilized warfare.

One important object was to open up Kentucky to a free and open communication with the Southern army, in which the sons of its citizens were serving. General Johnson, after recruiting about seven hundred men, conceived the plan of capturing Hopkinsville, on the line of route to the South, and which was heavily garrisoned, and in that way to effect a junction with Colonel

Thomas Woodward, another gallant partisan ranger, operating along the Tennessee and Kentucky line; and after the combination, attack and capture the important city of Clarksville, Tennessee, on the Cumberland river. By a forced march from his headquarters at Madisonville of forty-five miles, he reached Hopkinsville just before day, immediately charged the camp of the Federals, and put them to utter rout, and holding this town, was joined by Colonel Woodward. Clarksville, with much needed arms and munitions, was also captured, and the valuable supplies distributed among the needy Confederates.

General Johnson carried out his secret orders to the entire satisfaction of the authorities, and played as gallant a part in warfare as any hero in an army of heroes. To most men the loss of sight at his age would have been disheartening and so discouraging as to encourage inaction and loss of interest in the affairs of life. Not so with General Johnson. At the close of hostilities he returned to his home in Burnet, not the fine home with the thousands of acres of land he now possesses, but an humble home, and commenced most vigorously to repair his broken fortunes; and no man has succeeded more eminently than he has in accumulating a fortune, and of having been all along of the greatest importance and the main factor in developing the different material interests of Burnet county; and perhaps no man has led a more cheerful and happy life. His friends in Henderson bewailed the misfortune more on the ground of the deprivation to him of all happiness; but he has demonstrated the fact that he possesses a character so governed by the true philosophy of life that the physical loss of one of his senses has never clouded his mind with gloom or destroyed the joyousness of his spirits. As he enters into the business affairs of life, he enters into its social pleasures, and is one of the best informed and most agreeable conversationalists one will meet anywhere. In fact, he does as other men, and much better than most men, even, under his sad absence of sight.

He now, in 1904, seems to be in the full vigor and meridian of life, full of energy, enterprise, and action, with a promise before him of many useful years to his family and country.

INDEX